S0-AQP-764

LIST
PRICE

TIST
PRI $18.95

THEORIES OF
ORGANIZATIONAL
BEHAVIOR

JOHN B. MINER ——————

Research Professor of Management and
Coordinator of Doctoral Programs for
the College of Business Administration
Georgia State University

THE DRYDEN PRESS
HINSDALE, ILLINOIS

Copyright © 1980 by The Dryden Press
A division of Holt, Rinehart and Winston, Publishers
All rights reserved
Library of Congress Catalog Card Number: 79-64596
ISBN: 0-03-054721-0
Printed in the United States of America
012   038   987654321

DEDICATION

To the major theorists who made this book possible—

Abraham H. Maslow	Edwin A. Locke
Clayton P. Alderfer	B. F. Skinner
David C. McClelland	W. Clay Hamner
John W. Atkinson	Fred Luthans
Bernard Weiner	Arnold P. Goldstein
Frederick Herzberg	Melvin Sorcher
J. Stacy Adams	J. Richard Hackman
Basil S. Georgopoulos	Douglas McGregor
Victor H. Vroom	Raymond E. Miles
Jay Galbraith	Fred E. Fiedler
Larry L. Cummings	Robert J. House
Lyman W. Porter	Martin G. Evans
Edward E. Lawler	Frank A. Heller
George Graen	Robert Tannenbaum
Edward L. Deci	

—and the many who worked with them.

The Dryden Press Series in Management

William F. Glueck, Consulting Editor

Altman and Hodgetts
Readings in Organizational Behavior

Aronson
The Scorecard

Byars and Rue
**Personnel Management:
Concepts and Applications**

Duncan
**Essentials of Management,
2nd Edition**

Gaither
**Production and
Operations Management**

Gatza, Milutinovich and Boseman
**Decision Making in Administration:
Text, Critical Incidents and Cases**

Gellerman
Management of Human Relations

Gellerman
Management of Human Resources

Gellerman
Managers and Subordinates

Glueck
Management, 2nd Edition

Glueck
Management Essentials

Glueck and Jauch
**The Managerial Experience: Cases,
Exercises and Readings, 2nd Edition**

Grad, Glans, Holstein, Meyers, Schmidt
Management Systems, 2nd Edition

Greenlaw
**Readings to Accompany Modern
Personnel Management**

Greenlaw and Biggs
Modern Personnel Management

Hand and Hollingsworth
**Practical Readings in Small
Business Management**

Harbaugh, Byars, and Rue
**Readings and Cases in
Personnel Management**

Higgins
**Organizational Policy and Strategic
Management: Text and Cases**

Hodgetts
**The Business Enterprise:
Social Challenge, Social Response**

Hodgetts
**Management: Theory, Process, and
Practice, 2nd Edition**

Hodgetts
Modern Human Relations

Hodgetts and Altman
Organizational Behavior

Holley and Jennings
The Labor Relations Process

Hollingsworth and Hand
**A Guide to Small Business
Management: Text and Cases**

Karmel
**Point and Counterpoint in
Organizational Behavior**

Lindauer
**Communicating in Business,
2nd Edition**

McFarlan, Nolan and Norton
Information Systems Administration

Mayerson
**Shoptalk: Foundations of
Managerial Communication**

Miner
The Challenge of Managing

Miner
Theories in Organizational Behavior

Naumes and Paine
**Cases for Organizational Strategy
and Policy, 2nd Edition**

Paine and Naumes
**Organizational Strategy and Policy,
2nd Edition**

Paine and Naumes
**Organizational Strategy and Policy:
Text, Cases, and Incidents**

Robinson
**International Business Management,
2nd Edition**

Viola
**Organizations in a Changing Society:
Administration and Human Values**

PREFACE

The material presented here presupposes some prior work in such fields as management, organizational study, behavioral science, human relations, and the like. Given an introduction of this kind, however, the reader should find little in this book that overlaps with his or her prior learning. The reason is that basic courses typically take a content or problem centered approach dealing with what is known with regard to planning, organizing, leadership, motivation, and the like. In contrast, this book takes a very different tack. It focuses on the important theories in the field and the contributions these theories have made to our understanding of organizations, as well as to management practice. Since much of what we know about organizations derives from theory, this approach yields a very comprehensive coverage. Yet, embedding the discussion in theory also places considerable demand on the reader. It is for this reason that the book is advocated for the more advanced, second level student, who has already had some exposure to the field.

Secondly, it is important to recognize that the concern is with only part of the overall field of organizational study—the part that has come to be called organizational behavior, or micro-level analysis. For the purposes of this book organizational behavior refers to the individual and small group levels of consideration—an interpretation consistent with general practice in the field. In contrast, the field of organization theory, dealing as it does with macro-level analyses of inter-group relationships, organization-wide concepts, and organization-environment interactions, represents a quite different although related area of study.

A subsequent volume is planned to deal with theories at this macro-level covering matters of organizational process and structure. Thus, the works of Likert, Trist, Stogdill, Katz, Kahn, Thompson, Weber, Fayol, Argyris, Tannenbaum, Woodward, Lawrence, Lorsch, Bennis, March, Simon, Cyert, Chandler, and many others are not included here, simply because the field of organizational study has become too large to consider in a single presentation, and perhaps in a single course as well. The division between organizational behavior and organizational process and structure is indeed artificial, but it is essential to deal with the burgeoning body of theory and knowledge regarding how organizations operate.

My major debt in preparing this volume is acknowledged in the dedication. Without the efforts of the various theorists of organizational behavior there would be nothing to write about. I am also, once again, in the debt of Jack Neifert, my former editor, and of my wife Barbara Miner, who has done all the things beyond the actual writing that make the production of a book such as this possible. To all of these people I owe, and express, my very real appreciation.

J.B.M.

Atlanta, Georgia

CONTENTS

THEORY, RESEARCH, AND KNOWLEDGE OF ORGANIZATIONAL BEHAVIOR

1

The focus of this book is on theories of organizational behavior. It attempts to look at existing theories of behavior in organizations to determine what these theories can tell us that might prove useful to those who participate in organizations. Because we all participate in various organizations — schools, companies, hospitals, and so forth — throughout our lives, devoting a large percentage of our time to such participation, this obviously is a very important topic. Most people would like to function more effectively in organizations whether they are managers or subordinates; whether they are students attempting to deal with teachers or patients attempting to deal with doctors; or whether they are teachers or doctors themselves. Furthermore, it seems logical that the more we know about organizations and the way they operate, the better our chances of dealing with them effectively and achieving

1

our own goals within them. But what does this have to do with theory?

For many people the term theory evokes images of a speculative, ivory-tower world far removed from reality. "Theories" do not sound like things that would prove helpful in understanding the practical facts of organizational life. Yet one also hears statements made by presumably knowledgeable people, such as the eminent psychologist Kurt Lewin, that "nothing is so practical as a good theory." What Lewin means by a "good" theory, of course, is one that meets the test of adequate research validation. Thus, to be truly useful, a theory must be intimately intertwined with research. To the extent that it is, it has the potential for moving beyond philosophical speculation to provide a sound basis for action.

It is important, then, to understand what scientific theory is and what it is not, as well as how theory relates to research and how research either supports or fails to support theory. These are the concerns of this chapter. The intent is to provide a basic understanding of theory that can be drawn upon as specific theories are discussed in the remainder of the book.

THE NATURE OF SCIENTIFIC THEORY

The type of theory with which this book is concerned is one that can be tested through research studies and is therefore scientific in nature. Such theories have the same potential for practical use when applied to organizations as do the theories of physics and chemistry in developing new manufacturing technologies and consumer products or the theories of biology in advancing medical practice.

What Is Science?

Science has been defined as the enterprise by which a particular kind of ordered knowledge is obtained about natural phenomena by means of controlled observations and theoretical interpretations (Marx, 1963). The usually accepted goals of scientific effort are to increase understanding and to facilitate prediction (Dubin, 1969). At its best, science achieves both of these goals. However, there are many instances in which predictions have been realized with considerable precision even though true understanding of underlying phenomena is minimal; this is characteristic of much of the forecasting used by companies in planning, for example.

Similarly, understanding can be far advanced even though prediction lags behind. For instance, we know a great deal about the various factors that can combine to influence the level of people's work performance (Miner, 1975), but we do not know enough about how these factors combine in specific instances to be able to predict with high accuracy how well a certain individual will perform.

In an applied field, such as organizational behavior, understanding and prediction are joined by a third objective, which is the opportunity both understanding and prediction provide for influencing or managing the future. An economic science that permitted full understanding of business cycles and the precise prediction of fluctuations would represent a long step toward developing procedures for managing the economy to hold unemployment at a desired level. Similarly, knowledge of the dynamics of employee motivation and the capacity to predict when people will work hard would offer the prospect of engineering situations to maximize productivity. To the extent that limited unemployment or increased productivity is desired, science then becomes a means for achieving these goals. In fact, much scientific work is undertaken for just such purposes — to influence the world around us to achieve some desired end. When applied science meets such objectives, it does indeed achieve a major goal.

The Role of Theory in Science

Scientific method evolves in ascending levels of abstraction (Brown and Ghiselli, 1955). At the most basic level it utilizes *symbols* to portray and retain experience. The symbols may be mathematical in nature, but in organization study so far they have been primarily linguistic. Once converted to symbols, experience may be mentally manipulated and relationships established.

Description utilizes symbols to classify, order, and correlate events. It remains at a low level of abstraction and is closely tied to observation and sensory experience. It is a matter of ordering symbols to make them adequately portray events.

Explanation moves to a higher level of abstraction in that it attempts to establish meanings behind events. It attempts to identify causal or at least concomitant relationships so that observed phenomena make some logical sense.

At its maximal point explanation becomes *theory*. Theory is a patterning of logical constructs, or interrelated symbolic concepts, into which the known facts regarding a phenomenon, or theoretical domain, may be fitted. A theory is a generalization (applicable within stated boundaries) that specifies relationships between factors. Thus, it is an attempt to make sense out of observations that do not contain any inherent and obvious logic (Dubin, 1976).

Scientific Assumptions

In order to operate at all, science must make certain assumptions about the world around us. These assumptions may not be factually true and to the extent they are not, science has little value. However, to the extent that science operates on these assumptions and produces a degree of valid understanding, prediction, and influence, it becomes increasingly worthwhile to utilize the assumptions. Therefore, this kind of expediency appears entirely justified.

We assume first that certain natural groupings of phenomena exist so that classification can occur and generalization within a category is meaningful. For some years the field of business policy, for example, operating from the case method, assumed that each company is essentially unique. This assumption effectively blocked the development of scientific theory and research in the field. Now the assumption of uniqueness is disappearing, and generalizations applicable to classes of organizations are emerging (Steiner and Miner, 1977). As a result, scientific theory and research are burgeoning in the business policy field.

Second, we must assume some degree of constancy, stability, or permanence in the world. Science cannot operate assuming complete random variation; the goal of valid prediction is totally unattainable under such circumstances. Thus, objects and events must retain some degree of similarity from one point in time to another. This is an extension of the first assumption, but now it concerns time rather than units. For instance, if people did not retain any similarity in intelligence, motivation, and other personal qualities from the point of hiring through the ongoing work context, any scientific prediction of performance would be impossible. Fortunately, they do retain some similarity but not always as much as might be desired.

Third, science assumes that events are determined, that causes exist. This is the essence of explanation and theorizing. It may not be possible to prove a specific cause with absolute certainty, but evidence can be adduced to support certain causal explanations and reject others. If one does not assume some kind of causation, there is little point in scientific investigation; this assumption of determinism is what sparks scientific effort. For instance, one can assume that managerial behavior does not influence subordinate performance. If so, then the whole field of leadership moves outside the realm of scientific inquiry. Leadership theory must assume some causal impact from the leader to the follower. It then becomes the task of science to determine the nature of this impact.

Finally, because science is firmly rooted in observation and experience, it is necessary to assume some degree of trustworthiness in the human processes of perception, recall, and reasoning. This trustworthiness is always relative, but it must exist to some degree. The rules under which science operates are intended to increase the degree of reliability of scientific observation and recording. The objective is to achieve an unbiased rational, replicable result that will be convincing to those who are knowledgeable in the area of study.

The Rules of Scientific Inquiry

If the findings of research are to be replicated and valid generalizations made, concepts must be clearly defined in terms of the procedures used to measure them. This has been a major problem in the field of organizational study. Theoretical concepts often are stated so ambiguously and the conditions for their measurement left so uncertain that the researcher is hard put to devise an adequate test of the theory.

Second, scientific observation must be controlled so that causation may be attributed correctly. The objective is to be certain that an outcome is produced by what is believed to produce it and not by something else. Control of this kind is achieved through the use of various experimental designs, to be discussed later in this chapter, or through measurement and statistical adjustment. In the complex world of organizational functioning, establishing controls that are sufficient to define causation has proved to be a difficult task.

Third, because science is concerned with generalization to contexts that extend far beyond a given experiment, it is essential that research utilize adequate samples in terms of both the size and the conditions of selection. One must have confidence that the results obtained are generalizable and can be put to use outside the research situation. The field of statistics becomes important in organization study because of its potential for determining whether confidence should be placed in a particular research outcome.

Fourth, and worthy of continued emphasis, a scientist's propositions, hypotheses, and theories must be stated in terms that permit them to be tested empirically by others. This is where philosophy and science part company. Unfortunately, in the early years of its development organization study did not always clearly separate scientific from philosophical statements. The result has been considerable confusion and, on occasion, wasted effort in an attempt to test "theories" that were actually philosophies and not really testable.

Theory Building

A distinction is often made between deductive and inductive theory (Filley, House, and Kerr, 1976). In building a theory by deduction one starts by establishing a set of premises. Then certain logical consequences of these premises are deduced, and subsidiary concepts are established. The starting point is rational thought, and logical consistency is a major concern as the theory is developed. Often such theories are stated in mathematical terms.

Inductive theory, in contrast, builds up from observation and research, rather than down from a set of premises. Essentially, one puts together a theory that seems to offer the best explanation of what is known in a given area at the present time. New tests of this theory or of hypotheses derived from it must then be carried out just as if the theory were developed deductively.

A major pitfall in using the inductive approach (and we will consider instances of this in later chapters) is that the research from which the theory is induced may tend to become confused with an adequate test of the theory. Thus, the same research is used twice for two different purposes, and a self-fulfilling prophecy results. In the case of truly deductive theories this is not possible. When theories are developed inductively it is crucial that they be tested subsequently on a new sample in a manner that is entirely independent of the pre-theory research. If one goes back to a prior sample or to data used in developing the theory, anything that is unique and ungeneralizable (attributable to a chance fluctuation in that particular situation) is very likely to be confirmed by the test. As a result, an erroneous theory insofar as generalization and practical usefulness are concerned may well be accepted.

It is actually more useful to think of theories in terms of a deductive-inductive continuum than in distinct categories. Probably no theory is ever completely devoid of some inductive input. On the other hand, there are instances when an entirely inductive process is used. Such instances are often referred to by the term *dust-bowl empiricism* on the assumption that no theory is involved at all; however, the result may look very much like a theory, and we may not be entirely justified in rejecting the theory designation.

An example of *dust-bowl empiricism* would be a situation in which a great many measures, say several hundred, are obtained on a sample of individuals, groups, or organizations. Then these data are put into a computer, and closely related measures are identified through the use of correlation techniques, factor analysis, or some similar procedure. What emerges is a set of hypothesized relationships among variables, something very much like an inductively derived theory. This "theory" is then tested on a new sample using the appropriate measures to be sure that it does not incorporate relationships that represent mere chance fluctuations associated with the particular sample from which the theory was induced.

It should be emphasized that any theory, regardless of the method of its construction and the extent of current confirmation, is provisional in nature. Theories are constructed to be modified or replaced as new knowledge appears; this is the way science advances (MacKenzie and House, 1978). The modification process, furthermore, tends to be inductive from research rather than deductive. Findings emerge that do not quite fit the existing theory. Accordingly, the theory is changed so that these new data can be explained, and a test is then made of the revised theory. As a result of this kind of theoretical tinkering, even predominantly deductive theories may eventually take on a strong inductive element; if they do not, they may well be replaced.

What Is a Good Theory?

The objective of this book is to look at the field of organization study through the medium of its major theories. In the process we will attempt to evaluate these theories as to their current utility. To do this we need some criteria by which to decide whether a theory is good or not so good. It should be evident now that some explanatory statements may not meet the requirements of scientific theory at all, and that a theory that was good at some time in the past may be much less satisfactory some years later. How do we know a good theory when we see one?

First, theories should contribute to the goals of science. They should aid understanding, permit prediction, and facilitate influence. The more they do these things, the better they are. A theory that is comprehensive in relation to the phenomena that it explains is preferable to one that deals with only a very limited range of events. However, broad scope alone is not enough. Many so-called grand theories attempt too much and fail, simply because they do not thoroughly explain the wide range of phenomena they attempt to consider.

Second, there should be a clear delineation of the domain the theory covers. The boundaries of application should be specified so that the theory is not utilized fruitlessly in situations for which it was never intended. This has been an often neglected aspect of theory building in the social sciences generally (Dubin, 1969), including the field of organizational behavior.

Third, a good theory should direct research efforts to important matters. The number of research studies that could be done in the world is almost infinite. Yet most of these possible studies, even if the time and effort to carry them out were available, would not yield significant results in a statistical sense, and many of those that did would be trivial in terms of the usefulness of results. Good theory helps us to focus research efforts on salient variables, to identify important relationships, and to come up with truly *significant* findings. Basically, it protects a researcher from wasting time.

Fourth, theories at their best yield a value added above the research efforts alone. If a number of hypotheses derived from a theory are confirmed by research, then the whole body of the theory becomes available for use. Theory-based research thus has the potential not just for yielding a few isolated facts but for mobilizing the whole explanatory and predictive power of the theory across its domain. This aspect of good theory building is one of its most practical consequences.

Fifth, theories should be readily subject to test. It should be clear exactly what must be done to either confirm or disconfirm them. On occasion an experimenter will carry out a study that he believes to be an adequate test of a theory, only to have the theorist confront him with the statement, "That is not what I meant." When theory is well formulated, this type of situation should arise only rarely. Ideally, the theorist will identify the variables of the theory as specific measures, using operational terms.

Sixth, good theory not only is confirmed by research derived from it but is logically consistent within itself and with other known facts. In cases when theories are quite complex it is entirely possible to develop propositions that would predict diametrically opposed outcomes in the same situation. This is particularly likely to happen when one approaches the same subject matter from various directions using different concepts and assumptions. Such logical inconsistencies must be ironed out if the theory is to be of much use. Furthermore, theories do not exist in a vacuum; they are part of the total body of scientific knowledge. At a given point in time it may not be entirely clear how a particular theory fits into the larger scientific configuration, but a theory that from the outset quite obviously does not fit at all is deficient. Theories should build on what is known; they should not place us in the uneconomical situation of having to behold constantly the reinvention of the wheel.

Seventh, the best theory is one that is stated in the simplest terms. If a given set of phenomena can be explained tersely with only a few variables, that theory should be preferred over one that achieves the same level of explanation with a much more complex set of variables and relationships. Science does not value complexity for its own sake; there is enough of that in nature. Highly complex and involved theories are often very difficult to use. Thus, the ultimate objective must be to replace them with parsimonious explanations. Unfortunately, the process of inductive theory modification often involves the continual addition of new variables when unanticipated findings emerge and need to be explained. Under such circumstances a theory may fall of its own weight; it is just too cumbersome to be useful.

MEASUREMENT AND RESEARCH DESIGN

In large part the value of a theory resides in the research it sparks and in the extent of confirmation for the theory provided by this research. Research is possible only, however, to the extent that measures of the constructs of the theory are developed; that is to the extent the constructs are made operational. The twin topics of measurement and research concern us here, but the objective is not to provide a detailed treatment. However, in later chapters we will be asking questions such as "Does this measure effectively represent the constructs of the theory?" and, "Does this research provide an appropriate test of the theory?" As these questions are answered it will be necessary to draw on a degree of background knowledge of both measurement procedures and research design; accordingly, sufficient background must be provided.

Measuring Theoretical Constructs

Organizational research often has been conducted using measures that fall far short of what might be desired (Price, 1972). In part this is due to the newness of the field. In theories dealing with organizations, the major emerging constructs have typically been far removed from those previously measured in the social sciences. Thus, it has been necessary in many cases to start from scratch, and the development of reliable and valid measures of new constructs is a time-consuming process. Because many organizational measures are still at a primitive stage of development, the interpretation of research results may be seriously hampered.

Reliability. A major area of concern is the reliability of measurement. Measures must be sufficiently stable and unambiguous so that there are no sizable differences in score values if the measure is applied to the same phenomenon on separate occasions. The reliability of a measure is usually established by a correlation coefficient. There are a number of approaches used to determine this reliability coefficient, but all represent approximations to the ideal procedure of utilizing parallel forms of the same measure. Parallel forms exist when two indexes of the same construct that contain the same number of items of each type have been created, so that the measures concentrate equally on the various aspects of the construct, the same average scores, and the same distributions of scores through the range of possible values. Once such parallel measures have been developed, reliability is determined by administering both measures in the same sample and correlating the scores obtained on each.

The value of the reliability coefficient will fluctuate to some extent depending on whether the parallel form approach is used or one of the numerous approximations to it. Generally, if one wishes to use a measure in individual situations to measure the work motivation of a particular person, for instance, or to compute the average span of control in a certain company, reliability coefficients of .90 or above are required. If, however, one is concerned with group data, as when mean work motivation scores in two units of a company are compared, or when average spans of control in a number of companies are related to their profitability, values as low as about .70 or even less are considered acceptable.

The matter of reliability of measurement is important in research because if unreliable measures are used and statistically significant results are not obtained, it is impossible to interpret the outcome. The failure to obtain evidence of a relationship between two variables could be due to the fact that there is no real relationship. But if one or both measures of the two variables is very unreliable, it may well be that a relationship does exist in fact, although it has not been discovered due to the measurement inadequacy. The only satisfactory way to resolve this uncertainty is to develop and use measures of known high reliability; then if relationships are not found, it can be judged that they are not there.

Validity.   In considering the problems of theory construction, the need to create operational measures of theoretical constructs was emphasized. This means that the measures must truly reflect the underlying constructs; they must provide valid data regarding the phenomena that they are supposed to represent. If they measure something other than what they are intended to measure, a theory may well be assumed to be disconfirmed when it is actually correct. Worse still, a theory may be accepted when the variables of the theory have been stated incorrectly.

Taking an example from the author's own experience, a measure was developed that was presumed to provide an index of conformity to organizational norms. Subsequent research revealed that it was almost completely unrelated to any other measure of conformity that could be identified in the literature. However, moderate relationships with measures of intelligence were found. It became apparent that if the measure did tap some kind of tendency to conform, it was not the same construct that other researchers had in mind when they used the term. A much more likely interpretation was that a relatively unimpressive measure of intelligence had been developed.

This example does have value, however, in demonstrating how one goes about determining the validity of a construct measure. If the measure is what it purports to be, there are certain phenomena to which it should be related and certain others to which it should not be related. In the case of the "conformity" measure there were other indexes of the construct available; often when a new and highly innovative theory is under test this is not so. But it should nevertheless be possible to identify certain kinds of relationships that would be likely to appear. Thus, a measure of motivation to perform in a professional role should yield relatively higher scores among successful professionals than among either nonprofessionals or among beginning professional students, many of whom may never take up practice.

As we will see in considering the various theories, establishing the validity of a particular construct measure is not an easy task. To some degree the answer must always be inferred. Yet there certainly are organizational measures that merit considerable faith. At the other extreme, there are measures that leave considerable doubt as to their construct validity even after long years of use.

Designing Research

Research conducted to test theories is characteristically concerned with investigating hypothesized relationships among variables. It is first concerned with establishing whether a relationship exists at all and then with studying the causal path involved. Re-search focused on establishing whether relationships exist has proved to be relatively easy to conduct; however, the causal prob-lem is clearly much less tractable.

One reason for this situation is that the existence of relation-ships can be determined using data collected at one point in time. Studying causation typically requires the collection of data over time, on the premise that the cause must be shown to precede the effect. Actually, there are certain techniques such as those involv-ing path analysis that, given appropriate circumstances, can be used with concurrently obtained data to test causal hypotheses (Griffin, 1977). However, these techniques tend to require the col-lection of a considerable amount of data, and often they involve the conduct of complex statistical analyses. They also are subject to certain major pitfalls of interpretation (Young, 1977). It be-comes much easier to reject certain alternatives as possible causes than to establish the true causes. Thus, the use of concurrent ap-proaches to studying causation does not fully eliminate the diffi-culties inherent in causal research, which is very demanding of time, effort, and intellect.

A second factor that has served to make the identification of causal relationships difficult is the demand this type of research places on the researcher to establish adequate controls. Control may be accomplished statistically through procedures such as par-tial correlation and analysis of covariance, which measure un-wanted variables and then remove their effects from the relation-ships under study. However, these statistical techniques require assumptions about the nature of the data, and in many cases it is unclear if these assumptions can be met. The preferred alternative is to accomplish control through the original design of the study, which is not always easy.

Laboratory Experiments.   Much of the research that has been done focusing on causal relationships is of a laboratory nature. The extreme instance of this type of research is computer simula-tion, wherein there are no real subjects. More frequently the re-search is of a small group or group dynamics nature with the sub-jects often college sophomores. Here the experimental variables are introduced and the results measured under highly controlled conditions. Because the study is conducted outside the real world of ongoing organizations, it is easier to take longitudinal measures and to control unwanted variables. Yet, even here major difficul-ties in maintaining controls have been noted (Evan, 1971). Fur-thermore, the results are very much a function of the variables considered (this is particularly true of computer simulations). If the real world is not effectively modeled in the laboratory, the results of laboratory experiments will not transfer. This means that any type of laboratory experimentation should be extended to real organizations before the results are accepted. For example, some very significant results have emerged from studies of the decision-making process in business games, but we do not know whether these games contain all of the ingredients of real organizations. Until this is determined, game results cannot be considered complete tests of organizational theory.

Field Experiments. The ideal situation is to take the techniques of sample selection, repetitive measurement, and variable control associated with laboratory research into the real world of ongoing organizations and to conduct the same kind of research there. In such a context the myriad of variables that may really be important, not just assumed, do operate. Any results obtained can be expected to characterize the actual organizations to which any meaningful theory is addressed. The problem is that all the difficulties of designing and conducting good experiments that were so easily handled in the laboratory now become overwhelming. Real organizations have innumerable ways of resisting and undermining objective scientific research — not out of contrariness, but because their goals differ.

An Example of a Field Experiment. The difficulties of conducting causal research within organizations may be illustrated from a study (Belasco and Trice, 1969) dealing with whether a particular management development program produced changes in the managerial component of the organization. The study utilized 119 managers divided into four groups. Assignment to each of these groups was on a random basis within sex, type of work supervised, and department. This procedure was intended to hold as many factors as possible constant across the four groups and to control spurious factors that might contaminate the findings and make causal attribution difficult.

One group of managers went through a pretest measurement of knowledge, attitudes, and behavior, then received training, and finally was measured again with a post-test to see if a change had occurred.

A second group took the pretests, received no training, and then received the same post-tests. If this group changed as much as the first, then clearly the training was not the cause of change. If it did not change to the same extent, then the training remained a strong contender as a cause.

A third group also randomly selected underwent no pretest,

then received training, and finally took the post-test. By comparing the post-test result with that for the first group it was possible to determine whether any apparent change might be the result of a sensitizing effect of the pretest, which may have alerted the managers to what they were supposed to learn later in training.

The fourth such group also received no pretest, did not participate in the training, and therefore underwent only the "post-test." In comparison with the others this group yields an index of the effects of the passage of time only, therefore isolating the time factor from any impact that either repeated measurement or training might produce.

Clearly this kind of research requires a large number of subjects, the opportunity to assign them to groups as desired for research purposes, and a sizable measure of cooperation from the sponsoring organization. It could be argued that a fifth group should have been included to undergo training of a relatively neutral nature. Such a placebo situation would cancel out any so-called Hawthorne effect (receiving special attention). Thus even this very complex experiment cannot be said to have achieved an ideal level of control.

Patch-up or Adaptive Designs.   It is no accident that research of the kind Belasco and Trice conducted is rare in the literature. There are very few organizations that will permit the internal disruption for research purposes that this kind of study requires. In particular there are likely to be problems with random assignments to conditions, obtaining sufficient sample sizes, and leaving people out of a change effort (in the Belasco and Trice case management development), which usually must be proposed in the first place on the basis of some presumed potential value to the organization. Furthermore, there is the very real problem that organizations willing to go along with such studies might not be typical, and therefore the results may lack generality.

It has become quite evident that elegant research designs with all the possible controls are not likely to be implemented in a great number of ongoing organizations. Accordingly, certain variants are being proposed under such titles as patch-up (Evans, 1975) or adaptive (Lawler, 1977) designs. These designs represent major advances over the noncausal correlational analyses, but no one such study leaves all questions unanswered. Basically these studies utilize as many components of the ideal experimental design as possible, while recognizing that it is better to conduct some kind of research related to causes than to do nothing. Hopefully, the relative relaxation of control requirements will be compensated for by the larger number of research investigations carried out. It should then be possible to develop the same level of knowledge that one very elegant study might have given by conducting several interlocking investigations. As we shall see, most theoretical tests conducted in a field setting have been of a patch-up or adaptive variety.

THE STATE OF THEORETICAL KNOWLEDGE OF ORGANIZATIONS

As we enter upon our analysis of theories of organizational behavior, it may be useful to consider certain historical facts regarding the field and its scientist-practitioner nexus. There has not always been a consensus among scientist-researchers and practitioner-managers as to which theories dealing with organizations are most valuable. There is, if anything, a slight negative correlation. Those theories espoused by one group tend to be rejected by the other. One might think that such discord would arise because practitioners prefer the more useful theories while scientists remain guided by scientific values and theoretical sophistication. This is not entirely the case.

Some very insightful quotes from Robert Dubin's writing may help to explain what has happened:

> We live in a highly secular world. The morality of the Judeo-Christian tradition is no longer the consensual boundary within which practical decisions are taken in the operation and management of work organizations. Secular man, even though he is an executive and decision maker, is very much in need of moral guidelines within which to make his decisions .... Today's rational organizational decision makers avidly seek moral justification for their actions and are only too ready to see the new morals in the scientific theories of the applied behavioral scientists. ... Once this phenomenon is recognized, it becomes easier to understand how simple theories can often be widely accepted by practitioners at the very moment that they come under questioning and dispute among scientists (Dubin, 1976, p. 22).

As the Protestant ethic has paled in significance for them, many managers have turned to science for moral guidelines. In meeting this moral need they have been particularly attracted by relatively simple theories with strong humanistic overtones emphasizing the perfectability of mankind. These theories are not unlike religions but possess the added sanctions of science. Unfortunately, such theories often fail to meet scientific criteria for their endorsement and, in particular, may fail to meet the tests of research evidence. Thus, at the same time that more and more practitioners are learning about the theories and finding them attractive, any consensual support that may have existed originally among scientists is disappearing as additional research findings accrue. As more and more scientists withdraw their endorsements, such theories may ultimately fail to attract practitioner support. Or, and this is entirely possible, the theories will establish themselves as social philosophies, which many in large part often are, and continue to attract adherents regardless of the scientific world.

The high visibility of the humanistic philosophy-theory amalgams has led some to question whether the field of organizational behavior possesses any theories at all (Tosi, 1975). This negative position has received further support from some individuals, a number of them scientists, who place very little stock in theory building, preferring the slow but solid pace of untarnished empiricism. Yet there do appear to be some real scientific theories dealing with organizations, or at least advanced explanations that are so close to the level of theory that not to call them that is something of a quibble. These theories are not necessarily valid in all of their aspects; a number have not been fully tested but have contributed substantially to our knowledge of organizations.

The chapters that follow consider both philosophy-theories and theory-theories. They attempt to evaluate both types equally against the criteria of good science and good scientific theory. The selection of the theories for inclusion in this book was preceded by a search for nominations from recognized scholars in the field of organization study. More than 35 individuals responded by suggesting theories that they considered sufficiently important. All theories on which there was a sizable degree of consensus among these scholars are discussed here. Several others, while nominated less often, are included also because, in the author's opinion, they extend our knowledge in new directions or make particularly important contributions. A number of newer, promising theories that have stimulated very little research to date have been excluded on the grounds that it is too early to reach even a preliminary judgment. The author's own theoretical work has also been excluded because the needed objectivity cannot be assured. A review of this work, in many ways comparable to the chapters of this book, has been published elsewhere, however (Miner, 1978).

References   Belasco, James A. and Harrison M. Trice. *Assessment of Change in Training and Therapy.* New York: McGraw-Hill, 1969.

Brown, C. W. and Edwin E. Ghiselli. *Scientific Method in Psychology.* New York: McGraw-Hill, 1955.

Dubin, Robert. *Theory Building.* New York: Free Press, 1969.

Dubin, Robert. Theory Building in Applied Areas, In Marvin D. Dunnette (ed.), *Handbook of Industrial and Organizational Psychology.* Chicago: Rand McNally, 1976, pp. 17–39.

Evan, William M. *Organizational Experiments: Laboratory and Field Research*. New York: Harper and Row, 1971.

Evans, Martin G. Opportunistic Organizational Research: The Role of Patch-up Designs, *Academy of Management Journal*, Vol. 18 (1975), 98–108.

Filley, Alan C., Robert J. House, and Steven Kerr. *Managerial Process and Organizational Behavior*. Glenview, Ill.: Scott, Foresman, 1976.

Griffin, Larry L. Causal Modeling of Psychological Success in Work Organizations, *Academy of Management Journal*, Vol. 20 (1977), 6–33.

Lawler, Edward E. Adaptive Experiments: An Approach to Organizational Behavior Research, *Academy of Management Review*, Vol. 2 (1977), 576–585.

MacKenzie, Kenneth D. and Robert House. Paradigm Development in the Social Sciences: A Proposed Research Strategy, *Academy of Management Review*, Vol. 3 (1978), 7–23.

Marx, Melvin H. *Theories in Contemporary Psychology*. New York: Macmillan, 1963.

Miner, John B. *The Challenge of Managing*. Philadelphia: W. B. Saunders, 1975.

Miner, John B. Twenty Years of Research on Role Motivation Theory of Managerial Effectiveness, *Personnel Psychology*, Vol. 31 (1978), 739–760.

Price, James L. *Handbook of Organizational Measurement*. Lexington, Mass.: D. C. Heath, 1972.

Steiner, George A. and John B. Miner. *Management Policy and Strategy*. New York: Macmillan, 1977.

Tosi, Henry L. *Theories of Organization*. Chicago: St. Clair, 1975.

Young, Jerald W. The Function of Theory in a Dilemma of Path Analysis, *Journal of Applied Psychology*, Vol. 62 (1977), 108–110.

2 NEED HIERARCHY THEORY

The major figure associated with need hierarchy theory is the late Abraham Maslow, who spent much of his professional career on the faculty of Brandeis University. There were several people preceding Maslow who developed somewhat similar formulations, and in recent years certain variants on the basic theory have been put forth. However, the dominant contributor has been Maslow, and his views receive primary attention here; toward the end of the chapter we also will consider one of the recent variants.

Maslow was trained as a psychologist. His early work was in the field of comparative psychology and involved in particular research on primate behavior. However, his interests shifted increasingly to personality theory and to psychoanalysis. He became primarily a clinician, and we will see this influence in his theory.

Need hierarchy theory itself spans over 25 years of Maslow's life. Thus, the theory as set forth here is distinctly emergent. It was originally presented in the psychological literature as a general theory of motivation with little thought of specific applications to management and organizations. In fact, much of Maslow's writing on motivation took him into areas far removed from organizational behavior. The implications of the theory for organizations were first grasped by others, and it was not until the later years of his life that Maslow himself became interested in this type of theoretical application. Nevertheless, the focus here is exclusively on the theory as it applies to organizational matters.

STATEMENT OF THE THEORY

Maslow's first brief statement of need hierarchy theory occurred in a footnote appended to an article published in 1943 (Maslow, 1943a). Later that same year a more comprehensive presentation appeared (Maslow, 1943b).

The Basic Needs

The key variables of the theory are certain motives or needs that are posited as existing within an individual and that combine with biological, cultural, and situational factors to determine behavior. The motive state of a worker is not expected to equate with his or her performance, but it should be a major determinant of performance.

The needs of the theory are viewed as biological or instinctive in nature in that they characterize human beings in general and have a genetic base (Maslow, 1969). They often influence behavior unconsciously; the individual is usually totally unaware of the motivational origins of his behavior. In Maslow's view the number of needs that human beings are said to possess is largely a function of the level of abstraction used in describing them. Maslow prefers to utilize a relatively high level of abstraction and in reality presents a set of categories of human needs (Maslow, 1954, 1970).

The Physiological Needs. In the physiological category Maslow places the chemical needs of the body — sexual desire, hunger, sleepiness, activity needs, desired sensory satisfactions, and the like. Many but not all of these needs have a localized somatic base; such a base exists for hunger, thirst, and sex, but not for sleepiness. When these physiological needs are not satisfied the individual becomes totally preoccupied with the object involved. Thus, a very hungry person thinks of practically nothing except food.

The Safety Needs. The need to be free of danger can have the same pervasive quality as the physiological needs. People are motivated to avoid wild animals, extremes of temperature, assault, disease, and the like — things that might represent a threat to their safety. However, in adults in our society the expression of this type of motivation tends to be inhibited so that people try to show that they are not afraid for their safety; thus, the existence of such needs may not be evident on the surface. As a clinician Maslow devotes particular attention to the sense of insecurity and the consequent anxiety experienced by many emotionally ill individuals. He likens their need states to those of young children who have strong needs for protection against a threatening world.

The Love Needs. Maslow uses the word love in a very comprehensive sense to include affiliation and general belongingness. He has in mind the need for friends, spouses, children, parents, group membership, and the like. The love needs involve both giving and receiving. They should be clearly distinguished from sexual desire, which may be studied as a purely physiological need.

The Esteem Needs. Esteem needs fall into two broad categories. There is first the type that is essentially internal in orientation — desires for such feelings as strength, achievement, adequacy, confidence, independence, and freedom. In addition, esteem may derive from external sources, such as reputation, prestige, recognition, attention, importance, and appreciation. In either case, satisfaction of these needs results in self-confidence and a sense of adequacy; thwarting them produces feelings of inferiority and helplessness.

The Need for Self-Actualization. Self-actualization is both the most significant and the least clearly understood of Maslow's need groupings. It refers to the desire to realize or actualize one's full potential; in Maslow's words, "to become more and more what one is, to become everything that one is capable of becoming" (1943b, p. 382). Since Maslow recognizes sizable individual differences, this means that self-actualizing in one person can be quite different from that in another. In people with any creative potential, self-actualization means the manifestation of this potential. However, creative behavior may reflect needs other than self-actualization; noncreative people can also self-actualize. Since Maslow devoted considerable attention over the years to developing his concept of the need for self-actualization, we will return to this construct in later sections.

The Desires To Know and To Understand. Maslow is somewhat more tentative in his statements regarding the cognitive needs and does not always mention them in discussing his theory. However, when he does consider them, he clearly distinguishes two categories. Both appear to represent a motivational aspect of intelligence.

There is first the desire to know; this involves being aware of reality, getting the facts, and satisfying curiosity. Distinct from this is another set of needs that relates to understanding and explanation. Included in this category are desires to systematize, organize, analyze, and seek out relationships and meanings. Although Maslow does not say so, what he describes is closely allied to the goals of science.

The Aesthetic Needs. Maslow is not always clear in his discussion of aesthetic needs about whether or not they characterize all people. It is apparent that he has seen individuals in his clinical practice in whom these needs are strong, and he expands his theory in order to handle these cases. What he has in mind is a craving for beauty in one's surroundings and, when ugliness prevails, a real sense of deprivation, even sickness. Aesthetic needs may well overlap with cognitive needs. Overall, Maslow gives relatively little attention to aesthetic needs and does not define them or their role with great precision.

Deficiency and Growth Needs. In accordance with his view that need categories are a function of the level of abstraction employed, Maslow invokes a higher level of abstraction to separate the basic human needs into two groups — deficiency and growth. Generally the growth designation is reserved for self-actualization, and all other basic needs are treated as deficiency needs. However, Maslow is not entirely consistent in this usage. On occasion he notes specific needs (such as self-respect) that are not associated with self-actualization but do not qualify for the deficiency designation (Maslow, 1962, 1968). In any event, deficiency need deprivation is related to illness, either physical or psychological; thus, by satifying these needs an individual avoids pathological states. Growth needs, on the other hand, are on a different continuum; their satisfaction produces positive health. Although admitting the difficulty of dealing with the deficiency-growth distinction in the research context, Maslow introduces it to deal with certain qualitative differences in people noted in his clinical practice.

Relationships Among the Needs

Maslow arranges the physiological, safety, love, esteem, and self-actualization needs in what he calls a hierarchy of prepotency. In his hierarchy, physiological needs are the most prepotent; thus, they are lowest on the scale. If a person were totally deprived of need satisfactions, physiological desires would dominate his motivational life. Once physiological needs are reasonably well satisfied, safety needs take center stage, and so on. Thus, when a need is satisfied it disappears for all practical purposes as a motivating force and is replaced by needs at a higher level; the individual continues to be motivated, but the nature of that motivation changes. Should the more prepotent need subsequently be deprived again, it will shift back as the current need.

Degrees of Satisfaction. Various writers have interpreted Maslow's need hierarchy relationships in mutually exclusive terms. To do so certainly makes the conduct of research testing the theory much easier. However, this is not what the theory says, as indicated by the following statement:

> ... most members of our society who are normal are partially satisfied in all their basic needs and partially unsatisfied in all their basic needs at the same time. A realistic description of the hierarchy would be in terms of decreasing percentages of satisfaction as we go up the hierarchy of prepotency. For instance, if I may assign arbitrary figures for the sake of illustration, it is as if the average citizen is satisfied perhaps 85 per cent in his physiological needs, 70 per cent in his love needs, 40 per cent in his self-esteem needs, and 10 per cent in his self-actualization needs (Maslow, 1943b, pp. 388–389).

Furthermore, Maslow describes the emergence of higher level needs as a gradual process, extending over a considerable, unspecified time period. Thus, as a more prepotent need is increasingly satisfied, needs at the next higher level will attain a proportionately greater influence over behavior.

Exceptions to Strict Prepotency. Unfortunately for those who desire simplicity in their theories, Maslow's clinical experience leads him to the conclusion that the specified prepotency relationships among the five need categories, although to be expected on the average, do not hold for all individuals (Maslow, 1954, 1970). In some people, such as the chronically unemployed, higher level needs may become permanently deadened. Thus, these needs do not emerge with the satisfaction of more prepotent needs, and the individual continues to be quite satisfied with what others would consider to be very little.

Another exception occurs among certain people whose lower level needs have long been satisfied and who have lived for many years at the top of the hierarchy. Such people may assume a martyr role in accordance with their values and hold to these values in spite of considerable and extended lower level need deprivation. India's Gandhi would be an example.

Maslow also discusses several reversals where, for instance, esteem appears to be prepotent over love, but the theory is not very specific at this point, and it is not clear whether the reversals are real or only apparent. Throughout his writings Maslow often appears to be caught between theoretical orthodoxy and his clinical insights. The result is a much richer presentation at the expense of theoretical precision.

The Role of Cognitive and Aesthetic Needs. The cognitive and aesthetic needs have typically been ignored by writers and researchers who have concerned themselves with the Maslow theory; in fact, Maslow himself gave these needs relatively little attention. The result has been some confusion. One writer treats these needs as part of the prepotency hierarchy, inserting them after the esteem needs and before self-actualization in an order extending up from the desire to know, through understanding, to the aesthetic needs (Roe, 1956). This appears to be a misinterpretation.

Maslow views the cognitive needs to know and to understand as constituting a separate hierarchy, with knowledge prepotent over understanding. The relationship of this hierarchy and of the aesthetic needs to the other is simply not specified, except that all three types of needs are placed in the deficiency rather than the growth category.

Elaboration of the Self-Actualization Construct

Of all his theoretical formulations, the self-actualization or growth needs appear to have intrigued Maslow most. Over the years he elaborated this part of his theory most extensively. Yet he did not achieve the degree of scientific certainty that the extent of his writing would suggest. This is because he often moved outside the realm of science in discussing self-actualization into the philosophical domains of phenomenology and existentialism (Huizinga, 1970). At times Maslow comes very close to equating self-actualization with a type of religious conversion.

Although various people experience a degree of self-actualization at widely spaced points in their lives, this type of motivation typically becomes paramount as a lifestyle (in those relatively few in whom it is truly possible) only as a person nears the age of 50. In the healthy person physiological needs are predominantly satisfied in infancy, safety needs in childhood, love needs in adolescence, and self-esteem needs during adulthood. Thus, self-actualization is something that typically occurs late in life. When it does occur it is self-reinforcing; the more self-actualization is experienced, the stronger it becomes as a need. Thus, self-actualization is totally unlike the other needs; it is never fully satisfied and can only continue to grow. It is "intrinsic growth of what is already in the organism, or more accurately of what *is* the organism." Yet it takes a high degree of satisfaction of lower order needs before self-actualization emerges. It is very fragile in its prepotency, and only a limited number of people fully experience it.

In his later formulations Maslow did not consider self-actualization as a necessary consequence of satisfying lower level needs (Maslow, 1967). The move to a self-actualizing level can occur when a person is free of illness, gratified to a sufficient degree in lower level needs, positively using his capacities, *and* committed to a particular set of values. At this point, one's work becomes a calling or mission and is indistinguishable from play. Such a move to self-actualization and its values may, however, be totally suppressed in a particular culture or even organization; it is a potential, not an inevitable reality. The values involved are set forth in Table 2–1, along with some examples of their deprivation. It is indicative of Maslow's own uncertainty that some of these self-actualizing (growth) values overlap with the cognitive and aesthetic (deficiency) needs. Because he approaches his subject matter from different directions, Maslow does indeed reach different conclusions, and the inconsistencies are never resolved.

Finally, as further evidence of the convergence of the theory with religion, we might cite his concept of *eupsychia* — "the culture that would be generated by 1000 self-actualizing people on some sheltered island where they would not be interfered with" (Maslow, 1965). The parallel with various utopias and the kingdom of God is compelling. In this and other respects Maslow has

Table 2–1.   VALUES ESPOUSED BY SELF-ACTUALIZING PEOPLE AND EXAMPLES OF THEIR DEPRIVATION

Values	Deprivation
1. Truth	Dishonesty, disbelief, mistrust
2. Goodness	Evil, utter selfishness
3. Beauty	Ugliness, vulgarity
4. Unity, wholeness	Chaos, atomism, disintegration
5. Transcendence of dichotomies	Black and white dichotomies, polarization, low synergy
6. Aliveness, process	Deadness, emptiness, robotizing
7. Uniqueness	Sameness, uniformity
8. Perfection	Sloppiness, poor workmanship
9. Necessity	Accident, unpredictability
10. Completion, finality	Incompleteness, cessation of striving
11. Justice	Injustice, lawlessness
12. Order	Chaos, breakdown of authority
13. Simplicity	Overcomplexity, confusion
14. Richness, totality, comprehensiveness	Poverty, loss of interest
15. Effortlessness	Fatigue, strain, gracelessness
16. Playfulness	Grimness, depression, cheerlessness
17. Self-sufficiency	Dependence, contingency
18. Meaningfulness	Meaninglessness, despair

Adapted from Abraham Maslow. A Theory of Metamotivation: The Biological Rooting of the Value Life, *Journal of Humanistic Psychology*, Vol. 7 (1967), pp. 108–109.

a tendency to carry his concept of self-actualization into the domain of mysticism, and it is very difficult to decipher exactly what he means.

Implications of Need Hierarchy Theory for Organizations

Why is this kind of a theory important for the study of organizations? One answer is that it has been widely adopted by managers and used by them to guide their decisions about employees. There is little question that Maslow's original article (1943b) has been one of the most influential in the management field (Matteson, 1974).

However, the more basic consideration that makes need hierarchy theory important for organization study is that if the theory is valid it tells us some significant things about how organizations should be managed. Figure 2–1 presents one view of the relationships among company policies and leadership styles, the degree of activation and satisfaction of needs at various levels in the hierarchy, and productivity and turnover/absenteeisms. In this figure it is assumed that physiological needs are satisfied. The term membership is substituted for Maslow's love, and self-esteem is broken into its internal and external components. The implication is that

Conditions in the Work Group's Environment						
				Low Perceived Contribution Opportunity	High Perceived Contribution Opportunity	Company Perceived as Supportive
						High Perceived Contribution Opportunity
			Production-Centered Leadership	Accommodative Leadership	Accommodative Leadership	Group-Centered Leadership
		Low-Status Congruence	High-Status Congruence	High-Status Congruence	High-Status Congruence	High-Status Congruence
	Low Interaction Opportunity	High Interaction Opportunity	High Interaction Opportunity	High Interaction Opportunity	High Interaction Opportunity	High Interaction Opportunity
Low Employment Security	High Employment Security	High Employment Security	High Employment Security	High Employment Security	High Employment Security	High Employment Security

NEEDS

- Self-Actualization
- Status-Prestige
- Self-Esteem
- Membership
- Safety

(EFFECTS ON PRODUCTIVITY AND TURNOVER-ABSENTEEISM)

Productivity	High	Low	Low?	Low	Meets Minimum Requirements	High	High
Turnover-Abs.	Low	High	High	?	Average	Low	Low

Key: □ = need not activated   ▨ = need activated but relatively satisfied   ▥ = need activated but relatively frustrated

Figure 2-1. Some relations between conditions in the work group's environment, motivation, satisfaction, productivity and turnover/absenteeism. (James V. Clark. Motivation in Work Groups: A Tentative View. *Human Organization*, Vol. 13 (1960–61), p. 202.)

to the extent management can control conditions in the work group's environment, it can induce certain motivational patterns and obtain the resulting benefits of increased productive output and reduced turnover and absenteeism. Once one moves beyond the safety needs, it appears to be highly desirable to create conditions that activate the highest possible need level (Clark, 1960).

Other implications of the theory also have been noted. When job conditions are poor in terms of pay and security, the theory predicts that employees will focus on aspects of the work itself, and significant motivational consequences can be obtained only by making changes in this regard. As conditions improve, the behavior of supervisors takes on increased significance. Finally, with a much improved environment the role of the supervisor diminishes, and the nature of the work itself re-emerges as motivationally salient, but now in relation to self-actualization and not to physiological and safety need satisfaction (Campbell, 1971).

The theory also predicts that as people move up in the managerial hierarchy they will be motivated by higher and higher need levels; thus, managers at various levels should be treated differently. Furthermore, employees can be expected always to want more, no matter what the organization does, but the specific things desired will change. The organization cannot give enough by way of growth and development; it is the nature of the self-actualization need that once activated and satisfied, it becomes a stimulus to an even greater desire for satisfaction. Thus, it is a continuing source of motivation.

In his own writing in the field of management, Maslow is very clear that his theory indicates that companies should do all they can to provide the highest level of need satisfaction possible (Maslow, 1965). The self-actualizing manager is the best manager. Authoritarian leadership is rejected because it thwarts the esteem needs of subordinates. Yet Maslow is realistic: "Treating people well spoils them for being treated badly. That is, they become less contented and willing to accept lower life conditions." Once one takes the higher level need route in management, it will be difficult to go back.

Need hierarchy theory is attractive as a basis for managerial decision-making for a number of reasons, but one of the most important is that it is primarily an "on the average" theory. Except in the case of self-actualization, it does not stress individual differences nor require the measurement of each individual motivational pattern prior to action but rather considers groups of individuals as defined in part by external circumstances. In this regard it is particularly suited to the use of broad managerial policies (which also operate on the average) in dealing with human resource matters. Management by policy is the prevailing mode in organizations other than the very smallest.

Given the widespread acceptance of the theory by managers, and its attractiveness as a basis for formulating human resource policies, it becomes very important to assess Maslow's formulations in terms of their internal consistency, testability, and degree of research support. Can we then say this is good theory?

EVALUATION OF THE THEORY

Scientific, Philosophical, and Logical Considerations

Maslow's formulations are among those that border on the philosophical, especially in the treatment of self-actualization. They do have strong religious and moral overtones, and they are humanistic. Thus, a legitimate question is whether Maslow was writing in the realm of science or the realm of philosophy. On this point Maslow is quite specific:

> This book, like my previous one, is full of affirmations which are based on pilot researches, bits of evidence, on personal observation, on theoretical deduction and on sheer hunch. These are generally phrased so that they can be proven true or false. That is they are hypotheses, i.e., presented for testing rather than for final belief. They are also obviously relevant and pertinent, i.e., their possible correctness or incorrectness is important to other branches of psychology. They matter. They should therefore generate research and I expect they will. For these reasons I consider this book to be in the realm of science or pre-science, rather than of exhortation, or of personal philosophy, or literary expression (Maslow, 1962, pp. v–vi).

Thus, Maslow himself clearly opts for science. Yet he did only one research study bearing on his theory and did very little to establish operational measures of his major variables. There certainly are some logical inconsistencies in the theory, especially in relation to the deficiency-growth formulations. Furthermore, Maslow's treatment of self-actualizations does move into a mystical-religious arena where empirical tests of his propositions are almost impossible. There is a question whether the theory has been put forth in a manner that permits scientific confirmation or rejection.

A number of logical criticisms have been raised against need hierarchy theory (Locke, 1976). For example, the inherent nature and logical consistency of the various need groupings have been questioned. Above the physiological level little evidence exists for the basic nature of Maslow's needs, and in some areas he appears to be putting together "apples and oranges." The concept of self-actualization is never intelligibly defined. It is almost impossible to know when this motive is operating, because the real person must be established in advance, and this can vary individually. Ad hoc definitions are simply tautological (Miner, 1974). Furthermore, the theory continually confuses needs (what is good for a person) and values (what the person views as good), as in the case of aesthetic needs and beauty as a value.

There is little question that as a theoretical statement what Maslow has written leaves much to be desired. Yet one cannot read him without recognizing a genuine desire to grapple intellectually with extremely important topics and to consider anything that appears to offer contradictory evidence. His writings offer a stimulating portrayal of an outstanding mind in action and perhaps a self-actualizing person as well, although Maslow denies it. Even if parts of the theory are untestable and even unintelligible and major logical inconsistencies exist, there still remains a sizable body of theory that does not suffer from these deficiencies. Thus, the ultimate test must be empirical: Does the theory or a major part of it achieve the support of scientific research?

Measuring the Variables

The greatest obstacle to research on Maslow's formulations has proved to be measurement. With a few possible exceptions Maslow did not provide operational definitions of his variables. It was almost 20 years after the first publication of the theory before measuring instruments began to be developed. Accordingly, the theory went untested for a considerable period, during which it won increasing acceptance simply on its inherent appeal.

Maslow's Own Measures. The measures developed by Maslow are important not so much for themselves as for the approach he used in constructing them. One is a measure of self-esteem that was designed specifically for use with women (Maslow, 1942). The other is a measure of psychological security-insecurity that is intended to tap certain safety needs (Maslow, 1951). As a pure measure of a theoretical variable, however, this latter test suffers from a confounding of the safety need construct with the need for love (Huizinga, 1970).

Maslow's approach in developing these instruments was to identify a high and a low group of subjects (on the variable under study) based initially on clinical investigation. These extreme groups were then studied intensively, and a tentative measuring instrument was developed. Then the groups were purged of doubtful cases using the measuring instrument as a guide, and the measure was modified to better differentiate the groups. Through this iterative process extreme groups of subjects (who, for example, were all either very secure or very insecure) were finally established; items were included in the final test only if these two groups responded to them differently.

This is a time-consuming process but is clearly the one Maslow recommended for developing measures of his theoretical variables. Yet none of the measures developed since are based on such a process. It is entirely possible that many of the difficulties with measures that have occurred could have been avoided had Maslow's recommendations been followed.

The Porter Need Satisfaction Questionnaire.   One of the first and by far the most widely used measures was developed by Porter (1964). This is a 13-item instrument on which subjects indicate how much of the various listed characteristics exist in their current jobs, how much there should be, and how important the characteristics are to them. Some characteristics noted are: feeling of security, opportunity to develop close friendships, prestige of position, opportunity for independent thought and action, and feeling of worthwhile accomplishment. The physiological, cognitive, and aesthetic needs are not represented as such, and these latter two categories have not been explicitly included in any measure yet developed. Autonomy (independence) is separated from the esteem needs in a distinct departure from Maslow's categorization. For purposes of testing need hierarchy theory, the significant scores are the reported importance level for each need measured (on a 7-point scale) and the satisfaction index obtained by subtracting the reported "is now" amount of the characteristic from the "should be" amount.

This instrument, although it has yielded interesting data, is not adequate to provide a definitive test of the theory. The median test-retest reliability coefficient (R) of need measures over a 6-month period is only .38 (Lawler and Suttle, 1972). In addition, the method of obtaining satisfaction and importance scores at the same time from the same instrument introduces a response bias that makes interpretation of the results difficult; it is quite possible that the construct validities are not as high as might be desired (Wahba and Bridwell, 1976).

Other Measures.   Although the Porter questionnaire and derivatives of it have been by far the most widely used measures, a number of other measuring instruments have been developed. It has been shown that reliable instruments can be constructed (Beer, 1966). The various measures tend to concentrate on somewhat different needs even within the physiological-to-self-actualization hierarchy. Most commonly, the physiological level is neglected on the grounds that it is widely satisfied and thus of relatively little importance. However, a recent study conducted in Israel suggests that this may not always be so (Yinon, Bizman, and Goldberg, 1976). This same study also is noteworthy in that no attempt was made to measure self-actualization. In view of the logical problems with this construct and the fact that when attempts to measure it have been made the items have been written at a very high level of abstraction, the decision not to include such items in this study appears to be a wise one.

We are now at a point where the validity of Maslow's need categories can be studied by intercorrelating a number of the independent measures that have been developed. Indexes of the same need should relate more closely to each other than to measures of other needs. Very little of this research has been conducted; however, what has been done is not very encouraging for the Maslow constructs (Schneider and Alderfer, 1973). The need for more such research is clearly evident.

The Factor Analytic Studies

Another extensively used approach to testing Maslow's theory is to take some measure of the basic needs and conduct a factor analysis of the items to see if the resulting clustering is in accord with the Maslow formulations. Studies utilizing this approach (with the Porter questionnaire or a close facsimile) have uniformly yielded negative results (Wahba and Bridwell, 1976). One of the most confusing findings from this research has been the emergence of a clear "need to know" factor that appears to have much in common with the cognitive needs that Maslow described but was not intentionally included in the measure used for the research (Roberts, Walter, and Miles, 1971). This particular result begs further investigation, but to date has not received it.

Whether the overall lack of support for the theory resulting from the use of the Porter measure is a consequence of that instrument's deficiencies is difficult to say with certainty. The Porter questionnaire was an early effort to conquer measurement problems that the author of need hierarchy theory himself had not really attacked and that had been left uncontested for many years. As a pilot effort it succeeded admirably in that it did stimulate further study and the development of more useful instruments. This conclusion is affirmed by some later measures that have produced factor structures having much in common with the Maslow formulations (Beer, 1966; Huizinga, 1970; Mitchell and Moudgill, 1976).

On the other hand, the results of these more recent investigations do not prove the basic or instinctoid nature of the Maslow need categorizations. What comes out of a factor analysis is largely a consequence of what is put in. What has been demonstrated is that measures that produce factors matching the basic needs can be constructed if one works at it. Thus, the potential viability of Maslow's categories has been confirmed, but it has not been shown that these groupings are any more basic than other groupings. It seems likely that one could produce factors that matched a completely different theory of human needs if the initial items were selected with this intent in mind. The fact that autonomy factors that are quite separate from the esteem measures typically have been produced, even though Maslow himself did not make such a differentiation, attests to the extreme sensitivity of factor structures to initial item input.

Studies Dealing with Prepotency

A number of studies have used measures such as the one devised by Porter to rank the needs in terms of their average rated importance in a group. These rankings were compared with satisfaction levels on the assumption that the more the need is deprived or is a source of dissatisfaction, the more important it should be. Similar studies have compared satisfaction levels alone, with the expectation that higher order needs should be the least satisfied. The results obtained from this type of research are quite mixed, and no clear overall conclusions emerge (Wahba and Bridwell, 1976). However, if one follows Maslow closely, this is what might be expected. If higher level needs are not engaged or activated in people, it is meaningless to ask whether they are satisfied or dissatisfied; these needs simply do not exist as a factor in behavior. Thus, when one does ask a question related to higher level needs, the response obtained is very likely to be either a reflection of cultural stereotypes or a random "off the top of the head" reply that could be quite different tomorrow. In neither case is one getting at the true dynamics of the motives under study.

More significant research focuses directly on the prepotency question, preferably with an analysis over time. When a need moves toward satisfaction it should lose its importance proportionately, and the next higher need level should gradually increase in importance. Several studies have attempted to assess this aspect of the theory.

The Hall and Nougaim Research. A study was conducted with 49 young management level employees of one of the operating companies of the American Telephone and Telegraph Company (Hall and Nougaim, 1968). These individuals were followed over a 5-year period, and lengthy interviews were conducted with each on a yearly basis. These interviews were recorded and subsequently analyzed to yield measures of need strength and need satisfaction. When these scores were assigned by two independent coders it became evident that agreement was difficult. A median reliability coefficient of .57 was obtained.

An initial analysis was made for each year correlating the satisfaction scores for one need with the need strength scores for the next higher level need (e.g., safety satisfaction was correlated with affiliation strength). The correlations obtained were generally positive, as expected, but the median coefficient was only .20, and only 29 per cent of the correlations were statistically significant. In comparison, when need satisfaction and strength were correlated for the same need (excluding self-actualization), the values were also positive, with a median value of .24, and 43 per cent significant.

A similar analysis also was conducted using changes in scores from one year to the next. Thus, changes in safety need satisfaction during a given year were correlated with changes in affiliation need strength during that same year. This procedure provides a direct test of the Maslow formulations. As satisfaction of one need increases, the strength of the next higher need should increase. During the 5-year period of study, obvious increases in love, esteem, and self-actualization did occur, while the strength of safety needs declined. Nevertheless, the predicted correlations among change scores were not strong. The median figure was .18, and only 17 per cent of the correlations were statistically significant. These values compare with the same need changes, which had a median value of .34, with 75 per cent of the correlations significant.

Although the rather low correlations might be caused by difficulties in obtaining scorer reliability, this factor would not be expected to influence differently the predicted and nonpredicted correlations. The only conclusion warranted is that the study did not succeed in providing much support for the need hierarchy theory.

The Lawler and Suttle Research. This study was similar in many respects to that of Hall and Nougaim. A total of 187 managers in two organizations completed the Porter questionnaire at the same time; half of them then completed it again six months later and the other half a year later (Lawler and Suttle, 1972).

Without going into great detail, the results of this study are much the same as those of the preceding one. There are very few statistically significant findings. However, when significance is obtained it almost invariably involves the security need; and at least some of these correlations, although not all, are consistent with the Maslow theory. Furthermore, the security need measures are shown to be more reliable (median .67) than any of the others (love .42, esteem .41, autonomy .40, self-actualization .34). It is appropriate to speculate as to what the results for the needs above the security level might have been had their measures proved more reliable. Clearly, the Porter measure is not the instrument of choice in such studies. Yet even with its shortcomings, the fact that the Lawler and Suttle research using different samples, a different instrument, and in some respects different methods of analysis produced results similar to those of Hall and Nougaim must be taken as further reason to question the prepotency aspects of Maslow's theory.

Additional Research

There are many other studies that bear on aspects of the need hierarchy theory, although none represents the same kind of crucial test as those just cited. However, there are several, including one conducted by Maslow himself, that offer interesting insights and occasionally important information.

The Maslow Study of Self-Actualization. What Maslow set out to do was to identify a group of self-actualizing people and then study them clinically to try to get a clearer picture of what self-actualization is (Maslow, 1954). He may have had in mind as an ultimate goal the development of a measure similar to his tests of self-esteem and psychological security. However, this was not accomplished.

Initially, 3000 college students were screened, but only one was found to be truly self-actualizing. From this Maslow concluded that "self-actualization of the sort I have found in my older subjects was not possible in our society for young, developing people." In the end the sample was developed from among acquaintances and public or historical figures. There were 13 individuals who were considered certain self-actualizers, including Lincoln and Jefferson, 12 who fell short but were sufficiently close to provide some insights, and 26 who showed signs of developing toward self-actualization.

These people were studied by whatever methods were available, and a list of qualities of self-actualizing people was developed. There was much room for personal bias in both the selection of subjects and the identification of characteristics, and Maslow admitted this lack of adequate experimental controls. Nevertheless, as a pilot or exploratory effort the findings are of interest. The characteristics of self-actualizing people as reported by Maslow are as follows:

More efficient perceptions of reality and more comfortable relations with it

Acceptance of themselves, of others, and of the realities of life

Spontaneity and naturalness

A focusing on real problems outside themselves

The quality of detachment and a need for privacy

Autonomy and relative independence of the physical and social environment

Continued freshness of appreciation

Frequent mystic experiences

Feelings of identification, sympathy, and affection for mankind

Deeper and more profound interpersonal relationships

A democratic character structure

Strong commitment to ethical and moral standards

A philosophical, unhostile sense of humor

Creativeness

A certain resistance to or inner detachment from the prevailing culture

The capacity to resolve dichotomies

Mitchell's Study of Air Force Officers.   Mitchell's research is similar to that of a number of others, including Porter, in relating the various needs to characteristics of organizations. The Porter questionnaire has been widely used in these studies, and for this purpose it often has proved adequate. Mitchell (1970) administered the questionnaire to 675 Air Force officers and compared the need scores obtained at different grade levels as well as in line and staff positions.

The results of Table 2–2 indicate that in most instances the higher ranking officers (brigadier generals and colonels) experience greater need fulfillment and relative satisfaction in their work. In addition, those in command (line) positions are more fulfilled and satisfied than the staff officers. The only real exception to this pattern appears to be the social (love) needs, which vary very little with position level or type. There is very little evidence of hierarchical differences in need patterns. It should be understood that this type of research says nothing about whether those with certain motivational characteristics are more likely to attain or gravitate to certain positions or, as in Maslow, whether the positions elicit certain motivational responses.

Beer's Study of Leadership Style and Motivation.   It will be remembered that Clark (1960) hypothesized certain relationships between leadership style and need activation (Fig. 2–1). In particular, production-centered leadership was said to satisfy the safety needs and accommodative or group-centered leadership to satisfy needs at a higher level. Beer (1966) carried out a study of 129 insurance company clerical workers that bears directly on these hypotheses. He

Table 2-2. NEED FULFILLMENT AND SATISFACTION SCORES FOR AIR FORCE OFFICERS

Need Category	Rank				Position Type	
	Brigadier General or Colonel	Lieutenant Colonel or Major	Captain or Lieutenant		Line	Staff
Degree of Current Need Fulfillment in Position[*]						
Security	6.0	4.8	4.7		5.5	4.7
Social	5.6	5.3	5.2		5.5	5.2
Esteem	5.5	5.0	4.5		5.3	4.6
Autonomy	5.5	4.7	4.4		5.0	4.5
Self-actualization	5.3	4.8	4.5		5.3	4.6
Degree of Need Satisfaction Relative to What Is Desired[†]						
Security	.5	1.2	1.1		.6	1.2
Social	.6	.6	.6		.6	.6
Esteem	.9	1.1	1.3		1.0	1.2
Autonomy	.9	1.3	1.2		1.2	1.2
Self-actualization	1.0	1.5	1.6		1.2	1.5

[*] larger scores mean more fulfillment

[†] smaller scores mean more satisfaction

Adapted from Vance F. Mitchell. Need Satisfactions of Military Commanders and Staff. *Journal of Applied Psychology*, Vol. 54 (1970), pp. 284–285.

correlated various measures of leadership styles with his index of basic need satisfaction.

The results indicate that a highly structured leadership style (although not necessarily production centered) is associated with safety need satisfaction. A style that provides considerable freedom of action is positively related to autonomy need satisfaction. And highly considerate leadership is associated with both higher esteem and higher self-actualization. These results, although not identical with those hypothesized by Clark, are certainly consonant with them. They are also consistent with what Maslow (1965) might expect.

EXISTENCE, RELATEDNESS, AND GROWTH (ERG) THEORY

ERG theory was formulated by Alderfer (1972) to deal with certain of the shortcomings that have been noted in the original need hierarchy formulations. It is an attempt to revise Maslow's theory to make it agree more with the research findings. Perhaps Maslow would have developed a similar revision had he lived to do so.

Statement of the Theory

Alderfer's modifications involve a telescoping of the Maslow need categories, a change in the prepotency relationships, and certain additions to the theory.

Existence, Relatedness and Growth Needs.   The Alderfer theory corresponds to that of Maslow as follows:

Alderfer	Maslow
Existence needs	Physiological needs Safety needs of a material type
Relatedness needs	Safety needs of an interpersonal type Love or belongingness needs Esteem needs of an interpersonal type
Growth needs	Esteem needs that are self-confirmed Self-actualization

Relationships Among the Needs.   In its original form, ERG theory set forth seven basic propositions regarding need relationships:

1. The less existence needs are satisfied, the more they will be desired (follows Maslow).

2. The less relatedness needs are satisfied, the more existence needs will be desired (reverse of Maslow).

3. The more existence needs are satisfied, the more relatedness needs will be desired (same orientation as Maslow).

4. The less relatedness needs are satisfied, the more they will be desired (follows Maslow).

5. The less growth needs are satisfied, the more relatedness needs will be desired (reverse of Maslow).

6. The more relatedness needs are satisfied, the more growth needs will be desired (same orientation as Maslow).

7. The more growth needs are satisfied, the more they will be desired. (follows Maslow).

Going beyond the issues that were of concern to Maslow, Alderfer set forth a number of propositions dealing with the impacts of desires on satisfactions:

8a. When existence materials are scarce, then the higher chronic existence desires are, the less existence satisfaction.

8b. When existence materials are not scarce, then there will be no differential existence satisfaction as a function of chronic existence desire.

9a. In highly satisfying relationships there is no differential relatedness satisfaction as a function of chronic relatedness desires.

9b. In normal relationships, persons very high and very low on chronic relatedness desires tend to obtain lower satisfaction than persons with moderate desires.

9c. In highly dissatisfying relationships, then, the higher chronic relatedness desires, the more relatedness satisfaction.

10a. In challenging discretionary settings, then, the higher chronic growth desires, the more growth satisfaction.

10b. In nonchallenging, nondiscretionary settings, there will be no differential growth satisfaction as a function of chronic growth desires.

Alderfer's Research

Whereas Maslow did not make his theoretical variables operational in terms of specific measures (to any but a very limited degree), Alderfer constructed a specific measure of both desire and satisfaction for all three of his need categories. These scales generally contain items that can be grouped together in a factor analysis, are quite reliable, and are valid measures of the constructs involved.

A number of studies were conducted using these instruments in different settings to test the propositions. A given proposition typically was tested in several different samples. The samples consisted of: 34 managers in a medium-sized manufacturing firm; 138 employ-ees in the same firm; 60 managers in a medium-sized bank; 157 employees in the same bank; 57 members of a college fraternity; 46 members of another fraternity at the same college; 77 students at a boys' preparatory school; 46 teachers, ministers, and social workers in T-groups; 83 male and female preparatory school students in T-groups; 112 MBA students.

The results of this program of research are given in Table 2–3. Propositions 3 (satisfying existence needs activates relatedness needs) and 5 (depriving growth needs activates relatedness needs) clearly do not receive much research support. The other propositions that were tested generally received sufficient support to maintain their viability. However, in several cases the support was quite mixed.

Revised Propositions

In a number of instances when the research data did not consis-tently support ERG propositions, Alderfer felt he could identify certain factors that might account for obtaining support in one setting and not in another. Accordingly, he proposed several inductive revisions of his seven original theoretical statements. These are as follows:

2. When both existence and relatedness needs are relatively dissat-isfied, the less relatedness needs are satisfied, the more existence needs will be desired.

4. When relatedness needs are relatively dissatisfied, the less relat-edness needs are satisfied, the more they will be desired; when

Table 2–3. SUMMARY OF RESEARCH TESTING ERG THEORY PROPOSITIONS (ALDERFER, 1972)

Proposition Number	Number of Samples	Nature of Results
1	6	Consistent support in all samples
2	6	Supported in 5 samples
3	6	Not supported at all
4	8	Supported in 6 samples
5	6	Supported in 1 sample
6	8	Supported in 3 samples
7	8	Supported in 3 samples
8a	not tested	
8b	not tested	
9a	2	Supported in 1 sample
9b	3	Supported in 1 sample
9c	2	Supported in 1 sample
10a	2	Consistent support in both samples
10b	not tested	

relatedness needs are relatively satisfied, the more relatedness needs are satisfied, the more they will be desired.

6. When both relatedness and growth needs are relatively satisfied, the more relatedness needs are satisfied, the more growth needs will be desired.

7. When growth needs are relatively dissatisfied, the less growth needs are satisfied, the more they will be desired; when growth needs are relatively satisfied, the more growth needs are satisfied, the more they will be desired.

In presenting the propositions in curvilinear form, Alderfer has no doubt put them in closer alliance with his research data. Nevertheless, the propositions grew out of that data and must be subjected to subsequent independent tests. Furthermore, the revisions tend to upset the internal logical integrity of the original formulations. Thus, the revised theory is at a lower level of abstraction and tends to approach a set of empirical generalizations. Accordingly, it becomes more cumbersome to use ERG theory for managerial decisions.

Recent Research

The ERG theory and in particular its revisions are of sufficiently recent origin that very little research has been done. However, Alderfer, Kaplan, and Smith (1974) have provided confirmatory evidence for the revised proposition 4 in a carefully controlled laboratory study using practicing managers as subjects. The predicted curvilinear relationship between relatedness satisfaction and desire was obtained. Furthermore, Wanous, and Zwany (1977) obtained some evidence of curvilinear relationships in a study of 208 telephone company employees. This study is of additional significance because it utilized measures of ERG needs differing from those developed by Alderfer and still obtained a factor structure closely approximating the ERG classification.

CONCLUSIONS

Where then do need hierarchy theory and the ERG variant stand? The answer must differ depending upon what one intends to do with the results. For the purposes of science, where "I don't know" is the best answer until one is absolutely sure, it is desirable to be conservative. There is no need to make a decision immediately, and a premature wrong decision may foreclose further research in any area for years. For the purposes of operating organizations the situation is quite different. Decisions involving employee motivation must be made daily, and human resource policies can have tremendous impact on productivity. One must make the best decision possible, given the available information. Even if one ends by doing nothing, this is a decision that reinforces whatever implicit or explicit policies are in effect at that particular time. Thus, our conclusions must be considered separately relative to the goals of science and the goals of management.

Scientific Goals

It is clear that the available research does not support the Maslow theory to any significant degree. This does not imply that the theory is wrong, merely that it has not been supported. Other studies using other approaches might yield different conclusions, but for the moment the evidence is nonconfirming, and the longer this condition holds, the more scientific interest is likely to wane.

A number of suggestions can be made that might serve to produce better research tests of the theory; some of these derive from Maslow himself. As regards experimental design, Maslow (1943b, p. 387) says, "What we have claimed is that the person will *want* the more basic of two needs when deprived of both." This suggests that a truly elegant experiment would involve comparing the activated needs of groups of individuals deprived of two different types of needs. A series of such studies should establish any prepotency relationships once and for all.

Secondly, the measurement problem has not been solved fully. None of the existing measures achieves the degree of sophistication Maslow envisaged. It is clear from his discussion of the iterative approach that he had in mind the creation of lengthy, separate measures for each need category, and possibly even for groupings within categories. Furthermore, he viewed motivation as largely an unconscious process. Yet, the self-report measures that have been used rely on conscious processes. The method of choice in measuring unconscious motivation is some kind of projective technique. We will consider this whole matter in detail in the next chapter. It is sufficient to indicate now that no need hierarchy study has effectively utilized measures that tap unconscious motivation.

One of the most obvious measurement problems exists in the area of self-actualization, a very imprecise concept. Ideally, measures would utilize information on a person's capabilities and potential to construct a very individualized instrument. The alternative has been to use items at a high level of abstraction to obtain indexes of the desire for "growth," "development," and so forth. Such measures produce a rather large number of self-actualizers even in younger groups. But Maslow contends that self-actualization is a rare phenomenon and almost unheard of in the early years. Existing measures are not tapping the construct Maslow had in mind, although it is not certain if that construct was defined precisely enough to permit adequate operational use. Maslow's own research study indicates that he may have tried to create a measure and failed. One possible approach would be to use the values set forth in Table 2–1 to construct an appropriate measure of self-actualization.

It is noteworthy that research has focused entirely on the five basic needs in the hierarchy, ignoring completely the cognitive and aesthetic needs. This may have been unfortunate. The research does not prove that any specific set of needs is basic, and these other needs proposed by Maslow are equally worthy of consideration. It is evident that factor analysis can produce the Maslow categories, with autonomy added if desired, or the Alderfer ERG pattern. Thus, factor analysis will not tell us what to measure, only how to measure consistently what we want to measure.

Regarding the Alderfer theory, it is too early to reach a definite conclusion. This theory would not have been considered here were it not for its close relation to the Maslow constructs and the fact that ERG research is relevant to need hierarchy theory in general. It is evident that the original Alderfer theory has no more support for its validity than Maslow's. The revised theory may have, but in its present form it is merely a set of loosely related empirical generalizations. There is a need to organize these generalizations into a more powerful set of general propositions at a higher level of abstraction.

Managerial Goals

Many managers have used need hierarchy theories as an aid in understanding changing employee motivations as the industrial system of the United States has developed. In doing so they focus on the shift from physiological and safety needs to higher level needs as the primary basis for work effort; once the lower needs are satisfied in a relatively affluent industrial society, usually through the medium of compensation, higher needs come into play, and new types of incentives and satisfaction must be provided.

Thus, many managers have implicitly telescoped the need hierarchy into a dichotomy, with the cutting point quite low on the scale. In contrast, Maslow, in distinguishing between deficiency and growth needs, established a cutting point very high on the scale between esteem and self-actualization. This high level cutting point has not been supported by the research, although it is possible that with a more theoretically relevant measure of self-actualization it might yet emerge. On the other hand, a low-level cutting point does have considerable research support (Alderfer, 1972; Lawler, 1973; Mitchell and Moudgill, 1976).

For managerial purposes then, it does seem useful to think of at least some among the physiological and safety needs noted by Maslow and the existence needs described by Alderfer as dominating. When these needs are not satisfied they tend to dominate the personality in an all-pervasive manner, so that other types of striving are shut out. Although it might be argued that these types of needs are almost universally satisfied in our society, there is ample evidence that this is not true. One example might be a low pay, low seniority, low skill family breadwinner in an industry characterized by major cyclical swings, working in an area with sizable unemployment from which she cannot move because of family commitments. Other examples would be alcoholic and drug-using employees and neurotics suffering from severe phobias that are activated by the work situation. Then, too, there are jobs that must be performed under circumstances of real, continuing physical danger.

For those individuals whose physiological and safety needs are reasonably satisfied on a continuing basis, other needs do become important in determining behavior. In this instance only, there does appear to be some kind of prepotency. But what needs can be expected to emerge in what degree of dominance over behavior appears to depend on individual development experiences and to vary widely from person to person. Given the nature of the research evidence, it appears best for managers not to assume any certain need hierarchy above the most basic level. Thus, policy making should not adopt any such hierarchy.

Beyond this two-step differentiation, and the recognition that needs such as those for social relationships, self-esteem and dignity, autonomy, and creative challenge can be important in human behavior, need hierarchy theory has not yet contributed in a major way to a scientifically based managerial practice. Primarily its contribution is to the working theories that managers can use to understand, predict, and influence employee motivation and performance. In addition, the research generated by the theory relating certain needs to managerial level, line-staff status, company size, and the like (Porter, 1964; Mitchell, 1970) does provide useful guidelines as to the strong motives likely under certain circumstances.

The theory has not generated the kinds of original contributions to practice that we will see emerging from some of the other theories. The only such application of which the author is aware is a particular type of sensitivity training that focuses strongly on developing self-actualization and growth needs (Bugental and Tannenbaum, 1965). This approach appears to have been only partially successful and does not currently enjoy much managerial support.

References

Alderfer, Clayton P. *Existence, Relatedness, and Growth: Human Needs in Organizational Settings.* New York: Free Press, 1972.

Alderfer, Clayton P., Robert E. Kaplan, and Ken K. Smith. The Effect of Variations in Relatedness Need Satisfaction on Relatedness Desires, *Administrative Science Quarterly,* Vol. 19 (1974), 507–532.

Beer, Michael. *Leadership, Employee Needs and Motivation.* Columbus, Ohio: Ohio State University, 1966.

Bugental, J. F. T. and Robert Tannenbaum. Sensitivity Training and Being Motivation. *In* Edgar H. Schein and Warren G. Bennis (eds.), *Personal and Organizational Change Through Group Methods: The Laboratory Approach.* New York: Wiley, 1965, pp. 107–113.

Campbell, Douglas B. Relative Influence of Job and Supervision on Shared Worker Attitudes, *Journal of Applied Psychology,* Vol. 55 (1971), 521–525.

Clark, James V. Motivation in Work Groups: A Tentative View, *Human Organization,* Vol. 13 (1960–61), 199–208.

Hall, Douglas T. and Khalil E. Nougaim, An Examination of Maslow's Need Hierarchy in the Organizational Setting, *Organizational Behavior and Human Performance,* Vol. 3 (1968), 12–35.

Huizinga, Gerard. *Maslow's Need Hierarchy in the Work Situation.* Groningen, The Netherlands: Wolters, Noordhoff, 1970.

Lawler, Edward E. *Motivation in Work Organizations.* Monterey. Cal.: Brooks/Cole, 1973.

Lawler, Edward E. and J. Lloyd Suttle. A Causal Correlational Test of the Need Hierarchy Concept, *Organizational Behavior and Human Performance,* Vol. 7 (1972), 265–287.

Locke, Edwin A. The Nature and Causes of Job Satisfaction, *In* Marvin D. Dunnette (ed.), *Handbook of Industrial and Organizational Psychology.* Chicago: Rand McNally, 1976, pp. 1297–1349.

Maslow, Abraham. *The Social Personality Inventory: A Test of Self-esteem in Women.* Palo Alto, Cal.: Consulting Psychologists Press, 1942.

Maslow, Abraham H. Preface to Motivation Theory, *Psychosomatic Medicine,* Vol. 5 (1943a), 85–92.

Maslow, Abraham H. A Theory of Human Motivation, *Psychological Review.* Vol. 50 (1943b), 370–396.

Maslow, Abraham H. *The S-I Test.* Palo Alto, Cal.: Consulting Psychologists Press, 1951.

Maslow, Abraham H. *Motivation and Personality.* New York: Harper and Row, 1954, 1970.

Maslow, Abraham H. *Toward a Psychology of Being.* Princeton, N.J.: Van Nostrand, 1962, 1968.

Maslow, Abraham H.: *Eupsychian Management.* Homewood, Ill.: Irwin, 1965.

Maslow, Abraham. A Theory of Metamotivation: The Biological Rooting of the Value Life, *Journal of Humanistic Psychology,* Vol. 7 (1967), 93–127.

Maslow, Abraham. Toward a Humanistic Biology, *American Psychologist,* Vol. 24 (1969), 724–735.

Matteson, Michael T. Some Reported Thoughts on Significant Management Literature, *Academy of Management Journal,* Vol. 17 (1974), 386–389.

Miner, John B. *The Human Constraint.* Washington, D.C.: BNA Books, 1974.

Mitchell, Vance F. Need Satisfactions of Military Commanders and Staff, *Journal of Applied Psychology,* Vol. 54 (1970), 282–287

Mitchell, Vance F. and Pravin Moudgill. Measurement of Maslow's Need Hierarchy, *Organizational Behavior and Human Performance,* Vol. 16 (1976), 334–349.

Porter, Lyman W. *Organizational Patterns of Managerial Job Attitudes.* New York: American Foundation for Management Research, 1964.

Roberts, Karlene H., Gordon A. Walter, and Raymond E. Miles. A Factor Analytic Study of Job Satisfaction Items Designed to Measure Maslow Need Categories, *Personnel Psychology,* Vol. 24 (1971), 205–220.

Roe, Anne. *The Psychology of Occupations.* New York: Wiley, 1956.

Schneider, Benjamin and Clayton P. Alderfer. Three Studies of Measures of Need Satisfactions in Organizations, *Administrative Science Quarterly,* Vol. 18 (1973), 489–505.

Wahba, Mahmoud A. and Lawrence G. Bridwell. Maslow Reconsidered: A

Review of Research on the Need Hierarchy Theory, *Organizational Behavior and Human Performance*, Vol. 15 (1976), 212–240.

Wanous, John P. and Abram Zwany. A Cross-Sectional Test of Need Heirarchy Theory, *Organizational Behavior and Human Performance*, Vol. 18 (1977), 78–97.

Yinon, Yoel, Aharon Bizman, and Martha Goldberg. Effect of Relative Magnitude of Reward and Type of Need on Satisfaction, *Journal of Applied Psychology*, Vol. 61 (1976), 325–328.

3 ACHIEVEMENT MOTIVATION THEORY

Achievement motivation theory receives its name from the motive that has been the dominant focus of concern since 1948. In a sense, the designation is a misnomer at present. The theory has been developmental, undergoing considerable branching and, on occasion, revision. The achievement motivation construct has been stretched to include not only hope of success but also fear of failure and even fear of success. In addition, at least two other motives — those for power and for affiliation — must now be considered part of the theory. In recent years more attention has been given to the power construct than to achievement.

The domain of achievement motivation theory thus defined is much more limited than that of Maslow's theory. It focuses on three motives (often broadly stated) and relates them to organizational behavior or behavior that appears to have relevance for organizations. The theory follows the three motives well beyond the organizational context into a great variety of aspects of daily life; however, our concern will be only with achievement motivation theory as related to organizations.

The two major motives of the theory, achievement and power, would seem to fall within Maslow's esteem category, although achievement motivation has some aspects in common with self-actualization. Affiliation motivation would clearly fall in the social category. However, despite these overlaps and the origins of both theories in clinical psychology and personality theory, need hierarchy theory and achievement motivation theory represent distinctly different concepts of the motivational process.

MCCLELLAND'S CONTRIBUTIONS TO THE THEORY

Achievement motivation theory is the creation of David McClelland of Harvard University and of his students. The theory originated in an investigation into the relationship between hunger needs and the degree to which food imagery dominates thought processes (Atkinson and McClelland, 1948). It was found that the longer the subjects had gone without food, the more certain food-related words appeared in stories they wrote in response to various pictures. Subsequently, this arousal based approach to studying motives was extended to affiliation, power, aggression, sex, fear, and achievement. However, in the early years achievement motivation saw the greatest theoretical development (McClelland, Atkinson, Clark, and Lowell, 1953).

Achievement Motivation

In McClelland's view, all motives are learned, becoming arranged in a hierarchy of potential for influencing behavior that varies from individual to individual; thus Maslow-like fixed hierarchies of an instinctoid nature are rejected. As people develop, they learn to associate positive and negative feelings with certain things that happen to and around them. Thus, achievement situations such as a challenging task may elicit feelings of pleasure, and ultimately a person may be characterized by strong achievement motivation. For such a person, achievement is directed toward the top of the motive hierarchy; it takes only minimal achievement cues to activate the expectation of pleasure and thus increase the likelihood of achievement striving. Under such circumstances weaker motives are likely to give way to the achievement motive and assume a distinct secondary role in influencing behavior. Thus, if one asks such people to tell stories about a picture that contains potential achievement cues, their achievement motivations will be aroused, just as hunger was in the subjects deprived of food, and their stories will reflect what is on their minds — achievement.

Achievement Situations. McClelland (1961, 1962) specifies certain characteristics of the situations that are preferred by, and tend to elicit achievement striving from, people with a strong need for achievement. These situations permit a person to attain success through his own efforts and abilities rather than through chance. Thus these are situations in which it is possible to take personal responsibility and get personal credit for the outcome. The credit need not come from others. To such individuals, achieving through their own efforts is intrinsically satisfying.

Second, achievement situations are characterized by intermediate levels of difficulty and risk. Were the task to be too difficult, the chance of succeeding would be minimal and the probability of motive satisfaction low. Easy tasks represent things that anyone can do, thus there is little satisfaction in accomplishing them. Achievement motivated people tend to calculate the risks involved in situations and pick those situations where they anticipate feeling slightly overextended by the challenges, but not too overextended.

Third, the situation must be one in which there is clear and unambiguous feedback on the success of one's efforts. There is little opportunity for achievement satisfaction when a person cannot tell success from failure. Thus, the situation must provide for knowledge of results within a reasonable time.

In addition to these three major features, McClelland posits two other aspects of achievement situations. They permit innovation and novel solutions, thus allowing a greater sense of satisfaction when solutions are attained, and they also require a distinct future orientation, thinking ahead and planning, what McClelland calls "anticipation of future possibilities."

Quite apparently these various situational characteristics are epitomized in the entrepreneurial role, and indeed McClelland did have this role in mind as he developed his theory. In his view it is the prospect of achievement satisfaction, not money, that drives the successful entrepreneur; money is important only as a source of feedback on how well he is doing. To some extent then, the theory represents a deduction from a model of entrepreneurship, but also it is derived inductively from a wide range of prior research studies (McClelland, 1961).

Economic Development. The theory as stated to this point is important for organizational study because it tells about the motivation of the key individual in the founding and development of business organizations — the successful entrepreneur. However, McClelland goes on to relate achievement motivation to the economic growth and decline of whole societies, thus considerably extending the applicable scope of the theory.

The starting point for this set of propositions is Max Weber's (1904) theory that modern capitalism arose out of the Protestant Reformation in Europe. It was Weber's view that Protestantism, in contrast with the existing Catholicism, fostered self-reliance and working hard to make the most of what one had, as well as the rationalization of life through attempting to improve oneself in every way. As a sociologist, Weber formulated his theory in broad social terms:

Protestantism and the cultural $\longrightarrow$ Economic development
        values it produced

McClelland accepts this formulation but adds a level of psychological explanation:

Protestantism and its values
        $\downarrow$
Independence and mastery training by parents
        $\downarrow$
Development of achievement $\longrightarrow$ Economic development
        motivation in sons

As stated, this is a theory applicable to male children only. It assumes a generational lag (roughly 50 years) between the emergence of values fostering self-reliance and economic growth. Economic decline occurs with affluence, again with a generational lag. As parents become affluent they turn over child rearing to others, such as slaves, and the conditions for developing strong achievement motivation are lost. Lacking the driving force of the achievement need and its associated entrepreneurship, the society goes into economic eclipse.

In his formulations of the early 1960s McClelland does not clearly distinguish the domain of his theory, and he is not yet certain about the role of power motivation in the business world, although he does view it as important. These problems are related. At some points McClelland appears to equate entrepreneurship and the management of business organizations generally, making his theory of achievement motivation an overall theory of business development and management. Thus, little room is left for power motivation to play a significant role. At other times he sees some managerial jobs, such as those in marketing and sales, as more entrepreneurial than others, thus leaving a place for the power construct. In the end the matter is left open — "Whether n Power is an essential ingredient in managerial success, as we have argued n Achievement is, or an accidental feature of the private enterprise system, cannot be settled" (McClelland, 1961, p. 290). More recently the theory has been filled out in this regard.

Power Motivation

By the mid-1970s McClelland had moved to the position that achievement motivation was of organizational significance primarily within the limited domain of entrepreneurship, and that other constructs were needed to explain managerial effectiveness in large corporations. Thus "A high need to achieve does not equip a man to deal effectively with managing human relationships. For instance, a salesman with high n Achievement does not necessarily make a good sales manager" (McClelland, 1975). And again, "The good manager in a large company does not have a high need for achievement" (McClelland and Burnham, 1976).

Power and Performance. McClelland (1975) views power motivation as the essential ingredient for understanding and predicting managerial success, although such power needs must be couched in an appropriate motivational context to yield the desired result.

The revised theory states that power motivation may be manifested in behavior in a variety of ways and that different individuals develop different characteristic modes of expression, one of which is managing. In part at least the mode of expression is a function of the stage to which the power motive has developed in the individual; there is a hierarchy of growth of development, and people must experience one stage to reach the next. Adults may be at any one of the four stages at a point in time, and many never rise above the first level.

At *stage I* power motivation involves seeking to derive strength from others. Such people tend to attach themselves to strong people and obtain a sense of strength and power from that relationship. At *stage II* the source of strength shifts to the self, and a feeling of power is derived from being oneself and "doing one's own thing" (shades of self-actualization). Here power satisfaction does not involve influencing others at all. In contrast, *stage III* power motivation does involve impact on other people, including dominating them and winning out over them in competitive endeavor. Also included at this stage is the satisfaction of power needs through helping behavior, which clearly establishes the weaker status of the person helped. At *stage IV* the self moves into the background, and a feeling of power is derived from influencing others for the sake of some greater good, such as corporate success.

McClelland then distinguishes between what he calls personalized power and socialized power. The former is characterized by dominance-submission and win-lose. Satisfaction comes from conquering others. In an extensive series of studies McClelland and his colleagues have shown that this kind of power motivation can be related to heavy drinking, and that people with strong personalized power motivation experience considerable satisfaction from fantasies of power elicited under alcohol (McClelland, Davis, Kalin, and Wanner, 1972).

In contrast, socialized power involves a subtle mix of power motivation and inhibition, such that there is a "concern for group goals, for finding those goals that will move men, for helping the group to formulate them, for taking initiative in providing means of achieving them, and for giving group members the feeling of competence they need to work hard for them" (McClelland, 1975, p. 265). Power motivation is mixed with a degree of altruism and of pragmatism; it is satisfied in many ways that will work and get results, not just aggrandize the self.

Table 3–1 sets forth the theoretical relationships between the various types of power motivation and managerial performance. The effective organizational manager begins to emerge in late stage III with the advent of socialized power motivation (thus the addition of inhibitory tendencies). However, individuals at lower developmental stages may function effectively in some managerial roles.

It is important to note that affiliation motivation, which in earlier formulations had received relatively little attention insofar as theoretical statements involving the field of organizational

Table 3-1. *TYPES OF POWER MOTIVATION AND MANAGERIAL
PERFORMANCE

Maturity Stage	Motivational Pattern	Effect on Management
I	Desire to influence others is low. In this sense power motivation is low.	Generally not assertive enough to manage well.
II	Power motivation expressed in ways having little to do with others.	Not related to managing.
III (early)	High power motivation coupled with low inhibition and low affiliation motivation.	The conquistador pattern of the feudal lord.
III (late)	High power motivation coupled with high inhibition and low affiliation motivation.	The imperial pattern. Personalized power shades into socialized power.
IV	High power motivation of an altruistic type coupled with high inhibition and low affiliation motivation	Selfless leadership and efficient organizational management.

Adapted from David C. McClelland. *Power: The Inner Experience*. New York: Irvington, 1975, p. 264.

study were concerned, now assumes a significant role. If affiliative needs are too strong, the consequences for managerial effectiveness are said to be negative. McClelland and Burnham (1976, p. 103) explain this proposition as follows: "For a bureaucracy to function effectively, those who manage it must be universalistic in applying rules. That is, if they make exceptions for the particular needs of individuals, the whole system will break down. The manager with a high need for being liked is precisely the one who wants to stay on good terms with everybody, and, therefore, is the one most likely to make exceptions in terms of particular needs." In other words, strong affiliation motivation interferes with and subverts effective managerial performance. It may have similar effects on the relationship between achievement motivation and entrepreneurial success.

On the other hand, McClelland (1975) does accept a formulation originally put forth and documented by Litwin and Siebrecht (1967) that for managers who perform in an integrator role, such as project and product managers, a more balanced motivational pattern is desirable, perhaps even with affiliative needs stronger than power needs. Such individuals have little position power and need to work through personal relationships.

Varying Concepts of Power.   Not all theorists associated with the achievement motivation viewpoint have advocated stances identical to that of McClelland regarding the nature of power motivation. The positions taken by Winter (1973) and Veroff and Veroff (1972) vary at several points, even though both are generally aligned with the McClelland approach to motivation and its study.

The Veroffs take the position that power motivation is primarily a negative process involving the avoidance of feelings of weakness. Although McClelland would agree that such motivation exists, especially in the early stages of motivational development, it is certainly not his prevailing view of power needs in the organizational context.

Winter posits hope of power and fear of power as two distinct motivational processes, which appear to have much in common with the personalized and socialized categories but are not the same. Hope of power, for instance, is viewed as a source of excessive drinking *and* of organizational effectiveness. Fear of power is not entirely allied with altruistic power striving; it accounts for various kinds of emotional pathology as well. Thus, regarding the McClelland socialized/personalized differentiation, Winter (1973, p. 163) says, "I do not think that power can be so neatly divided into 'good' and 'bad' . . . both aspects of the power motive are mixed."

Motivational Change and Development

A final aspect of the McClelland theory relates to the acquisition of motives. Motives that are important for business development and effective continued operation, such as achievement needs and the socialized power motive, are said to be subject to the effects of appropriate educational processes (McClelland, 1965; McClelland and Winter, 1969). What is proposed is that these motives can be moved to a more dominant position in the individual motive hierarchy, and thus exert a more pervasive influence on behavior.

Educational efforts of this kind are considered most likely to "work" under certain circumstances:

1. When the person has numerous reasons to believe that he can, will, or should develop the motive.
2. When developing the motive appears to be rational in the light of career and life situation considerations.
3. When the individual understands the meaning and various aspects of the motive.
4. When this understanding of the motive is linked to actions and behavior.
5. When the understanding is closely tied to everyday events.

6. When the motive is viewed positively as contributing to an improved self-image.
7. When the motive is viewed as consistent with prevailing cultural values.
8. When the individual commits himself to achieving concrete goals that are related to the motive.
9. When the individual maintains progress toward attaining these goals.
10. When the environment in which change occurs is one in which the person feels supported and respected as an individual who can guide his own future.
11. When the environment dramatizes the importance of self-study and makes it an important value of the group involved in the change effort.
12. When the motive is viewed as an indication of membership in a new reference group.

THE ATKINSON AND WEINER THEORIES OF ACHIEVEMENT MOTIVATION

The McClelland formulations deal primarily with relationships between motives and organizational and societal factors. John Atkinson, who has spent most of his career at the University of Michigan and who has been associated with McClelland and his theories since the very early days at Wesleyan University, has focused more directly on the internal dynamics of achievement motivation. Bernard Weiner, an early student of Atkinson's and now at UCLA has done the same but from a somewhat different viewpoint. In most respects these theories supplement McClelland in areas where he has been less specific. They focus primarily on achievement, not power.

Atkinson's Contributions

Atkinson, like McClelland, has moved back and forth between theory and research, between deduction and induction. As a result, his theorizing has been evolutionary. In the early period he was concerned strictly with achievement, but he has moved increasingly toward a general theory of human motivation. Here, we will limit ourselves to what is relevant for organizational study (Atkinson and Raynor, 1974; Atkinson, 1977).

Initial Formulations. Atkinson's initial view was that the tendency to achieve success was a function of three factors:

Achievement motivation as it characterizes a particular individual

The individual's expectation that success will occur on the
particular task at hand

The incentive value of success on that task — how attractive
success is

As with McClelland, Atkinson considers a 50–50 chance of
success as the most achievement motivating. Too low or too high
a probability makes the task less attractive and does not engage
the achievement motivated person.

From the beginning Atkinson also has been concerned with
the fear of failure as a factor in total achievement striving. The
tendency to avoid failure is posited to be directly antithetical to
the tendency to achieve success; it leads one to avoid activities
that might contribute to success, and is thus inhibitory in nature
(Atkinson and Feather, 1966). Again the behavior manifestation is
a consequence of the motive strength (fear of failure), the expectation (perceived likelihood of failure), and the incentive value (to
what extent failure hurts).

Furthermore, the theory does recognize the role of external
factors such as pay. For instance, if the motivational forces to
achieve success and to avoid failure are equally strong, they will
counteract each other. What happens will be a consequence of the
extrinsic incentives.

The More General Theory. The initial formulations represent an extension of the views of McClelland, although it is clear
that both Atkinson and McClelland influenced each other in many
ways. However, it is with the collaboration of Atkinson and Raynor that the theory grew beyond a concept of simple task performance (often as epitomized in mundane laboratory experiments).

The concept of future goals was added. Performance on a task
was viewed as being often a means to an end rather than an end
in itself. Thus, such considerations as the motivation to achieve
career success and to avoid the shame of career failure, along with
expectations and incentive values related to career considerations,
became part of the calculation used to explain present achievement behavior.

This type of formulation has important implications for the
understanding of entrepreneurial behavior:

> Businessmen who are success-oriented should be much less speculative
> in their everyday (i.e., immediate) decisions which involve risk than
> McClelland's analysis suggests, since such activity is here conceived to re-
> present immediate activity in a long contingent path, where failure means
> loss of the opportunity to continue (i.e. bankruptcy) .... the career deci-
> sions of success-oriented individuals should not, according to the elaborat-
> ed theory, consist of a series of immediate risks in which there is a 50–50

> chance of failure, but rather should reflect a much lower degree of risk . . . . it is the future challenge which offers the moderate risk, given the necessity of guaranteeing "staying in the ballgame" long enough to achieve future career success (Atkinson and Raynor, 1974, pp. 146–147).

Another extension of the theory considers that achievement motivation does not occur in a vacuum. The individual is already active and actively motivated. Thus, an effective total theory must account for motivational change. Atkinson posits a consummatory force that operates to weaken a particular motive as it is expressed in a particular activity over time — i.e., the motive becomes satisfied. At some point the motive becomes weak enough so that distraction can occur and some other motive can take over the governance of activity. Thus, a highly achievement-oriented person may study hard for a considerable time impervious to events around him, but eventually he may turn to conversation with a friend as his achievement motivation is consumed and his affiliation motive is engaged. The distribution of time spent among various types of activities then may be taken as an index of the position of a motive in a person's motivational hierarchy. The more time spent consuming (satisfying) a motive, the higher its level.

Weiner's Contributions

Weiner has drawn certain concepts from the more general theory of motivation known as attribution theory and applied them to achievement striving. In doing so he attempts to enlarge upon McClelland's view that achievement motivated people prefer to attribute credit for outcomes to their own efforts rather than to chance or luck.

Weiner's (1972) theory deals with the degree to which people ascribe their successes and failures to:
1. Their own ability — viewed as a stable characteristic and inside oneself.
2. Their effort level — viewed as a variable factor, also inside oneself.
3. The difficulty of the task — viewed as stable and given, but external to the self.
4. Luck — viewed as variable and unstable, also external to the self.

Wide individual differences are postulated in the tendency to attribute what happens to a person to each of these factors. In particular, achievement-motivated people are expected to attribute their successes to their own efforts, and their failures to not trying hard enough. If they fail they are likely to try again because they tend to believe that with greater effort they can succeed. Thus, they consistently perceive their ability levels as being quite high. When they do succeed it is because they tried hard and used their abilities.

In contrast, those with a low need for achievement view effort as irrelevant. They attribute failure to other factors, in particular lack of ability, a condition that they believe is generally characteristic of themselves. Success is viewed as primarily a consequence of the external factors of easy tasks and luck.

Obviously, if one is interested in motivating a person to do something, what will work in dealing with an achievement oriented person may be absolutely useless in dealing with a person lacking achievement motivation. This suggests, as Weiner has indicated, that educational programs attempting to bring about motivational change and development in the achievement area should focus first on teaching the participants that effort does make a difference and that internal causation is a key factor mediating between a task and the level of performance on that task. Thus, establishing the importance of personal effort is added to the previously stated list of 12 circumstances under which motivational training is likely to work.

MEASURING THE THEORETICALLY RELEVANT MOTIVES

Achievement motivation theory had its origins in research that measured the effects of motive-arousing stimuli through the analysis of stories told by the subjects after they saw appropriate pictures. Thus, measures of major variables were present from the beginning, and the research-retarding effects of a lack of theory-based measures that plagued need hierarchy theory have not occurred. As achievement motivation theory developed new variables, one of the first steps was construction of appropriate measures. Yet, measuring and measuring well are not always the same thing, and there has been considerable contention that the achievement motivation theorists have not always measured well (Entwisle, 1972; Klinger, 1966).

Measurement Procedures

The preferred approach in measuring the various motives of the theory has been to utilize derivatives of the Thematic Apperception Test (TAT) originally developed by Henry Murray (1943) at the Harvard Psychological Clinic. Typically, from four to six pictures are used, selected to focus on the motive of greatest concern. Each picture is exposed briefly, from 10 to 20 seconds, and the subject is then asked to write a story about it within a specified time interval, usually 5 minutes. The story is to contain answers to the following questions:

1. What is happening? Who are the people?
2. What has led up to this situation? That is, what has happened in the past?
3. What is being thought? What is wanted? By whom?
4. What will happen? What will be done?

This procedure is much more structured than the traditional one used in clinical practice. There the pictures tend to be more ambiguous, there are no set time intervals for viewing the pictures and providing stories, the stories usually are given orally and recorded, and the instructions are not fully repeated for each picture. In addition, the original TAT contained 20 pictures. The achievement motivation theory TATs have the advantages of permitting group administration and greater manageability, but they lose something in the richness of fantasy content. Nevertheless, they remain projective in nature and thus do permit the measurement of unconscious motives.

Because they tap unconscious motives and allow the individual to exhibit thought processes that are relatively free of social desirability, conformity pressures, and defensiveness compared with objective tests (such as self-report tests that use the multiple choice format), TAT measures do not correlate well with other measures of the same motives (Hermans, 1970). In general, achievement motivation theorists have taken a very negative stance toward non-TAT measures. But Atkinson typically has used objective, self-report measures of anxiety to measure fear of failure and considers them entirely adequate for that purpose (Atkinson, 1977).

Scoring and Scorer Reliability

Projective measurement places heavy demands on the scorer. A coding system must be developed, learned, and applied consistently. In developing a coding system for a particular motive, the preferred approach among achievement motivation theorists has been to compare stories produced in neutral and motive arousal situations and generate a scoring system from the differences. An alternative occasionally used is to compare groups of known high and low characteristic motivational levels. In either case the coding systems are typically very detailed, and numerous examples are provided (McClelland et al., 1953; Winter, 1973).

When sufficient time is spent learning these coding systems, quite high levels of agreement can be achieved among different scores. A number of studies have dealt with this kind of scorer reliability. Heckhausen (1967) reports correlations ranging from .80 to .90 or better as typical. Atkinson (1977) reviews a number of studies in which the median correlation was in the upper .80s. On the evidence, the TAT protocols can be scored with considerable reliability. If they are not, continued learning by the scorer is recommended until they are. Scorer reliability of below .85 would appear to be unacceptable. Most published studies have exceeded that value.

Test Reliability

Questions regarding scorer reliability have been reasonably well resolved, but not so the overall reliability problem. One difficulty is that the TAT measures are not subject to quite the same evaluation procedures as many other psychological measuring devices. For one thing, responses may occur on a reciprocal or alternative basis so that if a subject manifests a motive in one way, other types of manifestation are less likely. This means that the use of factor analysis to define measures of variables is inappropriate (McClelland, 1975). Furthermore, the various internal consistency indexes of reliability are seriously compromised (Atkinson, 1977). Also, because the standard instructions ask for imaginative stories, subjects may shift away from a story (and a motive) previously given and remembered. On a second administration they opt for a story that manifests a motive somewhat lower on their individual hierarchies to demonstrate their originality.

Yet, it is incumbent on any measure to demonstrate its reliability in some manner, and there is sufficient evidence from varied sources, including the parallel form approach, to reach some conclusions. One extensive review estimated TAT reliability in the .30 to .40 range (Entwisle, 1972). Other studies suggest that values up to .50 or above are typical (Heckhausen, 1967). There seems to be little question that the TAT measures are not very reliable. Yet a very blunt instrument may separate manifestly distinct phenomena that have little overlap. The probable cause of measurement unreliability is the small number of pictures (stimulus situations, questions) used, and a return to something like the original 20-picture TAT would no doubt correct the situation. Nevertheless, the current (too short) measures have served to discriminate between arousal and nonarousal conditions and between certain different groups of subjects. For such an unstable instrument to do this, some very powerful forces would have to be at work. We turn now to the studies that bear on the validity of the achievement motivation theories.

THE RESEARCH EVIDENCE

Achievement motivation theory as it has developed is a set of loosely related formulations dealing with a variety of different theoretical domains. The lack of tight logical relationships cutting across these domains makes research more difficult, because tests must be carried out separately on each set of hypotheses. It is probably for this reason that a very large amount of research has been carried out instigated by the theory and related to it in one way or another.

Achievement Motivation and Entrepreneurship

If there is a key hypothesis in the theory, or at least in the McClelland formulations, it is that individuals who are high in achievement motivation should succeed in entrepreneurial activities. The data consistently support this expectation (McClelland and Winter, 1969; Steiner and Miner, 1977). A number of studies support the view that individuals who start their own businesses and make them succeed tend to have high levels of achievement motivation. Furthermore, the growth and success of such entrepreneurial enterprises also are closely related to the achievement needs of the founder. Thus, the prototype achievement situation (personal responsibility and credit, risk taking, feedback, opportunity for innovation, and future orientation) does turn out to provide fertile ground for the efforts of the high achievement-motivated person.

A characteristic study deals with relationships between entrepreneur motivations and sales growth rates for 51 small, technically based companies in the Boston area (Wainer and Rubin, 1969). The growth rates for firms headed by high achievement-motivated entrepreneurs were much higher than those headed by moderate or low need achievement individuals. In contrast, power motivation had little direct relationship to company success, and strong affiliation motivation was a negative factor.

Achievement Motivation and Economic Development

The primary source of data bearing on economic development is McClelland's most widely read and cited volume *The Achieving*

Society (1961). This work contains a mass of data focused primarily on the achievement motivation-economic development relationship. In some cases the presence or absence of entrepreneurship in a society is substituted for indexes of economic growth. Because TAT protocols on past societies were not available, various substitutes were used and scored in a manner as analogous to the TAT scoring procedure as possible. The objective was to utilize cultural products that represented distillations of the values and valued motives of the society, especially those related to transmitting the culture to future generations. Thus, indexes of achievement motivation were derived from folk tales, school readers for children, cultural artifacts, characteristic literature, and other sources.

Achievement Aspirations and Electric Power Output. The major analysis of modern industrial societies utilized achievement motivation scores from children's readers of the 1925 and 1950 periods and correlated them with indexes of electric power productivity gains over the intervening period. There is a sizable correlation for the 1925 data; none for the 1950 data. Thus, the predicted lag is in evidence. Table 3–2 contains data on 20 countries selected from a second study comparing the 1950 achievement motivation data with economic growth between 1952 and 1958. Again the relationship is sizable, even with the shorter lag. France and the U.S.S.R. do deviate rather markedly in the rankings, but the other countries exhibit reasonably close agreements.

Other Evidence. Similar results are reported by McClelland (1961) for earlier societies. An analysis of the folk tales of preliterate tribes indicates a relation between achievement striving and the presence of entrepreneurial activity. An analysis of the literature of ancient Greece shows a pattern of relationships between achievement imagery and the rise and fall of that civilization. Similar results were obtained for Spain and Great Britain.

Data on the United States from 1800 to 1950 have been developed using fourth grade readers to generate achievement motivation scores and the rate of recorded patents as an index of economic activity (deCharms and Moeller, 1962). The data show a steady rise in achievement imagery until 1890, and then a steady decline which by 1950 had reached the 1850 level. A similar curve was found for the patent data, but the familiar lag between the two indexes was much less in evidence, perhaps because patents must precede actual production by a number of years.

Although the support for an achievement motivation theory of economic development is strong, there is reason to believe that other factors, and even other motives, may also be involved (Barrett and

Table 3–2.   RANKING OF 20 SELECTED COUNTRIES IN TERMS OF
ACHIEVEMENT MOTIVATION LEVELS IN SCHOOL
READERS IN 1950 AND GAINS IN ECONOMIC
GROWTH FROM 1952 TO 1958

Country	Rank on Achievement Motivation	Rank on Economic Growth
India	1	4
Australia	2	8
France	3	14
Israel	4	2
Greece	5	3
Canada	6	11
U.S.A.	7	7
West Germany	8	6
U.S.S.R.	9	1
Portugal	10	5
Norway	11	17
Great Britain	12	9
Sweden	13	16
Mexico	14	10
The Netherlands	15	13
Italy	16	15
Japan	17	12
Switzerland	18	20
Denmark	19	18
Belgium	20	19

Adapted from David C. McClelland. *The Achieving Society.* Princeton, N.J.:
Van Nostrand, 1961, p. 100.

Bass, 1976). For instance, low levels of affiliation motivation have
consistently been found to be precursors of economic growth. Power
motivation appears to be an important factor in the larger countries,
particularly those already more industrialized. The role of affiliation
motivation is also in evidence in the study of the United States
(deCharms and Moeller, 1962), with lower levels of motivation
characterizing the period of greatest growth. McClelland himself
(1966) has shown that educational level operates independently of
achievement motivation, yet contributes sizably to economic
growth.

The Roles of Protestant Values and Independence Training

The McClelland theory of economic development is concerned
not only with achievement motivation but also with the roles that
Protestant values and independence training of sons play in the
development of that motivation. The research evidence, although

mixed, cannot be said to support the hypotheses dealing with Protestantism and independence training (Heckhausen, 1967; Weiner, 1972). In the world today the kind of Protestant-Catholic differences anticipated by the theory are not found with sufficient consistency to uphold McClelland's views. Furthermore, independence training now does not appear to play the pervasive role in the development of achievement motivation that early research suggested it might.

A more important consideration in the development of achievement motivation appears to be the degreee to which achievement values are transmitted directly by parents and the type of model provided by the father. It has been found, for instance, that the TAT achievement motivation scores of male seventh and eighth graders are strongly related to the fathers' occupations (Turner, 1970). The scores are much higher when the father is either a small business owner or holds a managerial position with considerable authority and autonomy in a large business. This difference remains even when social class is held constant. Exposure to a parental model of an entrepreneurial type appears to be the key factor that perpetuates the kind of achievement striving that fuels economic development.

Power Motivation and Organizational Management

It is not possible now to resolve the differences between proponents of different views regarding the nature of power motivation. McClelland, Winter, and the Veroffs offer theories that overlap but also diverge in certain areas. There is insufficient comparative research at present to say who is right and who is wrong, though it is possible to bring data to bear on the question of whether power motivation in general is related to managerial success.

The early research is quite mixed with regard to the relationships between both achievement and power motivation on the one hand, and performance in the managerial role on the other. Sometimes achievement motivation appears to be required (Cummin, 1967; McClelland, 1961) and sometimes it is not (Lichtman, 1970). Similarly, power motivation has been found to be related to managerial success in some instances (Cummin, 1967), yet in other cases it has nothing to do with managing (McClelland, 1961; Meyer, Walker and Litwin, 1961). The achievement motivation results appear to be best explained in terms of type of managerial role. There are managerial jobs in many companies in which the individual has profit center responsibilities and, in essence, manages a complete little business. Performances in these more entrepreneurial positions does seem to involve achievement motivation (Litwin and Siebrecht, 1967; Meyer, Walker, and Litwin, 1961), but many other managerial jobs clearly do not have any entrepreneurial potential. In addition, whether achievement or power motivation is important depends on the particular value system of the firm (Andrews, 1967).

With regard to power motivation, the McClelland (1975) theory would attribute the failure of the early studies to establish a relationship with managing to a failure to differentiate personalized from socialized power. However, the quantity of research dealing with this distinction and the managerial performance relationships posited by the theory fall short of what might be desired. What research has been carried out (McClelland, 1975; McClelland and Burnham, 1976) supports the theory both for power and for affiliation motivation. But this research is also intertwined with the development of the theory, and further independent tests are needed.

Some support for the power motivation formulations does derive, however, from a study reported by Winter (1973) in which the power motivation of various United States presidents was scored from their inaugural addresses. There was a correlation of .49 between the power motivation of eleven presidents and their prestige, as independently rated by historians. Presidents with strong power needs included Theodore Roosevelt, Kennedy, Truman, and Lyndon Johnson; Taft, Hoover, and Coolidge were relatively lacking in desire for power.

Research on Motivational Dynamics

A large amount of research has been conducted to test McClelland's hypotheses regarding the influences of factors in the achievement situation and the related theorizing of Atkinson and Weiner. The predominant approach in this research has been the laboratory study. Accordingly, control over relevant variables that might distort results has typically been good, but the somewhat artificial nature of some of the tasks does raise questions about generalizations to employee motivation in the real world.

Preference for Moderate Risks. The research generally supports the view that achievement motivated people prefer situations in which the risks are in the intermediate range, although not always exactly 50–50 (Hamilton, 1974). This research has considered the need for achievement and the fear of failure as separate contributory factors (as posited by Atkinson) in a sufficient number of instances to provide considerable validation for this differentiation; fear of failure does emerge as an important motivational construct.

Some question regarding the moderate risk theory has been raised by Locke, whose own research appears to indicate that more difficult (i.e., lower probability of success) goals are typically more motivating

(Locke, 1972). However, Locke's hypothesis and the research on it deal with "people in general," while Atkinson and McClelland are concerned with individuals having strong achievement motivation. Furthermore, Locke's views apply to those who accept and are committed to the goals, whereas achievement motivation theory extends on into the domain of task rejection and avoidance. Accordingly, the Locke data cannot be viewed as directly refuting the Atkinson-McClelland formulations.

Other Tests of the Atkinson Theory. As the Atkinson theory has evolved it has continually attempted to handle previously disconfirming research findings. There is no question that such findings have occurred with sufficient frequency to make modification of the theory necessary (Atkinson, 1977; Weiner, 1972).

In the more recent formulations the greatest support has been found for the role of future goals in achievement striving (Atkinson and Raynor, 1974). Performance in the present is not merely a function of the immediate situation. In achievement oriented people, in particular, the fact that current performance is a means to a future goal, such as entering a desired career, has a strong enhancing effect. Furthermore, the more long-term the goal, and thus the more steps needed to reach the goal, the more performance is affected.

A particularly interesting study relating achievement motivation to future orientation was carried out with college students (Mahone, 1960). High achievement motivation and high fear of failure students were compared as to realistic career aspirations. The achievement motivated students tended to pick careers that were appropriate to their abilities and general interests. Thus, their choices were in the moderate risk range, and they appear to have given considerable thought to their futures and to have collected the necessary vocational information.

The fear of failure students, on the other hand, chose quite unrealistic careers. Either they aspired to occupations that were well above them (high probability of failure) or well below what they could achieve (highly certain success). These students were carrying their avoidant tendencies into the career arena. They appeared not to have thought much about their occupational futures and not to have obtained much relevant information. The data suggest that they were afraid to try, not even obtaining information needed to make a realistic choice. The future and future goals are paramount in the minds of high achievement motivation people, but when fear of failure predominates, thoughts of the future are likely to be avoided.

Research on the Weiner Formulations. Although the relevant research has not been extensive, the Weiner formulations that explain certain of the dynamics of achievement motivation in terms of the attribution mechanism have been consistently supported (Weiner, 1972; Weiner and Sierad, 1975). Furthermore, the tendency of achievement motivated people to relate results to effort in their own minds is logically consistent with several of McClelland's propositions regarding the achievement situation, which generally have been supported by research (Heckhausen, 1967; McClelland, 1961).

Thus, the attribution view fits logically with the desire of high need achievement people to work in situations having a potential for personal responsibility and credit. In addition, the desire to develop novel solutions to problems makes sense with attribution concepts; novel solutions are more easily attributed to individual effort, since it is inherent in novelty that no one else had the idea. Finally, attribution to individual effort requires a situation of feedback on successes and failures. One cannot ascribe a success to what one has done if there is no clear basis for inferring that success has occurred at all.

Research Using Female Subjects

Achievement motivation theory as originally postulated by McClelland was a theory of male motivation and its development. Therefore, it is not surprising that attempts to apply the theory to females have not met with nearly the same degree of success. The typical arousal instructions have often failed to incite achievement imagery among females, and relationships between achievement motivation and performance have been found only infrequently in contexts where results for males would suggest that such relationships should have been found (Alper, 1974; Lesser, 1973; Stein and Bailey, 1973).

A number of factors appear to contribute to this result. One of the most apparent is that female goals are considerably more diverse than those sought by males. In particular, "it appears that attainment of excellence is often a goal of females' achievement efforts, but the areas in which such attainment is sought are frequently social skills and other areas perceived as feminine" (Stein and Bailey, 1973, p. 363). To the extent that the measures used to determine achievement motivation do not tap the goals toward which female achievement striving is channeled by culturally prescribed sex roles, the results for males and females will differ. Since the early arousal studies (on which TAT scoring is based) utilized male subjects, it does appear that this factor may account for much of the difference in findings for males and females.

An additional factor in these differential findings emerges from research that focuses on the fear of success (Horner, 1974). Fear of success has been found to be much more prevalent among females; this type of imagery appears quite rarely in the TAT stories of males. Furthermore, the large number of women who do experience fear of success tend to utilize their full potential in performance only when they are in relaxed, noncompetitive situations, and least of all when faced with male competition. The added ingredient of fear of success introduces a consideration into the performance of females that is rarely present among men. "It is, therefore, not surprising that the results of women in the past have not been consistent with the results of men" (Horner, 1974, p. 116).

Research on Motivational Development

The hypothesis that motives can be moved up the individual hierarchy, and thus made to exert more extensive influence on behavior through exposure to appropriate training, has been generally confirmed. Although most of the research has been conducted with achievement motivation training, there are some data on the development of power motivation.

Achievement Motivation Training. The major thrusts of achievement motivation training have been in the development of black capitalism in the United States, in stimulating economic growth in less developed countries, and in stimulating better performance from school children, especially disadvantaged children. Only the first two are relevant for organization study.

Figure 3–1 provides an outline for a typical achievement motivation course for prospective or present minority entrepreneurs. A particular course may be longer, or somewhat shorter, and it may be spread out in time rather than concentrated in a single period. However, the content tends to remain the same. The objective is to induce the 12 conditions hypothesized as conducive to motivational change (see earlier, pp. 53–54).

There is considerable evidence now that such achievement motivation training does increase the target motive, and that given appropriate external circumstances, this increased motivation will yield expanded entrepreneurial behavior (Durand, 1975; Timmons, 1971). Training of this kind has been provided quite widely in urban areas, often with federal government support.

Table 3–3 provides information on the effectivenes of an achievement motivation program conducted in India to foster entrepreneurship there. The comparisons of the trained group with a similar group that was not trained indicates that the training did stimulate desired

	Day 1	Day 2	Day 3
Morning			
Session I		Review and critique	Review and critique
Session II		Goal setting	Scoring own TATs for achievement needs
Session III		Discussion of self-perceptions and expectations	Goal setting
Afternoon			
Session I		Origin-pawn game	Goal setting: action team discussion
Session II		Lecture on achievement thinking and business success	General discussion of goal setting
Session III		Analyzing TATs for achievement thinking	Business game
Evening			
Session I	Introduction	Case discussions	Discussion
Session II	Complete TAT	Lecture on business and entrepreneurial leadership	Review and critique
Session III	The ring toss game as an index of risk taking	Review and critique	
Session IV	Organize action teams		

	Day 4	Day 5	Day 6
Morning			
Session I	Review and critique	Review and critique	Review and critique
Session II	Film on organizational climates	Business development case	Contest in achievement thinking
Session III	Personal managerial style: action team discussion	New enterprise case	Discussion of helping each other to achieve goals
Afternoon			
Session I	General discussion of personal managerial style	Goal setting	Discussion of helping each other to achieve goals
Session II	Goal setting	Goal setting: action team discussion	Development of follow-up plans
Session III	Goal setting: action team discussion	Individual planning	Course summary
Evening			
Session I	Disarmament game	The inner city investment game	
Session II	Review and critique	Review and critique	

Figure 3–1. Outline of an achievement motivation training program. (Adapted from Jeffry A. Timmons. Black Is Beautiful — Is It Bountiful? *Harvard Business Review*, Vol. 49, No. 6 (1971), pp. 93–94.)

Table 3–3. RESULTS OF ACHIEVEMENT MOTIVATION TRAINING CONDUCTED IN INDIA

	Two Years Before Course	Two Years After Course
Per cent active in business development		
Trained group (N=76)	18	51
Untrained controls (N=73)	22	25
Per cent increasing hours worked		
Trained group (N=61)	7	20
Untrained controls (N=44)	11	7
Per cent starting new businesses		
Trained group (N=76)	4	22
Untrained group (N=73)	7	8
Per cent making specific fixed capital Investment (in charge of a firm only)		
Trained group (N=47)	32	74
Untrained controls (N=45)	29	40
Per cent increasing number of employees (in charge of a firm only)		
Trained group (N=44)	35	59
Untrained controls (N=46)	31	33

Adapted from David C. McClelland and David G. Winter. *Motivating Economic Achievement.* New York: Free Press, 1969, pp. 213, 215, 217, 221, 226.

behavior, especially among individuals who were in charge of their own businesses and thus in the best position to foster business growth (McClelland and Winter, 1969). In this study the training was specifically designed to include the 12 conditions hypothesized to make it work, with the intent of subtracting various conditions in subsequent studies to determine which conditions were crucial. However, it was not possible to carry through on this subtractive design, so we are unable to evaluate the separate hypotheses.

Much of the training that has been conducted in this country and abroad has utilized the McClelland format, following generally the outline of Figure 3–1; it is this approach that has been studied most widely and that has received the strongest research support. However, a number of related, derivative techniques have also been developed, often under names such as personal causation training, self-esteem training, and the like. In some cases these, too, have been found to increase achievement motivation (Jackson and Shea, 1972).

Power Motivation Training. Attempts to develop power motivation in organizational managers are more recent than achievement motivation training, although the general format has much in common with the latter approach (McClelland and Burnham, 1976). Because the training is new, much less research has been conducted to evaluate it. One of the early efforts had the objective of shifting the power motivation of alcoholics from a personalized to a socialized mode, thus bringing about more mature and adaptive expression (McClelland et al., 1972). At present it is not possible, given available data, to say whether power motivation training works as effectively as achievement motivation training, or even if it works at all.

However, it is clear that the key to developing stable motives and retaining what has been developed over a considerable period of time is some kind of educational process. Merely exposing people for a similar time to a leadership style or organizational climate that is power or achievement oriented does not produce the same results (Litwin and Stringer, 1968). Thus, it appears that working in an organization that creates a climate in which power utilization or achievement motivated behavior is valued in its managers will not be sufficient to produce related motivational changes. There has to be a specific effort directed toward achieving motivational change.

CONCLUSIONS

In many respects achievement motivation theory has proved to be quite successful. It has generated a large amount of research, in part because its authors recognized the measurement need from the beginning, and much of this research has been supportive. It seems likely, however, that the success of the theory also may be attributable to its restricted objectives and focus, and thus its concentration on a specific domain. When the theory ventures outside this domain, it typically does less well.

Scientific Goals

One clear problem with achievement motivation theory is that it has had multiple contributors, and each has had a tendency to move off in directions that interest him without reference to the creation of a cohesive theory. It is not that there is logical inconsistency among the parts but rather a lack of consistent relationships. The greatest integrating forces have come from Atkinson and Weiner, but these have applied only to the internal dynamics of achievement motivation.

The close tie of achievement motivation theory with the domain of entrepreneurship is evident. Such concepts as moderate risk, attribution of causation to the self, future orientation, and feedback on results do meet the test of being important for high achievement-motivated people. They are also inherent in the entrepreneurial task, and achievement motivation does make for entrepreneurial success. The logical ring thus seems to close, and it makes sense that achievement motivation leads to success in founding and developing a small business.

Extensions of the theory into macro-economics also receive considerable support. The data on economic development indicate clearly that other factors such as educational level and affiliation motivation are involved. The achievement motivation theory of economic development is by no means a complete theory. But it does appear to be correct in positing an important casual factor in economic development. The most puzzling data are those related to lag. The time span between rises in motivation and measured economic growth are extremely variable in different studies. This is an area that needs further work.

Also, with the advent of multinational corporations and large stable bureaucratic organizations in the business world, individual entrepreneurial contributions to the gross national product may be less important than they have been in the past. In particular, a decline in achievement motivation and in the founding and development of new firms may be relatively unimportant insofar as a country's productive output is concerned (once large firms have been created). Thus the development curves may not show the same relationships as in the past. The theory would appear to need reconsideration in light of the advent of large multinational corporations. It may prove to be a theory of economic growth for less developed nations only. The concepts related to Protestantism, for example, already appear to be outdated.

Existing data on hierarchies of motives seem to favor McClelland-like concepts of varied individualized hierarchies (at least above the most basic survival level) over fixed hierarchies of the Maslow type. Atkinson's views about the perseveration and change of needs as a function of hierarchic position and consummatory forces are logically consistent with the individualized hierarchy construct. However, the research data tend to run somewhat thin in this area, and the Atkinson views in particular require more extensive verification.

The various power motivation formulations, especially as they relate to managerial performance in large corporations, are not nearly as strongly grounded in research as the achievement motivation theory of entrepreneurship. This suggests that the theory may have moved outside its domain, to limited advantage. There already exists a theory of the motivation or will to manage in large organizations that incorporates the power motivation dimension (among others) and that has received sizable support from research (Miner, 1965;

1977). It appears likely that power motivation is as important in corporate management as McClelland says it is, but the available research suggests that there is much more to a comprehensive and useful theory of managerial performance than that.

The same holds for power motivation training. The data are too sparse to advocate it, and approaches such as managerial role motivation training, which instill the more comprehensive motivation to manage, are much more thoroughly grounded in research. Achievement motivation training for developing people to serve in entrepreneurial positions, on the other hand, does appear to be much more logically consistent with the overall theory and more valid as a change procedure. A direct focus incorporating Weiner's views on learned attribution of effort could well make the training more effective.

It is apparent that achievement motivation theory, at least as currently operational in TAT measures, does not work well with females. However, females already engaged in entrepreneurial activities should fall within the domain of the theory. Studies of achievement motivation and other motives have consistently found that women who actually assume managerial roles have the same motivations as men and succeed on the same basis (Miner, 1977).

One of the major problems facing achievement motivation theory, its measurement procedures, is also one of its greatest strengths. The TAT method is valuable in that it delves into the unconscious motives of people, and this is an asset that many other theory-related measures do not have. However, the current measure appears to be unnecessarily lacking in reliability. As a result, important findings and differentiations probably are not being revealed. The solution may be either to move to a longer TAT with more pictures or to utilize a somewhat less cumbersome projective procedure, such as the sentence completion method, which makes it easier to incorporate more items in the overall instrument.

Managerial Goals

The great value of achievement motivation theory is that it provides major insights into what causes certain kinds of people (and often very important people) in the business world to behave as they do. Once one identifies a person as having high achievement motivation, a number of other characteristics follow; it should be relatively easy then to understand and predict that person's behavior. To a somewhat lesser degree the same is true of power motivation, affiliation motivation, fear of failure, and fear of success, which are the other major variables of the theory. These motivational constructs provide a useful framework for a working theory of business behavior. They should prove particularly useful in dealing with individuals at the managerial level, in negotiating, for instance, and in making staffing decisions related to various types of managerial positions.

It appears that managerial positions that represent a "small business within a business," such as those in venture management, should be staffed with high achievement-motivated people. In general, too great a desire for affiliation appears to be detrimental to managerial effectiveness. However, in certain kinds of project or product manager jobs with little position power per se, strong affiliation motivation can be useful.

One major application derived directly from the theory is achievement motivation training. On both theoretical and empirical grounds this approach appears to be extremely valuable for facilitating business and economic growth. On the other hand, it should not be used indiscriminately. Developing achievement motivation in an individual whose environment does not permit satisfaction of the motive can be self-defeating. In the past when this has been done, the people involved have either left the environment (quit to take more gratifying jobs) or attempted to change the existing environment through pressure tactics and other conflict-generating efforts (Jackson and Shea, 1972).

References

Alper, Thelma G. Achievement Motivation in College Women: A Now-You-See-It-Now-You-Don't Phenomenon, *American Psychologist*, Vol. 29 (1974), 194–203.

Andrews, John D. W. The Achievement Motive and Advancement in Two Types of Organizations, *Journal of Personality and Social Psychology*, Vol. 6 (1967), 163–168.

Atkinson, John W. Motivation for Achievement, *In* T. Blass (ed.), *Personality Variables in Social Behavior*. Hillsdale, N.J.: Erlbaum Associates, 1977, pp. 25–108.

Atkinson, John W. and Norman T. Feather. *A Theory of Achievement Motivation*. New York: Wiley, 1966.

Atkinson, John W. and David C. McClelland. The Projective Expression of Needs. II. The Effect of Different Intensities of the Hunger Drive on Thematic Apperception, *Journal of Experimental Psychology*, Vol. 38 (1948), 643–658.

Atkinson, John W. and Joel O. Raynor. *Motivation and Achievement*. Washington, D.C.: Winston, 1974.

Barrett, Gerald V. and Bernard M. Bass. Cross Cultural Issues in Industrial and Organizational Psychology, *In* Marvin D. Dunnette (ed.), *Handbook of Industrial and Organizational Psychology*. Chicago: Rand McNally, 1976, pp. 1639–1686.

Cummin, Pearson C. TAT Correlates of Executive Performance, *Journal of Applied Psychology*, Vol. 51 (1967), 78–81.

deCharms, Richard and Gerald H. Moeller. Values Expressed in American Children's Readers: 1800–1950, *Journal of Abnormal and Social Psychology*, Vol. 64 (1962), 136–142.

Durand, Douglas E. Effects of Achievement Motivation and Skill Training on the Entrepreneurial Behavior of Black Businessmen, *Organizational Behavior and Human Performance*, Vol. 14 (1975), 76–90.

Entwisle, Doris, R. To Dispel Fantasies

About Fantasy-Based Measures of Achievement Motivation, *Psychological Bulletin*, Vol. 77 (1972), 377–391.

Hamilton, J. Ogden. Motivation and Risk Taking Behavior: A Test of Atkinson's Theory, *Journal of Personality and Social Psychology*, Vol. 29 (1974), 856–864.

Heckhausen, Heinz. *The Anatomy of Achievement Motivation.* New York: Academic Press, 1967.

Hermans, Hubert J. M. A Questionnaire Measure of Achievement Motivation, *Journal of Applied Psychology*, Vol. 54 (1970), 353–363.

Horner, Matina S. The Measurement and Behavioral Implications of Fear of Success in Women, *In* John W. Atkinson and Joel O. Raynor (eds.), *Motivation and Achievement.* Washington, D.C.: Winston, 1974, pp. 91–117.

Jackson, Karl W. and Dennis J. Shea. Motivation Training in Perspective, *In* Walter Nord (ed.), *Concepts and Controversy in Organizational Behavior.* Pacific Palisades, Calif.: Goodyear, 1972, pp. 100–118.

Klinger, Eric. Fantasy Need Achievement as a Motivational Construct, *Psychological Bulletin*, Vol. 66 (1966), 291–308.

Lesser, Gerald S. Achievement Motivation in Women. *In* David C. McClelland and Robert S. Steele (eds.), *Human Motivation.* Morristown, N.J.: General Learning Press, 1973, pp. 202–221.

Lichtman, Cary M. Some Interpersonal Response Correlates of Organizational Rank, *Journal of Applied Psychology*, Vol. 54 (1970), 77–80.

Litwin, George H. and Adrienne Siebrecht. Integrators and Entrepreneurs: Their Motivation and Effect on Management, *Hospital Progress*, Vol. 48, No. 9 (1967), 67–71.

Litwin, George H. and Robert A. Stringer. *Motivation and Organizational Climate.* Boston: Graduate School of Business Administration, Harvard University, 1968.

Locke, Edwin A. A Comment on Atkinson's 'Motivational Determinants of Risk-Taking Behavior,' *In* Henry L. Tosi, Robert J. House, and Marvin D. Dunnette (eds.), *Managerial Motivation and Compensation.* East Lansing, Mich.: Graduate School of Busi-

ness Administration, Michigan State University, 1972, pp. 242–243.

Mahone, Charles H. Fear of Failure and Unrealistic Vocational Aspiration, *Journal of Abnormal and Social Psychology*, Vol. 60 (1960), 253–261.

McClelland, David C. *The Achieving Society.* Princeton, N.J.: Van Nostrand, 1961.

McClelland, David C. Business Drive and National Achievement, *Harvard Business Review*, Vol. 40, No. 4 (1962), 99–112.

McClelland, David C. Toward a Theory of Motive Acquisition, *American Psychologist*, Vol. 20 (1965), 321–333.

McClelland, David C. Does Education Accelerate Economic Growth? *Economic Development and Cultural Change*, Vol. 14 (1966), 257–278.

McClelland, David C. *Power: The Inner Experience.* New York: Irvington, 1975.

McClelland, David C., John W. Atkinson, Russell A. Clark, and Edgar L. Lowell. *The Achievement Motive.* New York: Appleton-Century-Crofts, 1953 and Irvington, 1976.

McClelland, David C. and David H. Burnham. Power is the Great Motivator, *Harvard Business Review*, Vol. 54, No. 2 (1976), 100–110.

McClelland, David C., William N. Davis, Rudolf Kalin, and Eric Wanner. *The Drinking Man: Alcohol and Human Motivation.* New York: Free Press, 1972.

McClelland, David C. and David G. Winter. *Motivating Economic Achievement*, New York: Free Press, 1969.

Meyer, Herbert H., William B. Walker, and George H. Litwin. Motive Patterns and Risk Preferences Associated with Entrepreneurship, *Journal of Abnormal and Social Psychology*, Vol. 63 (1961), 570–574.

Miner, John B. *Studies in Management Education.* Atlanta, Ga.: Organizational Measurement Systems Press, 1965.

Miner, John B. *Motivation to Manage: A Ten-Year Update on the "Studies in Management Education" Research.* Atlanta, Ga.: Organizational Measurement Systems Press, 1977.

Murray, Henry A. *Thematic Apperception Test Manual.* Cambridge, Mass.: Harvard University Press, 1943.

Stein, Aletha H. and Margaret M. Bailey.

The Socialization of Achievement Orientation in Females, *Psychological Bulletin*, Vol. 80 (1973), 345–366.

Steiner, George A. and John B. Miner. *Management Policy and Strategy.* New York: Macmillan, 1977.

Timmons, Jeffry A. Black Is Beautiful — Is It Bountiful? *Harvard Business Review*, Vol. 49, No. 6 (1971), 81–94.

Turner, Jonathan H. Entrepreneurial Environments and the Emergence of Achievement Motivation in Adolescent Males, *Sociometry*, Vol. 33 (1970), 147–165.

Veroff, Joseph and Joanne B. Veroff. Reconsideration of a Measure of Power Motivation, *Psychological Bulletin*, Vol. 78 (1972), 279–291.

Wainer, Herbert A. and Irwin M. Rubin. Motivation of Research and Development Entrepreneurs: Determinants of Company Success, *Journal of Applied Psychology*, Vol. 53 (1969), 178–184.

Weber, Max. *The Protestant Ethic and the Spirit of Capitalism.* (translated by Talcott Parsons). New York: Scribner, 1904, 1930.

Weiner, Bernard. *Theories of Motivation: From Mechanism to Cognition.* Chicago: Markham, 1972.

Weiner, Bernard and Jack Sierad. Misattribution for Failure and Enhancement of Achievement Strivings, *Journal of Personality and Social Psychology*, Vol. 31 (1975), 415–421.

Winter, David G. *The Power Motive.* New York: Free Press, 1973.

4 MOTIVATION-HYGIENE THEORY

The theory to which we now turn often is referred to as two-factor theory, a designation that has its rationale in the dual nature of its approach to the sources of job satisfaction, and ultimately job motivation. The prime generator of the theory, Frederick Herzberg, prefers the term motivation-hygiene; therefore, this designation is used here.

The initial source of the theory appears to be a comprehensive review of the literature on job attitudes and satisfaction undertaken by Herzberg and his associates at Psychological Service of Pittsburgh (Herzberg, Mausner, Peterson, and Capwell, 1957). This review revealed often conflicting results, although with some slight overall tendency for job satisfaction to be positively correlated with job performance levels. To this finding Herzberg added an insight derived from his background in the field of mental health — the idea that mental health is not just the obverse of mental illness but rather a totally separate process. He developed the hypothesis that a similar discontinuity exists in the field of job satisfaction (Herzberg, 1976). Subsequent research produced a list of factors that contribute to satisfaction at work (motivation factors), and another separate list of factors that contribute to dissatisfaction (hygiene factors). Thus, the theory is an amalgam of deductive and inductive components so closely intertwined with the early research that the two cannot be separated effectively (Herzberg, Mausner, and Snyderman, 1959). Accordingly, an independent test of the theory had to await later investigation.

Throughout the development of the theory and its later application in the field of job enrichment, Herzberg has remained its leading exponent, first at Case Western Reserve University in Cleveland (after leaving Psychological Service of Pittsburgh) and more recently at the University of Utah. His early collaborators have not been continuing contributors to the theory. Thus, because of its pattern of association with a single individual, motivation-hygiene theory has more in common with need hierarchy theory than with achievement motivation theory.

THE EVOLUTION OF THE THEORY

Motivation-hygiene theory is presented in three volumes (Herzberg, Mausner, and Snyderman, 1959; Herzberg, 1966, 1976). The most recent of these is primarily a compendium of articles previously published, the majority of them in the early 1970s. Although the basics of the theory established in 1959 have remained firm, Herzberg has elaborated considerably on them since then.

The Motivation To Work (1959)

The first volume promulgating the theory also contains a detailed report of the initial research. This research sought to explore two hypotheses:
1. The factors causing positive job attitudes and those causing negative attitudes are different.

2. The factors and the performance or personal effects associated with sequences of job events extending over long time periods differ from those associated with sequences of events of short duration.

Based on certain outcomes of this research, the factors leading to job satisfaction and to job dissatisfaction were specified and thus became part of the theory. Job satisfaction is viewed as an outgrowth of achievement, recognition (verbal), the work itself (challenging), responsibility, and advancement (promotion). These five factors are considered to be closely related both conceptually and empirically. When they are present in a job, the individual's basic needs will be satisfied, and positive feelings as well as improved performance will result. The basic needs specified are those related to personal growth and self-actualization, and these are said to be satisfied by the five intrinsic aspects of the work itself.

In contrast, job dissatisfaction results from a different set of factors, all of which characterize the context in which the work is performed. These are company policy and administrative practices, supervision (technical quality), interpersonal relations (especially with supervision), physical working conditions, job security, benefits, and salary. These dissatisfiers, or hygiene factors, when appropriately provided can serve to remove dissatisfaction and improve performance up to a point, but they cannot be relied upon to generate really positive job feelings or the high levels of performance that are potentially possible. To accomplish these outcomes, management must shift gears and move into motivation.

This means that good hygiene should be provided, but that it will yield benefits only up to a certain point. Beyond that the focus needs to be on the intrinsic aspects of the work itself, not on its context. ". . . jobs must be restructured to increase to the maximum the ability of workers to achieve goals meaningfully related to the doing of the job. . . . the individual should have some measure of control over the way in which the job is done in order to realize a sense of achievement and of personal growth" (Herzberg, Mausner, and Snyderman, 1959, p. 132).

Work and the Nature of Man (1966)

With the 1966 volume, Herzberg began to add philosophical embellishments to what had been an eminently scientific and testable theory. Thus, the fringe benefits and other hygiene factors provided by large corporations were equated with the welfare state, and the motivation-hygiene distinction was extended beyond the work context through the use of extensive biblical analogies. More specifically, mankind was described as possessing two sets of basic needs — animal needs relating to the environmental survival and human needs relating to "the tasks with which he is uniquely involved." The former needs are allied with the notion of mankind as sinful and perpetually condemned to suffer and avoid suffering, as epitomized by Adam's fall. In addition, mankind may be characterized, like Abraham, as a capable being possessing innate potential and created in the image of God.

Herzberg (1966, p. 56) summarizes his expanded position regarding human motivation:

> ... the human animal has two categories of needs. One set stems from his animal disposition, that side of him previously referred to as the Adam view of man; it is centered on the avoidance of loss of life, hunger, pain, sexual deprivation and in other primary drives, in addition to the infinite varieties of learned fears that become attached to these basic drives. The other segment of man's nature, according to the Abraham concept of the human being, is man's compelling urge to realize his own potentiality by continous psychological growth. ... these two characteristics must be constantly viewed as having separate biological, psychological and existential origins.

Although most people are best characterized in terms of both sets of needs, Herzberg also described individuals who are dominated by one set or the other. Thus, there are high growth-oriented people who actually experience what they interpret as unhappiness when deprived of motivators, and there are people who are fixated on hygiene seeking, such as the mentally ill.

Hygiene seekers are generally considered to be poor risks for a company, because they tend to be motivated over short time periods and require constant doses of external reward; they cannot be relied upon in crisis. Furthermore, a lack of motivators in a job tends to sensitize people to any lack of hygiene factors, with the result that more and more hygiene must be provided to obtain the same level of performance. Herzberg emphasizes strongly the need for companies to build motivators into their jobs.

To facilitate this he recommends that industrial relations departments be organized into two formal divisions, one to deal with hygiene matters and the other to deal with motivators. Assuming that most current departments are focused largely on hygiene, he devotes primary attention to what would be added with the division concerned with motivator needs. Among the tasks recommended are re-education of organization members to a motivator orientation (from the current welfare orientation), job enlargement, and remedial work in the areas of technological obsolescence, poor employee performance, and administrative failure.

The Managerial Choice (1976)

The most recent presentation of motivation-hygiene theory places much greater emphasis on job enrichment applications. However, it also extends the theory in several respects.

One such extension utilizes the two-factor concept to develop typologies of workers. The normal types are described as follows:

1. The person who has both hygiene and motivator fulfillment, who is not unhappy and is also very happy.
2. The person who is on both need systems but has little fulfillment in the hygiene area even though his motivator satisfaction is good. Such a "starving artist" is both unhappy and happy.
3. The person who is also on both need systems but whose satisfactions are reversed — hygienes are good, but motivators are poor; he is not unhappy but neither is he happy.
4. The down and out person who is lacking in fulfillment generally and is both unhappy and lacking in happiness.

To these four, Herzberg adds certain abnormal profiles that characterize people who are not actually on the motivator dimension at all and who attempt to substitute increased hygiene for this motivator deficiency. Such people may also resort to psychological mechanisms, such as denial of their hygiene needs and fantasied motivator satisfaction, which further compound their hygiene problems. In these pathological instances an inversion occurs in that fulfillment of hygiene needs may be viewed as satisfying, not merely as an avoidance of dissatisfaction.

A distinction is also made within the motivator factors. Achievement and recognition are described as preparatory in nature and as having, in common with hygiene factors, relatively short term effects. The work itself, responsibility, and growth and advancement are generators that truly motivate people. In job redesign, these latter factors should be emphasized.

Throughout his writings Herzberg has wrestled with the role of salary. The most frequently stated position is that it is a hygiene factor. Yet there are contradictory statements in the 1976 book, which contains articles published at different times. A 1971 article clearly states, "Money is a hygiene factor" (Herzberg, 1976, p. 305). But in 1974, the following statement appears, "Because of its ubiquitous nature, salary commonly shows up as a motivator as well as hygiene. Although primarily a hygiene factor, it also often takes on some of the properties of a motivator, with dynamics similar to those of recognition for achievement" (Herzberg, 1976, p. 71). It appears that the motivation-hygiene problem created by compensation is very similar to the problem created by power mo-tivation in the development of achievement motivation theory.

A final point needs to be made as we move to an evaluation of the motivation-hygiene theory. Herzberg has gradually become increasingly critical of his fellow social scientists and of alterna-tive theories. His justification is that he was attacked first. Others may well view what he considers attacks as merely the presenta-tion of objective scientific evidence. In any event, Herzberg (1976, pp. 54–55) has resorted to statements such as the following:

> Engrossed with their artificial measures and rarified statistics, social scien-tists have too long neglected the language and experiences of people at work. . . . Their error is attempting to manipulate their instruments to pro-duce a relationship that simply does not reflect the psychological and orga-nizational realities in many companies.

Are such statements attempts to play to the stereotypes of management practitioners, as some have charged, or do they rep-resent valid, scientific criticism? Certainly they reflect the exis-tence of considerable controversy. The answers, though, must be found in an objective evaluation of the research evidence.

HERZBERG'S RESEARCH AND THE RESEARCH OF OTHERS

It is to Herzberg's credit that he proposed measures of his the-oretical variables when the theory was first presented, and that he has conducted research on the theory from the beginning. As might be expected, these circumstances have served to stimulate considerable research by others. The result has been that both Herzberg's measures and his interpretation of his findings have been seriously challenged. To understand what has happened, it is necessary to start with the original research that spawned motivation-hygiene theory (Herzberg, Mausner, and Snyderman, 1959).

The Original Study

The measurement procedure developed by Herzberg and his associates was a derivative of the critical incident technique that had been utilized previously by Flanagan (1954), primarily in the evaluation of job performance. However, while Flanagan asked his subjects to focus on good and bad performance, Herzberg asked for incidents describing "a time when you felt exceptionally good or a time when you felt exceptionally bad about your job, either a long-range sequence of events or a short-range incident." Subjects were requested to provide several such incidents in as diverse an array of satisfaction levels and time durations as possible. In each instance a series of probing questions was asked regarding the incident to determine what factors were related to the job attitude expressed; these factors might be either antecedent objective occurrences (first level) or attributed internal reasons for the feelings (second level). Also, the perceived consequences or effects of the attitudes were explored with regard to such matters as job performance, tenure on the job, emotional adjustment, interpersonal relationships, and the like. The strength of feeling aroused by the incident was rated by the subject on a graphic scale.

These interview procedures emerged out of several pilot studies. The outcome is a set of stories from each subject specifying a factors-attitudes-effects sequence. These stories are somewhat similar to those elicited using the Thematic Apperception Test described in Chapter 3. However, there is no standardized external stimulus such as that provided by the TAT pictures, and a story here is about the subject himself rather than someone else. Both of these considerations reduce the psychological distance of the stories and thus increase the degree to which defensiveness may be manifested in them.

The Sample Studied.   In the major study this interview procedure was applied to 203 accountants and engineers employed by nine primarily manufacturing companies in the Pittsburgh area. The choice of these professional groups was dictated by earlier experiences in the pilot studies indicating that professionals gave much more vivid stories than did production or clerical workers. As the authors point out, "Since our study was still in the nature of any exploratory project, it was vital to us that we mine where the metal was richest."

The Analytical Approach.   The stories were scored using an approach to content analysis not unlike that used in scoring for the motives of achievement motivation theory. Since the theory called for measures of factors and effects as well as time durations and satisfaction levels, these become the focus of analysis. The specific categories of factors and effects were developed from the stories themselves.

In all, 39 scoring categories were developed. A check on scorer reliability, using independent coders, revealed an agreement rate of 95 per cent, certainly adequate to justify the procedure.

The basic procedure used in testing the theory was to determine how frequently a given type of factor appeared as a proportion of the total number of sequences in which it might have appeared. The theory predicts that certain kinds of factors would predominate in the satisfaction (motivator) sequences, and a completely different set would predominate in the dissatisfaction (hygiene) sequences. The same kind of differentiation should occur when short and long duration sequences are compared.

The Results. The data presented in Table 4–1 clearly indicate that recognition, achievement, responsibility, the work itself, and their related feelings are more commonly associated with job satisfaction than dissatisfaction. Advancement operates in a similar manner as a first level factor, but not at the second level. The

Table 4–1. PERCENTAGE OF SATISFACTION (N = 228) AND DISSATISFACTION (N = 248) SEQUENCES IN WHICH EACH TYPE OF FIRST LEVEL (OBJECTIVE SITUATIONAL) AND SECOND LEVEL (PERCEIVED INTERNAL MOTIVATIONAL) FACTORS FIGURED

Factor Designation	Per Cent Occurrence			
	Satisfaction Sequences		Dissatisfaction Sequences	
	First Level	Second Level	First Level	Second Level
Recognition	(33)*	(59)	18	26
Achievement	(41)	(57)	7	19
Possibility of growth	6	38	8	33
Advancement	(20)	3	11	2
Salary	15	19	17	13
Interpersonal relations—supervisor	4	†	(15)	†
Interpersonal relations—subordinates	6	†	3	†
Interpersonal relations—peers	3	†	(8)	†
Supervision—technical	3	†	(20)	†
Responsibility	(23)	(30)	6	7
Company policy and administration	3	†	(31)	†
Working conditions	1	†	(11)	†
The work itself	(26)	(29)	14	13
Factors in personal life	1	†	(6)	†
Status	4	18	4	10
Job security	1	7	1	9
Group feeling	†	(10)	†	4
Feelings of fairness or unfairness	†	3	†	38
Feelings of pride or shame	†	9	†	14

*Percentages given in parentheses are reported to be significantly higher for comparison within same factor level.
†Not a scoring category for this level of factor.
Adapted from Frederick Herzberg, Bernard Mausner, and Barbara S. Snyderman. *The Motivation To Work.* New York: Wiley, 1959, pp. 72, 77.

remaining significant differences all occur on factors that cannot be measured at both levels. Within this context, group feelings is a satisfier, whereas interpersonal relations with supervisors and peers, technical supervision, company policy and administration, working conditions, and factors in personal life are dissatisfiers. The data for second level factors also indicate that feelings of fairness and unfairness is a dissatisfier (although the statistical significance of this finding is not specifically noted).

The findings obtained are certainly consistent with the original hypotheses, and they largely fit the theory as it ultimately evolved based on interpretations of this study. On the other hand, the data yield several factors that emerge equally as satisfiers and dissatisfiers, among them the possibility of growth, salary, and status, and feelings of pride and shame. Furthermore, although dissatisfiers rarely yield meaningful frequencies as satisfiers, the reverse is not true. At one level or another, recognition, achievement, advancement, and the work itself all operate as dissatisfiers as well as satisfiers more than 10 per cent of the time.

Data on the factors associated with long- and short-term event sequences are not presented. The original hypothesis dealing with the differential causes and effects of sequences of job events extending over long and short time periods appears to have been dropped from the theory; it does not appear in later formulations.

The data on the effects consequent upon feelings of satisfaction and dissatisfaction are introduced quite tentatively: "Many readers will be skeptical of the validity of our respondent's reports that given behaviors are consequent upon their feelings about their jobs.... the lack of meaningful objective criteria makes it essential that we use what cues we have to the impact of people's attitudes on the way in which they behave in the work situation.... let us then present our data on effects in full knowledge of the fact that they were elicited by specific probes directed toward the kind of behavior with which we were concerned and that, therefore, they should not be considered direct evidence of the behavior of our respondents." (Herzberg, Mausner, and Snyderman, 1959, p. 84). Yet later, the authors make a number of much more definitive statements; for instance, "It is primarily the 'motivators' that serve to bring about the kind of job satisfaction, and as we saw in the section dealing with the effects of job attitudes, the kind of improvement in performance that industry is seeking from its work force" (p. 114).

It is clear that reports of satisfaction were associated with reports of positive effects, including improved performance, continued employment, improved attitude toward the company, improved mental health, better interpersonal relationships, and improved morale. In contrast, reports of dissatisfaction were associated with the reverse trends, although the overall results were less pronounced. These results "may be attributed to the unwillingness of some interviewees to admit to doing their jobs less well than usual."

Whatever the merits of this original study and of the interpretation the authors place on it, it is best viewed as an inductive source from which the theory was, if not totally generated, at least specifically delineated in terms of its operative variables. Given this situation, it is best to look to subsequent research for adequate empirical tests.

Findings from Studies Closely Allied to the Original Research

The major questions raised regarding research on the theory have revolved around what is and what is not an adequate test. One such question relates to whether comparisons should be made between data for all motivators and all hygienes combined, or independently for each specific variable (King, 1970). On this point it seems clear that the theory does specify factors, the 16 at the first level for instance, and that each of these variables should be tested separately. The combined hypotheses for motivators and hygienes overall would also be expected to hold if the preponderance of the individual variables operates as expected.

In the original research, comparisons were made on each factor between the frequencies obtained as a satisfier and as a dissatisfier; thus, this procedure would appear to provide an appropriate test of the theory. However, one may also ask whether individual motivators should consistently yield higher frequencies than individual hygienes as satisfiers and whether the reverse type of relationship should hold among individual variables when dissatisfaction is considered. In general, the theory does posit such a pattern; however, it also anticipates inversions, in which hygiene factors are frequently specified as satisfiers among the emotionally ill. Thus, in certain populations the usual motivation-hygiene differences in sources of *satisfaction* are not hypothesized.

The Early Research. A number of studies utilizing the methods of the original research, or minor variants, were conducted in the years immediately following and are summarized by Herzberg (1966) as providing support for his theory. Most of these studies did not consider effects, and a number did not deal with second level factors. Sequence duration was given practically no attention.

There is no question when statistically significant results are obtained in these studies they are much more likely to support the theory than refute it. It is evident also, as indicated in Table 4–2, that certain of the first level factors are much more likely to receive support from the data than others. Among the motivators, achievement and recognition are strongly supported, but possibility of growth is not supported at all. Among the hygienes, company policy and administration and also technical supervisions are supported but certainly not salary, status, and job security.

Another way of looking at the data is to ask how frequently motivators and hygienes act in a manner opposite to that hypothesized. The data indicate that frequently motivators may operate as dissatisfiers. Even when the analysis is restricted to those studies in which satisfier frequencies were significantly higher than dissatisfier frequencies, achievement served as a dissatisfier an average of 15 per cent of the time, the work itself 14 per cent, and recognition 8 per cent; the percentages for the remaining motivators were sufficiently low and based on a sufficiently small number of analyses so that chance errors of measurement might well account for them: advancement 6, responsibility 4, and possibility of growth 1.

The theory anticipates inversions wherein hygienes are speci-

Table 4–2.   PER CENT OF ANALYSES IN WHICH FACTOR FREQUENCIES ARE SIGNIFICANTLY HIGHER IN ACCORDANCE WITH PREDICTIONS FOR THE THEORY

	Per Cent Significant Findings
Motivators	
Recognition	60
Achievement	73
Possibility of Growth	7
Advancement	27
Responsibility	47
The Work Itself	27
Hygienes	
Salary	7
Interpersonal Relations—supervisor	20
Interpersonal Relations—subordinates	13*
Interpersonal Relations—peers	20*
Supervision—technical	60
Company Policy and Administration	87
Working Conditions	33
Factors in Personal Life	13
Status	7
Job Security	7

*In addition, one or more significant results the reverse of those predicted are also reported for these variables.

Adapted from Frederick Herzberg. *Work and the Nature of Man.* Cleveland: World, 1966, p. 124.

fied as satisfiers. These occurred relatively infrequently when the dissatisfier frequency was significantly higher. The highest average percentage was 9 (for salary in the one study in which it showed significance as a dissatisfier); all other values were 6 or less. However, interpersonal relations with subordinates and peers did yield significant reversals, with percentages ranging from 15 to 27.

Recent Studies. The method utilized in the original research has received continued use until the present. In general, the results have paralleled those of Tables 4–1 and 4–2. On balance the

Table 4–3. PER CENT OCCURRENCE AS SATISFIER AND DISSATISFIER FOR 16 FIRST LEVEL FACTORS IN THREE STUDIES

Factor Designation	Supervisors in State Government (N = 85) (Schwab and Heneman, 1970)		Black Working Poor (N = 50) (Karp and Nickson, 1973)		Greek Managers (N = 178) (White and Leon, 1976)	
	Satisfaction Sequence	Dissatisfaction Sequence	Satisfaction Sequence	Dissatisfaction Sequence	Satisfaction Sequence	Dissatisfaction Sequence
Motivators						
Recognition	(33)*	21	(15)	5	33	22
Achievement	(35)	12	(19)	4	(40)	14
Possibility of growth	1	5	(8)	0	(22)	3
Advancement	8	8	(5)	0	14	13
Responsibility	6	0	(12)	0	(26)	9
The work itself	1	0	(2)	0	(44)	21
Hygienes						
Salary	1	2	(24)	2	2	(23)
Interpersonal relations— supervisor	10	14			(28)	9
Interpersonal relations— subordinates	0	7	12	(33)	(11)	2
Interpersonal relations—peers	2	6			(17)	7
Supervision—technical	0	0	0	(4)	5	(25)
Company policy and administration	0	(17)	2	(24)	3	(42)
Working conditions	1	1	0	(27)	4	(18)
Factors in personal life	0	2	—	—	0	1
Status	0	5	(2)	0	14	6
Job security	0	0	—	—	3	(12)

*Percentages in parentheses are reported to be significantly higher for comparison within same factor level.

Adapted from Donald P. Schwab and Herbert G. Heneman, III. Aggregate and Individual Predictability of the Two-Factor Theory of Job Satisfaction. *Personnel Psychology*, Vol. 23 (1970), p. 61; H. B. Karp and Jack W. Nickson. Motivator-Hygiene Deprivation as a Predictor of Job Turnover. *Personnel Psychology*, Vol. 26 (1973), p. 382; Donald D. White and Julio Leon. The Two-Factor Theory: New Questions, New Answers. *Academy of Management Proceedings*, (1976), p. 358.

theory appears to be supported, but there are certain persistent problems. The studies providing the data of Table 4–3 have been selected to demonstrate these areas in which support is lacking. In two of the studies the tendency for motivators to appear frequently as dissatisfiers as well as satisfiers is clearly evident. This tendency to appear in the wrong context is less characteristic of the hygienes, unless (and this clearly does occur) a true reversal is in evidence. Such reversals (or inversions) can apparently appear for salary and the various interpersonal relations factors, and there they can be sizeable; they also may appear for status.

Performance Effects.   In view of Herzberg's own expressed concerns about the findings of the original study dealing with performance and personal effects, and the clear implications of these findings for the motivational as opposed to merely attitudinal hypotheses of the theory, it is surprising that so little research has focused on this area. A study conducted by Schwab, DeVitt, and Cummings (1971), utilizing essentially the same methods as the original research and dealing only with effects in the area of job performance, does serve to amplify the Herzberg findings. Favorable performance effects were reported often as an outgrowth of satisfying job experiences; to a lesser extent unfavorable performance effects were associated with dissatisfying experiences. This pattern is consistent with the one originally reported, and as Herzberg noted then, this "may be attributed to the unwillingness of some interviewees to admit to doing their jobs less well than usual."

One might assume from this result that the introduction of motivators is the key to improving employee performance. However, hygiene factors were occasionally reported as sources of satisfaction, and it was possible to determine in these instances that improved performance effects were reported to as great a degree as those for the motivators. Thus, it would appear that when hygiene factors operate as satisfiers, in this case interpersonal relations with a supervisor predominantly, they may be perceived as a source of performance stimulation just as much as motivators. Furthermore, when there is dissatisfaction, motivators can have just as negative an effect as hygienes. It is the level of job satisfaction-dissatisfaction that yields the reported performance effect, not the presence of motivators or hygienes.

Inversions in the Mentally Ill.   A study carried out by Herzberg, Mathapo, Wiener, and Wiesen (1974) bears upon the hypothesis that when hygienes are reported as sources of satisfaction, the inversions are characteristic of the mentally ill. Using the same method as in the previous research, hospitalized mental patients were found to attribute job satisfaction to hygiene factors 36 per cent of the time, as contrasted with an average of 19 per cent of the time for employed people. Furthermore, the evidence indicates that the frequency of inversions increases with the severity of the disorder. A second study of inversion percentages by the same investigators compared outpatients with varying degrees of diagnosed mental illness who were currently employed. Those with relatively minimal disturbances had an inversion percentage of 15, the more severely disturbed 27.

The results of these studies are certainly consistent with motivation-hygiene theory, and the research was indeed stimulated by the theory. The research design does not rule out other interpretations of the data, such as the possibility that the mentally ill might more easily tolerate and express certain kinds of logical inconsistencies. As the authors note, "The correlational results of this study could be explained, or predicted without resorting to the propositions and terminology of motivation-hygiene theory" (Herzberg et al., 1974, p. 418).

Research Utilizing Different Methodologies

In a number of its aspects, motivation-hygiene theory has received support from research utilizing the methods of the original study. Almost from the beginning, however, questions have been raised as to whether these methods might not somehow operate in and of themselves to determine the results; thus, the findings could be a direct consequence of the method per se, not the underlying attitudinal and motivational facts, and therefore might not be replicable when other methods are used. This concern is reflected in a review of the 1959 Herzberg volume:

> We may be seeing in the results some special characteristics of the nine Pittsburgh companies on which the Herzberg-Mausner research is based or some special characteristics of accountants and engineers. A more likely possibility, in my own opinion, is that these findings are in part the result of relying entirely on the respondent for a description of his job attitudes, the factors which occasioned them, and their behavioral consequences. For example, the factor which was coded most often as a reason for high job-attitude sequences was recognition, but the factor which was coded most frequently as a reason for low job-attitude sequences was *unfairness*. Now suppose that most respondents begin with the ego-protective notion that they are reasonably able and deserve recognition. The recognized respondent says, in effect: "I am meritorious and others perceive and reward my merit." The unrecognized respondent says: "I too am meritorious, but others fail to perceive and reward my merit. Hence, their unfairness and my low attitudes." I do not think that such an interpretation can be ruled out. . . . The replication and extension of these findings, especially with independent measures of environmental factors and of performance criteria, would be of major significance for the social psychology of large organizations (Kahn, 1961, p. 10).

In the following section we will examine what has been accomplished using other measures in ensuing years.

Other Methods — Pros and Cons.   In the period immediately after motivation-hygiene theory was proposed, a number of studies were conducted using a variety of methods to put the theory to a crucial test. Many of these studies now appear to have missed the mark. Some extended the theory beyond its limits, some dealt with satisfaction-dissatisfaction as a single factor, and so on (Bockman, 1971; King, 1970; Herzberg, 1976). It is not necessary to clamber through the labyrinth of conflicting arguments during this period. The findings were almost universally negative, but sufficient questions have been raised to make the irrelevance charge at least partially legitimate.

This point may be illustrated with a study conducted by Grigaliunas and Herzberg (1971) that sought to determine the legitimacy of using rating scale procedures to test the theory, a common practice in the early period. Here the standard incident method was compared with a rating scale approach wherein the subjects themselves indicated what factors were important to their feelings in the incidents. These latter, subject-attributed factors were evaluated by independent judges, and a score was obtained utilizing only data that were clearly relevant and logically appropriate to the particular incident.

The percentages of Table 4–4 indicate that only when the irrelevant rating scale data are purged do the findings conform to

Table 4–4.   PERCENTAGE OF MOTIVATOR AND HYGIENE SEQUENCES IN HIGH (SATISFYING) AND LOW (DISSATISFYING) INCIDENTS AS MEASURED BY DIFFERENT METHODS

Method of Measurement	Satisfying Incidents		Dissatisfying Incidents	
	Motivator	Hygiene	Motivator	Hygiene
Original incident method	71	29	21	79
Rating scale listing various statements relevant to motivator and hygiene factors and requiring a rating of the importance of each (statements rated as important)	71	29	61	39
The same rating scale procedure with only statements judged to be relevant to a subject's incident utilized	67	33	28	72

Adapted from Benedict S. Grigaliunas and Frederick Herzberg. Relevancy in the Test of Motivator-Hygiene Theory. *Journal of Applied Psychology.* Vol. 55 (1971). p. 76.

motivator-hygiene theory and to the results obtained with the original incident method. The authors interpret these findings as follows:

> When faced with an item, subjects seem to have a great deal of difficulty in focusing back to the incident and determining what is important in the incident as opposed to what is important to them generally. The force of social desirability or the pull of their value systems is stronger than the directions. Hence, quite automatically, subjects rate the general importance of the item to them rather than the importance of the item to the incident they have described (Grigaliunas and Herzberg, 1971, p. 78).

As research has progressed, many of these kinds of problems have been overcome. Yet the failure of research to support motivation-hygiene theory when alternative methods are employed continues. Table 4–5 contains the results of two studies in which satisfying and dissatisfying incidents reflecting the operation of two motivator factors and three hygiene factors were developed directly from training programs by trainees and trainers (Gordon, Pryor, and Harris, 1974). The subjects were asked to single out those specific incidents they had personally experienced during training. The average proportion of all possible incidents of each type is indicated in the

Table 4–5. PROPORTION OF INCIDENTS OF DIFFERENT TYPES EXPERIENCED BY TRAINEES IN A MANPOWER DEVELOPMENT PROJECT (N = 88) AND STUDENTS IN A VOCATIONAL TECHNICAL SCHOOL (N = 132)

	Manpower Development Project		Vocational-Technical School	
	Satisfying Incidents	*Dissatisfying Incidents*	*Satisfying Incidents*	*Dissatisfying Incidents*
Range of number of incidents included in scales for various factors	9–14	9–14	10–17	10–19
First level factors measured by scales	**Per Cent of Incidents Reported as Personally Experienced**			
Motivators				
Achievement	78	37	65	33
The work itself	75	35	74	33
Hygienes				
Company policy and administration	71	40	60	33
Interpersonal relations— supervisor and peers	67	29	69	28
Working conditions	55	40	73	34

Adapted from Michael E. Gordon, Norman M. Pryor and Bob V. Harris. An Examination of Scaling Bias in Herzberg's Theory of Job Satisfaction. *Organizational Behavior and Human Performance*, Vol. 11 (1974), pp. 110, 112, and 115.

table. The theory predicts that the incidents selected should be concentrated disproportionately in the satisfying-motivator and dissatisfying-hygiene categories. Certainly there is a tendency for satisfying motivator incidents to be selected more than dissatisfying motivator incidents. But this tendency is just as pronounced among the hygienes. The major findings are that in the two contexts studied satisfaction is more characteristic than dissatisfaction, and both are equally likely to be occasioned by the motivators and hygienes considered.

The Defense Mechanism Hypothesis.   Studies such as that conducted by Gordon, Pryor, and Harris do serve to question the validity of certain of the constructs of motivation-hygiene theory, but they do not speak to the question of *why* the original version of the incident method often yields disparate results. A considerable body of research has focused on this question, and in particular this research concerns itself with the kinds of issues raised by Kahn (1961) in his review (noted previously) of the Herzberg, Mausner, and Snyderman research.

One such study obtained a measure of defensiveness from employees of a single company. It related this to the degree of match obtained with motivation-hygiene theory predictions derived from the original critical incident method (Wall, 1973). Defensiveness was unrelated to the tendency to attribute satisfaction to motivator factors but strongly related to attributing dissatisfaction to hygiene factors. Composite findings combining both tendencies were intermediate. It is apparent that individuals who are more defensive do tend to blame unpleasant experiences on people and circumstances outside the self. A similar study reported by Herzberg (1976) utilizing students as subjects appears not to confirm these results. However, data for satisfying and dissatisfying incidents were not reported separately, and this may obliterate the unique role that defensiveness appears to play in the hygiene-dissatisfaction relationship.

Another research strategy does not involve measuring defensiveness and relating it to results obtained with the original measurement procedure, but rather utilizes a measurement procedure that increases psychological distance and thus decreases the need for defensiveness, and determines whether the results are supportive of motivation-hygiene theory. This is done by asking subjects to imagine an ideal way of making a living and then to list factors contributing to this satisfying state. A similar list is obtained of factors contributing to a dissatisfying way of making a living (Ondrack, 1974). The rank order of the frequency with which factors are noted, combining data from two samples, is as follows for the two conditions:

Factor	Source of Satisfaction	Source of Dissatisfaction
The work itself (motivator)	1	1
Salary (hygiene)	2	2
Interpersonal relations—peers (hygiene)	3	5
Responsibility (motivator)	4	3
Independence (new factor)	5	4
Achievement (motivator)	6	8
Recognition (motivator)	7	>10
Possibility of growth (motivator)	8	>10
Advancement (motivator)	9	7
Working conditions (hygiene)	10	>10
Supervision—technical (hygiene)	>10	6
Company policy and administration (hygiene)	>10	9
Socially useful work (new factor)	>10	10

This approach, being more removed from actual personal experience and thus more projective in nature, should reduce defensiveness and thus (according to the defense mechanism hypothesis) yield results less supportive of the theory. This is indeed the case. Motivators contributed more to both satisfaction and dissatisfaction, and to a roughly equal extent. In addition, three new factors were needed to account for the responses. Independence and socially useful work would appear to qualify as motivators, whereas travel ought to be a hygiene. In the preceding rankings, motivators and hygienes have practically equal average ranks as contributors to satisfaction and dissatisfaction. The factor rankings are quite similar for both types of feelings.

A somewhat different approach to investigating both defensiveness and the validity of motivation-hygiene theory constructs utilizes the original method of measurement but introduces a revised and more differentiated method of coding (Locke, 1975; Locke and Whiting, 1974). In this procedure first level factors are scored both for events (what event or condition occurred or was present) and agents (who or what caused the event or brought about the condition). Frequently mentioned event categories are working conditions, money, recognition, smoothness and amount of work; frequently mentioned agents are organizations, supervisors, nonhuman agents, and self.

When the analysis focuses on events, those of a motivator type consistently produce both greater satisfaction and greater dissatisfaction than the hygienes. Among the agents there is a clear tendency to credit the self for satisfying events, while others (nonself agents) are more likely to be blamed for dissatisfying events; this is consistent with the defense mechanism hypothesis. However, this kind of finding is not obtained at the lowest job skill levels. Although the coding system utilized by Locke has been challenged by advocates of the theory (Herzberg, 1976), it is still true that these results once again fail to provide evidence of construct validity.

JOB ENRICHMENT APPLICATIONS

From the very beginning, Herzberg has advocated restructuring jobs to place greater reliance on motivators. The techniques of this kind that evolved over the years are now designated by the term Orthodox Job Enrichment, to differentiate them from similar approaches that do not have their origins in motivation-hygiene theory. Although Herzberg has been a major influence in the development of job redesign procedures over the past 15 or 20 years, a great deal has happened in this area that is not attributable either to him or his theory. Furthermore, his self-designation "father of job enrichment" may be only partially correct, since efforts of this kind can be traced back many years.

However, the focus of the present discussion will be on applications and related research in which Herzberg himself has been involved or on which he has had a direct influence. Chapter 9 will deal with other approaches to job enrichment and enlargement as motivational techniques.

The Process of Orthodox Job Enrichment

Herzberg (1976) makes a strong point that what he is *not* talking about is participative management, sociotechnical systems, industrial democracy, or organizational development. Yet there is a marked tendency for a great variety of activities to creep into and become part of a job enrichment effort (Locke, 1975). Orthodox Job Enrichment by definition involves only the introduction of motivators into a job, not hygienes. Yet, pay raises and various interpersonal factors have accompanied such efforts on occasion. Accordingly, it is important to understand clearly what is implied by the term.

Herzberg (1976) has identified a number of factors that, although not limited to Orthodox Job Enrichment alone, are primary to the approach:

1. Direct feedback of performance results to the employee in a nonevaluative manner and usually not through a superior. An example would be targets on a rifle range that fall down when hit.
2. The existence of a customer or client either within or outside the organization for whom work is performed. The unit assemblers who depend on the output of various prior manufacturing opera-

tions fit this designation; so do a salesman's external customers.

3. The opportunity for individuals to feel that they are growing psychologically through new learning that is meaningful. For instance, a laboratory technician may be given a chance to learn many skills utilized by a research scientist.

4. Being able to schedule one's own work, with requirements set by realistic deadlines. Thus, work breaks might be taken when scheduled by the individual, not management.

5. Doing the job in one's own unique manner and utilizing time accordingly. As an example, individuals who finish their tasks ahead of time can be allowed to use the remaining work periods as they see fit.

6. Providing employees with minibudgets that make them directly responsible for costs. In this way cost and profit centers are pushed down to the lowest possible level, where employees may be authorized to approve expenditures within realistic limits.

7. Communication with the individuals needed to get the job done regardless of any possible hierarchic constraints. Accordingly, an employee whose work requires discussion with a supervisor in another department would be permitted to do so directly.

8. Maintaining individual accountability for results. For instance, responsibility for quality control may be taken away from a supervisor or external unit and built back into the job.

An indication of what these changes may involve is provided by a job enrichment program carried out within a sales unit:

1. Reports on each customer call were eliminated. Salesmen were to use their own discretion in passing on information to or making requests of management.

2. Salesmen determined their own calling frequencies and kept records only as might be needed for purposes such as staff reviews.

3. The technical service department agreed to provide service as needed by the individual salesman. Communication between salesman and technician was direct, with any needed paperwork cleared after the event.

4. If customers complained about product performance, salesmen could make settlements of up to 250 dollars if they considered it appropriate.

5. When faulty material was delivered or customers proved to be overstocked, salesmen could deal with these issues directly, with no limit on sales value of material returned.

6. Salesmen were given a discretionary range of about 10 per cent on quoted prices for most items, although quotations other than list did have to be reported to management.

Results at American Telephone and Telegraph

One of the first applications of job enrichment that was influenced by Herzberg's thinking occurred in the Bell system (Ford, 1969, 1973). The initial study was conducted in the treasury department among clerical personnel who answer inquiries from A. T. and T. shareholders. Job changes were introduced for certain employees with the objective of providing greater opportunities for achievement, recognition, responsibility, advancement, and psychological growth. The jobs of other employees remained unchanged. The results are described as follows:

> The achieving or experimental group clearly exceeded the control and uncommitted groups on a variety of criteria, such as turnover, the quality of customer service, productivity, lowered costs, lower absence rates, and source for managerial upgrading. . . . only the experimental group members felt significantly better about the task at which they work. The upward change in this group is most striking (Ford, 1969, p. 39).

Because of this result, the program was expanded into a variety of departments — commercial, comptroller, plant, traffic, and engineering. In most cases the practice of comparing experimental (enriched jobs) and control (job not enriched) groups was continued. The overall results were very favorable, although there were instances when job enrichment did not have much effect. Some supervisors clearly resisted it, and 10 to 15 per cent of the employees did not want the added responsibility. Blue collar jobs proved most resistant to enrichment.

More recent reports from A. T. and T. indicate continuing positive effects (Ford, 1973). In particular, success has been obtained by combining and reorganizing existing jobs to produce more meaningful work units, and by linking enriched jobs to produce internal customer or client relationships.

Results in the U.S. Air Force

Another program of job enrichment was initiated at Hill Air Force Base in Utah but has since spread to a number of other installations (Herzberg, 1976; 1977; Herzberg and Zautra, 1976). The enriched jobs vary from aircraft maintenance to keypunch operation and from contract document preparation to foreign military sales. Results obtained with the initial eleven jobs that were changed indicated savings of over 250,000 dollars in a ten-month period. The largest part of this saving occurred in two aircraft maintenance activities; several projects ran into considerable difficulty and did not yield tangible benefits. When tangible benefits were obtained, the

Table 4–6. PRE AND POST MEASURES OF JOB SATISFACTION FOR
                 JOB ENRICHMENT PROJECTS — PER CENT EXPERIENCING
                 INCREASE

Measure	Reported Increase Prior to Enrichment	Reported Increase During Enrichment
Overall satisfaction factors	33	76
Recognition for achievement	15	20
Achievement	28	67
Work itself	10	70
Responsibility	15	80
Advancement	23	62
Growth	30	72

Adapted from Frederick Herzberg and Alex Zautra. Orthodox Job Enrichment:
Measuring True Quality in Job Satisfaction. *Personnel*, Vol. 53, No. 5 (1976), p. 66.

return included reduced costs for materials, fuel, and personnel, and
increased units of production.

When the program was subsequently expanded:

> **The results were dramatic: a $1.75 million saving in 2 years on 29 projects that
> had matured to the point where careful auditing of savings was possible. The
> dollar benefits accrued from reduced sick leave, a lower rate of personnel
> turnover, less overtime and rework, a reduction in man-hours, and material
> savings (Herzberg, 1977, p. 25).**

Table 4–6 contains data on reported increases in job satisfaction
experienced over 12 months prior to job enrichment and again during
the months of job change. It is apparent that job satisfaction did
increase and that all motivators studied except recognition also
showed an increase. Data on hygiene factors were not obtained.

RELATED THEORIES

Like a number of the other theories considered here, motivation-
hygiene theory has spawned numerous revisions and restatements.
Many of these proposals are basically attempts to clarify the theory for
purposes of testing it and thus do not introduce sufficient modification to warrant calling them new theories. A few such efforts, however, contain significant changes and extensions of the Herzberg formulations. Generally, these theories have been conceived to deal with
disconfirming evidence for the original theory.

Need Gratification Theory

The similarities between need hierarchy theory and motivation-
hygiene theory have been noted by a number of writers including

Herzberg (1976). The most sophisticated attempt to tie the two theories together has been proposed by Wolf (1970), who faults Herzberg for equating satisfaction with motivation. Wolf accepts the Maslow theory, but for purposes of reconciling the two views he collapses the original need hierarchy into two levels, relating lower order needs to hygiene factors and higher order needs to motivators. The following hypotheses are proposed:

1. Those with ungratified lower order needs obtain both their satisfactions and their dissatisfactions from changes in gratification of their lower order needs (primarily from hygienes).

2. Those with conditionally gratified lower order needs obtain both their satisfaction and their dissatisfaction from changes in gratification of their higher order needs (primarily from motivators); dissatisfaction also may derive from threatened or actual disruption of lower order need gratification.

3. If lower order needs are fully and unconditionally gratified, then only higher order needs are relevant to satisfaction-dissatisfaction.

4. Dissatisfaction derives from frustrated gratification of whatever need is active.

5. Dissatisfaction also may result from an interruption or threatened interruption in the gratification of previously gratified lower order needs.

6. Satisfaction results from need gratification.

7. This satisfaction is greatest when a previously totally ungratified need is gratified.

8. For those whose lower order needs are largely gratified and whose higher order needs are active —
   a. hygiene factors are essentially unrelated to increased satisfaction;
   b. hygiene factors are strongly related to dissatisfaction if lower order need gratification is threatened;
   c. motivator factors are strongly related to both increased and decreased satisfaction, depending on the degree of higher order need gratification.

9. Job motivation is a consequence of a perceived opportunity to gratify an active need; its strength depends on the person's estimate of the probability that job-related behavior will yield the desired gratification.

10. Salary serves as a motivator when the person expects to be able to increase it through job related behaviors; otherwise, salary serves to lower satisfaction to the extent that it is seen as preventing the gratification of active needs.

Theoretical statements of this kind sharpen the distinction between job attitudes and motivation and provide more precise formulations regarding the role played by underlying needs than does motivation-hygiene theory. In addition, the final two hypotheses take the individual's expectations into account in establishing motivation levels.

The very considerable reliance of these hypotheses on need hierarchy theory raises a question whether research support can be anticipated. One test of the first two hypotheses, which are closely related to Maslow's concepts, failed completely to yield support for them (Neeley, 1973). Furthermore, Herzberg (1976) argues strongly that his theory should not be confused with Maslow's:

> The Maslow system, then, does seem appropriate, but it has holes in it. Lower order needs never get satisfied, as witness the constant demand for physiological and security guarantees, the continuing socialization of our society, and the never ending search for status symbols. This is evident even though we have recognized the importance of self-actualization as a potent force in the motivational make-up of people. The Maslow system . . . has not worked in application because the biological and psychological needs of man are parallel systems, rather than either one assuming initial importance (p. 48).

And again:

> It is true that Maslow's lower-order needs can be equated in some fashion to my hygiene needs and his higher order needs in some fashion to what I call the motivation needs of man. However, that is about as much connection between the two theories as is really relevant and pertinent (p. 317).

Hackman's Theory of Adult Work Motivation

Ray Hackman followed Herzberg as Research Director at the Psychological Service of Pittsburgh. His theory evolved out of certain reanalyses of the original Herzberg data. Subsequently he applied other instruments to the concepts thus derived, relying heavily on the use of factor analysis to identify his major theoretical variables (Hackman, 1969).

In reanalyzing the Herzberg data, Hackman distinguished between feelings and the events or conditions that stimulate them. He accepts the view that the sources of satisfaction are qualitatively distinct from the sources of dissatisfaction, and thus the idea of two separate continua. However, he substitutes the term stimulation seeker for motivation seeker, and he views Herzberg's hygiene seekers as essentially emotional responders, not really seekers.

The factors (and thus the dimensions of work motivation) emerging from each of the various types of measures Hackman used in his research differ somewhat. However, the theory in its most comprehensive form contains seven basic dimensions:
1. The characteristic level of activation or *stimulation*.
2. The extent to which this energy is *directed* to some work activity.

3. The extent to which work is viewed as a medium for exercising one's social, intellectual, perceptual, and motor skills to achieve closure experiences and the *accomplishment* of tasks.
4. The extent to which work is viewed as a medium for exercising *responsibility* over other people and their work.
5. The extent to which work is viewed as an instrumental means to gain goals extrinsic to the work, such as security, money, and *status*.
6. The extent to which the work situation is viewed as threatening and generates *anxiety*.
7. The extent to which the work situation is viewed as irritating and generates aggressive reactions and *hostility*.

The first five dimensions are positively related, both theoretically and empirically; they tend to be associated with satisfaction. The last two are also positively related to each other, but negatively with the preceding five; they tend to be associated with dissatisfaction. It is noteworthy that extrinsic, job context factors can generate satisfaction in the Hackman theory (item 5). Successfully employed adults show high levels of directed stimulation, and they satisfy their accomplishment, responsibility, and status needs through their work. Less successful employees evidence little directed stimulation at work and tend to experience anxiety or hostility easily. The latter are less mature motivationally. Somewhat tangentially, Hackman does invoke a hierarchy similar to Maslow's in which needs are arranged on a scale progressing from the lower level physiological drive system, through the intermediate emotional drive system to the highest intellectual level. People operating at this highest level are the true stimulation seekers.

As with Herzberg's original research, that reported by Hackman in his 1969 book must be considered to be the inductive source of his final theory rather than a test of it. Unfortunately, Hackman died shortly after completing the book, and although others at Psychological Service of Pittsburgh have been collecting data using his instruments, no body of research that might provide a definitive test of the theory has developed.

CONCLUSIONS

Motivation-hygiene theory has probably created more controversy than any other theory we will consider. There are a number of reasons for this, many having little relationship to either the scientific or the managerial usefulness of the theory. This condition does make objective evaluation more difficult. It is almost impossible not to be assigned an adversary position if one makes any kind of statement regarding the theory. Yet rational objective evaluation is crucial for both scientific advance and management practice.

Scientific Goals

The theory has been steadily losing components in subsequent tests and reformulations. Its focus has shifted, and even in the original study, data were collected without the results being reported. Concepts such as long- and short-term sequences, second level factors, and behavioral outcome effects have virtually disappeared from consideration. Ratings of the strength of feelings (importance) were included in the original data collection, but only frequency data were reported. By no means can all of this lost concepts phenomenon be attributed to the major theorist. Yet somehow a great deal of the original theory has disappeared; it is no longer tested nor mentioned. One gets the impression that this is by mutual consent.

This same phenomenon applies to the testing of the theory. The following statement is indicative:

> In an ideal world we would not only have been able to ask people about the times when they felt exceptionally good or bad about their jobs, but also to go out and find people who felt exceptionally good or bad about their job and watch them over long periods . . . such observation, especially when carried out by more than one observer to obtain measures of reliability, would be of great value (Herzberg, Mausner, and Snyderman, 1959, p. 19).

Similarly, Kahn (1961) asked for independent measures of environmental factors, job attitudes, and performance criteria. Yet neither Herzberg nor his advocates nor his critics have conducted research of the kind these statements imply. Thus, we have to rely on less than ideal data.

The incident technique as used in the original study must be considered most predisposed toward the theory. Yet this technique does yield certain findings inconsistent with that theory. The problem, at this level, appears to be not in the overall trend of the data but in the findings for specific factors. Abstractions such as content and context, motivators and hygienes, and the like simply do not hold when one gets down to specifics. Opportunity for growth, which should be the essence of a self-actualizing motivator, is no more a source of satisfaction than dissatisfaction. Salary, interpersonal relations, status, and security are not just sources of dissatisfaction; they are often equally likely to be sources of satisfaction, and in certain groups some of them may well be predominant sources of satisfaction. The Hackman (1969) reanalyses of the original study data clearly support these conclusions, and the revised theory takes them into account. Achievement and the work itself also are repeatedly found to be sources of dissatisfaction as well as satisfaction.

Yet certain other types of criticisms of the theory must be reject-ed. King (1970) and others question the theory on the grounds of coding bias. Hackman, using a different coding system, does support the basic two-factor concept, and there are data from Grigaliunas and Herzberg (1971) to indicate that the recommended procedure of having subjects classify their own stories is not any less error prone than coding by others. Furthermore, those who attempt to restrict the theory to job attitudes and matters of satisfaction and dissatisfaction misinterpret it (Lawler, 1973). From the beginning the theory has considered such concepts as needs, performance effects, and behav-ior in enriched jobs. One may be critical of the manner in which motivation and job behavior are handled theoretically, but it is not correct to say that these variables are not treated at all.

There is little question that motivation-hygiene theory is most vulnerable on the grounds that its support derives almost entirely from the critical incident method and that this method is subject to influence by defense mechanisms. Short of observational studies and entirely independent measures of variables, the weight of the evi-dence now clearly favors the defense mechanism interpretation in-sofar as the hygiene-dissatisfaction part of the theory is concerned. On theoretical grounds, given the very limited projective element in the incident measures and the reduction of psychological distance thus occasioned, one would expect defensiveness to manifest itself, as Kahn (1961) noted; the data from a number of studies utilizing quite varied research designs support this conclusion.

The self-report data on effects are particularly suspect on such logical grounds. And indeed the limited research that has been focused specifically on this matter raises serious questions as to whether the motivators do produce positive behavioral outcomes and the hygienes negative. The results of the job enrichment research have been invoked in support of the theory's hypotheses regarding performance effects (Herzberg, 1976). However, it is clear that these results could well be occasioned by other factors and that they apply only to certain of the motivator variables. In a number of areas the theory has great difficulty in dealing with hygiene-dissatisfaction re-lationships.

It seems that motivation-hygiene theory lacks the support needed to confirm it, in spite of an extended period of testing and a great deal of research. Rather surprisingly, the type of study recognized from the beginning as required to provide a definitive test has not been conducted. A new thrust in the research might, therefore, yield different conclusions.

The problem now is that researchers are losing interest in the theory, apparently assuming it is unlikely to yield valid predictions. In the last few years the number of related studies has dropped off sharply, and the level of scientific concern is now low. Thus, more elegantly designed tests may simply never be conducted. One could hope that the author of the theory might conduct these studies, but at present he is much more concerned with applications in the job enrichment area. It is as if the process of losing components noted at the beginning of this section has come to its ultimate conclusion. Now the applications may well have lost the entire theory. Even the Wolf (1970) and Hackman (1969) reformulations have not generated renewed hope. The researchers have simply gone elsewhere, leaving these revisions in limbo.

Managerial Goals

The tremendous appeal of motivation-hygiene theory for practicing managers over the past 15 or 20 years cannot be doubted. It appears simple, although Herzberg (1976, p. 323) admits to only partially understanding it himself. Its religious, ethical, and moral overtones may well fill a strong managerial need. Furthermore, the idea that investments in salary, fringe benefits, working conditions, and the like yield benefits only up to a point (and thus can be restricted on rational grounds) is bound to appeal to the cost conscious manager. These appeals are probably reinforced for some by the antiacademic, anti-intellectual thrust of much of Herzberg's recent writing.

Yet it is well to avoid uncritical acceptance. Salary is not just a dissatisfier; it clearly operates as a source of satisfaction in many cases, as do status, security, and interpersonal relationships. To believe otherwise may well lead one far astray. Whether these factors yield satisfactions or not depends very much on the individual; in some cases those who derive satisfactions from such factors may be mentally ill, but one should not apply such a blanket designation to all.

The suggestion that industrial relations departments be divided into motivator and hygiene units is interesting, but its validity rests on that of the underlying theory. That such an approach has not been widely adopted may be a result of misgivings on the latter score. It would appear that many industrial relations functions such as selection, training, compensation, and appraisal are so concerned with all aspects of motivation that an artifical separation could only be self-defeating.

But these matters are not of crucial significance. The major applied outgrowth of motivation-hygiene theory has been the rejuvenation, if not the creation, of job enrichment. This is an important accomplishment, and it justifies the emergence of the theory, no matter what its deficiencies. Job enrichment as a motivational technique can work — with some people, under certain circumstances, for some period of time — and Herzberg has been saying so for some 20 years.

Yet when one attempts to tie job enrichment back into motivation-hygiene theory, one encounters all kinds of difficulties. For example, job enrichment has nothing to do with hygienes at all; it involves adding only motivators to the job, and thus relates at best to half of the theory. Furthermore, the motivators emphasized are those called generators — the work itself, responsibility, opportunity for growth, and advancement; achievement and recognition are downplayed. However, achievement and recognition are by far the most strongly supported motivators when the incident method is used to test the theory (see Table 4–2).

The research indicates that even in the most appropriate context, 10 to 15 per cent of those exposed to job enrichment do not respond, and that in other contexts the total effect may be nil. Yet the theory provides no basis for predicting these failures and gives short shrift to the troublesome idea of individual differences.

Finally, one does not need motivation-hygiene theory to understand the job enrichment results. For example, what happens in orthodox job enrichment may be construed as a removal of hierarchic inducement of effort and an attempt to substitute the pushes and pulls inherent in the task itself (Miner, 1978). The job is thus moved much closer to that of the entrepreneur, who is pushed by the threat of bankruptcy and pulled by all kinds of inducements including the prospect of making a fortune. A job designed along these lines should be very attractive to those with high achievement motivation and much less attractive to those who are lacking it. Such a formulation does not require recourse to motivation-hygiene theory at all. We will await a more detailed treatment of job enrichment theory in Chapter 9 before attempting an evaluation of such alternative explanations. It suffices to note the very loose tie between motivation-hygiene theory and even orthodox job enrichment.

References

Bockman, Valerie M. The Herzberg Controversy, *Personnel Psychology*, Vol. 24 (1971), 155–189.

Flanagan, John. The Critical Incident Technique, *Psychological Bulletin*, Vol. 51 (1954), 327–358.

Ford, Robert N. *Motivation Through the Work Itself*. New York: American Management Association, 1969.

Ford, Robert N. Job Enrichment Lessons from AT&T, *Harvard Business Review*, Vol. 51, No. 1 (1973), 96–106.

Gordon, Michael E., Norman M. Pryor, and Bob V. Harris. An Examination of Scaling Bias in Herzberg's Theory of Job Satisfaction, *Organizational Behavior and Human Performance*, Vol. 11 (1974), 106–121.

Grigaliunas, Benedict S. and Frederick Herzberg. Relevancy in the Test of Motivator-Hygiene Theory, *Journal of Applied Psychology*, Vol. 55 (1971), 73–79.

Hackman, Ray C. *The Motivated Working Adult*. New York: American Management Association, 1969.

Herzberg, Frederick. *Work and the Nature of Man*. Cleveland: World, 1966.

Herzberg, Frederick. *The Managerial Choice: To Be Efficient and To Be Human*. Homewood, Ill.: Dow-Jones-Irwin, 1976.

Herzberg, Frederick. Orthodox Job Enrichment: A Common Sense Approach to People at Work, *Defense Management Journal*, April 1977, 21–27.

Herzberg, Frederick, J. Mathapo, Yoash Wiener, and L. Wiesen. Motivation-Hygiene Correlates of Mental Health: An Examination of Motivational Inversion in a Clinical Population, *Journal of Consulting and Clinical Psychology*, Vol. 42 (1974), 411–419.

Herzberg, Frederick, Bernard Mausner, R. O. Peterson, and Dora F. Capwell. *Job Attitudes: Review of Research and Opinion*. Pittsburgh: Psychological Service of Pittsburgh, 1957.

Herzberg, Frederick, Bernard Mausner, and Barbara S. Snyderman. *The Motivation To Work*. New York: Wiley, 1959.

Herzberg, Frederick and Alex Zautra. Orthodox Job Enrichment: Measuring True Quality in Job Satisfaction, *Personnel*, Vol. 53, No. 5 (1976), 54–68.

Kahn, Robert L. Review of *The Motivation To Work*, *Contemporary Psychology*, Vol. 6 (1961), 9–10.

Karp, H. B. and Jack W. Nickson. Motivator-Hygiene Deprivation as a Predictor of Job Turnover, *Personnel Psychology*, Vol. 26 (1973), 377–384.

King, Nathan. Clarification and Evaluation of the Two-Factor Theory of Job Satisfaction, *Psychological Bulletin*, Vol. 74 (1970), 18–31.

Lawler, Edward E. *Motivation in Work Organizations*. Monterey, Calif.: Brooks/Cole, 1973.

Locke, Edwin A. Personnel Attitudes and Motivation, *Annual Review of Psychology*, Vol. 26 (1975), 457–480.

Locke, Edwin A. and Roman J. Whiting. Sources of Satisfaction and Dissatisfaction Among Solid Waste Management Employees, *Journal of Applied Psychology*, Vol. 59 (1974), 145–156.

Miner, John B. *The Management Process: Theory, Research and Practice*. New York: Macmillan, 1978.

Neeley, James D. A Test of the Need Gratification Theory of Job Satisfaction. *Journal of Applied Psychology*, Vol. 57 (1973), 86–88.

Ondrack, D. A. Defense Mechanisms and the Herzberg Theory: An Alternate Test, *Academy of Management Journal*, Vol. 17 (1974), 79–89.

Schwab, Donald P., H. William DeVitt, and Larry L. Cummings. A Test of the Adequacy of the Two-Factor Theory as a Predictor of Self-Report Performance Effects, *Personnel Psychology*, Vol. 24 (1971), 293–303.

Schwab, Donald P. and Herbert G. Heneman, III. Aggregate and Individual Predictability of the Two-Factor Theory of Job Satisfaction, *Personnel Psychology*, Vol. 23 (1970), 55–66.

Wall, Toby D. Ego-defensiveness as a Determinant of Reported Differences in Sources of Job Satisfaction and Job Dissatisfaction, *Journal of Applied Psychology*, Vol. 58 (1973), 125–128.

White, Donald D. and Julio Leon. The Two-Factor Theory: New Questions, New Answers, *Academy of Management Proceedings*, (1976), 356–359.

Wolf, Martin G. Need Gratification Theory: A Theoretical Reformulation and Job Motivation, *Journal of Applied Psychology*, Vol. 54 (1970), 87–94.

5 EQUITY THEORY

Feelings of unfairness were the most frequently reported source of job dissatisfaction in the original Herzberg research. As indicated in Table 4–1, these feelings are a second level factor in the Herzberg model. Although motivation-hygiene theory gave relatively little attention to this finding, other theories have made this desire or need for fairness, or justice, or equity their focus.

Theories of this kind have been articulated by a number of individuals in a variety of forms. Basically, they are concerned with exchange relationships among individuals and groups, and the motivating effects of a perceived imbalance in the exchange. Applications of this type of theory have been extended beyond the organizational relationships that are of primary interest in this volume to other areas, notably exploitative relationships, helping relationships, and intimate relationships (Walster, Berscheid, and Walster, 1973).

The theory developed by Adams (1963a, 1965) appears to be not only the most relevant for an understanding of employee motivation but also the most fully articulated. It has been the source of a sizable body of research designed to test its various propositions and has been given considerable attention by wage and salary administrators. As Adams (1963a) has indicated, this so-called equity theory owes a strong intellectual debt to the prior, more general formulations of Festinger (1957) dealing with cognitive dissonance, and of Homans (1961) dealing with distributive justice.

THE ADAMS THEORY

Adams developed his theory and carried out the initial test studies while serving as a research psychologist with the General Electric Company in Crotonville, New York. More recently he has been on the faculty of the business school at the University of North Carolina. Although the term equity is usually used to describe the theory, it is at least as appropriate to describe it as *inequity* theory. The major motivating force considered is a striving for equity, but some degree of inequity must be perceived before this force can be mobilized.

Antecedents of Inequity

The theory starts with an exchange whereby the individual gives something and gets something in return. What the individual gives may be viewed as inputs to, or investments in, the relationship; examples are noted in Table 5–1. For such inputs to function they must be recognized as existing by the individual and must be considered relevant to the relationship. They may or may not be recognized and perceived as relevant by the other party, for instance, an employer. If they are not, a potential for inequity exists.

On the other side of the exchange are various things the individual may receive, the outcomes of the exchange relationship. As

Table 5–1. POSSIBLE INPUTS TO AND OUTCOMES FROM AN
EMPLOYMENT EXCHANGE NOTED BY ADAMS IN
VARIOUS WRITINGS

Inputs	Outcomes
Education	Pay
Intelligence	Intrinsic rewards
Experience	Satisfying supervision
Training	Seniority benefits
Skill	Fringe benefits
Seniority	Job status
Age	Status symbols
Sex	Job perquisites
Ethnic background	Poor working conditions
Social status	Monotony
Job effort	Fate uncertainty
Personal appearance	Herzberg's dissatisfiers
Health	
Possession of tools	
Spouse's characteristics	

with inputs, these must be recognized by the individual who receives them and considered relevant to the exchange if they are to
function effectively. Shared concepts of what are fair relationships
between these outcomes and various inputs are learned as part of
the overall socialization process.

The third type of theoretical variable, in addition to inputs
provided and outcomes received, is the reference person or group
used in evaluating the equity of one's own exchange relationship.
This reference source may be a coworker, relative, neighbor, group
of coworkers, craft group, industry pattern, profession, and so on.
It may even be the person himself in another job or another social
role. For an individual or group to operate in this capacity there
must be one or more attributes that are comparable to those of the
comparer. The theory is not more precise in specifying how the
appropriate reference source may be identified, although it is assumed that coworkers are commonly used.

The Definition of Inequity

Inequity is said to exist when the ratio of an individual's outcomes to inputs departs to a significant degree from the ratio perceived for the reference source. Thus, an individual may feel that
he is underrewarded in terms of what he puts into a job in comparison with what other workers are getting for their contributions. This might happen when the person considers himself a
much harder worker than other employees but is paid the same as
everyone else.

The theory is not limited to inequities that are unfavorable to the individual. Equity, balance, or reciprocity exists when outcome/input ratios for the individual and the reference source are equal, and the motivating force of inequity can arise when there is a departure either way from this steady state. Accordingly, a person might consider himself overrewarded, given his inputs, in comparison with others. This could be so if an individual perceived himself as working as hard as his coworkers but, for reasons he considered irrelevant, was in fact paid much more.

Since most exchanges involve multiple inputs and outcomes, these must be summed across all factors perceived to be relevant to arrive at operative ratios. The various components of those outcome and input totals also may not have the same utilities or valence for the person; in the mind of a given individual, education may predominate among the inputs noted in Table 5–1, and pay predominate among the outcomes. In such a case education and pay would be given disproportionate weight in their respective totals. Finally, "the thresholds for equity are different (in absolute terms from a base of equity) in cases of under- and overreward. The threshold presumably would be higher in cases of overreward, for a certain amount of incongruity in these cases can be acceptably rationalized as 'good fortune' without attendant discomfort" (Adams, 1965, p. 282). Thus, the motivational effects of a favorable inequity may remain immobilized at a degree of disparity that would be motivating if the disparity were unfavorable. This is an important consideration when testing the theory; overrewards must be sizable to have an effect.

The following schema indicating the relative amount of inequity experienced by an individual under varying conditions of total inputs and outcomes may prove helpful in understanding the proposed definition of inequity:

| | The Perception of the Reference Source | | | |
The Perception of Oneself	Inputs Low – Outcomes High	Inputs High – Outcomes Low	Inputs Low – Outcomes Low	Inputs High – Outcomes High
Inputs low – outcomes high	No inequity	Much inequity	Some inequity	Some inequity
Inputs high – outcomes low	Much inequity	No inequity	Some inequity	Some inequity
Inputs low – outcomes low	Some inequity	Some inequity	No inequity	No inequity
Inputs high – outcomes high	Some inequity	Some inequity	No inequity	No inequity

Reactions to Inequity

Inequity, when perceived, results in dissatisfaction either in the form of anger (underreward) or guilt (overreward). A tension is created in proportion to the amount of inequity. This tension in turn serves as a motivating force to reduce the inequity and move it to zero. A number of methods for reducing inequity tension are posited.

Altering Inputs. This involves changing inputs either upward or downward to what might be an appropriately equitable level. In the employment context this means altering either the quantity or quality of work to align them with reference source ratios. Certain inputs such as age cannot be modified in this manner, while others such as effort expansion or restriction can be.

Input alteration is likely to occur when there is a variation from the perceived inputs of the reference source, as opposed to discrepancies in outcomes. Lowering inputs can also be anticipated when the inequity is unfavorable to oneself; when the inequity is favorable, the inputs are likely to be increased. Restrictive production practices, as elaborated by the early human relations writers, then become a means of reducing inequity.

Altering Outcomes. Another approach to reducing felt inequity is to attempt to shift outcomes. Increasing outcomes, if achieved, will serve to reduce unfavorable inequities. Theoretically, attempts to decrease outcomes would be expected in cases involving favorable inequities. Charitable contributions often reflect this type of motivation, which, however, does not appear to be very common. The predominant mode in this instance appears to be the use of increased outcomes to reduce unfavorable inequity, as when union or other types of pressure are brought to bear to shift outcomes into balance with expectations.

Distorting One's Own Inputs and Outcomes. As opposed to actually altering inputs and outcomes, a person may cognitively distort them to achieve the same results. To the degree that reality is important to an individual, distortions of this kind become difficult. Thus, the absolute level of one's education as an input, or the amount of one's pay as an outcome, may be hard to distort perceptually. Yet even in these cases distortion can occur, though less objective inputs and outcomes are much more easily perverted. Furthermore, shifts in the relative weighting of inputs and outcomes can be used to achieve the same result, as when the value of one's education is exaggerated or the personal utility of pay misrepresented.

Leaving the Field. Another way of dealing with inequity is to reduce or entirely eliminate it through minimizing exposure to the inequity-producing context. This can occur through transfer, absenteeism, or even separation. Such responses are assumed to be relatively extreme and to occur only when the magnitude of inequity is sizable, or when the individual cannot deal with the inequity easily and flexibly.

Acting on the Reference Source. Distortion may be applied not only to one's own inputs and outcomes but also to those attributed to a reference individual or group. Similarly, attempts may be made to eliminate a reference source from one's environment, as when a coworker who has been used as a reference person is harassed out of his job. Or the actual inputs or outcomes of the reference source may be altered, as when a "rate buster" is induced to lower his efforts and productivity in response to strong individual and group pressure. Attempts to influence a reference source along these lines will vary considerably in their feasibility, but all are theoretically appropriate methods of reducing inequity.

Changing the Reference Source. It is possible to shift to a new reference source to reduce inequity. Thus, a person who previously compared himself to other similar professionals nationally may change from this cosmopolitan comparison to a local comparison utilizing only professionals in his own company. This strategy may be least viable when a prior reference source has been used for a considerable time.

Choices Among the Various Reactions. The theory is not as explicit as it might be about the circumstances under which the different reactions to inequity will emerge. However, Adams (1965) is well aware of the need for theoretical statements of this kind. He offers the following propositions:
1. Generally, an individual will attempt to maximize highly valued outcomes and the overall value of outcomes.
2. Inputs that are effortful and costly to change can be expected to increase only minimally.
3. Real and cognitively distorted changes in inputs that are central to one's self-concept and self-esteem will tend to be resisted. The same applies to the outcomes for a person when they have high relevance for the self.
4. The inputs and outcomes attributed to a reference source are much more easily distorted than those attributed to oneself.
5. Leaving the field will be utilized only when the inequity is sizable and other means of reducing it are unfavorable. Partial withdrawals such as absenteeism will occur at lower inequity levels than full withdrawals such as separation.

6. Changing the object of comparison, or reference source, will
    be strongly resisted once such a comparison has been stabi-
    lized over time.

Adams (1968a) also indicates that when the inequity tension
is sizable, the probability that more than one method of reducing
that tension will be utilized increases. However, individuals tend
to differ in tolerances for tension. A person with a high tolerance
level might not yet resort to multiple modes of inequity reduction
at a point where a person with a low tolerance level would long
before have mobilized more than one reaction. Adams notes further that these extensions to the theory remain speculative as long
as direct measures of inequity thresholds, tolerance for inequity
tension, and the tension itself are not available.

Extensions and Restatements

The nature and rationale of equity theory are expanded upon
in a series of four propositions set forth by Walster, Berscheid,
and Walster (1973). Since these propositions subsequently have
been endorsed by Adams (Adams and Freedman, 1976), it seems
appropriate to consider them part of the theory.

Proposition I. Individuals will try to maximize their outcomes
(where outcomes equal rewards minus costs). The term reward refers to positive outcomes and the term cost refers to negative outcomes.

Proposition IIA. Groups can maximize collective reward by
evolving accepted systems for "equitably" apportioning rewards
and costs among members. Thus, members will evolve such systems of equity and will attempt to induce members to accept and
adhere to these systems.

Proposition IIB. Groups will generally reward members who
treat others equitably and generally punish (increase the costs for)
members who treat others inequitably.

Proposition III. When individuals find themselves participating in inequitable relationships, they become distressed (the more
inequitable the relationship, the more distress). Anger and guilt
are two of the major forms of distress.

Proposition IV. Individuals who discover that they are in an
inequitable relationship attempt to eliminate distress by restoring
equity. The greater the inequity, the more distress, and the harder
they try to restore equity. There are two ways equity may be re-
stored. A person can restore actual equity by appropriately altering
his own outcomes or inputs or the outcomes or inputs of others. A
person can restore psychological equity by appropriately distorting the perceptions of his own or others' outcomes or inputs.

EARLY RESEARCH ON PAY

Studies conducted by and in association with Adams in the early 1960s have had a major influence on subsequent research intended to test his theory. Although the theory is not restricted to matters of compensation, this early research did tend to establish such a focus, and only a few studies since have departed from it. Furthermore, the type of experimental design utilized by the theory's author has had a strong influence on the designs used in subsequent investigations. There were five basic studies that tested the theory in the early period, and Adams has not published additional research in this area since then. All five studies deal with the most controversial aspect of the theory, the predicted effects of overreward inequity. Although the theory has undergone some elaboration and restatement since its creation, it was originally developed on the basis of formulations of Festinger (1957) and Homans (1961), and thus Adams' research can be considered as a true test rather than as an inductive theoretical source.

Experiment I

Adams and Rosenbaum (1962) reported a study conducted at New York University in which students referred by the university placement office were hired to conduct market research interviews. The advertised rate for the work was $3.50 per hour, and the initial implication was that the work would continue for several months.

The 22 students hired were split into two equal groups, and all were actually paid at the $3.50 per hour figure. At the time of hiring the experimental subjects were exposed to treatment intended to make them feel inequitably overcompensated for their work. They were told, "You don't have nearly enough experience in interviewing or survey work of the kind we're engaged in," but nevertheless, after some agonizing, they were hired. In contrast the control subjects were led to believe that their inputs were entirely appropriate to the pay and that they met all the qualifications. Thus, a condition of equity was established vis-à-vis "interviewers in general" as a reference source.

The interviewing job was terminated after roughly 2½ hours. Productivity in the experimental group, where presumably guilt had been induced, was significantly higher than that in the controls. This is what the theory predicts — in order to justify their inequitably high outcomes (pay), the experimental subjects should exert more effort to compensate for their lack of experience as an input, thus conducting more interviews in the allotted time.

Experiment II

A subsequent study conducted by Arrowood and reported by Adams (1963a) was designed to deal with a possibly confounding effect in Experiment I. It is possible that the experimental subjects worked harder, not to correct an inequity but to protect their jobs. The talk about their lack of qualifications may have made them feel insecure, with the result that they worked very hard to convince the experimenter to retain them.

To test this hypothesis a study was conducted in Minneapolis using much the same approach as that used in Experiment I except that half of the subjects mailed their completed work in a pre-addressed envelope to New York rather than merely turning it over to the experimenter. It was made clear that under these circumstances the experimenter never would know how many interviews had been produced; accordingly he would be in no position to fire anyone, and there would be no need to feel insecure.

Under the insecurity hypothesis, eliminating job insecurity should eliminate the difference between the experimental (inequity) and control (equity) groups. It did not. The tendency for experimental subjects to conduct more interviews than controls remained regardless of whether the completed forms were returned to New York. Thus, the results of Experiment I do not appear to be attributable to insecurity; they are more likely to have been caused by attempts to reduce inequity tension.

Experiment III

Whereas the preceding studies utilized an hourly compensation rate, another investigation explored the effects of paying on a piece rate basis (Adams and Rosenbaum, 1962). In most respects the procedure was the same as that in Experiment I. However, four groups were used, each containing nine subjects:

> Group 1. Overreward inequity; paid $3.50 per hour.
> Group 2. Equity; paid $3.50 per hour.
> Group 3. Overreward inequity; paid 30 cents per interview.
> Group 4. Equity; paid 30 cents per interview.

The use of piece rate payments adds a complicating factor in that exerting more effort to resolve the inequity will not solve the problem. Inputs do increase, but so do outcomes; thus the inequity remains and is exacerbated. As expected, the introduction of piece rate payment did have a markedly dampening effect on the tendency to produce more to eliminate inequity. In fact the overreward piece rate workers completed the fewest interviews of any group; increasing their outcomes was apparently the last thing they wanted to do.

The results of Experiment III tell much more about how people do not reduce inequity tension than about how they do. One hypothesis is that under this kind of inequity condition effort is increased but is put into improved quality of work that will not increase outcomes rather than into improved quantity that under piece rate payment will increase outcomes. Experiment IV attempts to test this hypothesis (Adams, 1963b). In this case procedures were introduced to permit measurement of interview quality, something that was not possible in Experiment III.

To do this interviewers were encouraged to obtain as much information as possible from respondents in reply to several open ended questions. Since lengthy responses (quality) inevitably limited the number of interviews obtained (quantity), following the directive to obtain more information should be an attractive approach to restoring equity. The results were indeed in accord with this expectation. Subjects in the overrewarded inequity condition obtained longer interviews on the average than those working under equitable payment, and they also completed fewer interviews.

A final study (Adams and Jacobsen, 1964) was conducted to provide a further check on the insecurity hypothesis considered in Experiment II. Sixty students from Columbia University who answered an advertisement for part-time summer work were hired to perform a proofreading task. Quantity of work was determined by the number of pages proofed and quality by the number of errors detected. Three different conditions related to equity were introduced:

1. Inequity was produced by such statements as, "you don't have nearly enough experience" and "your score on the proofreading test isn't really satisfactory," but payment was given at the full 30-cent per page rate initially quoted.
2. The same reduction of inputs noted above was combined with a compensating reduction of outcomes — "I can't pay you at the regular rate of 30 cents per page. I can pay you only 20 cents per page because your qualifications aren't sufficient."
3. Full equity was produced at the 30 cents per page figure —

Table 5–2. ERRORS DETECTED PER PAGE AND PAGES PROOFED
UNDER VARYING EXPERIMENTAL CONDITIONS

Conditions	Quality (Errors Detected)	Quantity (Pages Proofed)
1A. Inequity and insecure	7.9	8.7
1B. Inequity and secure	8.0	7.7
2A. Equity (at low pay) and insecure	4.7	11.3
2B. Equity (at low pay) and secure	4.9	11.8
3A. Equity and perhaps insecure	4.9	11.7
3B. Equity and secure	4.0	12.8

Adapted from J. Stacy Adams and Patricia R. Jacobsen Effects of Wage Inequities on Work Quality, *Journal of Abnormal and Social Psychology*, Vol. 69 (1964), pp. 22–23.

"You're just what we're looking for. You meet all the qualifications."

Within each of these three conditions two alternatives related to prospects for continued employment were introduced as follows:

A. "The book is only one of a series. . . there is a lot of work ahead. . . You may be able to help us in the future."

B. "Usually it isn't necessary to hire someone to proofread for us, but . . . we've got to get this particular book out . . . the job will take a short time only."

Thus, there were six different conditions with ten people in each. Equity theory predicts better quality work and lower quantity for both conditions 1A and 1B. The insecurity hypothesis predicts that conditions 1A and 2B, where there was a job to be lost and every reason to believe it might be lost, would produce the high quality, lower productivity response.

After one hour of work the study was terminated and the results reported in Table 5–2 were obtained. Questions asked of the subjects at that point indicated that the desired perceptions regarding qualifications, pay levels, and opportunity for continued employment had in fact been induced by the various treatments. The data are fully in line with equity theory predictions; they do not support the insecurity hypothesis.

However, Adams (1968a) notes that under the inequity conditions there were a few subjects who produced large quantities of relatively low quality work. These individuals were found to be economically deprived, needing the money badly. As a result they maximized their outcomes even though they were aware of the inequity. Adams interprets these data as indicating that for some people economic motivation may be dominant over equity motivation. It is apparent that equity theory is not an all-encompassing motivational theory but rather deals with one particular type of motivation that has major implications for behavior in the work-place. In this connection Adams (1964, p. 24) notes:

> ... overpayment by an employer need not necessarily increase his labor costs, provided he is primarily interested in quality, as opposed to produc-tion volume. If on the other hand the employer's objective is production volume, piecework overpayment may be very costly, especially for such work as inspection, quality control, finishing and other jobs that inherently permit considerable latitude in work quality.

OTHER RESEARCH TESTS

The early research dealt entirely with overreward, and we will first consider additional studies concerned with this issue. The discussion then turns to underreward, and finally to other considerations bearing on the validity of the theory. It is apparent that the Adams formulations have generated considerable scientif-ic interest.

Overreward Inequity

By no means has all of the research dealing with the effects of overreward inequity produced the same type of favorable results that Adams obtained originally. However, the theory itself posits a high threshold for overreward inequity, and there are data to sup-port this (Andrews, 1967; Zedeck and Smith, 1968). Thus, there is always the possibility (in a given study) that overreward thresh-olds were not consistently breached. Furthermore, a treatment or experimental manipulation might not be perceived as producing inequity at all, even though the researcher believed it should. Such might be the case, for instance, if what was thought to be an input manipulation (say changing the degree of job involvement) turned out to be an outcome manipulation (job involvement is considered a desirable opportunity for self-expression) for a siz-able number of subjects. This kind of interchangeability among individual inputs and outcomes of the type noted in Table 5–1 has been clearly established by research (Tornow, 1971). Given the variety of possible mitigating circumstances, it is important to consider the overall weight of the evidence in evaluating the theo-ry rather than relying on any individual study.

When this is done, there turns out to be considerable support for the overreward inequity proposition. In cases when the mo-tivational effects of overreward inequity were not demonstrated, there is good reason to believe that strong feelings of inequity were not mobilized (Goodman and Friedman, 1971).

Explanations Involving Insecurity and Self-Esteem. A question has been raised in several of the reviews of equity theory research as to whether the positive findings can be attributed to the causal influence of motivation to reduce inequity. Lawler (1968) emphasized the potential role of insecurity in this regard. The subjects may have experienced personal and immediate insecurity, which they sought to eliminate through various types of improved performance; this insecurity could have nothing to do with the long-term employment considerations Adams dealt with. Pritchard (1969) gives greater attention to the threat to self-esteem in many of the studies and the arousal of a need to prove oneself. In both instances the concern is with the true motivational impact of the "lack of job qualifications" treatment that Adams and others have used to create "inequity" conditions.

The solution has been to shift to some method of inducing inequity that does not denigrate or threaten the individual to see if the effects predicted by equity theory remain. If they do not, it would appear that insecurity or threatened self-esteem was the causal agent in the early studies, not inequity. In a number of cases these latter studies have failed to replicate the Adams findings. However, in eliminating the element of threat they also appear to have eliminated any perceived inequity.

One frequent procedure has been to attribute the overpayment to circumstances having nothing to do with the subject's qualifications, such as the availability of funds or governmental pay policies. As Adams (1968b) notes, this does not imply an unjust overpayment; the comparison is likely to be with others of similar qualifications, doing similar work, and paid at a similarly high rate. That this kind of experimental induction yields results identical with those of a lower paid equity condition is exactly what equity theory would predict. Yet this same procedure has continued in use and has continued to produce the same type of results (Moore and Baron, 1973).

A more appropriate approach is to expose subjects directly to a comparison source paid at a rate different from the subject, or to change the amount of payment arbitrarily in the middle of a study so that comparisons are made with past earnings. Therefore, outcomes, not inputs, are altered to produce the inequity, but reference source values are fixed rather than variable; job qualifications are not at issue. With some consistency, studies using this type of design do support equity theory predictions (Garland, 1973; Pritchard, Dunnette, and Jorgenson, 1972).

Garland (1973) hired students to work on a proofreading task at either 15, 30, or 60 cents per page. As they began the task they were exposed to another student (confederate of the experimenter) ostensibly just finishing up who said, "Well, good luck. One

Table 5-3. PROPORTION OF ERRORS DETECTED AND PAGES PROOFED UNDER VARYING EXPERIMENTAL CONDITIONS

Conditions	Quality (Per Cent of Errors Detected)	Quantity (No. of Pages Proofed)
Inequity — overpaid	.46	9.7
Equity	.42	13.0
Inequity — underpaid	.39	18.0

Adapted from Howard Garland, The Effects of Piece-Rate Underpayment and Overpayment on Job Performance: A Test of Equity Theory with a New Induction Procedure, *journal of Applied Social Psychology*, Vol. 3 (1973), pp. 330–331.

hour's not much time for this, but at 30 cents a page, I couldn't turn it down." Subsequent checks indicated that subjects did react to this direct exposure to an appropriate reference source with perceptions of overpayment, equitable payment, and underpayment. The data presented in Table 5–3 reflect the increased quality and decreased quantity with piece rate overpayment that equity theory predicts.

Findings of this kind do not indicate that the use of qualification questioning procedures cannot induce threats to security and self-esteem. There is good reason to believe they can. It is evident also that inequity alone can yield the hypothesized effects. Furthermore, there is considerable basis for concluding that the early results obtained by Adams and others are not fully explained by the artifactual influences of insecurity and lowered self-esteem (Goodman and Friedman, 1971).

Time Duration. Another set of questions regarding over-reward inequity has revolved around the time dimension. Given that the research has demonstrated the effects predicted by equity theory, it is still posited that these effects are transitory and have no real meaning in understanding ongoing motivation in organizations (Lawler, 1968).

The times utilized in the research have been short, at most several hours, in all but a very few studies. Furthermore, there are data indicating some decrease in effects over a time, although these may be attributable to various causes. Equity theory also offers a rationale for reduced performance effects over time. Under appropriate circumstances subjects can resort to altered perceptions of task difficulty and fair compensation, thus restoring equity through cognitive rather than behavioral processes (Gergen, Morse, and Bode, 1974). This could well be a gradual procedure, so that performance effects may give way to cognitive methods of restoring equity over time. Thus, an inequitable overpayment may at first influence performance levels but later be accepted as merely a just compensation for a task now perceived as more difficult and demanding. Should this be the case, overreward inequity would be of little practical significance; performance consequences would rapidly be replaced by psychological or cognitive ones. Put somewhat differently:

> Employers should not expect a long-term increase in morale or productivity as a result of providing an unexpected increase in wages for their employees. Rather, workers may be expected quickly to re-evaluate their work and their pay and to conclude that they are not being paid particularly well but are only receiving their due (Gergen, Morse, and Bode, 1974, p. 271).

Data on this point are sparse, reflecting the laboratory-type rather than real life nature of most research settings. The longest study extended over only six consecutive workdays of four hours each (Pritchard, Dunnette, and Jorgenson, 1972). In this case the cognitive dissipation hypothesis was not supported:

> Overreward feelings were not dissipated cognitively to any great degree. Instead, a more "costly" mode of inequity reduction (viz., sustained high effort) was used. Possibly, overreward performance effects are more permanent than has previously been suggested (Pritchard, Dunnette, and Jorgenson, 1972, p. 92).

The really long-term effects of overreward are not known. This uncertainty is compounded by the fact that the theory does not clearly indicate when various inequity reduction procedures of a behavioral or cognitive nature will be mobilized. Yet, behavioral effects of a week's duration have been established, and this same study indicates that overreward can create a sizable backlog of dissatisfaction.

Underreward Inequity

Although Adams did not create an underreward condition in his studies, other researchers have since conducted similar experiments that have extended the analysis to this condition. In addition to such pay-performance studies, there has been another research effort relating underreward to such inequity reduction strategies as absenteeism and job separation.

Research on Pay and Performance. With piece rate pay conditions, underrewarded individuals would be expected to increase the quantity of work in order to move total outcomes upward. At the same time, however, equity can only be achieved if inputs are not raised commensurate to the increase in outcomes. The most likely strategy for holding inputs down is to decrease the effort put into quality. The Garland (1973) data presented in Table 5–3 are entirely consistent with these theoretical expectations.

On an hourly pay schedule, underreward would be expected to result in less effort devoted to the work. Primarily this reduced input should yield a reduced quantity of work. On certain tasks, however, when quality is a major consideration, the reduced effort may well cause poorer quality work.

In general, the available research tends to support equity theory predictions for the underreward condition. This is the conclusion of the Goodman and Friedman review of 1971. Additional studies reported since then reinforce this interpretation (Garland, 1973; Kessler and Wiener, 1972).

Research on Absenteeism and Turnover. The research already considered has focused on alterations of inputs and outcomes as modes of inequity reduction. Another more extreme approach noted by Adams is that of leaving the field. This response has been investigated almost entirely under conditions of perceived underreward inequity, although there is no theoretical rationale for expecting this response to be so limited. Given the differential thresholds for under- and overreward inequities, it might be expected to occur more widely in the underreward context.

A study by Finn and Lee (1972) compares professional employees who do and do not report experiencing undercompensation inequity. Those who experience inequity do so because they view their inputs (education, professional status, performance) as relatively high and their outcomes (salary) as relatively low. There is evidence that they are dissatisfied with their jobs in a number of respects. However, the most important finding is that they are much more attracted than the equity group to a number of outcomes (increased pay, more interesting work) that might induce them to leave their current employment. They clearly have a high propensity for separation.

That this relationship between underreward inequity and propensity for separation extends to the actual separation response also has been demonstrated (Dittrich and Carrell, 1976; Telly, French, and Scott, 1971). Data from the former study are given in Table 5–4. Measures of perceived inequity in various areas were obtained from 158 clerical employees and correlated with absenteeism and turnover statistics over the ensuing eleven months. The most widespread procedure for reducing underreward inequity feelings was to reduce work effort (inputs) through absenteeism. However, in the case of pay inequities experienced in relation to others outside the organization, leaving the field completely through termination was also utilized.

Table 5-4.   STATISTICALLY SIGNIFICANT CORRELATIONS
BETWEEN AVERAGE PERCEIVED INEQUITY AND
ABSENTEEISM AND TURNOVER RATES IN 19
CLERICAL UNITS

Sources of Inequity	Correlation with Absenteeism Rate	Turnover Rate
1. Pay level relative to coworkers and rules used to grant pay increases and promotions	.47	—
2. Supervisor's administration of pay and promotion rules	—	—
3. Supervisor's requirements regarding pace of work	—	—
4. Pay level relative to others outside the organization	.58	.42
5. Supervisor's requirements regarding work behavior generally	.49	—
Overall inequity across all five areas noted above	.48	—

Adapted from John E. Dittrich and Michael R. Carrell Dimensions of Organizational Fairness as Predictors of Job Satisfaction, Absence and Turnover, *Academy of Management Proceedings* (1976), pp. 80–81.

Findings of this kind have been obtained in the simulated work studies dealing with pay and performance. It is not uncommon for some subjects in these studies to refuse further participation when faced with underreward inequity. Furthermore, if sizable inequities are made obvious and compelling through continued exposure to reference individuals known to be receiving greater compensation for the same work, expressions of anger and highly disruptive behavior may well occur (Hinton, 1972). When these more extreme methods of responding to perceived inequity are mobilized, they appear to supersede any performance effects.

Reward Allocation Research

A very different line of research has been concerned with testing the proposition that an individual will allocate rewards (outcomes) in a manner proportional to the inputs of the various parties. Designs call for some demonstration of actual inputs, usually for two people, and then as a dependent variable an allocation decision in accordance with perceptions of appropriate reward. The person making the allocation may be a third party or a person who has actually contributed inputs.

A common approach has been to lead a subject in a laboratory setting to believe he was performing a task with a partner and that there would be a monetary reward. The partner, who is said to be in another room, is fictitious, thus permitting the experimenter to vary performance levels according to a prearranged plan. The partner is also able to allocate the total compensation available to the subject and himself to create either equity in relation to the inputs of the two, or some kind of inequity. The test of equity theory then comes when the subject is given a chance to reallocate the money. If an inequity has been created, will the subject now act to restore equity? The answer appears to be that he will. Research of this kind has yielded strong support for equity theory (Leventhal, Weiss, and Long, 1969).

This type of research also reveals that allocation decisions may be motivated by considerations other than equity. When the research is designed to pit equity against some other desired circumstance such as conflict reduction (Leventhal, Michaels, and Sanford, 1972) or the prevention of waste (Leventhal, Weiss, and Buttrick, 1973), a number of individuals respond in terms of these other motives and not equity. Thus, there are differences in individuals in the strength of the need to achieve equity relative to other motives.

Reward allocation research also has produced considerable insight into the conditions under which equity motivation is mobilized (Cook, 1975). Results that support equity theory appear to depend on two conditions:
1. There must be a clear perception of the composition of the input dimensions (energy expenditure, performance level, prior qualifications) that are to be the basis for reward.
2. There must be a clear perception of one's position on these input dimensions relative to the reference source.

Without these conditions, when ambiguity prevails, subjects tend to adjust their input perceptions to whatever outcomes are received and do not actually enter a state of perceived inequity. Given the characteristic condition of partial knowledge of prior qualifications, performance levels, and even compensation that exists in most employment situations, it seems probable that equity motivation is not engaged as often as research results might indicate.

Research on Individual Differences

At a number of points in the prior discussion the existence of individual differences in the strength of equity motivation or at least in responsiveness to it has been noted. Although the results are somewhat spotty, there are some studies that provide certain insights into the kinds of individuals who are most likely to respond to inequities.

People who gamble frequently (risk takers) are less consistently committed to equity in allocations than those who gamble very little (Larwood, Kavanagh, and Levine, 1978). The gamblers appear more prone to accept outcome distributions that are not directly tied to concepts of equitable reward for performance, effort, and the like. Given the results of research on achievement motivation discussed in Chapter 3, it seems likely that those with the strongest equity motivation might often be people with higher levels of achievement motivation.

Although research conducted outside the United States is minimal, there is one study from the Netherlands suggesting that national differences in inequity motivation exist (Weick, Bougon, and Maruyama, 1976). In comparison with Americans, the Dutch were less motivated by inequities relative to others and generally more concerned about their inputs (at the expense of concern with outcomes). Therefore, equity motivation may be more difficult to arouse among Dutch workers.

There is also some evidence about the kinds of people who respond to underreward inequity with quantity increases and quality decreases (Lawler and O'Gara, 1967). High productivity increases are most characteristic of socially insecure people who lack self-assurance. Such people would be expected to be particularly sensitive to comparisons with others and to overrespond to disparities. The tendency to achieve quantity at the expense of quality is tempered by a strong sense of responsibility and maturity. People who have these characteristics feel a need to maintain quality work; those who lack them are much more prone to let quality deteriorate.

CONCLUSIONS

It is almost impossible to say what the impact of equity theory has been in applications. The theory is widely known among compensation specialists, and equity considerations typically are given major consideration in setting pay scales. Yet, it is hard to determine cause-and-effect relationships, and there is no generally established or widely publicized procedure that can be directly linked to Adams or to equity theory. It would appear that compensation practitioners have been well aware of the importance of equity considerations for their work for many years. The more recent and precise formulations of Adams and those who have followed his lead have had relatively little impact on existing practice. However, this situation says nothing about the *potential* utility of the theory in the future.

Scientific Goals

Obviously one factor contributing to the usefulness of equity theory is its scientific validity. In this respect the amount of research support is impressive. There are quite a number of studies that have failed to yield predicted results, but in most cases these failures can be attributed to inadequacies of conceptualization and design. The weight of the evidence is clearly in favor of the theory. Although not all of its propositions have been subjected to test, a number of the more central ones have been. Given the degree of internal consistency of the theoretical logic, it seems likely that the untested aspects would also obtain support.

The major difficulty with the theory appears to be not that it is wrong in any crucial respect but that there are a great many areas in which it does not yield precise hypotheses and predictions. These ambiguities have been evident from the beginning (Weick, 1966). The ensuing years have done little to clarify them.

There is little in the theory that would permit a prediction of what reference sources will be used for comparison purposes when a free choice and multiple sources exist. The research (with few exceptions) has tended to control rigidly the specification of a reference source, thus taking this variable out of the realm of investigation. There has been considerable argument that internal standards within the individual are a frequent comparison source (Pritchard, 1969), and Adams does indicate this as an alternative. Yet there is no basis for determining when this might be expected to occur; the theory is mute on this point. Extending the theory through a coupling with the concepts of internal versus external locus of control (Rotter, 1966) and local versus cosmopolitan reference groups (Gouldner, 1957) might well overcome this problem.

The theory also fails to provide a clear indication of what strategy a person might be expected to choose to reduce inequity, given that a number of reactions are possible. Adams has attempted to deal with this ambiguity, but there is still a lack of theoretical rigor. The research has tended to focus responses strongly on the performance relationship, thus permitting little opportunity to study other types of responses. When they are studied, as with absenteeism and turnover, they turn out to be important. But how do we know who will choose which inequity reduction strategy under what circumstances?

It is also unclear how people come to view various factors as inputs and outcomes. Tornow (1971) has shown that a number of variables can operate in either of these capacities. The theory offers no clear guidelines as to what specific factors can be expected to take on significant roles either as inputs or outcomes, and the research has tended to concentrate heavily on the input of energy expenditure and on the pay outcome. Presumably, answers in this area would require tying equity theory into a broader theory of significant human motives of the kind represented by need hierarchy theory or achievement motivation theory.

In any event, it is apparent that individual differences do pose a major problem for equity theory. Adams (1976) clearly recognizes the role of individual differences, but specific propositions about them are lacking in the theory. Individuals differ not only in the utilities or valences they impute to various potential inputs and outcomes but also in their inequity thresholds, tolerances for inequity tension, and the strength of their equity motivation relative to other types of motivation. It is not possible to predict from the theory who will respond to a particular inequity induction and who will not, although it is apparent that such individual differences exist.

Equity theory to date has not been seriously hampered by the lack of direct measures of its primary mediating variable, inequity tension, at least insofar as the conduct of significant research is concerned. However, this deficiency has now become a distinct limitation. Further progress in research requires the study of individual differences in inequity tension levels, thresholds, and tolerances, as well as the prevailing strength of equity motivation. The situation is not unlike that faced by achievement motivation theory in its early phases. Indeed, Thematic Apperception Test measures might provide a solution for equity theory.

It now appears that equity motivation can be conceptualized as a particular type of motive that exerts an important influence on work behavior in certain circumstances, in a manner quite analogous to achievement motivation. At least for measurement purposes it might be more fruitful to view it as consisting of two distinct motivational states, one a guilt or shame reduction motive and the other an anger or hatred reduction motive.

These problems now facing equity theory were (almost without exception) clearly recognized by Adams in his more recent writing on the subject (Adams and Freedman, 1976). Yet, it is not at all clear that he will provide a solution. Amendments to and extension of the theory have been relatively few in the past ten years, and Adams has had little direct involvement with motivational measurements. Furthermore, he has been almost exclusively concerned recently with organizational boundary role occupants and relationships (Adams, 1976).

Managerial Goals

In view of the level of research support for equity theory, one could hope that it might provide the basis for major breakthroughs in management practice. This expectation is further increased because the two motives involved, guilt and anger reduction, are major influences on what people do. There can be little doubt that the theory deals with motivational processes that relate to large segments of human behavior, not only in the organizational context but also outside it.

Performance Improvement.   One obvious application is to use the theory as a guide in introducing changed circumstances in the work place, so that improved quality or quantity of work will result. This was Adams' objective when as an employee of the General Electric Company he undertook the early research on pay-performance relationships, and his writing clearly indicates his belief that this is feasible. Yet there appear to be no accounts of this type of application in the literature. As far as can be determined, feasibility studies have not been conducted even though they could move us out of the laboratory and short-term simulation contexts into the real, ongoing work environment.

Thus, we can only guess at the results of such feasibility studies. It is doubtful whether overreward inequity could produce the theoretically anticipated consequences. The amount of inequity would have to be sizable in order to exceed threshold, and thus the cost would be considerable; many businessmen would question this initial outlay. More important, it is doubtful whether overreward inequity operates as a motivating force over long time periods; the guilt aroused may well give way to cognitive adjustments in most people. Thus, initial performance effects might be very short-lived. Research that would fully answer this question is nonexistent, although the limited evidence does suggest that overreward inequity is not entirely a transient matter.

Much more important, the research results have been obtained under highly structured circumstances with clearly established reference sources, input and outcome specifications, and rankings of inputs and outcomes. The experimenter has been free to adjust a wide range of factors and has chosen to hold many constant. In the ongoing organizational world these circumstances often do not exist because of union and competitive pressures. The ambiguity and uncertainty may be so great that it is impossible to focus the inequity reaction on a performance-related response.

Although in principle the equity concept is widely applicable, it might be difficult, if not impossible, to structure relationships and perceptions to make it work in a given circumstance. Yet, it is clear from studies such as that of Cook (1975) that without structuring that is analogous to that of the research situations, improved performance cannot be anticipated. This does not imply that equity theory adjustments in pay and other conditions cannot be used to improve performance. It does imply that the conceptual leap from existing knowledge to practical application is sizable, and that existing constraints may rule it out completely in many contexts. Without full knowledge of individual differences and their implications, it is questionable whether inequities should be introduced to spark performance improvements, even if they could be. Maximum returns would be anticipated only with certain types of individuals.

Achieving Equity. In contrast with attempts to introduce inequities through variations in pay plans, compensation levels, input perceptions, and the like, traditional compensation administration has sought to achieve equity through an adjustment of outcomes to perceived inputs, thus reducing the probability of absenteeism, turnover, disruptive behavior, and the like. The major concern has been to avoid underreward inequity. In addition, equity theory can be of considerable value in understanding the behavior that follows unintentional inequities. Full comprehension of equity theory can be useful to a manager and can help him deal with individual circumstances.

Among the major advocates of the use of inequity theory in designing compensation plans have been Belcher and Atchison (1976). In particular they have pointed out that important inputs and outcomes may vary from group to group and that organizations often provide "outcomes" that are not perceived as relevant by individuals.

Data obtained from a study conducted in a large public utility are given in Table 5–5. The inputs investigated were derived from the company's performance appraisal system and the outcomes from motivation-hygiene theory, a not inappropriate source in view of Adams' acceptance of the Herzberg outcomes. The clerical workers and production workers do differ in the importance they impute to various inputs and outcomes; the differences are particularly pronounced on the input side. Thus, an ideal compensation system would weight various inputs differently in the job evaluation process as applied to the two types of work (Atchison and Belcher, 1971; Belcher and Atchison, 1970). Although pay as an outcome is of major importance in both groups, other factors such as advancement do differ. In the production context, advancement opportunity might be used as an offset against pay, while still maintaining equity; this seems less feasible among clerical workers.

Belcher and Atchison also provide data indicating how well existing pay plans match an equity standard. Their approach measures existing perceptions in various groups and adjusts the compensation process to maximize equity, based on a knowledge of input and outcome utilities. Although this procedure does not include an explicit comparison, it does draw heavily upon the Adams formula-

Table 5–5. IMPORTANCE OF VARIOUS INPUTS AND OUTCOMES FOR CLERICAL AND PRODUCTION WORKERS

Inputs	Ranking Clerical Workers	Ranking Production Workers	Outputs	Ranking Clerical Workers	Ranking Production Workers
Quality of work performed	1	13	Job security	1	4.5
Reliability	2.5	2	Pay	2.5	1
Acceptance of responsibility	2.5	8	Competent supervisor	2.5	4.5
Job knowledge	4	13	Possibility of growth	4.5	2.5
Cooperation with others	5.5	10.5	Fair supervisor	4.5	6.5
Self-improvement	5.5	17.5	Recognition	7	8
Attitude	8	8	Adequate working conditions	7	11
Quantity of work performed	8	4.5	Interpersonal relations-supervisor	7	11
Initiative	8	13	Achievement	10	9
Adaptability-versatility	11	6	Interpersonal relations-peer	10	13.5
Judgment	11	16	Adequate planning and management	10	6.5
Intelligence	11	2	Adequate personnel policies	12	15.5
Experience	13	4.5	Amount of work	13	13.5
Personal appearance	14.5	15	Responsibility	14.5	11
Oral communication skill	14.5	17.5	Advancement	14.5	2.5
Education	16.5	10.5	Routine work	16	19
Written communication skill	16.5	8	Status	17	15.5
Personal involvement with task accomplishment	18	2	Difficult work	18	18
			Personal life	19	17

Adapted from D. W. Belcher and T. J. Atchison. Equity Theory and Compensation Policy, *Personnel Administration*, Vol. 33, No. 3 (1970), p. 28; and T. J. Atchison and D. W. Belcher. Equity, Rewards and Compensation Administration, *Personnel Administration*, Vol. 34, No. 2 (1971), p. 34.

tions and offers considerable promise as an adjunct to existing compensation approaches.

In contrast, the procedures developed by Jaques (1970), although incorporating an equity standard, do not assume an implicit motivational process. Jaques posits a single input, capacity, that is channeled through the amount of individual discretion that the person is allowed to exercise in the job. The longer the period of time a person is expected to exercise independent judgment in his work, the higher the pay level should be to be perceived as equitable. In general, this time span of discretion increases with occupational level.

Although Jaques' views have received considerable criticism, and the measurement of time spans of discretion has proved difficult, the approach has much in common with equity theory and receives support from the research reported in this chapter (Gray, 1976). The major advance provided is the emphasis on time span of discretion, or freedom to act independently as a major factor conditioning input perceptions. In this respect the theory has contributed a concept of considerable value for compensation administration.

Other Contributions. To the extent that equity theory deals with strong and prevalent human motives, it should have wide application in understanding organizational behavior. At the present time its most unique contribution appears to be in explaining and predicting reactions to perceived overreward inequity. It simply is not true that offering the 'carrot' (more money) will inevitably produce more and better performance; the nature of human motivation is more complex.

An analogous phenomenon exists in the field of consumer behavior (Jacoby, 1976). Various products come to have a perceived fair price attached to them. Major price reductions, if they violate the equitable price range, do not necessarily increase demand; they can in fact decrease it. If it has accomplished nothing else, equity theory has performed a useful service in pointing up phenomena of this kind and in providing guides to the circumstances under which they might be expected to occur.

References

Adams, J. Stacy. Toward an Understanding of Inequity, *Journal of Abnormal and Social Psychology*, Vol. 67 (1963a), 422–436.

Adams, J. Stacy. Wage Inequities, Productivity and Work Quality, *Industrial Relations*, Vol. 3 (1963b), 9–16.

Adams, J. Stacy. Inequity in Social Exchange, In Leonard Berkowitz (ed.), *Advances in Experimental Social Psychology*. Vol. 2. New York: Academic Press, 1965, pp. 267–299.

Adams, J. Stacy. A Framework for the Study of Modes of Resolving Inconsistency, In Robert P. Abelson, et. al. (eds.), *Theories of Cognitive Inconsistency: A Sourcebook*. Chicago: Rand, McNally, 1968a, pp. 655–660.

Adams, J. Stacy. Effects of Overpayment: Two Comments on Lawler's Paper, *Journal of Personality and Social Psychology*, Vol. 10 (1968b), 315–316.

Adams, J. Stacy. The Structure and Dynamics of Behavior in Organizational Boundary Roles, In Marvin D. Dunnette (ed.), *Handbook of Industrial and Organizational Psychology*. Chicago: Rand, McNally, 1976, pp. 1175–1199.

Adams, J. Stacy and Sara Freedman. Equity Theory Revisited: Comments and Annotated Bibliography. In Leonard Berkowitz and Elaine Walster (eds.), *Advances in Experimental Social Psychology, Vol. 9*. New York: Academic Press, 1976, pp. 43–90.

Adams, J. Stacy and Patricia R. Jacobsen. Effects of Wage Inequities on Work Quality, *Journal of Abnormal and Social Psychology*, Vol. 69 (1964), 19–25.

Adams, J. Stacy and William B. Rosenbaum. The Relationship of Worker Productivity to Cognitive Dissonance About Wage Inequities, *Journal of Applied Psychology*, Vol. 46 (1962), 161–164.

Andrews, Irving R. Wage Inequity and Job Performance: An Experimental Study, *Journal of Applied Psychology*, Vol. 51 (1967), 39–45.

Atchison, T. J. and D. W. Belcher. Equity, Rewards and Compensation Administration, *Personnel Administration*, Vol. 34, No. 2 (1971), 32–36.

Belcher, D. W. and T. J. Atchison. Equity Theory and Compensation Policy, *Personnel Administration*, Vol. 33, No. 3 (1970), 22–33.

Belcher, D. W. and T. J. Atchison. Compensation for Work, In Robert Dubin (ed.), *Handbook of Work, Organization and Society*. Chicago: Rand McNally, 1976, pp. 567–611.

Cook, Karen S. Expectations, Evaluations and Equity, *American Sociological Review*, Vol. 40 (1975), 372–388.

Dittrich, John E. and Michael R. Carrell. Dimensions of Organizational Fairness as Predictors of Job Satisfaction,

Absence and Turnover, *Academy of Management Proceedings*, (1976), 79–83.

Festinger, Leon. *A Theory of Cognitive Dissonance*. Evanston, Ill.: Row, Peterson, 1957.

Finn, R. H. and Sang M. Lee. Salary Equity: Its Determination, Analysis, and Correlates, *Journal of Applied Psychology*, Vol. 56 (1972), 283–292.

Garland, Howard. The Effects of Piece-Rate Underpayment and Overpayment on Job Performance: A Test of Equity Theory with a New Induction Procedure, *Journal of Applied Social Psychology*, Vol. 3 (1973), 325–334.

Gergen, Kenneth J., Stanley J. Morse, and Katherine A. Bode. Overpaid or Overworked? Cognitive and Behavioral Reactions to Inequitable Rewards, *Journal of Applied Social Psychology*, Vol. 4 (1974), 259–274.

Goodman, Paul S. and Abraham Friedman. An Examination of Adams' Theory of Inequity, *Administrative Science Quarterly*, Vol. 16 (1971), 271–288.

Gouldner, A. W. Cosmos and Locals: Toward an Analysis of Latent Social Roles, *Administrative Science Quarterly*, Vol. 2 (1957), 281–306, 444–480.

Gray, Jerry L. *The Glacier Project: Concepts and Critiques*. New York: Crane, Russak, 1976.

Hinton, Bernard L. The Experimental Extension of Equity Theory to Interpersonal and Group Interaction Situations, *Organizational Behavior and Human Performance*, Vol. 8 (1972), 434–449.

Homans, George C. *Social Behavior: Its Elementary Forms*. Harcourt, Brace, and World, 1961.

Jacoby, Jacob. Consumer and Industrial Psychology: Prospects for Theory Corroboration and Mutual Contribution. In Marvin D. Dunnette (ed.), *Handbook of Industrial and Organizational Psychology*. Chicago: Rand, McNally, 1976, pp. 1031–1061.

Jaques, Elliott. *Equitable Payment*. London: Heinemann, 1970.

Kessler, John J. and Yoash Wiener. Self-Consistency and Inequity Dissonance as Factors in Undercompensation, *Organizational Behavior and Human Performance*, Vol. 8 (1972), 456–466.

Larwood, Laurie, Michael Kavanagh, and Richard Levine. Perceptions of Fairness with Three Different Economic Exchanges, *Academy of Management Journal*, Vol. 21 (1978), 69–83.

Lawler, Edward E. Equity Theory as a Predictor of Productivity and Work Quality, *Psychological Bulletin*, Vol. 70 (1968), 596–610.

Lawler, Edward E. and Paul W. O'Gara. Effects of Inequity Produced by Underpayment on Work Output, Work Quality, and Attitudes Toward the Work, *Journal of Applied Psychology*, Vol. 51 (1967), 403–410.

Leventhal, Gerald S., James W. Michaels, and Charles Sanford. Inequity and Interpersonal Conflict: Reward Allocation and Secrecy About Reward as Methods of Preventing Conflict, *Journal of Personality and Social Psychology*, Vol. 23 (1972), 88–102.

Leventhal, Gerald S., Thomas Weiss, and Richard Buttrick. Attribution of Value, Equity, and the Prevention of Waste in Reward Allocation, *Journal of Personality and Social Psychology*, Vol. 27 (1973), 276–286.

Leventhal, Gerald S., Thomas Weiss, and Gary Long. Equity, Reciprocity, and Reallocating Rewards in the Dyad, *Journal of Personality and Social Psychology*, Vol. 13 (1969), 300–305.

Moore, Loretta M. and Reuben M. Baron. Effects of Wage Inequities on Work Attitudes and Performance, *Journal of Experimental Social Psychology*, Vol. 9 (1973), 1–16.

Pritchard, Robert D. Equity Theory: A Review and Critique, *Organizational Behavior and Human Performance*, Vol. 4 (1969), 176–211.

Pritchard, Robert D., Marvin D. Dunnette, and Dale O. Jorgenson. Effects of Perceptions of Equity and Inequity on Worker Performance and Satisfaction, *Journal of Applied Psychology*, Vol. 56 (1972), 75–94.

Rotter, J. B. Generalized Expectancies for Internal Versus External Control of Reinforcement. *Psychological Monographs*, Vol. 80 (1966).

Telly, Charles S., Wendell L. French, and William G. Scott. The Relationship of Equity to Turnover Among Hourly Workers, *Administrative Science Quarterly*, Vol. 16 (1971), 164–172.

Tornow, Walter W. The Development and Application of an Input-Outcome Moderator Test on the Perception and Reduction of Inequity, *Organizational Behavior and Human Performance*, Vol. 6 (1971), 614–638.

Walster, Elaine, Ellen Berscheid, and G. William Walster. New Directions in Equity Research, *Journal of Personality and Social Psychology*, Vol. 25 (1973), 151–176.

Weick, Karl E. The Concept of Equity in the Perception of Pay, *Administrative Science Quarterly*, Vol. 11 (1966), 414–439.

Weick, Karl E., Michael G. Bougon, and Geoffrey Maruyama. The Equity Context, *Organizational Behavior and Human Performance*, Vol. 15 (1976), 32–65.

Zedeck, Sheldon and Patricia Cain Smith. A Psychophysical Determination of Equitable Payment: A Methodological Study, *Journal of Applied Psychology*, Vol. 52 (1968), 343–347.

EXPECTANCY THEORIES

6

In contrast to the theories considered previously, the expectancy approach to employee motivation cannot be associated with a single individual. The central constructs of the theory have a long history in psychology and may be traced back at least to Tolman's (1932) early work in the field of learning. Much of the early

133

research was carried out with animals, and the first application in the field of organizational behavior did not occur until the late 1950s. During the 1960s a number of variants of the theory were proposed, and a rather sizable amount of research was initiated. Among scholars in the field, expectancy concepts now appear to provide the most popular approach to understanding employee motivation. In part this is because a number of widely known and respected individuals have become identified with the theory. However, applications face a number of difficulties (Pinder, 1977), and practitioner acceptance does not appear to be extensive.

Of the theories considered so far, only Atkinson's formulations regarding achievement motivation have much in common with the expectancy theory approach. Atkinson (1977) utilizes concepts such as expectancy, valence, incentive value, and contingent path, which clearly identify him with many of the viewpoints considered in this chapter. The fact that he does not specifically label his theory with the term "expectancy" makes little difference. Theories of this kind carry a wide variety of titles, although most utilize some combination of the words expectancy, instrumentality, valence, path, and goal.

THEORETICAL STATEMENTS AS APPLIED TO WORK MOTIVATION

There is no consensus on how many different versions of expectancy theory exist; different reviewers come up with somewhat different lists (Campbell and Pritchard, 1976; Mitchell, 1974; Wahba and House, 1974). There are four such theories that have been given sufficient attention to consider here. These are the formulations of Vroom; Galbraith and Cummings; Porter and Lawler (later extended by Lawler); and Graen. The early proposals by Georgopoulos should be added also, even though they do not constitute a formal theory, simply because of their groundbreaking nature. Additional extensions of expectancy theory into the realm of leadership are considered in later chapters in this book.

The Georgopoulos, Mahoney, and Jones Hypotheses

The Georgopoulos, Mahoney, and Jones (1957) study was conducted as part of a research program of the Survey Research Center at the University of Michigan. It aimed at identifying factors associated with high and low levels of employee productivity. This program as a whole was focused primarily on the role of supervisory practices but in the present instance dealt only with the motivation-productivity relationship. The theoretical hypotheses were formulated as derivations from prior work in the field of psychology and guided the conduct of the research. They were intended to deal only with the conscious, rational aspects of employee motivation.

The major variables considered are:

1. Individual needs as reflected in the goals sought. Examples of these goals would be making more money or getting along well in the work group.
2. Individual perceptions of the relative usefulness of productivity behavior (high or low) as a means of attaining desired goals (in theoretical terms the instrumentality of various productivity levels or the extent to which they are seen as providing a path to a goal).
3. The amount of freedom from restraining factors the individual has in following the desired path. Examples of constraining factors might be supervisory and work group pressures or limitations of ability and knowledge.

The basic hypothesis is as follows:

> **If a worker sees high productivity as a path leading to the attainment of one or more of his personal goals, he will tend to be a high producer. Conversely, if he sees low productivity as a path to the achievement of his goals he will tend to be a low producer (Georgopoulos, Mahoney, and Jones, 1957, p. 346).**

This relationship between motivation and performance is moderated by the amount of freedom to act. When freedom is high, motivation will readily appear in productivity levels. When barriers operate, the hypothesized relationships will be disrupted and the motivation-performance correlation reduced. Path-goal perceptions are conceived as expectancies or estimated probabilities that there will be a given amount of payoff as a consequence of certain types of job behavior. Accordingly, high productivity may be viewed as likely to produce a desired goal (thus having a positive valence) or to impede goal attainment (thus having a negative valence).

Vroom's Theory of Work and Motivation

The initial, preliminary statements of Vroom's expectancy theory appear in the published version of his doctoral dissertation (Vroom, 1960). These statements have much in common with the views of his University of Michigan colleagues in the Georgopoulos, Mahoney, and Jones article and in the early statements of Atkinson's theory. Subsequently, Vroom expanded his ideas into a more formally stated expectancy theory of work and motivation (Vroom, 1964). Thus, all of the original thinking regarding applications of expectancy theory to employee motivation emanated from the University of Michigan. Vroom then moved to the University of Pennsylvania, and at the time of his 1964 book he was at Carnegie-Mellon University. He is now on the faculty at Yale University.

Vroom's theory starts with the idea that people tend to prefer certain goals, or outcomes, over others. They thus anticipate experiencing feelings of satisfaction should such a preferred outcome be achieved. The term valence is applied to this feeling about specific outcomes. If there is positive valence, having the outcome is preferred to not having it. If negative valence exists, not having the outcome is preferred. Outcomes may require valence either in their own right or because they are expected to lead to other outcomes that are anticipated sources of satisfaction or dissatisfaction. Thus the accumulation of earnings per se might be viewed as inherently satisfying to one person, but to another it is important as a means to the end of buying a sports car.

As a basis for establishing the valence of a specific outcome, Vroom sets forth the following proposition:

> The valence of an outcome to a person is a monotonically increasing function of the algebraic sum of the products of the valences of all other outcomes and his conceptions of its instrumentality for the attainment of these other outcomes.

Thus the size of the valence of an outcome is dependent on the extent to which it is viewed as a means to various other outcomes and the valence of the other outcomes. Since the proposition calls for the multiplication of the perceived instrumentality by the valence of each other outcome, any such outcome that has no valence for a person or that has no instrumental relationship to the outcome whose valence is being computed takes on a zero value, adding nothing to the final sum. An outcome with a large valence would tend to be one that is linked to many other outcomes, one that is considered highly instrumental to the attainment of a large number of these other outcomes, and one that is linked to other outcomes having large valences. Vroom specifically applies this first proposition to the topics of occupational choice (calculation of the valence of an occupation), job satisfaction (calculation of the valence of a job held), and job performance (calculation of the valence of effective performance in a job held). The latter was the single concern of Georgopoulos and his associates.

An additional and central variable in the theory is expectancy. People develop varying conceptions of the probability or degree of certainty that the choice of a particular alternative action will indeed lead to a desired outcome. In contrast to instrumentality, which is an outcome-outcome link, expectancy involves an action-outcome linkage. Expectancies combine with total valence to yield a person's aroused motivation or potential for a given course of action. Vroom uses the term *force* to describe this combination and offers the following proposition:

> The force on a person to perform an act is a monotonically increasing function of the algebraic sum of the products of the valences of all outcomes and the strength of his expectancies that the act will be followed by the attainment of these outcomes.

The total force for an action is uninfluenced by outcomes that have no valence and also by outcomes that are viewed as totally unlikely to result from the actions, since again a multiplicative relationship between the two variables is posited. People are expected to choose among action alternatives in a rational manner to maximize force (in a positive direction). When an action is linked to many very positively valent outcomes by strong expectations that it will yield these outcomes, the force can be sizable. The theory makes specific statements with regard to the implications of the second proposition for occupational choice (calculation of the force on a person to enter an occupation), job satisfaction (calculation of the force on a person to remain in a job held), and job performance (calculation of the force on a person to exert a given amount of effort in the performance of a job held). Since the last of these statements has been the subject of considerable further theorizing and research, it is given in full:

> The force on a person to exert a given amount of effort in performance of his job is a monotonically increasing function of the algebraic sum of the products of the valences of different levels of performance and his expectancies that this amount of effort will be followed by their attainment.

Galbraith and Cummings' Extensions

The major contributions by Galbraith and Cummings (1967) were in making explicit several ideas that were not fully developed by Vroom. While Vroom (1964) notes that certain "things are desired and abhorred for their own sake" rather than for their expected consequences and in fact conducted a study earlier dealing with the role of this kind of ego-involvement in job performance (Vroom, 1962), he does not incorporate this concept directly in his first proposition. Galbraith and Cummings provide for such a situation by adding into the total valence of an outcome a valence figure representing the internalized or intrinsic motivation involved. Thus, if doing good quality work and performing at a particular job have acquired valence in their own right and thus are anticipated to be a source of satisfaction, these valence figures are added to the valence-instrumentality products for "other outcomes" to obtain the total valence for good work or job performance.

Vroom's propositions clearly do deal with focal and "other" outcomes. Other outcomes assume significance if they have valence and instrumentality. Galbraith and Cummings explicitly identify focal outcomes such as performance levels as first level, and the valent outcomes for which the first level outcomes are perceived to be instrumental as second level. Pay, fringe benefits, support from a supervisor, work group acceptance, and the like might operate as significant second level outcomes for job performance levels (first level). The model as developed can be schematized as follows:

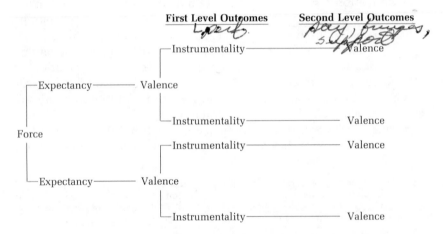

It should be noted that a recent publication by Galbraith (1977) holds to essentially this same theoretical position while raising certain questions about whether intrinsic valences should simply be added into the total valence as indicated in the 1967 article or be treated in some other manner. There has been some research on this matter in the interval, and we will consider it in greater detail later.

The Porter/Lawler Model

Porter and Lawler (1968) present a model that draws heavily on Vroom but goes beyond the limited concept of motivational force to performance as a whole. Vroom (1964) himself moves in this direction by stating that ability and motivation relate to performance in a multiplicative manner:

Vroom

$$\text{Performance} = f(\text{Ability} \times \text{Motivation})$$

At the time their book was published, Porter was at the University of California at Irvine, and Lawler was at Yale University. Lawler subsequently moved to the University of Michigan, and more recently to the University of Southern California. The variables of the Porter/Lawler theory are as follows:

1. Value of reward — how attractive or desirable an outcome is (valence).
2. Effort-reward probability — a perception of whether differential rewards are based on differential effort. This breaks down into effort-performance (expectancy) and performance-reward (instrumentality) components.
3. Effort — the energy expended to perform a task (force).
4. Abilities and traits — the long-term characteristics of a person.
5. Role perceptions — the types of effort a person considers necessary to effective job performance.
6. Performance — a person's accomplishment on tasks that comprise the job.
7. Rewards — desirable states of affairs received from either one's own thinking or the actions of others (intrinsic and extrinsic outcomes).
8. Perceived equitable rewards — the amount of rewards a person considers fair.
9. Satisfaction — the extent to which rewards received meet or exceed the perceived equitable level (dissatisfaction results from underreward inequity only).

In line with prior formulations the first two variables (value of reward and effort-reward probability), when multiplied together, are said to produce the third variable (effort). Following Vroom, abilities and traits also have a multiplicative relationship to effort in determining performance. A similar relation to effort (in establishing performance level) holds for role perceptions. Because of the intervention of such factors between effort and performance, the latter two cannot be expected to be perfectly related.

Porter and Lawler also posit certain feedback loops that make their theory more dynamic over time than Vroom's. First, to the extent that performance does result in reward, the perceived effort-reward probability is increased. Second, when satisfaction is experienced after receiving a reward, it tends to influence the future value (valence) of that reward. The nature of this effect varies with the particular reward (outcome).

More recently Lawler has modified this theory in several respects, although the overall change is not marked. He has elaborated certain factors that may influence effort-reward probabilities and thus has continued the tendency to make the model dynamic over time, in contrast to Vroom's static approach (Lawler, 1971, 1973). The most important change is an additional feedback loop from performance to effort-reward expectancy to the effect that within normal limits heightened performance will yield greater self-esteem and thus subsequently higher expectancy. In addition, a much clearer distinction is made between intrinsic and extrinsic rewards.

Graen's Modifications

Graen (1969) who was at the University of Illinois until his recent move to the University of Cincinnati, has extended the basic Vroom model considerably and thereby made it quite complex. Many of these modifications extend the theory beyond motivation into the leadership realm; these will not be given much attention at this point. Graen has taken the role perception variable as noted in the Porter/Lawler model and developed it into a much more central concept of the theory. In the process he has added a dynamic or developmental dimension through the use of feedback concepts.

The important Graen modifications occur between force and first level outcomes. He introduces the concept of *work role*, defined as:

> A set of behaviors expected by the organization and considered appropriate of an incumbent of a position within the organization. Examples: incumbent of a particular job, effective job performer, occupational group member.

Outcomes then accrue to a person from the attainment or maintenance of these work roles (doing what is expected). The model for the effective job performer would look as follows:

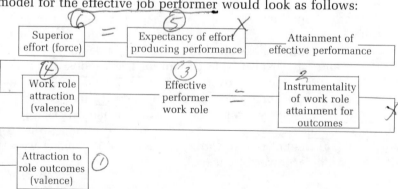

Attractions to the various role outcomes are multiplied by their instrumentalities to establish work role attraction, in this case attraction to the effective performer role. Work role attraction level (the valence of the work role) is then multiplied by expectancy to determine whether superior effort can be anticipated. A feedback process is hypothesized in that whenever a role outcome is achieved following the attainment of a work role (effective performance), the level of instrumentality is elevated so that the work role is now seen as more likely to yield that outcome.

Although this basic model has been differentiated further by Graen (1969) and others, as with the specification of various types of task goals within a work role (Campbell and Pritchard, 1976), the variables and relationships noted are the essence of the modified theory. The next step is to look at the initial research evidence presented by the authors of these five versions of expectancy theory.

RESEARCH BY PROPONENTS OF VARIOUS THEORETICAL VERSIONS

Most of the versions of expectancy theory that have been considered were introduced preliminary to a research study testing the theoretical formulation. These seminal studies are important not only because they bear directly on matters of theoretical validity but also because they have tended to set the scene (particularly in experimental design and measurement) for almost all of the research that has followed.

The Georgopoulos, Mahoney, and Jones Research on Productivity

As noted, Georgopoulos, Mahoney, and Jones (1957) formulated their hypothesis as part of a study of motivation-performance relationships. The sample consisted of production workers for a household appliances company. The measures used were all derived from a questionnaire and thus constitute entirely conscious self-reports of the variables.

The goals studied were the three ranked as most important by all the subjects out of a list of ten. These same rankings were used to determine whether each of the three was important to an individual subject. The three goals were:

1. Making more money in the long run.
2. Getting along well with the work group.
3. Promotion to a higher base rate of pay.

The instrumentality of either high or low productivity for attaining these goals was established through a rating scale extending from "helping," through a neutral value, to "hurting." For instance, high productivity might be rated as helping a great deal to make more money and low productivity as hurting a little in achieving the same goal.

Productivity was reported in terms of per cent of the standard usually achieved, on the basis of the standard hour incentive system in effect in the company. Freedom from restraining factors was established according to both reported freedom and amount of job experience.

As indicated in Table 6–1, the data tend to confirm the basic instrumentality hypothesis in that those who view performance levels as instrumentally related to goals in a positive sense are more likely to be high producers. However, the differences are not pronounced, and only three of the six differences attain accepted levels of statistical significance. Other data indicate that the presence of a stronger need to achieve a goal tends to be associated with an increase in relationship between instrumentality and productivity; freedom from restraining factors also tends to have the same facilitating effect. Again the differences are often small, and consistent statistical significance occurs only for the "making more money in the long run" goal. Overall, the results do support expectancy theory, but not strongly.

Table 6–1. PERCENTAGE OF THOSE WITH VARIOUS INSTRUMENTAL PERCEPTIONS WHO ARE HIGH PRODUCERS

| | Instrumental Perceptions | | | |
Goal Involved	High Productivity Helps to Achieve the Goal	High Productivity Hurts Achieving the Goal	Low Productivity Hurts Achieving the Goal	Low Productivity Helps to Achieve the Goal
More money in the long run	(38	21)*	(30	22)
Getting along well with the work group	32	23	33	28
Promotion to a higher base rate	26	23	(32	12)

*Differences in parentheses are statistically significant.

Adapted from Basil S. Georgopoulos, Gerald M. Mahoney, and Nyle W. Jones. A Path-Goal Approach to Productivity, *Journal of Applied Psychology*, Vol. 41 (1957), p. 349.

Vroom's Research on Organizational Choice

Although Vroom does not present any research of his own on expectancy theory in his 1964 volume, he did publish an article two years later that bears on the subject (Vroom, 1966). This research is related only to the first of his basic propositions, since it does not concern itself with expectancies and deals only with the occupational choice question, not with job satisfaction or job performance.

The subjects were business students about to obtain masters degrees from Carnegie-Mellon University. The objective was to predict the attractiveness of various potential employing organizations (and ultimately the choice itself) from a knowledge of what goals were important to the individual and how instrumental membership in each organization was perceived to be as a means of achieving each goal. Questionnaire ratings on a number of variables were obtained prior to choice. Job goals or outcomes such as a chance to benefit society, freedom from supervision, high salary, and the like were rated in terms of their importance to the person. The three organizations in which the subject was most interested were then evaluated to establish the degree to which the student thought each might provide an opportunity to satisfy each type of goal. Combining these two variables, an instrumentality-goal index was calculated for each organization and related both to the attractiveness rating given the organization and to the subsequent choice.

The results indicate clearly that organizations viewed as providing a means to achieving important goals were considered more attractive. Eliminating organizations that ultimately did not make an offer, 76 per cent of the students subsequently chose the organization with the highest instrumentality-goal score. Although providing only a partial test of the theory, Vroom's research results are entirely consistent with it. Similar support of the theory was obtained in a follow-up study conducted several years after actual employment (Vroom and Deci, 1971).

The Galbraith and Cummings Study of Productivity

Galbraith and Cummings (1967) used as subjects 32 operative workers for a heavy equipment manufacturing firm. Productivity figures maintained by the company were related to measures of valence, instrumentality, and ego involvement; the latter measure was included to indicate the internalization or intrinsic nature of

motivation. The expectancy component of the theory was not actually measured but was assumed to have been held constant by
the fact that all of the workers performed independent tasks and
thus "were dependent on no one other than themselves in achieving a performance outcome." Furthermore, performance figures
were corrected for the effects of extraneous factors such as machine breakdown, and the jobs allowed incumbents to vary their
work pace.

The valence and performance-instrumentality levels for six
possible second-level outcomes were obtained through a self-
report questionnaire. The outcomes were (1) being popular with
coworkers, (2) a pay increase, (3) the support and consideration of
a supervisor, (4) promotion, (5) greater fringe benefits, and (6) a
reduced work load with more free time. Ego involvement was
measured through responses to a question about the tendency to
think about unsettled work problems after work.

The only consistently significant finding was for the supervisory support and consideration outcome, for which a combination
of high valence and performance instrumentality was associated
with high productivity. Apparently, those who wanted support
from their supervisors and had been convinced by them that good
performance was a means to that end were more productive. The
implication is that supervision can make a difference. On the
other hand, the relative lack of results with other outcome measures does not bode well for the theory. There is some evidence
that the outcome variables themselves may not have been well
chosen, and some of the measures used had low reliability. Furthermore, the small sample size militates against obtaining statistical significance. There are other possible explanations for the lack
of results, including the possibility that expectancies regarding
the effort-performance relationship were not actually held constant as assumed. In any event, this study does not yield strong
evidence for the validity of expectancy theory.

The Porter/Lawler Studies

The most extensive investigation by Porter and Lawler and
the one that is presented immediately after the major elaboration
of their theory was conducted among the managers of seven different organizations — three state government departments (employment, conservation, retail liquor) and four private firms (a
large processor of canned goods, a large chemical firm, an aero-
space company, and a utility). In all, some 563 managers below
the officer level were included (Porter and Lawler, 1968).

The study focuses primarily on pay as an outcome. Questionnaire measures of a number of theoretical variables were obtained from the managers, including measures of value of reward, effort-reward probability, effort, role perceptions, performance, rewards, perceived equitable rewards, and satisfaction. Ratings of effort and performance also were obtained from the managers' immediate supervisors.

Insofar as pay is concerned the data do support the hypothesis that value of reward and perceived effort-reward probability combine to influence effort. Those who view pay as important and who consider pay to be tied to their efforts put more effort into their work, and this is true whether self or superior perceptions of effort are used. The same relationship also holds for performance but to a somewhat lesser degree. This, too, is what the theory predicts, since additional factors intervene between effort and performance in the model. Among these are role perceptions; data are presented indicating that certain kinds of role perceptions (when combined with the effort measures) do increase the precision with which performance level is predicted.

In another study of 154 managers in five organizations, the authors collected and analyzed data using several outcomes in addition to pay, such as promotion, friendship, and opportunity to use skills and abilities (Lawler and Porter, 1967). Basically the approach was the same as that used in the preceding research except that data for more outcomes were combined in the predictors. As indicated in Table 6–2, including value of reward (valence) in the

Table 6–2. MULTIPLE CORRELATIONS FOR SEVEN OUTCOMES OF EFFORT-REWARD PROBABILITIES ALONE AND IN COMBINATION WITH VALUE OF REWARD AS PREDICTORS OF JOB EFFORT AND PERFORMANCE

Ratings	Effort-Reward Probability Alone	Effort-Reward Probability Multiplied by Value of Reward
By the manager's superior		
Job effort	.22	.27
Job performance	.17	.18
By the manager's peers		
Job effort	.25	.30
Job performance	.21	.21
By the manager himself		
Job effort	.32	.44
Job performance	.25	.38

Adapted from Edward E. Lawler and Lyman W. Porter. Antecedent Attitudes of Effective Managerial Performance, *Organizational Behavior and Human Performance*, Vol. 2 (1967), p. 136.

prediction formula did make a difference; the correlations are consistently higher than without it. Job effort was consistently predicted more accurately than the further removed job performance. Yet the overall level of the coefficients is quite low for multiple correlation analyses. Only the four values of .30 or above are statistically significant. Considering that three of these four significant correlations involve self-ratings whose independence of the measures can be questioned, the overall results do not offer strong support of the theory.

In a later study Lawler (1968a) used some of the same managers and obtained his measures twice, with a one-year interval between measurements. This time the multiple correlations were higher, and statistical significance was much more frequently attained. The data over time are consistent with the hypothesis that pre-existing perceived probabilities and valences of outcomes tend to exert a causal influence on subsequent performance.

A final early study related to the Porter/Lawler version of expectancy theory was conducted by Hackman and Porter (1968) with telephone company service representatives as subjects. A variety of performance criteria were predicted using effort-reward probability multiplied by value of reward as the predictor. In this instance, the rewards (or outcomes) considered were generated directly by the service representatives themselves in interviews; thus, they were the rewards the subjects perceived to be actually present. The correlations with performance criteria are significant in almost all instances. On the other hand, the median value is only .27.

Overall these various studies by Porter and Lawler do provide considerable support for the expectancy theories. Yet, given that this theoretical approach has identified an important way of looking at motivation at work, even Porter and Lawler appear puzzled by the low correlations found in many of the investigations.

Graen's Simulation Study

Graen's (1969) research had much in common with the early equity theory studies. Women were hired on a part-time, temporary basis to perform a clerical task. There were two work sessions, and certain experimental manipulations were introduced in the interval: one group of subjects received verbal recognition that was tied directly to their prior performance; a second group received a pay increase "in the hope that you will do much better"; and a third group received no special treatment. Questionnaire measures of the variables of the theory were obtained as well as indexes of job satisfaction and performance on the clerical tasks. Four hypotheses derived from the theory were tested.

Hypothesis I. If a role outcome is attained following the attainment of the role of job incumbent, higher perceived instrumentality of that role for the attainment of like outcomes will result; this is a feedback hypothesis. (This hypothesis was supported. Giving recognition for achievement did enhance the perceived instrumentality of the work for achievement feedback and recognition; giving money enhanced the instrumentality for salary.)

Hypothesis II. Satisfaction with the work role of job incumbent is a monotonically increasing function of the products of the attraction of each role outcome, and the perceived instrumentality of that work role for the attainment of like role outcomes summed over all role outcomes. (This hypothesis was supported quite consistently for the group receiving recognition for prior performance but not for the others. In addition, the instrumentality component was more strongly related to satisfaction than attraction [valence].)

Hypothesis III. If a role outcome is attained following the attainment of the role of effective performer, higher perceived instrumentality of that role for the attainment of like outcomes will result; this is a feedback hypothesis for the effective performer role rather than for the mere job incumbent. (This hypothesis was supported in that the perceived instrumentality of effective performance for achievement feedback and recognition was enhanced in the group that received performance recognition, and that group only.)

Hypothesis IV. Job performance is a monotonically increasing function of the product of the attraction of the work role of effective performer and the perceived expectancy that increased effort will lead to effective performance. (This hypothesis was only partially supported. Only *improvements* in performance from the first to second sessions [not absolute performance levels] were predicted, and then only in the group that received recognition for improved performance in the interim.)

The author summarizes his results as generally favorable to the theory but adds:

> Only in the achievement feedback treatment was the contingency between effective performance and the attainment of a favorable role outcome established in a concrete manner — presenting the achievement feedback contingent upon effective performance . . . Therefore, an important boundary condition for instrumentality theory is that contingencies must be established in a concrete manner between effective job performance and attaining favorable role outcomes (Graen, 1969, p. 19).

LOGICAL AND EMPIRICAL EVALUATIONS

The early research provided overall support for expectancy theory formulations, although the level of support was uneven. In addition, a number of questions were raised regarding the nature and operationalizing of constructs, boundary conditions for the theory, and the like. During the 1970s a sizable amount of additional research has appeared bearing on the validity of the theory. Questions have been raised also regarding the philosophical underpinnings and basic assumptions of expectancy theory, especially as they relate to decision theory.

Philosophical and Logical Questions

A major critique of the basic assumptions of the theory has been presented by Locke (1975). Of the points made by Locke the one that receives the most attention is that the concept of hedonism, as incorporated in the expected satisfaction definition of the valence variable, is untenable. Locke raises a number of the same arguments against the view of man as a satisfaction maximizing being that philosophers have raised for centuries. The essence of these arguments is that much human behavior is in fact self-punitive. It is the difficulty of dealing with behavior of this kind and with reactions to guilt of the type considered by equity theory that casts doubt on the strictly hedonistic formulations. Furthermore, there is reason to believe that many people do not attempt to maximize even when they do strive for satisfaction but rather accept some lesser level of effort. Issues like this have not really been faced by expectancy theorists. At the very least they suggest that there are behaviors, and perhaps people, to whom the theory may apply in a very limited way.

Locke also questions whether human beings can engage in the cognitive processes implied by the theory, such as weighting all possible outcomes as they contribute to other outcomes, and then others, to the point of infinite regress, or multiplying valences and instrumentalities in a manner that, according to the theory, assumes very complex internalized measurement processes. He also notes the fact that the theory assumes common tendencies to project one's thoughts into a future time span and to search for alternatives for all human beings, since it is silent on individual differences in these respects. Yet, it is apparent that people do differ in both time perspective and the proclivity for search. Finally, individuals do act on occasion out of unconscious motives and in ways that cannot be based on the calculative, highly rational processes that expectancy theory specifies; impulsive behavior, the repetition compulsions of neurotic individuals, and the like are examples.

These questions do not void expectancy theories as useful methods of predicting and understanding work behavior. They do suggest that the theories may deal with only part of organizational behavior and that their propositions may well represent only approximations of human motivational processes (perhaps overly complex in certain respects and overly simplistic in others). Under these circumstances the theories could still work quite well in the theoretical domains to which they apply.

Another line of questioning to which Locke alludes, although he does not develop it fully, has to do with the extent to which expectancy theories must meet the various rationality assumptions that have been developed for formal decision theory. Vroom (1964) notes certain similarities between his formulations and those of subjective, expected utility theory. Others have drawn out these parallels more fully, even to the point of considering expectancy theories of motivation as special cases within the broader context of decision theory (Mitchell, 1977).

Attempts to relate expectancy theories to rationality assumptions or postulates taken from decision theory have not always come to identical conclusions (Behling and Starke, 1973; Wahba and House, 1974). However, if such assumptions are to be considered part of the theory or implicit in its basic propositions, then the range of empirical support required to validate these propositions is greatly expanded. Furthermore, those who have compared expectancy theories to criteria derived from decision theory clearly imply that expectancy theories are wanting in these respects.

On the other hand, strong arguments have been advanced that expectancy theories need not meet all of the tests derived from decision theory. For instance, it has been contended that the theory presupposes a lack of correlation (independence) between expectancy and valence and that such independence probably does not exist in reality (Behling and Starke, 1973). Regardless of the empirical facts, there is reason to conclude that independence is not necessary for the propositions of expectancy theory to prove valid (Liddell and Solomon, 1977b).

Another assumption, transitivity, is generally conceded to be necessary for expectancy theories. Accordingly, if an outcome A is preferred to another outcome B, and B in turn is preferred to C, then A must be preferred to C. If this is not the case and C has greater valence than A, then intransitivity exists. To the extent that people actually think in intransitive terms, expectancy theory, with its strong reliance on rationality, is in trouble. Luckily for the theory, the best evidence currently available suggests that intransitivity is a relatively uncommon phenomenon (Liddell and Solomon, 1977a).

It seems appropriate to conclude that a number of rationality assumptions derived from decision theory do not represent necessary conditions for expectancy theories. If the theory works in the prediction of performance, effort expenditure, job satisfaction, occupational choice, and the like, then it is not necessary to give major attention to these considerations. To the extent that it fails to predict, such factors then become likely causes that require exploration.

Research Related to Performance and Satisfaction

The general emphasis of research during the 1970s has been on understanding why the earlier studies produced the results they did and on using that understanding to improve those results. In large part this has meant that measurement and design considerations have received the greatest attention.

Reliability of Measures. The early studies utilized rather simple (and often quite short) measures of the expectancy theory variables. Given the limited number of items per measure, one might have anticipated that there would be considerable concern over the reliability of the measures involved; this is particularly true since the use of unreliable measures hinders the identification of significant relationships, even when they are present. Yet most of the early studies do not report reliability information, and when it is reported, the results are not consistently encouraging. Galbraith and Cummings (1967) obtained a test-retest reliability of .80 for their instrumentality measure but only .50 for valence. Because of a lack of independence of measures, these figures are almost certainly inflated in an absolute sense; however, the difference between them appears stable. Graen (1969) reports equally variable reliabilities for his criterion measures of performance, with many of the values well below an acceptable level.

More recent research has been focused directly on the reliability issue. DeLeo and Pritchard (1974) report median reliability coefficients of .60 for valence, .52 for instrumentality, and .64 for expectancy measures. When different operational definitions of these variables (all drawn from the existing research literature) were compared, the evidence for construct validity was quite weak — .58 for valence, .46 for instrumentality, and only .10 for expectancy. It is apparent that different researchers are not always measuring the same things, even when they use the same terms.

A second study, also using repeat measurements over a short time span, obtained a median reliability figure for expectancy measures of .68 and for valence measures of .63 (Berger, 1976). In this and the preceding study, a number of low coefficients (below .50) were reported, while values above .85 were nonexistent.

These and other similar results (Mitchell, 1974) raise serious questions about the measures often used to test expectancy theories. They may well account for a number of the failures to support the theory. Furthermore, they suggest a reason why different components of the theory tend to emerge as the best predictors in different studies. The reliabilities for measures of different variables often vary considerably within a single investigation; this in turn should influence the predictive correlations. If valence is unreliable in a particular study relative to other measures, it should contribute relatively little to the predictions, while in another study with a highly reliable valence measure, it should contribute a great deal. Certainly such variations in predictive power from study to study do occur; they may well be a function of the reliabilities of the measures used.

Methods of Generating Outcomes. Most of the early studies utilized lists of outcomes developed by those conducting the research. In the case of the Georgopoulos, Mahoney, and Jones (1957) study, this list was pruned further with information provided by the subjects. In the Hackman and Porter (1968) study, outcomes generated by the service representatives themselves were used to develop a standard list; otherwise, the outcomes specified were entirely the product of the researchers.

This question of who should generate the outcomes and how long the list should be has been the subject of considerable discussion (Connolly, 1976; Mitchell, 1974). Various versions of the theory are primarily concerned with motivational processes rather than with the kinds of motivational contents emphasized in theories such as need hierarchy, achievement motivation, and motivation-hygiene. Thus, the question of what is a relevant outcome under given circumstances is left open. From a theoretical viewpoint, any outcome could be tried, since those that lack instrumentality or valence would reduce to zero in any event. Yet, the practicalities of research argue against the use of lengthy lists containing many outcomes that will prove to be irrelevant for most subjects. In the end, decisions in this area must be based on empirical evidence.

Data of this kind from two studies (Matsui and Ikeda, 1976; Oliver, 1974) are given in Table 6–3. In all instances expectancy theory predictions that were derived from a limited set of outcomes specified by each subject outperform the predictions made

Table 6–3. CORRELATIONS BETWEEN PREDICTORS DERIVED FROM EXPECTANCY THEORY AND CRITERIA USING SELF-GENERATED AND STANDARD OUTCOME LISTS

Criterion Measure	Subjects	Self-Generated Outcomes	Standard Outcome List
Effort — average daily hours on home work	High school students	.44	.28
Performance — grades on most recent exams	High school students	.36	.23
Performance — total six month sales volume	Life insurance agents	.27	.17
Performance — ratio of this volume to personal objective	Life insurance agents	.25	.14

Adapted from Tamao Matsui and Hiroshi Ikeda. Effectiveness of Self-Generated Outcomes for Improving Predictions in Expectancy Theory Research, *Organizational Behavior and Human Performance*, Vol. 17 (1976), p. 292; and Richard L. Oliver. Expectancy Theory Predictions of Salesmen's Performance, *Journal of Marketing Research*, Vol. 11 (1974), p. 249.

from a longer, entirely researcher established, standard list. These and other findings in the studies argue for the use of an individualized approach to outcome generation. However, one may wish to focus research attention on specific types of motivation, as Porter and Lawler (1968) did with pay as an outcome. In such cases, researcher designation of outcomes is entirely appropriate.

The Within Persons Problem. Vroom (1964, p. 19) states that "... people choose from among alternative acts, the one corresponding to the strongest positive (or weakest negative) force." The implication is that force values for various alternative acts should be computed for each subject; the highest would then be predicted to result in behavior. Yet the approach used in all of the early research (and much of the research since) has been to develop only one force prediction per subject and then run correlations with criterion measures across a number of subjects. In contrast to this typical across-subjects approach, the within-subjects procedure yields separate correlations between predicted force and criterion values for each subject. These latter correlations may then be averaged to get a composite measure.

In one case, college students provided separate expectancy theory measures and ratings of the effort they put into each course (the criterion) for all courses they were taking. The average predictor-criterion correlation was .52. In contrast, when the students provided the same data for only their 'course work in general' and a single correlation was computed across all subjects, the value was .31 (Muchinsky, 1977). In another study, life insurance sales representatives provided expectancy theory data on each of six different types of policies they could sell, and the resulting force predictions were correlated with the actual number of policies of each type sold in a given period for each representative. The average of these correlations was .50, well above the typical value of .25 to .35 obtained in across-subject analyses (Matsui, Kagawa, Nagamatsu, and Ohtsuka, 1977). It appears that the use of a within-person approach, which is consistent with most versions of the theory, does yield a higher level of theoretical confirmation.

The Establishment of Boundary Conditions. Of the early studies, the one by Graen (1969) contributes most toward establishing the boundaries or domain of expectancy theory. Graen concludes that if expectancy theory is to prove valid, there must be a clearly established contingency relationship (in the minds of the subjects) between attaining effective job performance and attaining desirable outcomes. This conclusion subsequently received considerable support from a study of employees in two manufacturing plants by Dachler and Mobley (1973), who reported the following:

> The fact that the pattern of results obtained from Plant 1 employees supported every prediction derived from the present VIE model, whereas the pattern of results from Plant 2 employees in nearly all cases did not bear out these predictions provides a strong argument for the possibility that certain organizational characteristics in Plant 2 acted as boundary conditions . . . the piece-rate system used in Plant 1 specified the contingencies between levels of performance and obtained salaries . . . employees in Plant 2 were not exposed to any incentive plan . . . the organizational conditions of Plant 1 were more structured, less complex, and more "assessable" so that it was easier to form accurate perceptions about the organizational conditions and contingencies as well as to accurately perceive how much they could actually achieve in the existing situation . . . 36 of 45 performance-outcome contingencies were stronger in Plant 1 (Dachler and Mobley, 1973, p. 415).

A later study by Reinharth and Wahba (1975) similarly indicates that expectancy theory predictions may prove valid in certain companies but totally invalid in others. This particular study does not permit further specification of the theory's appropriate domain. However, other multi-company research does (Kopelman, 1976; Kopelman and Thompson, 1976).

These latter studies were conducted using engineers as subjects, and expectancy theory measures were obtained twice, with a four-year interval between; three companies were involved. The data clearly indicate that motivational levels (as defined by expectancy and valence measures) were higher, and the relationships between motivation and performance closer, the more the company had established a "strong, concrete performance-reward contingency." Such contingencies exist when:

1. People are rewarded in proportion to the excellence of their performance.
2. Merit increase percentages are an accurate reflection of relative performance.
3. The promotion system helps the best person to the top.
4. Salary increases are viewed as based on performance.
5. Reward and recognition are given for good work.
6. People with ability have a promising future.

Again, it appears that expectancy theory only "works" where a context conducive to it has been created.

Research Related to Occupational Choices

Of the early studies only Vroom's (1966) deals with occupational choice. However, subsequent research has concentrated considerable attention on this area. It appears that the results are at least as good as those emerging from the performance and satisfaction research, and probably somewhat better (Mitchell and Beach, 1976). Not only are the correlations between expectancy variables and occupational decisions respectable, but the inconsistency of the results reported using performance-related criteria is not present among the occupational choice studies.

In Table 6–4 data related to business career choices are presented for college students majoring in either business or psychology (Bartol, 1976). The findings are given separately for the simple expectancy theory model and for an expanded model that includes variables similar to the role perceptions included in the Porter and Lawler (1968) performance model. In general, the expanded model, which takes into account the pressures experienced from family and peers, does a better job of predicting the choice of a business career but adds nothing in predicting attitudes toward business. Thus, these outside pressures appear to be focused primarily on whether one should elect to work in a business environment. Both kinds of predictions are more effective in predicting the attitudes of college males than of females.

The results of Table 6–4 deal with the anticipated, not actual, choice of an occupation. However, a study of the actual decisions made by senior naval officers regarding whether they would retire or not at the end of 20 years yields very similar results. Expectancy

Table 6–4. CORRELATIONS OF EXPECTANCY THEORY PREDICTIONS ALONE AND IN COMBINATION WITH FAMILY AND PEER PRESSURES WITH OCCUPATIONAL CHOICE AND ATTITUDE TOWARD BUSINESS

Predictors	College Student Sample	Choice of Business Occupation	Attitude Toward Business
Predictions from expectancy theory variables alone	Female	.38	.39
	Male	.38	.69
Predictions from expectancy theory plus family and peer expectations and their rated importance	Female	.64	.41
	Male	.54	.70

Adapted from Kathryn M. Bartol. Expectancy Theory as a Predictor of Female Occupational Choice and Attitude Toward Business, *Academy of Management Journal*, Vol. 19 (1976), p. 672.

theory predictions yielded a correlation of .42 with the fact of retirement (Parker and Dyer, 1976). In this instance also the addition of information on family pressures to the basic expectancy theory model increased this correlation.

THE RELATIONSHIP OF EXTRINSIC AND INTRINSIC MOTIVATION

One of the major extensions to expectancy theory proposed by Galbraith and Cummings (1967) involved the explicit differentiation of intrinsic outcomes from extrinsic outcomes and the specification of an additive relationship between the valences of these two outcomes. This formulation appears to be entirely consistent with Vroom's (1964) propositions. Yet subsequent theorizing and research has brought it into question.

DeCharms (1968) contends that the introduction of extrinsic reward (such as pay) for behavior that was previously intrinsically rewarding tends to decrease the overall level of motivation. This happens because the individual experiences a loss of control over his own behavior so that the pre-existing intrinsic motivation is sharply diminished. Similarly, the elimination of extrinsic rewards can operate to shift the perceived locus of causation of behavior from the external world into the self, thus liberating intrinsic motivation and increasing the overall motivational force. Hypotheses such as these do not fit the strictly additive assumption of expectancy theory.

Deci's Theory and Research

Deci has built upon the original formulations of deCharms and advanced a formal theory of the relationships between intrinsic and extrinsic motivation; he has also conducted considerable research to test his theory (Deci, 1975, 1976). The result must be considered a major threat to some of the basic tenets of expectancy theories.

The propositions set forth by Deci deal with the situation in which the pre-existing state of affairs is one of intrinsic motivation:

1. One process by which intrinsic motivation can be affected is a change in perceived locus of causality from internal to external (Subjects engaged in the behavior in order to feel competent and self-determining, but when rewards were introduced they began to perceive that they were performing the activity in order to make money). This will cause a decrease in intrinsic motivation and will occur, under certain circumstances, when someone receives extrinsic rewards for engaging in intrinsically motivated activities.

2. The second process by which intrinsic motivation can be affected is a change in feelings of competence and self-determination. If a person's feelings of competence and self-determination are enhanced, his intrinsic motivation will increase. If his feelings of competence and self-determination are diminished, his intrinsic motivation will decrease.

3. Every reward has two aspects, a controlling aspect and an informational aspect which provides the recipient with information about his competence and self-determination. The relative salience of the two aspects (external controlling and internal informational) determines which process (that of proposition 1 or that of proposition 2) will be operative. If the controlling aspect is more salient, it will initiate the change in perceived locus of causality process. If the informational aspect is more salient, the change in feelings of competence and self-determination process will be initiated (Deci, 1975, pp. 139–142).

To test these propositions Deci conducted a number of studies, primarily with college students in a laboratory context. The task was a puzzle that college students typically found intrinsically interesting. In the prototype experiment some of the students would work on the puzzles without any extrinsic reward and some would work with pay geared to their success levels (contingent reward). After the standard sessions, both groups of students were allowed free time with the puzzles. The amount of this free time that they used for puzzle solving was used as a measure of their remaining intrinsic motivation. The hypothesis was that those who received the extrinsic pay reward would experience diminished intrinsic motivation and thus spend less free time on the puzzles.

This hypothesis appeared to have been confirmed. A variety of different extrinsic factors were studied with much the same results. Deci interpreted his findings as follows:

> ... intrinsic motivation appears to be affected by two processes: a change in perceived locus of causality and a change in feelings of competence and self-actualization. Intrinsic motivation decreases when a person's behavior becomes dependent on extrinsic rewards such as money or the avoidance of punishment. It also decreases when a person receives negative feedback about his performance on an intrinsically motivated activity. But it increases as a result of positive feedback and interpersonal supportiveness (Deci, 1976, p. 70).

When pay is given merely for being present and is in no way tied to performance (thus is noncontingent), the effects on intrinsic motivation appear to be minimal.

Subsequent Research and Conclusions

Since Deci published his findings, a number of questions have been raised about both his interpretations of his data (Hamner and Foster, 1975) and the appropriateness of his statistical procedures (Farr, Vance, and McIntyre, 1977). It is apparent that well-controlled research can yield very similar results. Thus, Pritchard, Campbell, and Campbell (1977), using chess problems as the intrinsically motivated activity and comparing no-pay and pay-for-performance groups, found clear evidence of a decline in free time devoted to chess problems in the group working under extrinsic conditions even a week after the extrinsic reward had been experienced. Several extensive reviews of the research conducted to date show that the nonadditivity of extrinsic and intrinsic rewards is a real phenomenon that has been sufficiently established to at least partially refute expectancy theory in this area (deCharms and Muir, 1978; Jones and Mawhinney, 1977).

On the other hand, certain studies that depart from the Deci paradigm do not yield similar results. This was true for instance when performance level at familiar work, rather than free time expenditure, was used as a dependent variable (Hamner and Foster, 1975). Furthermore, very high intrinsic motivation levels appear to be quite resistant to the detrimental impacts of extrinsic factors (Arnold, 1976). In contrast the average intrinsic motivation level mobilized in Deci's research appears to have been only intermediate. Extrinsic rewards such as advancement and pay may not operate or be experienced in the same way in ongoing organizations as in the laboratory experiments (Dermer, 1975). Thus, a perception of stronger contingencies between the budget performance of department store managers and both advancement and pay was found to be associated with *higher* levels of reported intrinsic motivation. From the Deci results one might have expected that the presence of strong perceived extrinsic contingencies would have affected intrinsic motivation negatively, not positively.

The intrinsic-extrinsic problem is a product of the 1970s, and it is too early for knowledgeable conclusions. There has not been time for needed thought and research to accrue. However, as an interim conclusion, the position taken by Staw (1977, p. 76) appears to have considerable merit:

> The task for which external rewards are administered must be interesting, the rewards themselves must be salient, and there should be no preexisting norms for payment. Without these necessary conditions, one is more likely to find a reinforcement effect. The necessary conditions for the over justification effect (as that effect is stated by Deci) reduce its applicability to industrial work organizations. First, within industrial organizations, a large number of jobs are not inherently satisfying enough to foster high intrinsic interest. . . . Second, even when an industrial job is inherently interesting, there exists a powerful norm for extrinsic payment.

If research continues to support these conclusions, the phenomenon first identified in the Deci experiments may well turn out to be largely esoteric — real enough but having little pragmatic value for employing organizations. There simply may not be many instances outside the laboratory when it can occur. As noted in Chapter 1, findings from the laboratory require testing in the organizational context before they can be accepted.

SUGGESTED APPLICATIONS

Much of the writing and research on expectancy theories gives only fleeting attention, if any, to practical applications. The major exception to this generally nonpractice oriented approach is a series of statements about the administration of compensation and other reward systems initiated in the Porter and Lawler (1968) volume and continuing through a number of subsequent publications by Lawler (1971, 1973, 1974).

Expectancy Theory-Based Compensation and Reward

Four recommendations for practice grew out of the original Porter and Lawler research, although the fourth is not a direct derivative of the theory per se:

1. Companies should collect systematic information as to what employees want from their jobs (value of rewards or valence) and their perceived probabilities of obtaining rewards relative to the effort they put out. This information could then be used in designing reward systems.
2. Companies should make sure that employees understand the role prescriptions for their jobs so that efforts are not misdirected and thus wasted.
3. Companies should take steps to tie rewards to performance in the minds of employees (to establish perceived contingencies). This argues against giving pay increases across the board, cost of living raises, and also against incentive raises that are kept secret, thus preventing any relative evaluation of their value. It argues for:
   a. tailoring rewards to what the individual wants.
   b. giving more extrinsic rewards and more opportunities to obtain intrinsic rewards to superior performers than to inferior performers.
   c. permitting employees to see and believe that high performance results in high reward; thus, for example, secrecy about pay should be removed so that contingencies can be observed, and the best and most credible source of information should be used to evaluate performance, even to the point of obtaining peer- and self-ratings.
4. Continuously measure and monitor employee attitudes.

In his subsequent writings Lawler has placed particular emphasis on procedures that create performance-outcome contingencies and on individualized approaches that, among other things, adjust rewards to valent outcomes. His most unique contributions in these respects have been the emphasis on eliminating pay secrecy and a call for the use of "cafeteria" compensation systems, which permit employees to structure their own compensation (pay and benefits) packages to place the greatest relative emphasis on what they desire the most. This latter approach should help to maximize effort expenditure by focusing on outcomes that are anticipated to yield the most satisfaction.

The Advisability and Use of the Suggested Applications

The re-emphasis on tying pay to performance (as epitomized in various incentive pay and bonus plans) that has emerged from expectancy theories has faced its share of criticism, and a variety of arguments have been advanced against it (Meyer, 1975; Pinder, 1977). Some contend that expectancy theory has not yet met the test of research and that applications based on it are premature. Others view the processes involved as representing threats to human dignity and self-esteem.

Almost universally critics now point to Deci's research as evidence of the negative consequences of contingent extrinsic reward for intrinsic motivation. Deci (1976) himself advocates avoiding the creation of perceived performance contingencies in administering extrinsic rewards and using job enrichment and participative management to increase intrinsic motivation wherever possible. Ultimately the question is how the research on expectancy theory is to be viewed and interpreted, and this includes the research on intrinsic-extrinsic relationships. We will return to this issue in the next section.

Both the resort to an open pay policy and the use of an employee choice, "cafeteria" approach in allocating compensation dollars have met considerable resistance (Miner and Miner, 1977). Pay secrecy may well perform a useful function, at least when openness would result in increased feelings of inequity. There appears to be relatively little sentiment favoring an open policy, even among those who receive the greatest rewards. Cafeteria approaches face sizable obstacles, not only from the employing companies themselves because of increased administrative costs but also from the insurance companies who write group policies and from the Internal Revenue Service, which must decide what is and is not taxable income.

As to the actual adoption of these approaches, the evidence is mixed. There is little basis now for concluding that arguments from expectancy theory have produced much change in pay secrecy (Miner, 1974). Relatively few firms have a truly open policy, and a great many do not even make rate ranges available. The cafeteria approach has produced a certain amount of experimentation, and a number of attempts to move in this direction have been described in the literature (Miner and Miner, 1977). The cafeteria concept seems more likely to receive widespread acceptance than an open pay policy.

CONCLUSIONS

Perhaps because of its strong ties to prior theories of motivation and learning that have achieved widespread credence in psychology, expectancy theory has obtained considerable acceptance among students of organizational behavior. It is, however, primarily a theory for the scholar and the scientist rather than for the practitioner. This fact is manifested in the continued outpouring of expectancy theory research and the almost total lack of applications that can be clearly traced to the theory. It is becoming increasingly evident, though, that applications are possible and that they might well prove very fruitful.

Scientific Goals

Although a number of different versions of expectancy theory have been proposed, the core elements of all are very similar. Thus, the various versions do not appear to conflict with one another, and tests of any one version are in large part tests of all others.

These research tests have now yielded sufficient theoretical support so that it seems safe to conclude that expectancy theories are on the right track. They certainly do not explain all motivated behavior in all types of work organizations, but they do explain enough to be worth pursuing further. The early research was far from conclusive in that the theory often emerged as invalid in a specific context and even when validity was established the correlations tended to be low. Now, enough is known so that studies can be designed that will yield not only significant results but also correlations well above those in the .20s that plagued the early research.

As Graen (1969) first indicated, expectancy theory works best when contingencies can be established "in a concrete manner between effective job performance and attaining favorable role outcomes." In other words, people have to see that putting out effort to do what the job requires will give them what they want. When rewards are not so structured or existing performance-reward relationships are so ambiguous that they are not readily perceived, the theory appears to predict very little.

In addition to observing this boundary condition for the theory, a test also must utilize measures that are not only reliable but valid operationalizations of the theoretical variables. In the past these measurement requirements have not always been met, but it is now apparent that they can be met if sufficient attention is given to the selection or initial development of the measures. Furthermore, research that has utilized individualized outcome indexes tailored to the specific motives that have achieved salience or dominance for a given person has tended to yield higher correlations. So too has research that employs *within person* analyses to differentiate among various alternative behavior patterns.

It is apparent also that correlations can often be raised by including measures of variables that are extraneous to the basic expectancy theory formulations — for instance, the family and peer pressure indexes utilized in certain of the occupational choice studies. To do this certainly contributes to our overall understanding of human motivation; however, extending the research in this manner contributes little to our understanding of expectancy theory and of how and why its component variables work. There is a real risk that the expectancy concepts may become lost in a melange of other constructs so that true understanding of the basic theory is impaired (Miner and Dachler, 1973). It is important that research remain focused on central concepts such as valence, instrumentality, expectancy, outcome, effort (force), and the like.

Limitations of the Theory.   It appears that, given our current state of knowledge, the theory can consistently yield correlations with relevant independent criteria rising into the .50s. Relative to research on other motivational theories this is a sizable accomplishment; relative to explaining and predicting all of human behavior at work it leaves much to be accomplished. It is apparent that the theory simply fails to handle a number of aspects of human motivation.

Expectancy theory is a hedonistic, maximizing theory. To the extent that human motivation is neither hedonistic nor maximizing, and under many circumstances it appears to be neither, the theory simply will not work. Furthermore, expectancy theory presents a highly rational, conscious model of human motivation, and its measures (which are almost always of a self-report nature) reflect this fact. Whenever unconscious motives deflect human behavior from what a knowledge of conscious processes would predict, expectancy theory misses its mark. There is good reason to believe this is not an uncommon occurrence.

These appear to be the major limitations of current versions of expectancy theory as applied to the organizational work setting. Deci's (1975) arguments regarding the subtractive impact of extrinsic factors on intrinsic motivation may indicate other limitations. However, it is doubtful if this phenomenon has much practical relevance. Many jobs, such as those of a managerial, professional, and entrepreneurial nature, frequently appear to engage such high levels of intrinsic motivation that performance is impervious to any possible negative extrinsic impact. Also, some kind of explicit or implicit inducement-contribution contract involving extrinsic inducements including pay is the prevailing norm in the world of work, and under such circumstances the phenomenon described by Deci on the current evidence does not appear to operate.

Another limitation that has been proposed is the failure of expectancy theories to handle assumptions derived from formal decision theory. Yet it is apparent that expectancy theory does yield valid results sufficiently often to raise serious questions about these criticisms. It is important to understand that the critics are not contending that expectancy theory is logically inconsistent within itself, but rather that when it is extended to include the decision theory assumptions it is incorrect as a descriptive theory. However, a number of these assumptions, although perhaps necessary to a normative theory, are not required to achieve valid descriptions of human motivation and sound predictions.

Whatever certain of the major theorists such as Vroom (1964) may have originally implied, it does not now seem necessary to add much of the "excess baggage" of decision theory to the expectancy theory propositions. It would appear much more fruitful to concentrate on understanding how expectancy formulations can work as well as they do.

Expectancy Theory and Equity Theory.   It would certainly appear that some of the concepts and research from equity theory, especially in the area of overreward inequity, are distinctly in conflict with expectancy theory. Under certain circumstances equity theory predicts (and the research seems to substantiate) that people do not strive to maximize rewards.

This problem has been given some attention by expectancy theorists (Campbell and Pritchard, 1976; Lawler, 1968b). Their position is that the equity theory results can be incorporated within the larger framework of expectancy theory if certain assumptions are made regarding the way valences are formed or operate. In discussing this matter Lawler (1968b, p. 609) says:

> There are two ways in which equity can come into play as a determinant of the valence of certain rewards. One way concerns the possibility that increasingly large piece-rate rewards could have a decreasing valence for subjects. That is, rewards that are seen as too large, and therefore inequitable, may have a lower valence than rewards which are perceived as equitable. A second point concerns the effect of the amount of a reward that has been received on the valence of additional amounts of the reward. It seems reasonable that once a perceived equitable level of rewards has been achieved future rewards will have lower valences.

Formulations of this kind, whatever their attractiveness, are clearly post hoc. Expectancy theory is completely silent on what effects of this kind would be predicted, while equity theory is quite explicit. That certain phenomena can possibly be explained within a certain theoretical orientation does not mean that they are best explained in that manner. It would seem most appropriate to view the two theories as separate and distinct but with partially overlapping domains. This conclusion is reinforced by the fact that when equity and expectancy theories are tested together they tend to emerge as complementary, with each expanding the predictive power of the other (Dansereau, Cashman, and Graen, 1973; Klein, 1973). In fact there is a possibility that the behavior of certain kinds of people may be best predicted from expectancy theory, and that of others from equity theory.

Managerial Goals

Suppose one wanted to use expectancy theory to produce a highly motivated employee work force. What should one do? For one thing, conditions should be established that emphasize performance-outcome contingencies and make them highly visible, thus operating within the boundaries of the theory. These conditions have been described by Dachler and Mobley (1973) and by Kopelman (1976). In many respects they are consistent with the original recommendations made by Porter and Lawler (1968) regarding applications. Although complete openness regarding pay and cafeteria compensation procedures can contribute to creating an optimal environment for expectancy theory, there is ample evidence that the theory can work in contexts in which neither is present. Thus, if the use of these approaches does not seem feasible, it should still be possible to structure a situation in which contingencies are clear and valent outcomes attainable.

In certain respects the highly rationalized organization that expectancy theory demands seems comparable to the ideal bureaucracy of organizational theory. Yet writers such as Mitchell (1973) have allied expectancy theory with participative management. Either form can probably be compatible with expectancy theory, provided decisions are made in some manner, and those decisions emphasize performance-reward contingencies. It would appear that such decisions might be somewhat easier to obtain in the hierarchic context of a bureaucracy but that if such contingencies do emerge from participative processes, the latter will facilitate the kind of information exchange that causes the contingencies to be widely recognized.

Creating the conditions required by expectancy theory may have certain negative side effects, as indicated by Meyer (1975) and Deci (1976). The extent to which these effects can be expected is uncertain, although their possibility should be recognized. It does appear, however, that some of these problems can be handled by selecting employees who are likely to have high scores on the various expectancy theory measures and who thus will bring a maximal amount of effort or force to the work context. Such individuals should be most responsive to a situation within the domain of expectancy theory and least susceptible to any detrimental side effects.

A rather sizable body of research indicates that the people who bring the most motivational energy to their work (as that energy is determined from expectancy theory) are those generally referred to as internals. These people believe that events in their lives are largely subject to their own influence; in contrast, externals see themselves as largely at the mercy of fate, luck, and more powerful individuals. Given the rational, hedonistic emphasis of expectancy theory, it is not surprising that internals tend to emerge as strongly motivated in these terms. The research consistently yields this result (Broedling, 1975; Lied and Pritchard, 1976; Szilagyi and Sims, 1975). Accordingly, it should be possible through the use of a measure of internality to select people who perform best in the expectancy context.

Unfortunately there is no research comparing productivity figures for a deliberately structured expectancy theory context staffed with the appropriate types of people with similar figures for a control condition. One would expect a sizable advantage for the expectancy theory approach, even with the theory's limitations, given the convergence of the research evidence. However, the crucial application experiment remains to be performed.

References

Arnold, Hugh J. Effects of Performance Feedback and Extrinsic Reward upon High Intrinsic Motivation, *Organizational Behavior and Human Performance*, Vol. 17 (1976), 275–288.

Atkinson, John W. Motivation for Achievement, In T. Blass (ed.), *Personality Variables in Social Behavior*. Hillsdale, N.J.: Earlbaum Associates, 1977, pp. 25–108.

Bartol, Kathryn M. Expectancy Theory as a Predictor of Female Occupational Choice and Attitude Toward Business, *Academy of Management Journal*, Vol. 19 (1976), 669–675.

Behling, Orlando and Frederick A. Starke. The Postulates of Expectancy Theory, *Academy of Management Journal*, Vol. 16 (1973), 373–388.

Berger, Chris J. Reliability and Validity of Expectancy Theory Constructs, *Academy of Management Proceedings*, (1976), pp. 74–78.

Broedling, Laurie A. Relationship of Internal-External Control to Work Motivation and Performance in an Expectancy Model, *Journal of Applied Psychology*, Vol. 60 (1975), 65–70.

Campbell, John P. and Robert D. Pritchard. Motivation Theory in Industrial and Organizational Psychology, In Marvin D. Dunnette (ed.), *Handbook of Industrial and Organizational Psychology*. Chicago: Rand, McNally, 1976, pp. 63–130.

Connolly, Terry. Some Conceptual and Methodological Issues in Expectancy Models of Work Performance Motivation, *Academy of Management Review*, Vol. 1, No. 4 (1976), 37–47.

Dachler, H. Peter and William H. Mobley. Construct Validation of an Instrumentality - Expectancy - Task Goal Model of Work Motivation: Some Theoretical Boundary Conditions, *Journal of Applied Psychology Monograph*, Vol. 58 (1973), 397–418.

Dansereau, Fred, James Cashman, and George Graen. Instrumentality Theory and Equity Theory as Complementary Approaches in Predicting the Relationship of Leadership and Turnover Among Managers, *Organizational Behavior and Human Performance*, Vol. 10 (1973), 184–200.

deCharms, Richard. *Personal Causation: The Internal Affective Determinants of Behavior.* New York: Academic Press, 1968.

deCharms, Richard and Marion S. Muir. Motivation: Social Approaches, *Annual Review of Psychology*, Vol. 29 (1978), 91–113.

Deci, Edward L. *Intrinsic Motivation.* New York: Plenum, 1975.

Deci, Edward L. The Hidden Costs of Rewards, *Organizational Dynamics*, Vol. 4, No. 3 (1976), 61–72.

DeLeo, Philip J. and Robert D. Pritchard. An Examination of Some Methodological Problems in Testing Expectancy-Valence Models with Survey Techniques, *Organizational*

Behavior and Human Performance, Vol. 12 (1974), 143–148.

Dermer, Jerry, The Interrelationship of Intrinsic and Extrinsic Motivation, *Academy of Management Journal*, Vol. 18 (1975), 125–129.

Farr, James L., Robert J. Vance, and Robert M. McIntyre. Further Examinations of the Relationship Between Reward Contingency and Intrinsic Motivation, *Organizational Behavior and Human Performance*, Vol. 20 (1977), 31–53.

Galbraith, Jay R. *Organization Design*. Reading, Mass.: Addison-Wesley, 1977.

Galbraith, Jay and Larry L. Cummings. An Empirical Investigation of the Motivational Determinants of Task Performance: Interactive Effects between Instrumentality-Valence and Motivation-Ability, *Organizational Behavior and Human Performance*, Vol. 2 (1967), 237–257.

Georgopoulos, Basil S., Gerald M. Mahoney, and Nyle W. Jones. A Path-Goal Approach to Productivity, *Journal of Applied Psychology*, Vol. 41 (1957), 345–353.

Graen, George. Instrumentality Theory of Work Motivation: Some Experimental Results and Suggested Modifications. *Journal of Applied Psychology Monograph*, Vol. 53, No. 2 (1969).

Hackman, J. Richard and Lyman W. Porter. Expectancy Theory Predictions of Work Effectiveness, *Organizational Behavior and Human Performance*, Vol. 3 (1968), 417–426.

Hamner, W. Clay and Lawrence W. Foster. Are Intrinsic and Extrinsic Rewards Additive? A Test of Deci's Cognitive Evaluation Theory of Task Motivation, *Organizational Behavior and Human Performance*, Vol. 14 (1975), 398–415.

Jones, W. David and Thomas C. Mawhinney. In Interaction of Extrinsic Rewards and Intrinsic Motivation: A Review and Suggestions for Future Research, *Academy of Management Proceedings*, (1977), pp. 62–65.

Klein, Stuart M. Pay Factors as Predictors to Satisfaction: A Comparison of Reinforcement, Equity, and Expectancy, *Academy of Management Journal*, Vol. 16 (1973), 598–610.

Kopelman, Richard E. Organizational Control System Responsiveness, Expectancy Theory Constructs, and Work Motivation: Some Interrelations and Causal Connections, *Personnel Psychology*, Vol. 29 (1976), 205–220.

Kopelman, Richard E. and Paul H. Thompson. Boundary Conditions for Expectancy Theory Predictions of Work Motivation and Job Performance, *Academy of Management Journal*, Vol. 19 (1976), 237–258.

Lawler, Edward E. A Correlational-Causal Analysis of the Relationship between Expectancy Attitudes and Job Performance, *Journal of Applied Psychology*, Vol. 52 (1968a), 462–468.

Lawler, Edward E. Equity Theory as a Predictor of Productivity and Work Quality, *Psychological Bulletin*, Vol. 70 (1968b), 596–610.

Lawler, Edward E. *Pay and Organizational Effectiveness: A Psychological View*. New York: McGraw-Hill, 1971.

Lawler, Edward E. *Motivation in Work Organizations*. Monterey, Calif.: Brooks/Cole, 1973.

Lawler, Edward E. The Individualized Organization: Problems and Promise, *California Management Review*, Vol. 17, No. 2 (1974), 31–39.

Lawler, Edward E. and Lyman W. Porter. Antecedent Attitudes of Effective Managerial Performance, *Organizational Behavior and Human Performance*, Vol. 2 (1967), 122–142.

Liddell, William W. and Robert J. Solomon. A Total and Stochastic Test of the Transitivity Postulate Underlying Expectancy Theory, *Organizational Behavior and Human Performance*, Vol. 19 (1977a), 311–324.

Liddell, William W. and Robert J. Solomon. A Critical Reanalysis of 'A Test of Two Postulates Underlying Expectancy Theory.' *Academy of Management Journal*, Vol. 20 (1977b), 460–464.

Lied, Terry L. and Robert D. Pritchard. Relationships Between Personality Variables and Components of the Expectancy-Valence Model, *Journal of Applied Psychology*, Vol. 61 (1976), 463–467.

Locke, Edwin A. Personnel Attitudes and Motivation, *Annual Review of Psychology*, Vol. 26 (1976), 457–480.

Matsui, Tamao and Hiroshi Ikeda. Effectiveness of Self-Generated Outcomes for Improving Predictions in Expectancy Theory Research, *Organizational Behavior and Human Performance*, Vol. 17 (1976), 289–298.

Matsui, Tamao, Makoto Kagawa, Jun Nagamatsu, and Yoshie Ohtsuka. Validity of Expectancy Theory as a Within-Person Behavioral Choice Model for Sales Activities, *Journal of Applied Psychology*, Vol. 62 (1977), 764–767.

Meyer, Herbert H. The Pay-for-Performance Dilemma, *Organizational Dynamics*, Vol. 3, No. 3 (1975), 39–50.

Miner, John B. and H. Peter Dachler. Personnel Attitudes and Motivation, *Annual Review of Psychology*, Vol. 24 (1973), 379–402.

Miner, Mary Green. Pay Policies: Secret or Open? And Why? *Personnel Journal*, Vol. 53 (1974), 110–115.

Miner, Mary Green and John B. Miner. *Policy Issues in Contemporary Personnel and Industrial Relations.* New York: Macmillan, 1977.

Mitchell, Terence R. Motivation and Participation: An Integration, *Academy of Management Journal*, Vol. 16 (1973), 670–679.

Mitchell, Terence R. Expectancy Models of Job Satisfaction, Occupational Preference, and Effort: A Theoretical, Methodological, and Empirical Appraisal, *Psychological Bulletin*, Vol. 81 (1974), 1053–1077.

Mitchell, Terence R. Expectancy and Expected Value: Decision Models for Organizations, *Organization and Administrative Sciences*, Vol. 8 (1977), 97–115.

Mitchell, Terence R. and Lee Roy Beach. A Review of Occupational Preference and Choice Research Using Expectancy Theory and Decision Theory, *Journal of Occupational Psychology*, Vol. 49 (1976), 231–248.

Muchinsky, Paul M. A Comparison of Within-and Across-Subjects Analyses of the Expectancy-Valence Model for Predicting Effort, *Academy of Management Journal*, Vol. 20 (1977), 154–158.

Oliver, Richard L. Expectancy Theory Predictions of Salesmen's Performance, *Journal of Marketing Research*, Vol. 11 (1974), 243–253.

Parker, Donald F. and Lee Dyer. Expectancy Theory as a Within-Person Behavioral Choice Model: An Empirical Test of Some Conceptual and Methodological Refinements, *Organizational Behavior and Human Performance*, Vol. 17 (1976), 97–117.

Pinder, Craig C. Concerning the Application of Human Motivation Theories in Organizational Settings, *Academy of Management Review*, Vol. 2 (1977), 384–397.

Porter, Lyman W. and Edward E. Lawler. *Managerial Attitudes and Performance.* Homewood, Ill.: Irwin, 1968.

Pritchard, Robert D., Kathleen M. Campbell, and Donald J. Campbell. Effects of Extrinsic Financial Rewards on Intrinsic Motivation, *Journal of Applied Psychology*, Vol. 62 (1977), 9–15.

Reinharth, Leon and Mahmoud A. Wahba. Expectancy Theory as a Predictor of Work Motivation, Effort Expenditure, and Job Performance, *Academy of Management Journal*, Vol. 18 (1975), 520–537.

Staw, Barry M. Motivation in Organizations: Toward Synthesis and Redirection, *In* Barry M. Staw and Gerald R. Salancik, (eds.), *New Directions in Organizational Behavior.* Chicago: St. Clair, 1977, pp. 55–95.

Szilagyi, Andrew D. and Henry P. Sims. Locus of Control and Expectancies Across Multiple Occupational Levels, *Journal of Applied Psychology*, Vol. 60 (1975). 638–640.

Tolman, Edward C. *Purposive Behavior in Animals and Men.* New York: Appleton-Century-Crofts, 1932.

Vroom, Victor H. *Some Personality Determinants of the Effects of Participation.* Englewood Cliffs, N.J.: Prentice-Hall, 1960.

Vroom, Victor H. Ego-Involvement, Job Satisfaction, and Job Performance, *Personnel Psychology*, Vol. 15 (1962), 159–177.

Vroom, Victor H. *Work and Motivation.* New York: Wiley, 1964.

Vroom, Victor H. Organizational Choice: A Study of Pre- and Postdecision Processes, *Organizational Behavior and Human Performance*, Vol. 1 (1966), 212–225.

Vroom, Victor H. and Edward L. Deci. The Stability of Post-Decision Dissonance: A Follow-up Study of the Job Attitudes of Business School Graduates, *Organizational Behavior and Human Performance*, Vol. 6 (1971), 36–49.

Wahba, Mahmoud A. and Robert J. House. Expectancy Theory in Work and Motivation: Some Logical and Methodological Issues, *Human Relations*, Vol. 27 (1974), 121–147.

7

GOAL SETTING THEORY AND MANAGEMENT BY OBJECTIVES

In this chapter the discussion focuses on two motivational approaches that are conceptually similar but have emerged through distinctly dissimilar historical paths. In previous treatments it has been the pattern to consider theories first and then applications that developed from them, as was done for instance, with achievement motivation training. However, goal setting theory, although it has produced more direct applications of its own, did not spawn the most widely utilized application of its underlying principles—management by objectives (MBO). Management by objectives preceded the more recent and most fully developed formulation of goal setting theory by a number of years. MBO and goal setting theory now have converged, to their mutual benefit, with the former thus acquiring a theoretical base and the latter being a very popular arena of application.

Modern goal setting theory, although it has multiple historical origins, probably owes most to the formulations of Kurt Lewin (1935, 1938). Lewin's views resulted in a sizable amount of research on the determinants of the level of aspiration (or goal setting) as a dependent variable (Lewin, Dembo, Festinger, and Sears, 1944). The current resurgence of interest in this area (dating from the middle 1960s) delves into the *effects* of goal setting on performance (Locke, 1966a).

Management by objectives, in contrast, dates its current popularity to Drucker's (1954) writings and to a later article by McGregor (1957). Its historical antecedents, however, may be traced back through the classical and scientific management literature and through management practice to the early 1900s, especially as the literature and practice deal with planning and its related activities (LaFollette and Fleming, 1977).

LOCKE'S THEORY OF GOAL SETTING

The discussion here focuses primarily on the theory of goal setting that has been developed by Edwin Locke, now a professor at the University of Maryland. There are a number of reasons for this choice. Foremost is the fact that Locke's views have attracted considerable attention, predominantly in the academic world at first, but now increasingly among practitioners. In addition, much research has been conducted by both Locke and others bearing on his formulations. Whether these formulations should be considered a true motivational theory is open to some question. At one time Locke considered such a designation appropriate, but more recently he states, "Goal-setting is more appropriately viewed as a motivational technique rather than as a formal theory of motivation, despite previous suggestions to the contrary" (Locke, 1975, p. 465). In any event, the Locke hypotheses come closer to representing a viable theory than any other formulations in this particular area.

It should be recognized, however, that Locke's thinking is strongly intertwined with that of Thomas Ryan (1970). Although

Ryan's views on the significant role that intentions play in human behavior were not formally published until 1970, they were available in an earlier mimeographed version in 1964. Locke was exposed to these views as a graduate student at Cornell (where Ryan was on the faculty) well before that time. Locke acknowledges his debt to Ryan in numerous publications. Thus, goal setting theory or technique, in its basic concepts, is very much a joint product of these two people.

The Early Research-Guiding Hypotheses

The first theoretical statements appear in published versions of Locke's doctoral dissertation. Initially the stated research objective was merely to determine "how the level of intended achievement is related to actual level of achievement" (Locke, 1966a, p. 60), although there was an implicit hypothesis that higher levels of intended achievement would contribute to higher levels of performance. Soon thereafter this hypothesis was made explicit, with the added proviso that when an individual had *specific* goals or standards of performance to meet, the performance effects would be more pronounced than when specific goals were lacking (as with the instruction "do your best") (Locke and Bryan, 1966a).

In another paper this hypothesis regarding the superiority of specific over ambiguous goals was extended to task interest. "It was hypothesized ... that working toward a determinate goal would lead to a higher level of task interest than would be the case with an abstract goal such as do your best" (Locke and Bryan, 1967, p. 121). Thus, the presence of specific hard goals should reduce boredom at work.

This emphasis on the significant motivational effects of specific goals that are difficult to achieve was extended to explain various other motivational phenomena. The first such extrapolation was to the area of knowledge of results or feedback on the effectiveness of performance. More specifically, it was hypothesized that knowledge of results achieves its motivational effects through the incorporating of goal setting and that in the absence of such performance intentions, knowledge of results does not contribute to the level of work output (Locke and Bryan, 1966b).

The highly popular Parkinson's Law (1957) is also explained as a goal setting phenomenon (Bryan and Locke, 1967a). This law indicates that work expands to fill the time available for its completion; more generally it can be hypothesized that "effort (or work pace) is adjusted to the perceived difficulty of the task undertaken." This process is said to be mediated by goal setting, and accordingly a goal setting process is assumed to intervene between task perception and actual performance. The following quote not only explains how this might occur but also provides a first glimpse of the broader theoretical framework that emerged later:

> ... adjustment (of effort to difficulty level) requires first that the subject perceive the task, that he be conscious of the fact that there is a task to be performed and that he have some idea or knowledge of what the task requires of him. Then, depending upon the situation and the individual's perception of it in relation to his own values, he will set himself a goal or standard in terms of which he will regulate and evaluate his performance.... This goal-setting procedure can vary widely in the degree to which it is conscious or subconscious, explicit or implicit ... but once the goal is set, it is argued that effort and performance level will be regulated by and with reference to this goal (Bryan and Locke, 1967a, p. 260).

A similar explanation in terms of goal setting is applied to the relationships between monetary incentives and work performance. The specific hypotheses are:

1. Goals and intentions will be related to behavior regardless of incentive conditions; that is goals and intentions will be related to behavior both within and across different incentive conditions.
2. When incentive differences do correlate with behavior differences, these differences will be accompanied by corresponding differences in goals and intentions.
3. When goal or intention differences are controlled or partialed out, there will be no relationship between incentive condition and behavior (Locke, Bryan, and Kendall, 1968, p. 106).

More Comprehensive Formulations

The theoretical statements considered to this point were all presented as hypotheses that were tested immediately in research. However, beginning in 1968 Locke began a series of attempts to pull his ideas together within a more comprehensive framework. That seven years later he still had serious doubts as to whether these efforts had amounted to a true theory does not deny the fact that something more than a set of loosely related first-order hypotheses was achieved.

Clearly the formulations Locke presents are limited in various respects (Locke, 1968a). Little attention is given to the developmental causes of particular goals, and thus to why a person comes to try consciously to do what he does. Furthermore, goals are viewed as having significance for performance only to the extent that they are actually accepted by the individual; thus the theory is one of accepted or internalized goals. Very difficult goals might well fail to achieve acceptance, and if this were the case the positive relationship between goal difficulty and performance would no longer be expected to hold. On almost any task there is a hypothetical level of difficulty beyond which goal acceptance will not occur. At this point a boundary condition of the theory has been reached. One of the key reasons monetary incentives work with regard to performance levels is that they contribute to task and goal acceptance, or commitment.

In the early statements, goal setting was introduced as an explanation not only of the effects of monetary incentives but also of knowledge of results and variations in available time. Later this list was expanded to several additional areas (Locke, 1968a, 1970b). The performance effects of participative management are attributed in part to explicit or implicit goal setting. Competition is viewed as a case in which the performance of others serves to establish goals that arouse individuals to higher levels of performance. Praise and reproof may well induce people to set hard performance goals, although it is apparent also that this need not necessarily occur; the theory is not specific as to when, under such circumstances, hard or easy goals will emerge.

Goals have two major attributes — content and intensity. Content refers to the nature of the activity or end sought. Intensity relates to the level of importance of the goal to the person. Goal content exerts a primarily directive influence, and it also serves to regulate energy expenditure because different goals require different amounts of effort. Goal intensity can also influence both the direction and level of effort. Important goals are more likely to be accepted, to elicit commitment, and thus to foster persistent striving.

Job Satisfaction.   The theory treats job satisfaction in the short range as a function of the size of the perceived discrepancy between intended and actual performance. Goal achievement leads to the pleasurable emotional state we call satisfaction; failure to achieve a goal leads to the unpleasurable state of dissatisfaction (Locke, 1969, 1970a).

However, job satisfaction is usually viewed in a wider context than individual goal accomplishment. In this broader context abstract job values serve in the manner of goals. "Job satisfaction and dissatisfaction are a function of the perceived relationship between what one wants from one's job and what one perceives it as offering or entailing" (Locke, 1969, p. 316). *Values* establish what one wants. Like the more immediate goals, they are characterized by content and intensity (importance). Thus the achievement of more important values (financial security, for instance) will yield greater satisfaction, and the same value-percept discrepancy will produce more dissatisfaction if the value is important than if it is not. Beyond these directional hypotheses, the theory does not indicate in specific detail the relationships involving values, discrepancies, importance, and satisfaction-dissatisfaction. It does, however, view job satisfaction as primarily a product or outcome of goal or value-directed effort, and thus a consequence of performance.

The Theoretical Model. Locke, Cartledge, and Knerr (1970) have proposed a theoretical model to explain how the various types of variables specified in Locke's theoretical formulations interact:

existents⟶ cognition⟶ emotional⟶ goal⟶ action
(such as in- (evaluation   reactions   setting
centives or   against
previous   values)
outcomes)

The most immediate determinant of action is the individual's goal. External incentives influence action through their impact on the individual's goals. Emotional reactions result from evaluations in which the person cognitively compares the existents against standards established by relevant values.

As an example of how these processes work, let us take an examination situation:

existent:⟶ cognition:⟶ emotion:⟶ goal:⟶ action:
grade of C+ C+ evaluated dissatis-   improve improved
             as too low   faction   on next examination
             relative to   exami-   performance
             B value   nation
             standard

Improved performance should result ultimately in greater satisfaction.

Locke, Cartledge, and Knerr (1970) also extend this basic model to include anticipated existents and emotions as well as the judged instrumentality of anticipated goals. Subgoal attainment is valued to the extent it is seen as instrumental for an overall goal. Although these formulations regarding anticipatory states and subgoals add a degree of complexity to the model, they are nevertheless handled within the basic framework discussed above.

LOCKE'S PRIMARILY LABORATORY STUDIES

As previously noted Locke's formal theoretical statements emerged gradually and were intertwined closely with his research. This might represent a major problem in evaluating the theory against these research results were it not for several considerations. One is that Locke appears to have operated from an implicit theory that influenced the design of his research and the selection of research topics from the beginning, long before he made this theory explicit; this implicit theory clearly owes much to Ryan. Second, Locke has typically conducted many studies in each area he has investigated, thus replicating his results several times. Accordingly the theoretical hypotheses cannot be dismissed on the grounds that they incorporate empirical fluctuations attributable to chance on an ad hoc basis.

Research Focused on Performance

An initial series of studies utilized brainstorming tasks in which subjects were to list objects or things that could be described by a given adjective, or to give possible uses for certain objects (Locke, 1966a). Goal levels (easy or hard) typically were set by the experimenter, and performance was measured in terms of numbers of objects or uses noted in a given time period over a number of trials. The subjects were all college students.

Performance was consistently higher when harder goals existed. This was true even when the goals were set so high that they could actually be reached less than 10 per cent of the time. In the one instance when subjects were permitted to set their own goals, they chose relatively easy ones, and their performance reflected this.

A similar experiment was conducted later using a complex psychomotor task involving adjusting certain controls to produce a pattern of lights to match a standard. The more matches achieved in a set time period the better the performance (Locke and Bryan, 1966a). Comparisons were made between the results achieved when specific, hard goals were set by the experimenter and those achieved when the student subjects were merely told to do their best. The results provided strong support for the hypothesis that specific hard goals improve performance.

These results were extended to various clerical tasks of a numerical nature in another series of studies (Locke and Bryan, 1967). In this instance subject acceptance of goals was essential for goal setting effects to occur. In certain instances when post-experimental questions indicated that subjects had not accepted the specific, hard goals assigned, performance was not superior. The introduction of a monetary incentive appears to have been effective in gaining the necessary commitment in one study, although other studies were able to produce similar results without incentives. Data obtained with an interest questionnaire indicated that subjects working for hard goals were significantly less bored than subjects working without specific goals. These findings are consistent with numerous reports from industrial contexts that goal setting can function as an antidote to boredom.

Comparisons of initially highly motivated subjects who did not set goals with low motivation subjects who did (in terms of performance on numerical tasks) indicate that almost complete convergence can be expected over time (Bryan and Locke, 1967b). The introduction of specific, hard goals dramatically improved the performance of the initially less motivated subjects.

Practically all of Locke's studies utilized college student subjects working on laboratory tasks. A partial exception occurred in one instance when performance of college students was measured in terms of course grades (Locke and Bryan, 1968a). The basic design called for obtaining goal statements early in the semester and relating these to accomplishments at the end of the semester (both in terms of grades). The results obtained for a history course, which are typical, are given in Table 7–1. It is apparent that regardless of the exact method of goal setting, higher goals lead to higher grades. This result was obtained not within the relatively short time span of the typical laboratory experiment but over a semester of more than four months. Furthermore, it is apparent from Table 7–1 that although trying to reach a harder goal yields better performance, this occurs at the expense of sharply reduced probabilities of actually reaching the goal.

A final series of studies focuses not on the energizing function of goals but on the manner in which they direct effort to certain aspects of a task (Locke and Bryan, 1969a). The tasks used were a routine numerical calculation and driving a car around a standard course. In the first instance, the effects of quality versus quantity goals were investigated. In the latter the effects of instructions to reduce either steering or accelerator reversals were studied. In both the results were clear. Directive goals that focused on specific parameters of the tasks did indeed tend to influence performance on those parameters, but not others.

Research Dealing with Motivational Phenomena

For a number of years Locke has attempted to utilize his goal setting formulations to explain the results of other thrusts in mo-

Table 7–1. OBTAINED GRADES AND PROBABILITY OF SUCCESS IN REACHING
GRADE GOALS IN A HISTORY COURSE FOR STUDENTS WITH
DIFFERENT GOALS

Method of Setting Goal	Grade Goal Indicated	Mean Obtained Grade*	Mean Probability of Reaching or Exceeding Grade Goal
Grade hopes to make	C	2.0	.77
	B	2.4	.43
	A	2.9	.26
Grade expects to make	D	1.5	1.00
	C	2.2	.89
	B	2.7	.58
	A	3.4	.50
Minimum grade would be satisfied with	D	1.9	1.00
	C	2.4	.96
	B	2.9	.70
	A	3.1	.40
Grade actually tried for	C	2.2	.70
	B	2.3	.35
	A	2.9	.24

*Computed on a scale of:
   D = 1
   C = 2
   B = 3
   A = 4

Adapted from Edwin A. Locke and Judith F. Bryan. Grade Goals as Determinants of Academic Achievement, *Journal of General Psychology*, Vol. 79 (1968), p. 225.

tivational research and (on occasion) to explain the results derived from other motivational theories. His actual research, however, has dealt only with knowledge of results, time durations, and monetary incentives.

Knowledge of Results. Studies of the extent to which findings usually attributed to knowledge of results can be explained in goal setting terms have been a major focus of Locke's research program (Locke, 1966b, 1967, 1968b; Locke and Bryan, 1966b, 1968b, 1969b). In addition he has written a major review on this topic (Locke, Cartledge, and Koeppel, 1968). The conclusions presented in the latter publication provide an overall statement of the experimental results:

> The present review found none of the evidence to be inconsistent with the notion that the effects of motivational knowledge of results depend upon the goals a subject sets in response to such knowledge. Most previous studies failed to separate the effects of knowledge qua knowledge from those of goal setting. . . . When the two effects are separated, there is no effect of knowledge of results over and above that which can be attributed to differential goal setting (Locke, Cartledge, and Koeppel, 1968, p. 482).

In experimental terms this means that if subjects set specific, hard goals, they obtain results similar to those obtained in many studies of knowledge of results; when the goals are less specific and easier, the results approximate a knowledge of results condition from which goal setting has been explicitly excluded. All the studies used college student subjects in a laboratory context. The tasks were primarily clerical and required numerical skills, although in certain instances the range of activities was extended (to psychomotor reaction times, for instance).

In a typical experiment college student subjects solved a large number of addition problems (Locke and Bryan, 1969b). Subjects were assigned to one of four groups to equalize ability they exhibited during a preliminary trial period:

1. *No knowledge of scores and easy goals.* Subjects were not told how many problems they had completed or how many they had done correctly at any time, and their goal levels were established at two-thirds of what they accomplished in the trial period.
2. *No knowledge of scores and hard goals.* The same as above except that goal levels were established at the same level as the subject achieved in the trial period.
3. *Knowledge of scores and easy goals.* Subjects were given the number of problems completed at frequent intervals and the number correct at the end of each of the five trials; goals were set as in 1 above.
4. *Knowledge of scores and hard goals.* The same as 3 above except that goals were set as in 2 above.

When the results were analyzed statistically it was found that hard goals produced a larger number of problems completed than easy goals, regardless of the amount of knowledge of scores. However, no such differences in problems completed were found when knowledge of score and no knowledge conditions were compared. The level of goal setting, rather than knowledge of results per se, provided the major explanation of the findings.

Parkinson's Law.   The research on Parkinson's Law and the effects of different time limits on work performance also utilized college students solving addition problems in a laboratory setting (Bryan and Locke, 1967a). Comparisons were made between an excess time condition and a minimum time condition with the difficulty of the task held constant. The subjects in the excess time conditions actually expanded the time they took to complete the assigned problems over several trials to the point where they were taking significantly longer than the minimum time subjects setting harder goals. Also it was found that even with the same goals, the excess time subjects worked at a slower rate.

These findings are interpreted as not only supporting Parkinson's Law (in that the excess time subjects slowed their work pace to fill the available time when they found they had more time than needed to complete the problems) but providing evidence that goal setting mediates this effect. The additional finding that the context (time provided) can affect performance even under the same goal conditions was not predicted by the theory.

Monetary Incentives. The research on monetary incentives was conducted with college students using a variety of tasks — brainstorming uses for objects, assembling objects from Tinker Toy sets, and word unscrambling (Locke, Bryan, and Kendall, 1968). All five studies involved comparisons of the effects of goal setting and monetary incentives on an outcome variable to determine which would most effectively account for the outcome variations. In a typical study analyses were conducted comparing subjects working on the brainstorming task under the following four conditions:

1. *Assigned hard goals and all-or-none incentive.* Subjects were given goals that exceeded their performance in a trial period and paid a five cent bonus when they reached this goal.
2. *Assigned hard goals and no incentive.* The same as above, but with no bonus.
3. *Self-set goals and piece-rate incentive.* Subjects indicated their own goals that turned out to be well below those in 1 and 2 above and were paid at a bonus rate per use proposed that resulted in an average total payment equal to that of 1 above.
4. *Self-set goals and no incentive.* The same as 3 above, but with no bonus.

Performance was measured in terms of increases in the number of uses for objects from the beginning of the experiment to the end. Such increases were found to be entirely attributable to the assigned hard goals; incentives exerted no independent influence at all. These results and those of the other studies reported are consistent with the interpretation that whenever performance effects of monetary incentives are found, they are likely to be attributable to built-in goal setting factors.

Research Focused on Job Satisfaction

Locke has undertaken a number of studies to test his formulations regarding job satisfaction, all with undergraduate subjects and most in a laboratory setting. One series of studies bears on the hypotheses related to goal-performance discrepancies as sources of satisfaction-dissatisfaction (Locke, Cartledge, and Knerr, 1970). The authors reach the following conclusion from this research:

> Our findings confirm previous work (Locke, 1969) showing that satisfaction with performance is a function of the degree to which one's performance achieves one's desired goal or is discrepant from one's value standard. The present results also extend the earlier findings which dealt only with goals as ends in themselves to include goals which are a means to an end. Subgoal attainment is valued to the extent that it is seen as instrumental in achieving one's overall (end) goal (pp. 152–153).

The bases for these conclusions may be illustrated by the one study that extended beyond the laboratory setting. Students in an industrial psychology course completed a questionnaire dealing with grade goals and satisfaction levels at the time their first hourly examination of the semester was returned to them. As indicated in Table 7–2, those who reached or exceeded their grade goals on the exam were more satisfied; those who fell short of their goals were dissatisfied. Furthermore, those who fell below their goals on the first exam were most likely to set higher goals for the next exam, presumably in an effort to reduce or eliminate their dissatisfaction.

Table 7–2 also contains data on the perceived instrumental value of the first exam as a means or subgoal contributing to final course goal achievement. It is apparent that high instrumentality goes with high satisfaction; those who attained or bettered their goal on the first exam see it as more valuable in contributing to the grade they desire in the course. Thus they are more satisfied. They also apparently see less need to improve on the next exam. All of these results are consistent with theoretical expectations.

Another series of studies dealt with the hypothesized tendency for goal or value importance to increase satisfaction and dissat-

Table 7–2. CORRELATIONS INVOLVING GOAL-PERFORMANCE DISCREPANCY, SATISFACTION, INSTRUMENTALITY, AND FUTURE GOALS

	Satisfaction with grade on first exam	Algebraic difference between grade on first exam and goal for second
Algebraic difference between grade goal for first exam and obtained grade	.84	−.92
Rated instrumentality of first hour exam for attaining course grade goal	.89	−.84
Satisfaction with grade on first exam	—	−.83

Adapted from Edwin A. Locke, Norman Cartledge, and Claramae S. Knerr. Studies of the Relationship Between Satisfaction, Goal-Setting, and Performance, *Organizational Behavior and Human Performance,* Vol. 5 (1970), p. 151.

isfaction levels (Mobley and Locke, 1970). Subjects were college students. In most of the studies the students provided information (on a questionnaire) regarding their reactions to various aspects of either jobs they had actually held or hypothetical jobs. In one instance importance levels were actually experimentally varied, and resulting satisfaction score levels were compared. Regardless of the design used, the data do support the hypothesized tendency for importance to exaggerate emotional reactions. It can be assumed that existing measures of satisfaction with different job aspects incorporate reflections of the perceived relative importance of these aspects.

LABORATORY RESEARCH AND FIELD APPLICATIONS OF GOAL SETTING

Data bearing on the validity of goal setting theory derive from three sources. First, there are the laboratory studies such as those conducted by Locke. Second, there are a number of field studies conducted in ongoing organizational contexts that represent direct extensions of the laboratory research. Finally, there is a limited group of studies in which the goal setting occurs within the framework of a formal management by objectives program. In this section we will consider the first two, focusing primarily on research that has been conducted subsequent to Locke's basic studies. Research on MBO is considered later in this chapter.

The Results of Laboratory Studies

Much of the laboratory research by others has followed in Locke's footsteps, and tends to use similar tasks and experimental designs. The research deals with many of the same topics that Locke considered — goal specificity, difficulty and acceptance, knowledge of results, and incentives. Relatively little has been done following up on Locke's hypotheses and studies in the area of job satisfaction, but there has been a concern with the consequences of participative goal setting, as opposed to the assigned approach typically used in Locke's studies (Steers and Porter, 1974).

Goal Specificity. There is additional laboratory evidence supporting Locke's conclusions regarding the facilitating effects of setting very specific quantitative performance goals (White, Mitchell, and Bell, 1977). At least one study has failed to yield such a relationship when the task involved was of a repetitive nature with highly prescribed procedures. It appears from the results of this study that on occasion tasks can be so uninteresting that even setting specific goals has little influence on performance (Frost and Mahoney, 1976).

A more troublesome finding for the theory and its practical application emerges from a simulation study in which subjects made production-related decisions for manufacturing plants (Baumler, 1971). Comparisons were made between subjects who were given fixed production goals and those who were not. Some subjects worked on a simulation that required very little interaction with other subjects to perform well; others worked on a simulation involving considerable interdependence and coordination of effort. The results were not the same. Specific goals facilitated performance in the independent situation, but when the work required considerable coordination of effort the goal setting had a detrimental impact. There was evidence that with goal setting, needed communication with others was reduced and that subjects tended to focus individually on the goal to the exclusion of others. The necessary teamwork did not occur and performance dropped.

Goal Difficulty. Locke (1968a) reports a linear correlation of .78 between goal difficulty and performance across twelve studies that he conducted. Similar findings have been reported by others. Campbell and Ilgen (1976) found that performance in solving chess problems increased with increasing difficulty of the goal assigned (proportion of the problem to be solved), and that this was true regardless of the actual difficulty level of the problems themselves. In another study the task was a bargaining exercise involving a buyer and a seller. The goals (earnings) were established by the subjects rather than being set by an experimenter (Hamner and Harnett, 1974). Yet the higher, more difficult goals continued to contribute to better performance.

These findings must be contrasted with those of several studies that failed to find a positive relationship between goal difficulty and performance at relatively high levels of goal difficulty. This failure to find the predicted relationship has occurred with a clerical task involving the completion of time sheets (Oldham, 1975), with a reading task, and with a jigsaw puzzle (Frost and Mahoney, 1976). These researches only considered assigned goals in the range from moderate to very difficult.

Acceptance of Goals. Locke (1968) argues that deviations from his theory in the upper difficulty range reflect a failure to fully accept the goals assigned. People who "stop trying when confronted by a hard task are people who have decided the goal is impossible to reach and *who no longer are trying for that goal.*" In his own studies Locke believes that the assigned goals were for the most part accepted. In studies that appear to contradict his findings, such as some in support of achievement motivation theory (Atkinson and Feather, 1966). Locke attributes the apparent contradiction to a lack of goal acceptance. There were instances in some of his own studies when apparently negative results were found subsequently to be attributable to a lack of acceptance (Locke and Bryan, 1967). When the data were reanalyzed based on the subjects' reports of goal acceptance rather than goal assignment alone, the theory was supported.

Yet in the two studies noted previously that failed to yield the expected goal difficulty-performance relationships, attempts to establish goal acceptance as a key contributor to the results were not successful; goal acceptance did not appear to be a very important factor (Frost and Mahoney, 1976; Oldham, 1975). Thus, one is left with some uncertainties based on the laboratory research. There is, however, a possibility that the nonsupportive studies failed to really engage the subjects, and that assigned goals (regardless of difficulty level) were not taken very seriously. It is known that laboratory studies can possess a strong demand character, and that experimenter authority can be great (Milgram, 1974), but the conditions for this kind of authority may not always be present.

Feedback and Incentives. Relatively little has been done subsequently to test directly Locke's hypotheses regarding the key role of goal setting in feedback or knowledge of results. However, one laboratory study does indicate that for knowledge of results to have a maximal effect it must be complete and correct (Cummings, Schwab, and Rosen, 1971). If the knowledge fed back is only partial and thus insufficient to evaluate one's performance, or erroneously low, difficult goals will not be set, and performance will be affected accordingly.

Research on goal setting and incentives provides considerable support for Locke's hypotheses related to goal difficulty and the directing or work focusing effects of goals. However, it does not support his explanation of the motivational effects of incentives in terms of the goal setting variable (Pritchard and Curts, 1973; Terborg, 1976). It would appear that in Locke's research the monetary incentives were set at too low a level to mobilize their full, independent motivational potential. Subsequent research has shown that sufficiently large monetary incentives can exert a significant independent impact on performance above and beyond goal setting. Thus, in the work situation it would not appear to be desirable to substitute nonmonetary goal setting programs for incentive systems; the best results would be expected when the two are used jointly.

Assigned and Participative Goal Setting. Goals may be established by another person such as an experimenter (as in many of Locke's studies) or a supervisor; also they may be established by the performer without any outside influence. In between there can be any one of a range of degrees of influence from the two sources. It can be assumed that to the degree goals are self-generated, they are more likely to be accepted (Oldham, 1975). It is clear from the research that a similar degree of acceptance is possible even when goals are totally externally assigned.

In Locke's own studies, when self-generated goals were elicited they tended to be consistently rather easy, and the motivational and performance levels obtained were not high. This would appear to argue for assigned goals. On the other hand, in the Hamner and Harnett (1974) research, which utilized an interpersonal bargaining task and which provided for an actual financial return proportional to the individual's bargaining effectiveness, a number of subjects did set rather difficult goals. These goals were reflected in their earnings. Thus, it is apparent that under appropriate circumstances participation by the individual in the goal setting process need not have negative consequences. Since much of the research bearing on this subject has been conducted in field settings, we will delay further discussion until the next section.

Goal Setting Research in the Organizational Context

Laboratory studies are valuable because they permit considerable control of relevant variables, but they cannot provide an ultimate test. Practically all of the early research on goal setting theory was of the laboratory variety, but increasingly during the 1970s the theory has moved into a field setting and, in particular, into business organizations.

Goal Specificity. Reviews of the field research consistently have concluded that setting specific goals yields positive consequences, thus bearing out the laboratory findings (Latham and Yukl, 1975b; Steers and Porter, 1974). One of the most impressive series of studies has been carried out within the logging operations of wood products companies. In the first study of this kind it was found that productivity (mean cords per day) was highest not only when specific production goals were assigned but also when the crew supervisor stayed at the work site to encourage goal acceptance (Ronan, Latham, and Kinne, 1973).

In a second study, ten matched pairs of logging crews were compared over a 14-week period. One of each pair was exposed to preliminary training in goal setting, and the other was not. Appropriate specific production goals were established for all crews each week, but only in the case of the previously trained crews were these goals communicated; thus only one of each pair was actively engaged in goal setting, although the performance of both crews could be measured relative to goals (Latham and Kinne, 1974). The results appear in Table 7–3. It is clear that the goal setting crews exceeded their goals more often and usually outperformed the nongoal-setting crews.

A similar approach was utilized in a study by Latham and Baldes (1975) to induce logging truck drivers to carry heavier loads to the mill. A goal of 94 per cent of the legal weight limit was assigned. At the beginning of the period the trucks were averaging 60 per cent. With the introduction of the goal, performance improved sharply and by the end of nine months had stabilized at over 90 per cent. "Without the increase in efficiency due to goal setting it would have cost the company a quarter of a million dollars for the purchase of additional trucks in order to deliver the same quantity of logs to the mills" (p. 124).

A particularly intriguing test of the theory involved the establishment of a company to hire part-time workers to identify and code parcels of land with zoning codes for a county government (Umstot, Bell, and Mitchell, 1976). Workers assigned specific individual quotas (set to represent difficult goals) were compared with

Table 7–3. MEAN DEVIATION FROM PRODUCTION GOALS (CORDS PER MAN HOUR) FOR GOAL SETTING AND NONGOAL-SETTING LOGGING CREWS

Matched Pair Number	Goal Setting Crew	Nongoal-Setting Crew
1	+.23	+.09
2	−.09	−.09
3	+.05	−.08
4	+.05	−.07
5	+.04	+.01
6	+.13	−.02
7	+.08	−.16
8	+.22	+.24
9	+.08	−.07
10	+.11	+.13
Mean for 10 crews	+.09	−.002

Adapted from Gary P. Latham and Sydney B. Kinne. Improving Job Performance Through Training in Goal Setting, *Journal of Applied Psychology*, Vol. 59 (1974), p. 189.

workers who did not experience goal setting. As Locke's theory would predict, performance was superior under the goal setting condition.

These consistently positive results receive a degree of qualification from a series of studies conducted with samples of maintenance technicians who had operated under an assigned goal setting program for several years. In two of these studies a measure of perceived goal clarity, which appears to reflect specificity, proved to be totally unrelated to any of the six performance indexes. However, the expected performance relationships were found for a subset of the total sample having strong higher order needs (in Maslow's sense) (Ivancevich and McMahon, 1977b), and also among the less well educated technicians (Ivancevich and McMahon, 1977a). In a third analysis dealing with blacks and whites a significant goal clarity-performance relationship was found in the total sample; however, this finding was predominantly attributable to the black group (Ivancevich and McMahon, 1977c). At the very least, findings such as these suggest that goal setting may be more effective with some people than with others.

Goal Difficulty and Acceptance. The research involving maintenance technicians also utilized a measure of goal challenge, which appears to reflect difficulty, and a measure of goal acceptance — the goal setting program used assigned goals. Only in the study dealing with racial differences did the challenge measure yield an overall correlation with performance, and subsequent analyses indicated this occurred largely in the white group (Ivancevich and McMahon, 1977c). Also, challenge was positively related to performance among better educated technicians (Ivancevich and McMahon, 1977a) and among those with strong higher order needs (Ivancevich and McMahon, 1977b). Reported goal acceptance was associated with better performance only for those with relatively weak higher order needs; otherwise it did not matter. Overall these data continue to support the idea that individual differences are important.

Other field research has more frequently produced evidence of an overall positive relationship between goal difficulty level and performance. However, in many of the studies moderator effects of the kind noted by Ivancevich were found, with the result that certain groups did not exhibit the predicted relationship (Latham and Yukl, 1975b; Steers and Porter, 1974). This could be attributable to the difficult goals being viewed as impossible and, accordingly, not being accepted; this is what goal setting theory would anticipate. However, the majority of the field studies have not incorporated measures of goal acceptance in a manner adequate to test this hypothesis. There is also some evidence that the motivating effects of difficult goals may be diminished over time periods extending well beyond those of the laboratory experiments.

Feedback, Incentives, and Time Limits. Locke's hypotheses regarding the important mediating role played by goal setting in determining the effects of knowledge of results, incentives, and time variation have not received much investigation in the field setting. The results of one study of performance feedback are important, however (Kim and Hamner, 1976). Here, telephone plant employees at four locations were studied over a three-month period. At one location assigned goal setting occurred, but no formal feedback was provided. At the other locations, varying amounts and types of formal feedback were introduced in addition to the goal setting. Performance differences were studied on several different dimensions. Based on these analyses the authors conclude that "it is possible for goal setting alone to enhance performance without a formal feedback program, but when self-generated knowledge of results plus supervisory generated knowledge of results and praise are added to a formal goal setting program, performance was generally enhanced even more" (p. 56). The data appear to indicate that feedback has motivational effects above and beyond goal setting per se, although it is possible that these effects occur in goal acceptance.

There also is evidence from a study in a corporate research and development department that monetary incentives (a bonus ranging from 3.5 to 9 per cent of salary) can yield performance effects above those attributable to goal setting (Latham, Mitchell, and Dossett, 1978). This finding is consistent with those of laboratory research cited previously and again raises a question about whether the various motivational phenomena in the employment situation can be explained entirely through goal setting.

A study of the effects of time limits indicated that when pulp and paper mills restrict their buying of wood from independent logging crews to one or two days a week, they implicitly urge higher production goals (Latham and Locke, 1975). The crews harvest at a more rapid rate, attempting to produce in the few days available what they would otherwise produce in five days. Thus the time quotas curtail overproduction, but by no means in direct proportion to the amount of the time reduction. Work does tend to expand or contract to fill the time available.

Assigned and Participative Goal Setting. Locke attributes much of the impact of participative leadership to implicit goal setting. On this particular point solid research evidence is lacking. There are data bearing on the degree to which participation in goal setting influences performance, a point upon which goal setting theory per se is mute, except perhaps to imply that goal acceptance is more certain under participative conditions.

Data from the Ivancevich studies of maintenance technicians indicate that perceived participation in goal setting is positively related to performance outcomes, but primarily among blacks (Ivan-cevich and McMahon, 1977c). A study carried out by Latham and Yukl (1975a) yields similar results — participation level makes a difference for blacks, but not whites.

There are studies that indicate that participative goal setting can prove effective in white samples as well; thus it may only be *more* effective among blacks. In the Latham, Mitchell, and Dossett (1978) research participative goal setting among research and development personnel was highly effective, and these results appeared to be attributable to the setting of more difficult performance goals (contrary to what Locke found in his laboratory experiments). No clear difference between participative and assigned goal setting manifested itself in performance. On balance in this study one is not more effective than the other.

There is additional research. However, since these studies utilized management development programs to install goal setting (and appear to resemble the typical MBO effort) they are considered in the next section.

THE NATURE AND VALUE OF MANAGEMENT BY OBJECTIVES

Locke (1968a), in concluding a review of his work, notes:

Finally, a word is in order about the possible industrial application of the finding that goal setting is a major determinant of task performance. There are two recent trends in industry, which, although they were not inspired by this research, are quite congruent with its implications. One is a motivational program called *Zero Defects*. The purpose of a zero-defects program is basically to reduce errors in workmanship (i.e. increase the quality of work) by persuading workers to adopt higher goals with regard to quality . . . a second major trend is called *Management by Objectives*. The key element in this system is the setting of specific performance goals by executives and managers (p. 186).

Of these two, MBO has received by far the most attention and has generated the largest amount of research. In addition it seems on *a priori* grounds to have the closest relationship to goal setting theory. Accordingly, it is the major focus of consideration here.

The Nature of MBO

Management by objectives typically is described as a series of steps to be carried out. The steps noted by different writers are not the same, nor are those utilized in different companies. Several fairly typical descriptions of the steps in the process are given in Figure 7–1.

Raia (1974, pp. 18–22)

1. Formulate long-range goals and strategic plans.
2. Develop the specific objectives to be achieved within the given time period.
3. Establish derivative objectives and subobjectives for major departments and subunits.
4. Set realistic and challenging objectives and standards of performance, for members of the organization.
5. Formulate action plans for achieving the stated objectives.
6. Implement and take corrective action when required to ensure the attainment of objectives.
7. Review individual and organizational performance in terms of established goals and objectives.
8. Appraise overall performance, reinforce behavior, and strengthen motivation through effective management training and development, compensation and career planning.

Odiorne (1965, p. 78)

1. Organization's common goals measures of organization performance.
2. Revisions in organization structure.
3. Superior sets down goals and measures for subordinates and/or subordinate proposes goals and measures for his job.
4. Joint agreement on subordinates' goals.
5. Feedback of interim results against milestones.
6. Cumulative periodic review of subordinate results against targets.
7. Review of organization performance.

Chung (1977, pp. 222–231)

1. Arrange organizational goals in means-end chain.
2. Identify key performance responsibilities.
3. Assign priorities to key responsibilities.
4. Define the expected outcomes of key responsibilities.
5. Assign specific tasks to employees.
6. Define authority and responsibility relationships.
7. Develop time schedules for performing key responsibilities.
8. Perform assigned tasks and integrate them into overall goals.
9. Undertake periodic performance process reviews.
10. Conduct annual performance review session.

Figure 7–1.   Steps in management by objectives as described by different writers.

In these, as in most other descriptions, the key elements appear to be:
1. Setting objectives.
2. Working toward the goals.
3. Reviewing performance (Wikstrom, 1968).

Beyond this basic goal setting-feedback nexus, a tremendous amount of diversity emerges. Among the components of MBO noted in Figure 7–1 are strategic planning, performance appraisal, management development, compensation administration, career planning, organization planning, job design, and coaching. A review of individual company programs suggests that the following should also be added: control systems design, organization development, manpower planning, job enrichment, leadership style change, and changes in organizational climate (Wikstrom, 1968). It is clear that beyond its core elements, management by objectives is many things to many people.

This diversity of elements can be a strength in that it is possible to tailor a program to the needs of a specific company. But from the point of view of evaluation, it creates major problems. Even if an MBO program is shown to yield positive results, it is very difficult to know what factors were responsible, or to compare one study with others. In any given instance it may be goal setting that is the cause of a motivational effect, but it also may be any one of the other aspects of the program. Thus research on MBO must be viewed with some caution; variables are typically confounded, and implications for goal setting theory tend to be indirect at best.

Some Specific Research Studies

Research on MBO typically utilizes a longitudinal design that permits monitoring of performance and attitudinal effects from the time of introduction to some subsequent point. Ideally a control situation that did not contain the various aspects of the MBO program would be studied as well, to at least narrow the number of possible causal factors. However, studies that contain this element are relatively few.

The General Electric Research.   One of the first studies of MBO focused on various aspects of goal setting interviews conducted by managers at General Electric (French, Kay, and Meyer, 1966). In these interviews certain problem areas yielded specific goals for improvement, whereas others did not. Furthermore, some of the subjects engaged in highly participative goal setting, while others were assigned goals during the interviews by their superiors. Performance improvement was rated by superiors and subordinates 12 weeks after goal setting interviews.

The findings yield strong support for the setting of specific goals for improvement as opposed to mere criticism and discussion. They also tend to give some support for participative goal setting, at least when the individual is accustomed to a certain amount of participation. However, this support is not strong and is clearly limited to certain individuals. It is also possible that factors other than participative goal setting in the interview might have caused the obtained results.

The Purex Studies.   The Purex Corporation MBO program has been described by Raia (1974). The program moved from the top down and had considerable support from the chief executive; it apparently never did have much impact at lower management levels. Follow-up studies involving interviews and the collection of production data were carried out 18 months after initiation and again a year later. Production was decreasing 4/10 of one per cent per month prior to the introduction of MBO. During the following 18 months this pattern was reversed, and an increase of 3/10 of one per cent per month occurred. In the ensuing year production remained high but did not continue to increase. Goal setting was done largely in an assigned manner, and goal acceptance was not always obtained. Over a time the MBO program "gradually lost its identity as a driving force in the organizational environment."

The program, with all its imperfections, appears to have been successful — or at least something was; but without control data for a company situation where MBO was not introduced, it is impossible to attribute causation to MBO with any certainty.

The Black and Decker Research.   Carroll and Tosi (1973) report on an extensive study of an MBO program introduced at the Black and Decker Company. Their data were collected through interviews and questionnaires administered at an 18-month interval. The program itself had been in existence for some time prior to the first phase of the research; a major effort to improve the program intervened between the two phases.

Figure 7–2 reports a number of the findings. In general, subordinate participation in goal setting made little difference, although, as in the General Electric research, there was a slight tendency for positive results to accrue when a participative relationship had already been established. Goal clarity was consistently associated with positive outcomes. Goal difficulty appeared to act positively on confident, mature managers but could have negative consequences for the less self-assured.

The University of Kentucky and University of Houston Studies.   This program of research has been conducted primarily by John Ivancevich, who moved to the University of Houston in the early 1970s. The basic approach has involved comparisons of satisfaction and productivity data obtained in a time series design. The first study dealt with satisfaction levels prior to an MBO training program and at subsequent intervals extending over a 20-month period in two companies (Ivancevich, 1972). Such improvements as occurred were found immediately after training and were much more pronounced in one company than in the other. However, six months later this increase in satisfaction had disappeared entirely.

In a subsequent study, performance data were obtained and comparisons were made among three plants: one with MBO training only, one with MBO training and continuing reinforcement (follow-up letters, meetings, and consultative advice), and one with no MBO (Ivan-

The Goal Setting Process

1. More difficult goals are associated with subordinate managers being more positive toward the program.
2. As goals increase in perceived clarity and importance, subordinate managers become more positive to the program and also report improved relations with superiors.
3. The amount of subordinate influence in establishing goals is not significantly related to MBO success.

The Review Process

1. Higher feedback frequencies are associated with higher satisfaction with the program, higher reported goal accomplishment, and improved relations with superiors.
2. Strong perceptions that the superior is concerned with goal accomplishment are associated with more positive feelings about the program.

Superior Conduct

Higher goal clarity, goal difficulty, and frequency of performance review, and thus greater overall MBO effectiveness, are associated with—
1. Higher amounts of perceived organizational support for the MBO program by the superior
2. Greater job satisfaction for the superior
3. Greater amounts of decisiveness as opposed to cautiousness for the superior
4. Greater amounts of self-assurance for the superior

Figure 7–2.   Selected general findings from the Black and Decker study.

(Adapted from Stephen J. Carroll and Henry L. Tosi. *Management by Objectives: Applications and Research.* New York: Macmillan, 1973, pp. 35–39.)

cevich, 1974). Measures were obtained at intervals over a three-year period. Again training effects were in evidence, but a tendency to revert to pre-MBO performance levels was also present. This tendency was considerably more pronounced in one experimental plant than in the other. The findings are consistent with the view that reinforcement (evidence of renewed top management interest) rekindles the motivational effects of MBO.

Two other studies by Ivancevich, one dealing with sales personnel (1976) and the other with skilled technicians (1977), compare MBO programs utilizing participative and assigned goal setting with a control condition. Both productivity and attitudinal data over a period of one year are presented. In both cases improvements occurring at the time MBO was initiated had dissipated by the end of the 12-month period. In neither case did the institution of participative goal setting yield results superior to an assigned approach. In fact among the technicians who were not accustomed to participative procedures, the assigned procedure proved superior in several respects.

Other Research Evidence.   Of the remaining somewhat scattered recent studies on MBO effectiveness, three stand out either because of design characteristics, criterion measures, or both. Muc-zyk (1976) conducted studies using hard and relevant criterion meas-ures and control conditions in a branch banking system and in the repair shops of a railroad. MBO was introduced to the experimental units in both instances through a training program widely utilized in the business world. In neither case was there evidence of an impact on performance over periods of 12 and 8 months respectively. This lack of results could be attributable to many factors, including the failure of the MBO induction to "take" in these companies. Perhaps there were some short-term gains of the kind noted by Ivancevich. This may well have occurred in the bank, since the first follow-up did not occur for six months. Nevertheless, the final outcome is clear and is consis-tent with other well controlled studies such as those reported by Ivan-cevich.

A study by Steers (1975) was carried out in a company in which a well-organized MBO program was already in place; there could be no question that the induction had "taken." Various indexes of aspects of the individual's goal-setting situation were correlated with perfor-mance measures. Except for a low positive correlation involving participation, the overall performance results were lacking in signifi-cance. Goal difficulty was totally unrelated to performance. When the data for managers high and low on achievement motivation were analyzed separately, a quite different picture emerged, as indicated in Table 7–4. Participation was important for the less motivated, while other goal setting aspects were important for the more motivated. Individual differences play an important role.

A clear need from the research cited to this point is for an instrument that will indicate whether MBO actually exists, or whether the training induction has "taken" in an organization. Such a measure has been developed by Kirchhoff (1975). Studies with this measure indicate that MBO training may well have a short-term effect that dissipates rather quickly. Ivancevich reports no performance and attitudinal effects a year later; Kirchhoff reports that there may be no

Table 7–4. CORRELATIONS WITH OVERALL PERFORMANCE MEASURES FOR VARIOUS ASPECTS OF THE INDIVIDUAL GOAL SETTING SITUATION

| Aspect of the Goal Setting Situation | Correlation with Performance | | |
	All Subjects	High Achievement Motivation	Low Achievement Motivation
Participation	.20	.09	.41
Feedback	.13	.27	−.04
Goal difficulty	.02	.14	−.19
Goal specificity	.12	.22	−.05

Adapted from Richard M. Steers. Task-Goal Attributes, n Achievement, and Supervisory Per-formance, *Organizational Behavior and Human Performance*, Vol. 13 (1975), pp. 398–399.

MBO. With reinforcement, Ivancevich (1974) finds a renewed motivational impact. Kirchhoff notes that an organization that did not exhibit a decline in MBO "take" after two years "modified its appraisal system and reorganized its profit centers to reinforce the use of goals in managing. In addition, the organization initiated at least one goal setting or goal use activity every year to provide added reinforcement" (p. 363). But then what is the key ingredient — goal setting, performance appraisal, compensation, or some other aspect of the total MBO program? The data cannot tell us.

CONCLUSIONS

Goal setting theory has experienced a great deal of success — both in the laboratory and more recently in the field. Furthermore, it has a considerably intuitive appeal, in part at least because of its apparent simplicity. In spite of Locke's recent disclaimers, it is not so simple as to be considered a technique only. There is a basic theory here, and it is important to consider it on the same basis as other theories.

Scientific Goals

To say that goal setting theory is a theory is not to say that it is a complete theory. There are significant gaps, and Locke clearly recognizes this fact (as well as the difficulty of filling them). The theory does not really provide an understanding of how goals are developed and how goal acceptance occurs. This lack leads to some ambiguity regarding what can be anticipated at high levels of goal difficulty and also regarding the relative status of assigned and self-generated goal setting. There is a need for an explicit theory of when and how goals will be created and an individual becomes committed to them (Dobmeyer, 1972). In particular we need formulations regarding the emergence of easy and difficult goals. In all likelihood a theory of goal development and acceptance will place much greater emphasis on individual differences than Locke has done to date. Simply to move this problem back from individual goals to personal values is not sufficient. It then becomes important to specify the origins of the values in order to predict them and the goal-based behavior they generate.

There are also certain gaps in the research that relate closely to the theoretical needs. For instance, the theory posits an important role for values and also views them as operating in large part parallel with goals. Yet the theory-based research deals entirely with the more behaviorally proximate goals and intentions. Studies at the level of values using the goal paradigm might well yield very powerful results covering a wide range of work behaviors.

Locke's hypotheses regarding job satisfaction also have received relatively little research attention beyond his own basic studies. Is it true, for instance, that the gap between goal and results, or value and results, is sufficient as an explanation of job satisfaction-dissatisfaction in the complex milieu of an ongoing work situation? In this area, simple extrapolation from the laboratory studies is not adequate. The same holds for goal importance. There is a hint in some of the nonconfirming research that the failures may have occurred because the goals studied generally lacked sufficient importance to motivate behavior. Yet goal importance has received little explicit study, although Carroll and Tosi (1973) did note that establishing goal priorities in MBO was associated with positive outcomes. It would be valuable to learn how work-related goals achieve importance for the individual and to have information on the extent to which low importance might account for the occasional failure of specific hard goals to motivate behavior.

This point appears closely related to the problems that individual differences create for goal setting theory. It is evident now that goal specificity, goal difficulty, and participation in setting goals affect various individuals differently. This finding could well be mediated by variations in the importance certain people attach to particular goals, or at a more abstract level, values. In any event there are some distinct variations in the kinds of individuals who react differently to aspects of the goal setting process. Some of Locke's own findings now appear to be due at least in part to the fact that his research subjects were college students.

If we pull together the diverse research results it becomes apparent that goal specificity is particularly likely to be associated with high performance levels among people with strong higher order needs and with considerable achievement motivation. Similarly, goal difficulty yields a sizable performance relationship among those with strong achievement motivation, more confidence and self-assurance, and a greater degree of maturity (also among whites rather than blacks and among the better educated). Participation in goal setting, which Locke did not specifically consider in his theorizing but which in his research turned out to be associated with easy goals and low performance, appears to be particularly valuable among the less well educated, blacks, individuals with relatively weak achievement motivation, and those who are accustomed to participation. Within these groups it seems to generate more difficult goals and better performance.

All of these findings appear consistent with the view that Locke's research was conducted with a group for which the theory was particularly appropriate. The only evidence seemingly contrary to this interpretation is the finding that goal specificity is most important among the less well educated and among blacks — groups either not studied or underrepresented in Locke's work with college students. It seems very possible that goal setting theory is subject to certain boundary limitations regarding to whom it applies, or at least among whom it works best.

The research raises another question about goal setting theory's interpretation of the effects of motivational phenomena such as knowledge of results, time limits, and the like. It is apparent that feedback, incentives (or at least sizable incentives), and time limits can exert influences beyond those attributable to goal setting; goal setting per se cannot explain all of what happens. Although research on the goal setting interpretation of the effects of participative management and peer competition is lacking, it seems likely that these phenomena will prove also to have performance consequences not attributable to the goal setting factor. This is not to say that goal setting does not exert considerable influence on various motivational phenomena, and Locke has performed a useful service in demonstrating this.

When goal setting theory takes on concepts such as instrumentality of anticipated goals and the role of subgoals, it appears to assume characteristics of expectancy theory, and, in fact, the major reviews of the goal setting literature conclude with arguments for the integration of the two theoretical approaches (Latham and Yukl, 1975; Steers and Porter, 1974). Locke (1975) notes a number of difficulties for such an attempt at integration. Among these are the varying orientations of the two theories with regard to hedonism and unconscious processes. Also the two theories posit (and the research each has generated partially supports) conflicting views regarding the expectancy-performance relationship. Expectancy theory views the relationship as a positive one. Goal setting theory states that "harder goals (with lower expectancies) lead to higher performance than easier goals (with higher expectancies)" (Locke, 1975, p. 468). Attempts to reconcile these differences and explain the disparate experimental results are not entirely convincing. There is a distinct tendency for expectancy theory advocates to attempt to subordinate goal setting within the expectancy framework and for goal setting advocates to do the reverse. If, as seems likely, the two theories operate at maximum efficiency within different domains, neither type of integration can be expected to prove fruitful.

As noted in the discussion of Atkinson's formulations regarding achievement motivation, his theory indicates a decrease in performance beyond a certain level of task difficulty, at least among high achievement-motivated individuals. Locke's views would lead one not to anticipate such a decline. The research evidence seems to be mixed. However, there are so many differences between the studies in terms of measuring the exact level of difficulty (actual or perceived), the amount of goal setting, the amount of goal acceptance, and the achievement motivation level of the subjects, that explanation is almost impossible. At present we are at a theoretical impasse until more comprehensive studies are conducted that measure all theoretically relevant variables.

Managerial Goals

The clear implication of goal setting theory for managing organizations is that getting people to set and strive to attain specific, relatively hard goals can well exert a strong motivational force. Whether this force results in greater overall *organizational* goal accomplishment is another matter. In work situations when coordination with the activities of others is not required and when there are only a few relevant goals operating, goal setting would appear to have considerable value. In contrast, in interactive contexts such as those experienced by many managers, especially those who are not at the very top levels, the increased effort along specific goal dimensions may create problems. It is *focused* motivational effort that makes organizations successful. Diversified goal setting by the various members of an interacting component can have negative consequences. Some of the difficulties that MBO programs have had may be attributable to this.

Another problem for MBO is that the motivating effects of difficult goals appear to be particularly susceptible to dissipation over time, even among the particular kinds of individuals who are most responsive to them. To counteract this tendency, goal setting must be reinforced frequently, often by approaches that are not really embodied in goal setting theory. Thus if the need is for an immediate burst of energy due to declining profits or shrinking markets, MBO can prove very valuable. For the long term it is less likely to maintain effort levels unless it is possible to reactivate goals frequently and perhaps to shift the actual content of certain goals (and thus introduce new jobs) at periodic intervals.

These considerations suggest that goal setting for particular, relatively isolated operations is most likely to yield favorable results. In contrast, a comprehensive top down MBO program can run into difficulties that will hamper its operations. Locke (1970b) has noted the value that goal setting may have when an individual supervisor deals with subordinates; there is also research evidence to support these conclusions (Oldham, 1976). In this limited context it can be adjusted to the individual characteristics of the subordinate to stay within the boundaries of theoretical application and establish appropriate priorities. An overall MBO program for a company, however, may well miss the mark with so many people that it ultimately loses its legitimacy, goal importance, and motivational impact for almost everyone. Many may feel they have been duped into setting certain goals only to have them "thrown in their face" months later (when they are almost forgotten) as justification for a denied promotion or salary raise.

Whether goals should be assigned by a superior or set participatively is also an individual matter. Assigned goals appear to achieve much the same level of impact in hierarchic organizations as in the laboratory context, presumably because legitimate authority and the demand character of experiments operate in much the same manner. Assigned goals work best with those who are already intrinsically motivated and who thus find the assigned goals less onerous. Participative goal setting works best if people are accustomed to and comfortable with it, and when intrinsic motivation to perform is at a low level, thus requiring an added inducement.

Overall, goal setting procedures appear to have considerable motivational potential with the right people under the right circumstances. Difficulty, specificity, and acceptance of goals are important. Goal setting within the context of a comprehensive MBO program is a much more uncertain matter, especially over the long term. The ideal approach would seem to be to train individual supervisors of relatively independent jobs in the techniques of goal setting, as well as when, how, and when not to use them. This should create the maximum motivational impact without the cumbersome and often detrimental effects, including the paperwork, of management by objectives.

References

Atkinson, John W. and Norman T. Feather. *A Theory of Achievement Motivation.* New York: Wiley, 1966.

Baumler, John V. Defined Criteria of Performance in Organizational Control, *Administrative Science Quarterly,* Vol. 16 (1971), 340–349.

Bryan, Judith F. and Edwin A. Locke. Parkinson's Law as a Goal Setting Phenomenon, *Organizational Behavior and Human Performance,* Vol. 2 (1967a), 258–275.

Bryan, Judith F. and Edwin A. Locke. Goal Setting as a Means of Increasing Motivation, *Journal of Applied Psychology,* Vol. 51 (1967b), 274–277.

Campbell, Donald J. and Daniel R. Ilgen. Additive Effects of Task Difficulty and Goal Setting on Subsequent Task Performance, *Journal of Applied Psychology,* Vol. 61 (1976), 319–324.

Carroll, Stephen J. and Henry L. Tosi. *Management by Objectives: Applications and Research.* New York: Macmillan, 1973.

Chung, Kae H. *Motivational Theories and Practices.* Columbus, Ohio: Grid, 1977.

Cummings, L. L., Donald P. Schwab, and Marc Rosen. Performance and Knowledge of Results as Determinants of Goal Setting, *Journal of Applied Psychology,* Vol. 55 (1971), 526–530.

Dobmeyer, Thomas W. A Critique of Edwin Locke's Theory of Task Motivation and Incentives, In Henry L. Tosi, Robert J. House, and Marvin D. Dunnette (eds.), *Managerial Motivation and Compensation.* East Lansing, Mich.: Graduate School of Business Administration, Michigan State University, 1972, pp. 244–259.

Drucker, Peter F. *The Practice of Management*. New York: Harper, 1954.

French, John R. P., Emanuel Kay, and Herbert H. Meyer. Participation and the Appraisal System, *Human Relations*, Vol. 19 (1966), 3–19.

Frost, Peter J. and Thomas A. Mahoney. Goal Setting and the Task Process. I. An Interactive Influence on Individual Performance, *Organizational Behavior and Human Performance*, Vol. 17 (1976), 328–350.

Hamner, W. Clay and Donald L. Harnett. Goal Setting, Performance and Satisfaction in an Interdependent Task, *Organizational Behavior and Human Performance*, Vol. 12 (1974), 217–230.

Ivancevich, John M. A Longitudinal Assessment of Management by Objectives, *Administrative Science Quarterly*, Vol. 17 (1972), 126–138.

Ivancevich, John M. Changes in Performance in a Management by Objectives Program, *Administrative Science Quarterly*, Vol. 19 (1974), 563–574.

Ivancevich, John M. The Effects of Goal Setting on Performance and Job Satisfaction, *Journal of Applied Psychology*, Vol. 61 (1976), 605–612.

Ivancevich, John M. Different Goal Setting Treatments and Their Effects on Performance and Job Satisfaction, *Academy of Management Journal*, Vol. 20 (1977), 406–419.

Ivancevich, John M. and J. Timothy McMahon. Education as a Moderator of Goal Setting Effectiveness, *Journal of Vocational Behavior*, Vol. 11 (1977a), 83–94.

Ivancevich, John M. and J. Timothy McMahon. A Study of Task-Goal Attributes, Higher Order Need Strength, and Performance, *Academy of Management Journal*, Vol. 20 (1977b), 552–563.

Ivancevich, John M. and J. Timothy McMahon. Black-White Differences in a Goal Setting Program, *Organizational Behavior and Human Performance*, Vol. 20 (1977c), 287–300.

Kim, Jay S. and W. Clay Hamner. Effect of Performance Feedback and Goal Setting on Productivity and Satisfaction in an Organizational Setting, *Journal of Applied Psychology*, Vol. 61 (1976), 48–57.

Kirchhoff, Bruce A. A Diagnostic Tool for Management by Objectives, *Personnel Psychology*, Vol. 28 (1975), 351–364.

LaFollette, William R. and Richard J. Fleming. The Historical Antecedents of Management by Objectives, *Academy of Management Proceedings*, 1977, 2–5.

Latham, Gary P. and J. James Baldes. The Practical Significance of Locke's Theory of Goal Setting, *Journal of Applied Psychology*, Vol. 60 (1975), 122–124.

Latham, Gary P. and Sydney B. Kinne. Improving Job Performance Through Training in Goal Setting, *Journal of Applied Psychology*, Vol. 59 (1974), 187–191.

Latham, Gary P. and Edwin A. Locke. Increasing Productivity with Decreasing Time Limits: A Field Replication of Parkinson's Law, *Journal of Applied Psychology*, Vol. 60 (1975). 524–526.

Latham, Gary P., Terence R. Mitchell, and Dennis L. Dossett. Importance of Participative Goal Setting and Anticipated Rewards on Goal Difficulty and Job Performance, *Journal of Applied Psychology*, Vol. 63 (1978), 163–171.

Latham, Gary P. and Gary A. Yukl. Assigned Versus Participative Goal Setting with Educated and Uneducated Woods Workers, *Journal of Applied Psychology*, Vol. 60 (1975a), 299–302.

Latham, Gary P. and Gary A. Yukl. A Review of Research on the Application of Goal Setting in Organizations, *Academy of Management Journal*, Vol. 18 (1975b), 824–845.

Lewin, Kurt. *A Dynamic Theory of Personality*. New York: McGraw-Hill, 1935.

Lewin, Kurt. *The Conceptual Representation and the Measurement of Psychological Forces*. Durham, N.C.: Duke University Press, 1938.

Lewin, Kurt, Tamara Dembo, Leon Festinger, and Pauline S. Sears. Level of Aspiration, *In* J. McVicker Hunt (ed.), *Personality and the Behavior Disorders*. New York: Ronald, 1944, pp. 333–378.

Locke, Edwin A. The Relationship of Intentions to Level of Performance, *Journal of Applied Psychology*, Vol. 50 (1966a), 60–66.

Locke, Edwin A. A Closer Look at Level of Aspiration as a Training Procedure: A Reanalysis of Fryer's Data, *Journal of Applied Psychology*, Vol. 50 (1966b), 417–420.

Locke, Edwin A. Motivational Effects of

Knowledge of Results: Knowledge or Goal Setting, *Journal of Applied Psychology*, Vol. 51 (1967), 324–329.

Locke, Edwin A. Toward a Theory of Task Motivation and Incentives, *Organizational Behavior and Human Performance*, Vol. 3 (1968a), 157–189.

Locke, Edwin A. Effects of Knowledge of Results, Feedback in Relation to Standards, and Goals on Reaction-Time Performance, *American Journal of Psychology*, Vol. 81 (1968b), 566–574.

Locke, Edwin A. What is Job Satisfaction? *Organizational Behavior and Human Performance*, Vol. 4 (1969), 309–336.

Locke, Edwin A. Job Satisfaction and Job Performance: A Theoretical Analysis, *Organizational Behavior and Human Performance*, Vol. 5 (1970a), 484–500.

Locke, Edwin A. The Supervisor as Motivator: His Influence on Employee Performance and Satisfaction, In Bernard M. Bass, R. Cooper, and J. A. Haas (eds.), *Managing for Task Accomplishment*. Lexington, Mass.: Heath, 1970b, pp. 57–67.

Locke, Edwin A. Personnel Attitudes and Motivation, *Annual Review of Psychology*, Vol. 26 (1975), 457–480.

Locke, Edwin A. and Judith F. Bryan. Cognitive Aspects of Psychomotor Performance: The Effects of Performance Goals on Level of Performance, *Journal of Applied Psychology*, Vol. 50 (1966a), 286–291.

Locke, Edwin A. and Judith F. Bryan. The Effects of Goal Setting, Rule Learning, and Knowledge of Score on Performance, *American Journal of Psychology*, Vol. 79 (1966b), 451–457.

Locke, Edwin A. and Judith F. Bryan. Performance Goals as Determinants of Level of Performance and Boredom, *Journal of Applied Psychology*, Vol. 51 (1967), 120–130.

Locke, Edwin A. and Judith F. Bryan. Grade Goals as Determinants of Academic Achievement, *Journal of General Psychology*, Vol. 79 (1968a), 217–228.

Locke, Edwin A. and Judith F. Bryan. The Goal Setting as a Determinant of the Effect of Knowledge of Score on Performance, *American Journal of Psychology*, Vol. 81 (1968b), 398–406.

Locke, Edwin A. and Judith F. Bryan. The Directing Function of Goals in Task Performance, *Organizational Behavior and Human Performance*, Vol. 4 (1969a), 35–42.

Locke, Edwin A. and Judith F. Bryan. Knowledge of Score and Goal Level as Determinants of Work Rate, *Journal of Applied Psychology*, Vol. 53 (1969b), 59–65.

Locke, Edwin A., Judith F. Bryan, and Lorne M. Kendall. Goals and Intentions as Mediators of the Effects of Monetary Incentives on Behavior, *Journal of Applied Psychology*, Vol. 52 (1968), 104–121.

Locke, Edwin A., Norman Cartledge, and Claramae S. Knerr. Studies of the Relationship Between Satisfaction, Goal Setting, and Performance, *Organizational Behavior and Human Performance*, Vol. 5 (1970), 135–158.

Locke, Edwin A., Norman Cartledge, and Jeffrey Koeppel. Motivational Effects of Knowledge of Results: A Goal Setting Phenomenon, *Psychological Bulletin*, Vol. 70 (1968), 474–485.

McGregor, Douglas. An Uneasy Look at Performance Appraisal, *Harvard Business Review*, Vol. 35 (1957), 89–94.

Milgram, Stanley. *Obedience to Authority.* New York: Harper and Row, 1974.

Mobley, William H. and Edwin A. Locke. The Relationship of Value Importance to Satisfaction, *Organizational Behavior and Human Performance*, Vol. 5 (1970), 463–483.

Muczyk, Jan P. MBO in a Bank and a Railroad Company: Two Field Experiments Focusing on Performance Measures, *Industrial Relations Research Association Proceedings*, Winter (1976), 13–19.

Odiorne, George S. *Management by Objectives.* New York: Pitman, 1965.

Oldham, Greg R. The Impact of Supervisory Characteristics on Goal Acceptance, *Academy of Management Journal*, Vol. 18 (1975), 461–475.

Oldham, Greg R. The Motivational Strategies Used by Supervisors: Relationships to Effectiveness Indicators, *Organizational Behavior and Human Performance*. Vol. 15 (1976), 66–86.

Parkinson, C. N. *Parkinson's Law and Other Studies in Administration.* Boston: Houghton-Mifflin, 1957.

Pritchard, Robert D. and Michael I. Curts. The Influence of Goal Setting and Financial Incentives on Task Performance, *Organizational Behavior and Human Performance*, Vol. 10 (1973), 175–183.

Raia, Anthony P. *Managing by Objectives.* Glenview, Ill.: Scott, Foresman, 1974.

Ronan, W. W., Gary P. Latham, and S. B. Kinne. Effects of Goal Setting and Supervision on Worker Behavior in an Industrial Situation, *Journal of Applied Psychology*, Vol. 58 (1973), 302–307.

Ryan, Thomas A. *Intentional Behavior: An Approach to Human Motivation.* New York: Ronald, 1970.

Steers, Richard M. Task-Goal Attributes, Achievement, and Supervisory Performance, *Organizational Behavior and Human Performance*, Vol. 13 (1975), 392–403.

Steers, Richard M. and Lyman W. Porter. The Role of Task-Goal Attributes in Employee Performance, *Psychological Bulletin*, Vol. 81 (1974), 434–452.

Terborg, James R. The Motivational Components of Goal Setting, *Journal of Applied Psychology*, Vol. 61 (1976), 613–621.

Umstot, Denis D., Cecil H. Bell, and Terence R. Mitchell. Effects of Job Enrichment and Task Goals on Satisfaction and Productivity: Implications for Job Design, *Journal of Applied Psychology*, Vol. 61 (1976), 379–394.

White, Sam E., Terence R. Mitchell, and Cecil H. Bell. Goal Setting, Evaluation Apprehension, and Social Cues as Determinants of Job Performance and Job Satisfaction in a Simulated Organization, *Journal of Applied Psychology*, Vol. 62 (1977), 665–673.

Wikstrom, Walter S. *Managing by- and with-Objectives.* New York: National Industrial Conference Board, 1968.

BEHAVIOR MODIFICATION AND OPERANT LEARNING

8

For many years the concepts of behaviorism have permeated psychological thought; in fact various behavioristic "schools" have characterized the field almost from its beginnings. In recent years, however, behaviorism in psychology and the name of B. F. Skinner have become almost synonymous. Skinner's publications on the subject now span almost 50 years of a career that started at

Harvard, extended to the universities of Minnesota and Indiana, and then in 1948 shifted back to Harvard.

Originally Skinner's research and thinking focused on animals, and he gave little attention to practical applications of his ideas. Gradually his horizons expanded, a change that is readily apparent if one traces the development of his ideas through his books. Of these *Science and Human Behavior* (Skinner, 1953), *Beyond Freedom and Dignity* (Skinner, 1971), and *About Behaviorism* (Skinner, 1974) provide the most comprehensive statements regarding matters that have significance for the study of organizations.

Skinner himself, however, has written little and conducted no research dealing directly with organizational topics; his concerns have been either with individual behavior or with the broad spectrum of culture and societal functioning. Thus, it has fallen to others to extrapolate Skinner's ideas into the organizational setting and to conduct research related to those extrapolations. Skinner indicates his own relationship to the field of organizational study in the following quote from one of the two interviews that represent his only specific published contributions to the field (Skinner and Dowling, 1973; Skinner and Hall, 1972):

> I'm not a specialist in industrial psychology. I have only a casual acquaintance with the kinds of things done by Douglas McGregor and Abe Maslow. They do not strike me as being particularly effective. You can classify motives and still neglect contingencies of reinforcement, and the contingencies are the important thing. Behavior modification is beginning to get into industry, and that may mean a change. Up to now it's been most effective in psychotherapy, in handling disturbed and retarded children, in the design of classroom management, and in programmed instruction. It is possible that we're going to see an entirely different kind of psychology in industry. Unfortunately there are not yet many people who understand the principle. It is not something that can be taken over by the nonprofessional to use as a rule of thumb. In the not-too-distant future, however, a new breed of industrial manager may be able to apply the principles of operant conditioning effectively (Skinner and Dowling, 1973, p. 40).

EXTRAPOLATIONS FROM SKINNER TO THE ORGANIZATIONAL CONTEXT

A number of different individuals have published extensions of Skinner's ideas to the organizational domain, most of them during a relatively brief period in the late 1960s and early 1970s. The industrial *Zeitgeist* appears to have been ripe for this kind of approach, since an earlier effort (Aldis, 1961) had almost no impact. Some of these extrapolations are presented as direct restatements of Skinner's previously published views; others do not even acknowledge a debt to Skinner. But all are directly concerned with the process of influencing employee behavior to desired ends using techniques of behavior modification.

The initial statement appears to be that of Nord (1969). This in turn elicited various extensions and replies (Heiman, 1975; Jablonsky and DeVries, 1972). Shortly thereafter came articles by Luthans and White (1971) and Sorcher (1971). Hamner (1974) presented a particularly comprehensive statement of Skinner's views as applied to the organizational context that appears to provide the best starting point for the present discussion in that it is most closely allied to the Skinnerian origins. Hamner has served on the faculties of several universities including Michigan State, Northwestern, and most recently Duke.

Hamner's Formulation of Reinforcement Theory

The basic concept of the theory is *learning*, defined as "a relatively permanent change in behavior potentiality that results from reinforced practice or experience" (Hamner, 1974, p. 87). Performance is the translation of what is learned into practice. Through reinforcement certain behaviors are strengthened and intensified and thus occur more frequently.

Behavior may occur in a reflex manner in response to changes in the environment. This type of behavior is of little concern for the theory. What is important is *operant* behavior, behavior emitted by a person that influences or has an effect upon the individual's outside world. Operant behaviors are learned as consequences accrue in the form of rewards and punishments that are applied contingent upon whether certain behaviors do or do not occur. Thus, the role of the supervisor becomes one of orchestrating reinforcements to produce desired behaviors at a high frequency; this is how performance can be improved.

Operant learning involves a process whereby reinforcers are applied to initially randomly emitted behaviors. Accordingly, to understand a person's behavior one must know the situation in which the behavior occurs, the nature of the behavior, and the reinforcing consequences. To influence a person's behavior in a desired direction one must know how to arrange correctly the contingencies of reinforcement. The major hypotheses of the theory relate to the relative effectiveness of manipulating the contingencies of reinforcement in different ways.

Types of Contingencies. Four different types of arrangements of contingencies are specified. Two serve to strengthen desired behavior (positive reinforcement and avoidance learning) and two serve to weaken undesired behavior (extinction and punishment). "A *positive reinforcer* is a stimulus which, when added to a situation, strengthens the probability of an operant response" (Skinner, 1953, p. 73). Certain reinforcers such as food, water, and sex are innate and thus operate independent of past experiences. In the work context, however, the important reinforcers are learned such as advancement, praise, recognition, and money. What is a reinforcer for one person may not be for another; it depends on the individual's past reinforcement history.

Hamner (1974) describes three steps in the successful application of reinforcement theory in the work environment:

1. Select reinforcers that are powerful and durable for the individual.
2. Design contingencies so as to make the occurrence of reinforcing events contingent upon desired behavior.
3. Design contingencies so that a reliable procedure for eliciting the desired behavior is established.

The third point is important because if one cannot ever find the desired behavior to reward, learning cannot occur. Training thus becomes a method of *shaping* behavior so that it can be controlled by reinforcement procedures. Separate aspects and approximations of the total desired behavior are reinforced until finally the behavior as a whole is shaped; learning to drive a car might be an example.

Avoidance learning operates in a manner similar to positive reinforcement except that the desired behavior serves to prevent the onset of a noxious stimulus, or, in a variant, terminates such a stimulus that already exists. In the workplace, supervisory criticism is often such a noxious stimulus. Although avoidance learning is effective under certain circumstances, many behavior modification advocates, including Skinner, much prefer positive reinforcement.

Extinction occurs when a previously utilized positive reinforcer is withheld. Under such circumstances the behavior involved may continue for some time, but as the reward continually fails to appear, the behavior diminishes and ultimately is extinguished entirely. This approach is appropriate when an individual brings undesired behaviors to the job or when an undesired behavior has inadvertently been reinforced in the past.

Many behavior modification advocates prefer extinction to *punishment* as a method of influencing behavior, on the grounds that punishment may have certain negative side effects. Skinner himself does not favor the use of punishment. There are, however, many behavior modification approaches in use that draw heavily on the reinforcement effects of punishment. There is no unanimity on this matter.

Hamner (1974) and Hamner and Hamner (1976) present several rules for using operant conditioning techniques, which might best be considered as hypotheses with regard to how desired behaviors may be obtained.

1. Do not give the same level of reward to all; differentiate based on some performance standard.
2. Failure to respond to behavior has reinforcing consequences; these consequences should be recognized, and nonactions as well as actions adjusted to the desired ends.
3. Tell a person what behavior gets reinforced.
4. Tell a person what he or she is doing wrong.
5. Do not punish in front of others; there may be undesirable side effects not only for the person punished but for the others as well.
6. Make the consequences equal to the behavior.

Schedules of Reinforcement. Although a variety of different reinforcement schedules are possible, certain ones are of particular theoretical and practical relevance. *Continuous reinforcement* occurs when every instance of the desired behavior is followed by the reinforcer. This approach often is not practical in a complex work environment in which managers supervise many employees. Although continuous reinforcement fosters rapid learning, it also produces behavior that is subject to rapid extinction, should the reinforcer be removed for any reason. Overall some kind of *partial reinforcement* schedule is recommended.

Partial reinforcement, when reinforcement does not occur after every emergence of an operant, is relatively slow but has the advantage of considerable permanence. Four such schedules require discussion:

Fixed interval — reinforcement occurs when the desired behavior manifests itself after a set period of time has passed since the previous reinforcement.

Variable interval — reinforcement occurs at some variable interval of time around an average.

Fixed ratio — reinforcement occurs after a fixed number of desired behaviors are produced.

Variable ratio — reinforcement occurs after a number of desired responses, with this number changing from one reinforcement to the next, varying around an average.

These schedules are presented in order of anticipated increasing effectiveness. Fixed interval procedures tend to yield cyclical fluctuations with desired behaviors maximized just prior to reinforcement. In general the variable approaches produce slower extinction and more stable performance levels. The variable ratio schedule is considered to be particularly attractive, although it may not be as easy to implement. In all instances it is important that the reinforcer follow the desired behavior as closely as possible.

Stages in Developing a Positive Reinforcement Program. Hamner (1977) and Hamner and Hamner (1976) have set forth certain steps or stages that should be followed in introducing a positive reinforcement program in a company. In essence this is an applied theory of performance maximization. Underlying these statements is the view that positive reinforcement should be maximized and punishment minimized. Furthermore, worker attitudes as a cause of behavior are ignored on the grounds that behavior can be fully explained in terms of the work situation and the contingencies of reinforcement.

The *first* stage is to define performance in strictly behavioral terms and to conduct a performance audit with the objective of establishing a *baseline* for measuring future performance. This procedure makes it possible to determine what the current performance situation is, in as objective a manner as possible.

The *second* stage involves setting specific and reasonable performance goals for each worker, expressed in measurable terms. These goals, however they may be established, are external to the individual; there is no invoking of experiential concepts such as intentions, expectations, and the like.

The *third* stage is to have the employee maintain a continuing record of work, a schedule of reinforcements. This way it is possible for the individual to picture how current work contrasts with that of the performance audit stage and with the goals established in stage two. The objective is to create a situation in which behavior that will warrant positive reinforcement occurs. One way of doing this is to shorten the time intervals of measurement as much as possible.

The *fourth stage* is described as follows:

> The supervisor looks at the self-feedback report of the employee and/or other indications of performance (e.g. sales records) and then praises the positive aspects of the employee's performance (as determined by the performance audit and goals set). This extrinsic reinforcement should strengthen the desired performance, while the withholding of praise for the performance which falls below the goal should give the employee incentive to improve that level of performance. Since the worker already knows the areas of his or her deficiencies, there is no reason for the supervisor to criticize . . . use of positive reinforcement leads to a greater feeling of self-control, while the avoidance of negative reinforcements keeps the individual from feeling controlled or coerced (Hamner, 1977, p. 261).

Although the above discussion focuses on reinforcement by praise, other approaches may be used as appropriate to the individual's reinforcement history, including money, freedom to choose one's activities, opportunity to see oneself achieving, higher status on some dimension, and power over others.

Luthans' Organizational Behavior Modification

Luthans, who has published with several different co-authors, has spent most of his professional career at the University of Nebraska. His formulations parallel those of Hamner in a number of respects, not surprising because both draw heavily from Skinner. However, Luthans treatment is more comprehensive, dealing with a wider range of topics and with some of Hamner's topics in greater depth (Luthans and Kreitner, 1975).

Furthermore, Luthans is even more explicit in following Skinner with regard to the rejection of internal states (attitudes, motives, feelings, and the like) as causes of behavior. Behavior is said to be strictly a function of its consequences, not of internal motives; thus the theory is really one of learning, not motivation, although the ultimate outcome remains performance, as in the preceding theories. Unobservable internal states are irrelevant to understanding behavior and generally are mere concomitants of the behaviors themselves. Inner state constructs such as achievement motivation, expectancy, intentions and goals, self-actualization, feelings of equity, and so on have no place in the theory. At least they are said not to. In this sense it represents a radical departure from previous theories; many consider the formulations essentially untheoretical.

Luthans, in contrast to some others who generally espouse behaviorist views but include internal variables in their formulations (see Jablonsky and DeVries, 1972), would thus fully accept the following quote from Skinner (1975, p. 43):

> What we feel are conditions of our bodies, most of them closely associated with behavior and with the circumstances in which we behave. We both strike *and* feel angry for a common reason, and that reason lies in the environment. In short, the bodily conditions we feel are *collateral products* of our genetic and environmental histories. They have no explanatory force; they are simply additional facts to be taken into account.

Stages of the Behavioral Contingency Management Model. Luthans and Kreitner (1975) present an approach to identifying and managing the critical performance-related behaviors of employees in organizations. They call this approach the behavioral contingency management model for organizational behavior modification. This model presents a series of stages not unlike those suggested by Hamner:

1. Identify performance-related behaviors using the following questions as guidelines —
   a. Can the behavior be reduced to *observable* behavioral events?
   b. Can one *count* how often each behavior occurs?
   c. *Exactly* what must the person do before a behavior is recorded?
   d. Is a key *performance-related* behavior involved?
2. Measure to establish the baseline frequencies of behaviors using such procedures as tally sheets and time sampling.
3. Identify existing contingencies of reinforcement to determine where the behavior takes place and what its consequences are by —
   a. Analyzing histories of reinforcement.
   b. Using self-report measures.
   c. Resorting to systematic trial and error to identify reinforcers.
4. Carry out the intervention process as follows —
   a. Develop an intervention strategy considering such environmental variables as structures, processes, technologies, groups, and tasks.
   b. Apply the appropriate strategy using suitable types of contingencies.
   c. Measure to establish the frequencies of behaviors after intervention.
   d. Maintain desired behaviors through the use of appropriate schedules of reinforcement.
5. Evaluate the overall performance impacts.

Obviously there are differences in this approach as opposed to Hamner, such as with regard to establishing goals and the techniques of measurement used. But overall the similarities are greater than the differences. The two together provide a reasonably good picture of how behavior modification theory can reduce to practice.

Shaping, Modeling, and Self-Control. Shaping, which is considered only relatively briefly by Hamner, is described in a step-by-step manner in Figure 8–1. The following quote serves to amplify that statement:

> Closer approximations to the target response are emitted and contingently reinforced. The less desirable approximations, including those reinforced earlier in the shaping process, are put on extinction. In this manner, behavior may actually be shaped into what is desired. Shaping solves the problem of waiting for the opportunity to reinforce a desired response. It is a particularly important technique in behavior modification if a desired response is not currently in a person's behavior repertoire (Luthans and Kreitner, 1975, p. 55).

Shaping	Modeling
1. Define the performance-related target behavior.	1. Identify the target behavior desired.
2. If the target behavior is a complex chain, reduce it to a discrete, observable, and measurable sequence of steps.	2. Select the appropriate model and its medium, such as in-person demonstration, training film.
3. Be sure the individual is able to meet the skill and ability requirements of each step.	3. Be sure the individual is capable of meeting the skill requirements of the target behavior.
4. Select appropriate positive reinforcers based on the individual's history of reinforcement.	4. Structure a favorable learning, context with regard to attention, participation, and the target behavior.
5. Structure the contingent environment so that antecedent conditions will foster desired behavior.	5. Model the target behavior and support it by activities such as role playing; demonstrate the positive consequences of the modeled behavior.
6. Make all positive reinforcements contingent on increasingly close approximations to the target behavior so that the behavioral chain is built gradually.	6. Reinforce all progress of the modeled behavior.
7. Once the target behavior is achieved, reinforce it at first continuously and then on a variable basis.	7. Once the target behavior is achieved, reinforce it at first continuously and then on a variable basis.

Figure 8–1. Strategies for shaping and modeling.

(Adapted from Fred Luthans and Robert Kreitner. *Organizational Behavior Modification.* Glenview, Ill.: Scott, Foresman, 1975, pp. 132–133, 140–141.)

Figure 8–1 also sets forth the steps in modeling, a type of learning that has a somewhat uncertain status in behavior modification. Note that phrases such as attention, participation, and demonstration of positive consequences come into the discussion — implying internal causal states that a true behaviorist should consider irrelevant to theory construction. It is difficult to deal with modeling or imitation without resort to such constructs; yet complex behaviors do become learned rather quickly, obviously too quickly to be a result of shaping. Luthans and Kreitner (1975) follow Bandura (1971) in making this kind of learning part of their theory even though it is almost impossible to handle it without resort to internal constructs such as imagination, memory, and the like. At this point a certain amount of logical inconsistency is introduced into their theory.

This same problem plagues the discussion of *self-control* as well, another concept of somewhat uncertain status in behavior modification theory. In the strict behavioral sense, self-control involves the manipulation of environmental consequences by the individual to determine his own behavior. However, most who try to put the idea to use in the employment context, including Luthans and Kreitner, find it impossible not to invoke internal constructs.

The Use of Punishment. As Hamner notes, punishment as a type of contingency can have certain negative side effects that make it relatively unattractive. In contrast Luthans is more accepting of the use of punishment, while recognizing its limitations. Four such side effects are noted:

1. Punishment serves to suppress behavior temporarily rather than to change it permanently, with the result that a method of continued punitive reinforcement must be devised; often this requires a manager's continued presence.
2. Punishment generates emotional behavior, often against the punisher.
3. Punishment may serve not to suppress behavior temporarily, but to stifle it permanently under any and all circumstances, thus producing a degree of behavioral inflexibility.
4. A frequently punishing individual may assume the role of a conditioned aversive stimulus, with the result that he or she disrupts self-control efforts and cannot effectively administer positive reinforcers.

These considerations generally are consistent with those discussed by Nord (1969), who also indicates that punishment does not necessarily produce the desired behavior, only the cessation of the punished behavior. Another undesired behavior may be next in the response hierarchy, replacing the one punished. Yet, given all these arguments punishment is still widely used in managing organizations and in behavior modification (Luthans and Kreitner, 1973).

Goldstein and Sorcher's Applied Learning

Goldstein, a professor of psychology at Syracuse University who previously had worked primarily on the clinical applications of behavior modification, and Sorcher, a psychologist with General Electric, have developed an approach to supervisory training that relies heavily on modeling techniques (Goldstein and Sorcher, 1974). Their approach, called *applied learning*, represents essentially a theory of how behavior may be changed to yield more effective (desired) supervisory performance and ultimately subordinate performance. Clearly the concepts are closely allied to those of behavior modification, but the strong emphasis on modeling puts the approach somewhat on the periphery of that theoretical framework rather than in the mainstream as with the approaches of Hamner and Luthans. This peripheral status is evident in that Goldstein and Sorcher do not mention Skinner in their book and also by their explicit utilization of internal variables.

Modeling. The technique starts with the presentation of a display, usually filmed, that depicts effective supervisor-employee interactions. This situation is designed to maximize attention to a few major learning points. Attention is enhanced when the model is of high status, competent, and of the same age and sex as the supervisor, and when the model is depicted as rewarded for the desired, learning point behaviors.

Effective learning by modeling requires that learning point behaviors be retained in memory; this is facilitated by fostering both covert, internal rehearsal in the mind and overt, behavioral rehearsal. Furthermore, for these learned behaviors to manifest themselves on the job there must be an anticipation of reward. This is most likely when the model receives large, consistent, immediate, and frequent rewards for the desired behavior.

Role-playing. The next component of applied learning is role-playing, in which the supervisors participate in the practice and overt rehearsal of the learning point behaviors. Successive approximation to the desired behavior of the model is enhanced by giving the supervisor a choice regarding role-playing participation, having the role-playing done publicly before the other supervisors in training to increase behavioral commitment, providing opportunities to improvise in the role-playing situation, and introducing reinforcement of the desired role-play behaviors. The objective is to produce stable behavior change and thus increase the supervisor's repertoire of behaviors that he can use on the job.

Social Reinforcement. Social reinforcement in such forms as praise and constructive feedback is applied to the role-play behavior by both the trainer and the other supervisors participating in the training. The theoretical guidelines for application of this reinforcement are essentially those of behavior modification theory in general. Regarding reinforcement, Goldstein and Sorcher (1974, p. 55) note:

> Though it is largely true that reinforcement alone is more likely to lead to *enduring* behavior change than either modeling or role-playing alone, it is also true that the behaviors to be reinforced must occur with sufficient correctness and sufficient frequency for reinforcement to have its intended effect. Modeling can provide the correctness; role-playing can provide the frequency.

Transfer Training.   Ultimately the objective of the total training process is to achieve transfer or generalization of the new behaviors from the classroom to the job setting. In applied learning, four approaches are incorporated toward this end:

1. General principles or advance organizers regarding satisfactory performance are provided before the model display and during role-play to make it easier to apply what is learned to specific job situations.
2. High levels of practice and overlearning are utilized to maximize response availability on the job.
3. The training context is made as much like the job as possible, thus maximizing the number of identical elements.
4. Conditions are established to provide continued social reinforcement on the job after training, such as having several levels of management within a department all experience the same training.

ORGANIZATIONALLY RELEVANT RESEARCH

In the preceding section a number of theoretical statements were presented, not in hypothetical form but as principles already established by research. The reason for this method of presentation is that considerable research support developed over a long period of time prior to any attempt to extrapolate behavior modification theory to the organizational context. Much of this research involves laboratory work with animals only, and all of it is at most tangentially relevant to organizational functioning. Since the focus of this volume is on organizational behavior, all of the theoretical statements made by Hamner, Luthans, Goldstein and Sorcher, and others become subject to new test, regardless of their status in other contexts. We are interested in how well reinforcement theory, organizational behavior modification theory, and applied learning theory work in organizations and in comparing them with other theories designed for the same ends. Our intent is not to evaluate Skinnerian behaviorism. The research on that theoretical orientation is not relevant for our purposes, since it has been carried out almost without exception in less complex environments than the functioning organization.

Schedules of Reinforcement

Some of the research conducted to evaluate other theories bears on behavior modification theory as well, although typically it does not yield a preference for a particular theoretical alternative. Thus research dealing with contingent rewards from an expectancy theory orientation may be just as relevant for behavior modification theory while providing no greater support for one theory than the other, since both emphasize the value of rewards that are contingent on desired behaviors (Schneier, 1974).

Studies dealing with the relative effectiveness of various types of schedules of reinforcement do separate the two theories, with expectancy theory tending to favor continuous reinforcement and behavior modification theory partial reinforcement, especially that of the variable ratio variety. Thus, it becomes particularly important to determine how schedules of reinforcement operate in work settings.

The early research dealing with this factor was plagued with a number of difficulties and did not yield conclusive results. It has not proved easy to conduct studies of this kind in either simulation or field settings, and sample sizes often have been small. However, a consistent pattern of findings has now begun to emerge.

A field study in which workers planted pine seedlings under various alternating schedules of reinforcement (base pay and incentive bonuses) indicated that incentive reinforcement did yield higher productivity (trees per man hour). However, the variable ratio schedule was not better than continuous reinforcement; if anything it was less effective. This was true despite the fact that the planters made more money under variable ratio conditions (Yukl, Latham, and Pursell, 1976).

A simulation study in which part-time student workers coded attitude questionnaire data on IBM coding sheets also failed to provide evidence of the superiority of variable ratio over continuous scheduling. Performance improved over the baseline period when incentives were introduced but not significantly more sharply in the variable ratio groups (Berger, Cummings, and Heneman, 1975). Another simulation study, also utilizing part-time workers, required the learning of programmed instructional materials in the field of electronics. Comparisons were made among hourly, fixed ratio, variable ratio, and variable ratio-variable amount schedules. The evidence favored the ratio schedules over hourly payment, but no significant differences were found among the three ratio schedules — the variable schedules were not superior (Pritchard, Leonard, Von Bergen, and Kirk, 1976).

A final study provides some possible insight into the preceding findings. The subjects were trappers paid to catch rats that eat young trees planted for reforestation purposes. After a baseline period at their regular hourly pay, half of the group went to an hourly pay plus continuous reinforcement schedule (a set bonus per rat trapped) and half to an hourly pay plus variable ratio schedule (bonus paid for an average of every fourth rat); later these reinforcement schedules were reversed (Latham and Dossett, 1978). The findings under the various conditions are given in Table 8–1.

For the group as a whole the incentive conditions produced improved performance. Even with additional bonus costs the total cost of catching a rat dropped from $16.75 prior to the study to $12.86. Once again continuous reinforcement was at least as effective as variable ratio. However, when the trappers were split into experienced and inexperienced groups, the variable ratio schedule exhibited clear superiority among the more experienced. These individuals already had learned the job well, and thus the impact of the variable ratio bonus must have been on performance only. The less experienced were presumably still learning, and here the continuous schedule operated more effectively. Given that in the three previous studies the subjects were all temporary or part-time workers, most of them somewhat inexperienced, it is not surprising that they also did as well or better under continuous or fixed schedules. It would appear that certain kinds of individual differences may mediate the effects of the various schedules. However, it is not clear exactly when experience might be expected to moderate the effects of reinforcement schedules.

Improving Attendance and Performance

There is a gradually evolving field research literature pointing to the effectiveness of behavior modification and operant learning procedures in organizational management. In general these studies compare conditions during a baseline period with those existing subsequent to the introduction of behavior modification proce-

Table 8–1.   RATS TRAPPED PER MAN HOUR ON VARIOUS REINFORCEMENT SCHEDULES

	Baseline Period	Continuous Reinforcement	Variable Ratio Reinforcement
	Hourly Pay Only	*Beyond Hourly Pay*	*Beyond Hourly Pay*
All trappers	.44	.67	.58
Trappers of above average experience		.48	.72
Trappers of below average experience		.70	.63

Adapted from Gary P. Latham and Dennis L. Dossett. Designing Incentive Plans for Unionized Employees: A Comparison of Continuous and Variable Ratio Reinforcement Schedules, *Personnel Psychology,* Vol. 31 (1978), pp. 53–54.

dures. In some but not all instances, control groups not exposed to behavior modification are included in the analysis.

A study that did include a control condition was carried out in five manufacturing/distribution facilities of a single company (Pedalino and Gamboa, 1974). A procedure intended to reduce absenteeism was introduced in one facility but not in the other four. No change in absenteeism over the period of study occurred in the four control facilities. The baseline absenteeism rate in the experimental facility was 3.01 per cent. Then a procedure was introduced whereby when an employee came to work on time each day he chose a card from a deck of playing cards. The individual from each work group with the best poker hand at the end of the week received a $20 bonus; thus there was partial reinforcement. Absenteeism dropped to 2.38 per cent. When the reinforcement was stretched to two weeks, by running the program every other week, a rate of 2.51 per cent was maintained. After the program was terminated absenteeism went back up to 3.02 per cent.

A second study dealt with various performance measures in two small businesses (Komaki, Waddell, and Pearce, 1977). The first analysis was conducted in a neighborhood grocery store with two employees performing sales clerk and stocking duties. Performance was monitored by intermittent observation in terms of clerk presence, assistance given customers, and completeness of stocking. After a baseline period, the clerks were trained in desired behaviors through discussion, modeling, and role-playing. Reinforcement was through time off with pay, visually presented feedback, and the clerk's own self-recordings. Performance improvements averaged 38 percentage points on the three criterion variables after the behavior modification interventions were introduced, and follow-up data indicated that these changes were maintained.

A similar analysis was conducted with a single attendant at a game room in a downtown area. Again highly specific desired behaviors were defined and observation was used to obtain measures. Reinforcement was in terms of pay differentials on a contingent basis and goal clarification discussions. Baseline and behavior modification conditions were alternated twice. The average baseline performance level was 63 per cent; the average level under behavior modification procedures was 95 per cent. It was quite apparent that when behavior modification procedures were in effect performance improved, and when they were not it returned to baseline.

Research in Quality Control

Research in quality control has been stimulated in large part by the popularity of Zero Defects programs in industry. These programs

are not necessarily congruent with any particular theoretical orientation, although a strong goal setting emphasis would appear to be
present frequently. Nevertheless, behavior modification advocates
have exhibited considerable interest in determining whether the
kinds of improvements in production quality attempted through Zero
Defects can be achieved through reinforcement schedules.

The initial research was conducted in laboratory settings with
student subjects and produced mixed results. However, one such
study by Johnson (1975) did yield certain promising findings. The
task involved the use of IBM keypunch equipment. Subjects initially
received monetary reinforcement for quantity of output on a fixed
interval schedule. Subsequently, some subjects were exposed to
persuasive influence attempts involving quality, of the kind used in
Zero Defects programs; then some subjects continued on the quantity
reinforcement schedule, while others were shifted to a fixed interval
schedule that made pay levels contingent on performance quality.
The persuasive influence variable proved to have little effect. However, reinforcing quality did result in a reduction of errors, although at
the expense of a relatively lower quantity performance level than that
for the subjects staying on quantity reinforcement whose quantity of
output continued to improve but with decreasing quality. The quality
changes, although statistically significant, were not large.

A later study attempted to extend these findings to the field
setting (Adam, 1975). After baseline measurement, a behavior modification program involving supervisory feedback and verbal reinforcement on a fixed interval schedule was introduced in the three shifts of
a diecasting manufacturing facility. The verbal reinforcement, although not ignoring quantity, gave particular attention to reducing
scrap and thus improving quality. As indicated in Table 8–2, this
quality emphasis was not effective; if anything the scrap rates increased, but performance quantity did improve. The overall result of
the program was an estimated 77,000-dollar per year saving. At the
present time it appears that the amount of output is much more easily
influenced by behavior modification than the quality of output.

Table 8–2. QUALITY AND QUANTITY OF DIECASTING PERFORMANCE
BEFORE AND AFTER 30 WEEKS OF BEHAVIOR MODIFICATION

	Quality (per cent scrap saved)		Quantity (per cent performance)	
	Before	*After*	*Before*	*After*
Shift 1	6.8	7.3	89.4	95.0
Shift 2	6.0	6.0	89.5	97.1
Shift 3	4.1	4.9	93.4	97.4
All Shifts	5.5	6.0	90.9	96.6

Adapted from Everett E. Adam. Behavior Modification in Quality Control, *Academy of Management Journal*, Vol. 18 (1975), p. 671.

Modeling and Applied Learning

There is good evidence that modeling on the behaviors of superiors perceived as effective is an important method by which managers develop their own leadership styles (Weiss, 1977). Thus the underlying premise of the applied learning approach is upheld. In addition, the few studies that have been undertaken to evaluate the approach in terms of its impact on performance are generally favorable.

The first such study was conducted at General Electric to facilitate the retention of disadvantaged employees (Goldstein and Sorcher, 1974). Parallel films were developed for both the employees and their supervisors. The supervisor films modeled and depicted reward for tact, coolness, patience, thoroughness, and control; the employee films emphasized that it takes courage to succeed, the value of working at a job, and job success. The situations dealt with were: not quitting, how to teach a task, developing trust, pride in work, reactions to ostracism, the new environment, absenteeism, and lateness. Each film was introduced and summarized by a narrator of high status, such as the plant manager for the supervisors and a famous black athlete for the employees. Role-playing was interspersed with the films, and continuous social reinforcement from the instructors and other training group members was provided for role-playing behaviors that were similar to or identical with those of the model. In all there were five two-hour sessions in both the supervisor and the disadvantaged employee programs.

Comparisons were made between those new employees who went through the applied learning sessions and a comparable group who were oriented in a more conventional manner. The major evaluation was in terms of turnover rates, since the experimental program was initiated to reduce separations. After six months, 72 per cent of the applied learning group were still on the job, in contrast to only 28 per cent of the control group. Subsequently the program was extended to first-line supervisors at GE, regardless of whether they had hard-core employees.

A similar program for supervisors at A.T. and T. was initiated with special attention to methods of dealing with minority and female employees (Moses and Ritchie, 1976). Again trained and untrained control groups were compared in terms of rated performance in a specially devised assessment center. The evaluations, which were made two months after completion of training, are summarized in Table 8–3. Although the design is of the "after only" type and thus does not indicate with certainty that the two groups started at the same point, there is reason to believe that the training produced a real change in performance potential. Whether it influenced on-the-job performance is unknown.

Table 8–3. DISTRIBUTIONS OF SUBSEQUENT ASSESSMENT CENTER RATINGS FOR SUPERVISORS WHO HAD AND HAD NOT UNDERGONE APPLIED LEARNING TRAINING

Assessment Center Rating	Trained Supervisors (N = 90)	Matched Controls (N = 93)
Exceptional	26	8
Above average	50	21
Average	9	33
Below average	5	27
Poor	0	4

Adapted from Joseph L. Moses and Richard J. Ritchie. Supervisory Relationships Training: A Behavioral Evaluation of a Behavioral Modeling Program, *Personnel Psychology*, Vol. 29 (1976), p. 342.

Comparative Studies

One argument against the applications of behavior modification in industry is that what is being done is not very new and that the approaches used depart so far from the basic tenets of behavior modification as expounded by Skinner that the findings cannot provide a real test of that theory (Locke, 1977). One way of assessing this type of argument is to compare predictions from behavior modification theory with those from other theories. If behavior modification predictions are independent of those from other theories and account for a large amount of criterion variance, then the arguments must be dismissed.

A limited amount of research has been conducted along these lines producing comparisons with expectancy theory and goal setting theory. A study already discussed dealing with alternative reinforcement schedules contains additional data on the relative effectiveness of expectancy theory predictions (Berger, Cummings, and Heneman, 1975). In this instance performance predictions from expectancy theory data appear to be superior to those from behavior modification theory. In fact behavior modification theory with expectancy relationships removed did not yield any significant results. However, small sample sizes and a lack of consistency in the findings hamper the interpretation of this study or at least the expectancy theory aspects of it.

In another instance goal setting and behavior modification were compared. Managers in management development were exposed to role-playing exercises; in addition some experienced delayed appraisal and goal setting back on the job, where telecoaching reinforcement was also used in conjunction with the role-playing. This latter is a behavior modification technique described as follows:

> . . . a trainer attempts to reinforce effective behaviors and modify ineffective behaviors by providing verbal feedback. The feedback, received by the trainee

through an ear device, is immediate in nature and behavioral in context. Specifically, the trainer provides verbal reinforcement, cuing, and shaping to the trainee via a small microphone device kept in the trainee's ear while he performs the role-playing exercises. The reinforcement, mostly positive, is given continuously at first and later intermittently. The trainer cues the trainee's behavior by not always waiting for the desired responses to be emitted, but by suggesting to the trainee ways in which he could be more effective. The trainer shapes the trainee's behavior by reinforcing successively closer approximations to the desired response (Wexley and Nemeroff, 1975, pp. 447–448).

The results of these various treatments, as viewed through the eyes of the managers' subordinates, are given in Table 8–4. In general, the delayed appraisal and goal setting procedures appear to have produced results above and beyond those achieved from mere role-playing. But the behavior modification approach adds nothing, and regarding work satisfaction it has a negative impact.

Table 8–4. AFTER ONLY DATA OBTAINED TWO MONTHS AFTER TRAINING FOR THREE DIFFERENT SUPERVISORY TRAINING METHODS (OBTAINED FROM SUPERVISORS' SUBORDINATES)

	Training Method		
	Role-Playing Delayed Appraisal Goal Setting	Role-Playing Delayed Appraisal Goal Setting Telecoaching Reinforcement	Role-Playing Only (Control)
Subordinates' rating of supervisors'—			
Consideration (regards the comfort, well-being, status, and contributions of followers)	34.1*	35.4*	30.5
Integration (maintains a closely knit group and resolves intermember conflicts)	16.7*	15.7*	14.2
Production emphasis (applies pressure for productive output)	29.6	27.7	27.9
Initiating structure (clearly defines own role and lets subordinates know what is expected)	37.1	36.3	34.4
Subordinates' satisfaction—			
With work	35.8*	30.0	29.2
With supervision	38.7	41.1	36.5
Subordinates' absenteeism	1.1*	1.2*	2.2

*Differs significantly from control group

Adapted from Kenneth N. Wexley and Wayne F. Nemeroff. Effectiveness of Positive Reinforcement and Goal Setting as Methods of Management Development, *Journal of Applied Psychology*, Vol. 60 (1975), pp. 448–449.

The Kim and Hamner (1976) research considered in the previous chapter tends to suggest a somewhat more positive role for variable interval positive reinforcement of a verbal nature. The results seem to indicate that the reinforcement procedures add something beyond goal setting alone. However, it is not entirely clear how this "something" was added; it may well have been greater goal acceptance and thus entirely explainable within the confines of goal setting theory. Overall, the results of this study support the use of feedback in addition to goal setting, but they do not specifically support the use of the kinds of feedback advocated by behavior modification theory. Thus, again the data do not indicate any relative advantage for behavior modification.

BROAD SCALE APPLICATIONS

During the late 1960s and 1970s a number of organizations have undertaken sizable, continuing applications of behavior modification with the objective of reducing absenteeism, increasing output, achieving cost savings, and the like. These applications typically involve specific, relatively large components within the organization. In most instances they do not represent controlled experiments so much as demonstrations of behavior modification's feasibility. Frequently hard data on successes and failures are lacking, and one must rely on testimonials. A recent survey of ten organizations known to have instituted behavior modification procedures indicated that nine of them considered the procedures to have been successful in some degree (Hamner and Hamner, 1976). The following descriptions provide some indication of the range of applications utilized. An effort has been made to select examples in which the consequences are reasonably well documented.

Leading Hardware and Metropolitan School

Nord (1970) describes two programs instituted to reduce absenteeism, one in a six-store hardware chain and the other in a large city school district. The hardware program was a lottery in which perfect attendance for a given period made an employee eligible to draw for a prize and also caused his or her name to be printed in the company newspaper. During the first year this program was estimated to have reduced absenteeism to one-fourth its baseline level; however, subsequent results were not as pronounced, with a trend back toward the original level.

The metropolitan school program was for teachers only, and provided a fixed interval monetary award for perfect attendance. Over a five-year period the program was clearly successful. Yet most of the improvement occurred in the second year, and there was a gradual return to the first-year level after that. Again the effects appear to have peaked at a relatively early point and then declined.

Emery Air Freight

The Emery Air Freight behavior modification applications were widely publicized in the early 1970s (Feeney, 1973), and more recent data are provided by Hamner and Hamner (1976). The procedures are typically applied to operations in which the biggest payoff can be anticipated — usually areas with relatively poor baseline performance. Initially these were sales and sales training, customer service, and containerized shipping.

The two major characteristics of the programs appear to be detailed, continuing measurement of the performance factor to be improved with daily feedback and the use of praise and recognition by supervisors. Supervisors are trained extensively in techniques of administering these positive reinforcements. They are to apply them at least twice a week in the early period and thereafter on a stretched variable interval schedule. In a three-year period an estimated 3 million dollar company saving resulted. However, a subsequent report from the president of the company raises some questions:

> **Inasmuch as praise is the most readily available no-cost reinforcer, it tends to be the reinforcer used most frequently. However, the results have been to dull its effect as a reinforcer through its sheer repetition, even to risk making praise an irritant to the receiver (Hamner and Hamner, 1976, p. 15).**

Organizational Behavior Modification Programs

Luthans and Kreitner (1975) document the use of their approach in a number of contexts including the customer service group of a major airline, a food processing company, and a U.S. Army battalion. However, these examples contain little information on results. Such information is provided in the case of a program introduced into a single plant engaged in light manufacturing (Luthans and Kreitner, 1975; Ottemann and Luthans, 1975).

One group of first-line supervisors was taught and coached in the previously described organizational behavior modification procedures over a ten-week period; a comparable group did not receive training. Although measured direct labor effectiveness in the production units of the trained and untrained supervisors was almost identical at the beginning, a significant difference emerged during training and was clearly in evidence two months after training was completed. The effectiveness percentage for the experimental units was 91, as opposed to 81 for the controls.

In addition to these composite data on overall performance, individual supervisors maintained measures against baseline with reference to specific problems they had during the training period. One was able to reduce the complaints of a problem employee dramatically by ignoring the complaints (extinction) and positively rewarding satisfactory production and constructive suggestions with praise. Another achieved a considerable reduction in group scrap rate, and another improved internal quality control by contingency contracting for expanded coffee breaks. Overall the supervisors definitely appear to have learned some techniques that they could put to good use on the job.

CONCLUSIONS

Evaluating behavior modification and operant learning theory in the organizational context is complicated by differences between Skinner and his extrapolators — and even among the extrapolators. Radical behaviorism of the Skinnerian variety is not identical with the theories of even those who claim to follow Skinner, especially in the area of internal or "mind" variables. These variations in theoretical position make it possible for advocates to attribute their results to some kind of behavior modification theory relatively easily; if one variety of the theory will not fit, another can be grasped. Such circumstances make the theory appear more broadly valid than has been demonstrated. This state of affairs is not attributable to Skinner. His stance is clear and, as theoretical positions go, quite unambiguous.

Scientific Goals

The most consistent criticisms of behavior modification theory as extrapolated to organizations are that its approach is not new and that as theory it is less adequate to explain behavior than other theories. Several authors have argued that what is done in the name of organizational behavior modification is very close to what Frederick Taylor and other advocates of scientific management extolled at the turn of the century (Fry, 1974; Locke, 1977).

There is considerable evidence that a theory that ignores cognitive variables does not work very well in explaining behavior when it moves into the realm of complex organizations (Mitchell, 1976). Consistently the extrapolators have felt compelled to repudiate the radical behaviorism of Skinner and introduce internal, cognitive factors. One reason for this is that under Skinnerian assumptions the only true way to understand and predict behavior, taking into account individual differences, is to comprehend the person's full reinforcement history. But this is a practical impossibility for mature working adults. Cognitively based theories typically view present thoughts, feelings, attitudes, and the like as providing an adequate representation of past experience and learning; accordingly, they offer a feasible method of dealing with factors that radical behaviorism cannot deal with practically.

Behaviorists argue that their theoretical approach has the advantage of parsimony. But in science, parsimony is a positive value only "all else being equal." In this case all is not equal; cognitive theories add something above and beyond the strict behaviorist approach in the areas of understanding, prediction, and managing the future. That is why when behavior modification moves into organizations, cognitive variables tend to emerge even when the theorists do their best to avoid them. This appears to be particularly true in dealing with such clearly important phenomena as modeling or imitation and self-control. But the question then becomes whether behavior modification and operant learning theory are needed at all. As a number of writers have indicated, expectancy theory and goal setting theory, perhaps even equity theory, may be more suitable (Klein, 1973; Korman, Greenhaus, and Badin, 1977; Locke, 1977). When one looks at the limited amount of comparative research available, the data do tend to favor expectancy and goal setting formulations over those of behavior modification. Thus, on the evidence, there is good reason to question whether behavior modification *theory* makes a useful independent contribution.

Empirically evaluating a theory is not simply a matter of determining whether other theories do a better job; it also involves testing the theory itself. A number of questions have been raised regarding the design and interpretation of results from behavior modification research (Locke, 1977; Mawhinney, 1975). In general the uncertainties thus created can be resolved by other studies now available. However, there is one problem that emerges with sufficient consistency to warrant serious consideration. Operant learning is by definition and experimental example a gradual process that requires considerable time and numerous reinforcements, on whatever schedule, to achieve its results. Yet some of the changes attributed to it appear to have occurred almost instantaneously or before reinforcement was presumed to intervene (Feeney, 1973; Otteman and Luthans, 1975; Pedalino and Gamboa, 1974). Such results are much more appropriately explained in terms of expectancies and intentions than by schedules of reinforcement.

A key aspect of the theory relates to the use of various schedules of reinforcement. In general this research strongly supports the use of contingent reinforcement, but this fact is just as consistent with other theoretical positions as with behavior modification. Beyond this finding, however, behavior modification theory does not receive strong support; continuous reinforcement appears to be much more effective than the theory predicts. There is some evidence from the Latham and Dossett (1978) research that variable ratio schedules can be highly effective with experienced workers. The timing of this phenomenon suggests a motivational rather than a learning impact. The result might have been predicted from such formulations as the Luthans and Kreitner (1975) admonition to reinforce target behaviors "at first continuously and then as on a variable basis." However, Luthans and Kreitner are not specific as to the time spans in their formulations, and thus one cannot say with any certainty whether the Latham and Dossett data offer support for this particular version of behavior modification theory. The current evidence does not credit behavior modification theory in the area of schedules of reinforcement, although it is possible that long-term longitudinal research would yield somewhat more favorable results. The looseness of the theory as regards time factors does present a problem.

The most favorable findings for the theory appear to occur in highly controllable contexts such as very small business, and with variables that are independent and separate such as absenteeism. As research moves to more complex situations involving quantity-quality interactions, interdependent work, and the like, the theory predicts less well, if at all. Furthermore, almost all of the research has focused on relatively low level employees rather than on managers or professionals. The greater control and lower job complexity at this level should facilitate obtaining positive results. Yet even when favorable findings do occur and can realistically be attributed to behavior modification procedures, there is reason to believe that the improvements may dissipate over a time if the procedures were instituted on a continuing basis. Whether the improvements represent essentially a temporary Hawthorne effect attributable to increased managerial attentions, as some have suggested, is unclear (Fry, 1974). In any event this diminishing effect is not something the basic theory would predict; it thus becomes additional negative evidence.

Managerial Goals

Whatever its status as a theory of organizational functioning, behavior modification has generated some useful inputs to managerial practice. Korman, Greenhaus, and Badin (1977, p. 189) provide a good description of the current situation:

> It is clear that the principles of operant conditioning are being applied in organizations at an accelerating rate . . . many of the techniques of OB Mod [organizational behavior modification] are hardly new to the organizational

behavior literature. Tying valued outcomes to desired behavior is the corner-stone of expectancy theory. The use of rewards as opposed to coercive power also has a rich history of research and theory, as does the importance of goal setting and the provision of clear feedback. Where then lies the distinctiveness of the OB Mod approach? Its major characteristic may be the mental set with which the manager approaches a situation. OB Mod requires the manager to observe quantifiable behaviors, to establish base rates in order to determine the extent of the problem, to determine what reinforcers are supporting the unde-sirable behaviors, to estimate what stimulus will reinforce the desired behav-ior, and to chart the frequency of the desired behavior after the reinforcement intervention. It is this critical look at behaviors and contingencies that prom-ises to provide a refreshing addition to the organizational behavior litera-ture.

Practical Considerations.   Given that a manager has developed the mental set implied by organizational behavior modification, where is the approach likely to work best? One requirement is that precise behavioral measures of the central performance variables in the work be possible. This is much more feasible for manual work than for managerial and professional positions. In any job there is always the risk that one will measure and reinforce behavior that is easily measured but contributes little if anything to actual perfor-mance.

Another requirement is that it be possible to control the contin-gencies of reinforcement. Much of the success of behavior modifica-tion has been achieved with children, often in schools, with hospital-ized mental patients, with prisoners, and of course originally with animals. In these cases control is relatively easy. In many jobs it is not; for instance, when reinforcements administered by coworkers have long been a primary influence on individual performance. A major factor contributing to the fact that operant learning procedures have been applied almost exclusively to lower level job incumbents is the relative ease of achieving the necessary control there. Modeling approaches have been used with managers, primarily at the first level, but even here the procedures are applied in the highly controlled environment of the management development program.

This need for control capability is closely related to a need for simplicity and independence. Developing an appropriate reinforce-ment approach becomes increasingly difficult as jobs become more complex, involving interacting performance dimensions, and relate to other jobs as subsystems of a larger whole (Whyte, 1972; Schneier, 1974). Behavior modification risks producing sufficient behavior rigidity so that the individual follows one particular course at the expense of other important goals. This problem is similar to that noted for goal setting; in interactive situations calling for coordinated effort, both approaches can well yield something less than an optimal overall result.

Goal setting and organizational behavior modification also share another common problem, further substantiating the view that they are much the same thing (Locke, 1977). In both cases long-term application appears to result in the dissipation of effects. In management by objectives it has been found possible to counteract this tendency by introducing new sources of reinforcement. These are often drawn from outside management by objectives (compensation change, job enrichment, for example). This same type of change in approach may be required also to maintain the effects of organizational behavior modification — shifting from reinforcement by praise to monetary reward, for instance.

In general the positive results obtained with behavior modification procedures have utilized externally administered reinforcers — praise, pay, recognition, extra free time, and the like. In a number of studies there has been self-recording of target behaviors, but even then rewards of an external nature have been introduced contingent upon the recording of desired behaviors. Thus, although self-control is theoretically entirely possible, and in fact has been used in industrial applications, the research evidence to evaluate it does not now exist (Blood, 1978). Management probably would be best advised to rely on externally administered or extrinsic reinforcers for the time being, while recognizing that certain negative effects on intrinsic motivation as discussed in Chapter 6 may conceivably occur.

Like self-control, the use of punishment as a reinforcer has undergone little test in the organizational context. In other contexts, in spite of the frequent disclaimers of behavior modification advocates, punishment has been used widely and with considerable success within the operant learning paradigm. For instance, bedwetting by children can be effectively stopped by a device that administers an unpleasant stimulus (such as a mild shock) when it becomes wet. Would a similar approach work in industry, if it realistically could be applied? Do the negative side effects of punishment noted by Hamner, Luthans, Nord, and others really operate in the organizational environment? Systematic study in this area is completely lacking. It appears best to rely primarily on positive reinforcement and extinction at present, simply because such an approach has been found to work under appropriate circumstances.

Practical experience indicates that teaching managers to utilize behavior modification techniques effectively is not easy. At a minimum it requires a sizable investment in management development procedures of the kind discussed by Luthans and Sorcher. The latter's use of modeling, as in the applied learning procedure, appears to have considerable promise; however, it is not clear that behavioral modeling as utilized in the role-play component of the training is a necessary condition for behavioral change. Considerable evidence, of the type noted in Chapter 3 in connection with the discussion of achievement motivation training, indicates that mental modeling in a person's mind alone can achieve similar results. Thinking one's way into a role initially, based on lectures, discussions, examples, and the like, may be less threatening and thus even more effective. Such an approach is totally inconsistent wth the tenets of behaviorism and thus is unlikely to be used by behavior modification advocates; even the behavior modeling approaches tend to stretch the original theory almost to the breaking point.

Ethical Considerations. One of the reasons that behavior modification's organizational advocates often do not mention Skinner and attempt to disassociate themselves from his views is that certain of Skinner's writing such as *Beyond Freedom and Dignity* (1971) have elicited strong negative reactions on strictly ethical grounds. There has been a distinct tendency to avoid this "bad press" by using terms other than behaviorism and operant conditioning. Yet it is important for a manager to understand and evaluate these ethical considerations wherever they may be involved. Court decisions related to the use of behavior modifications procedures in the treatment of the emotionally ill have begun to appear with some frequency (Stolz, Wienckowski, and Brown, 1975). There is a real possibility that this situation may extend to the business world before long. Thus both ethical and legal considerations are involved, at least potentially.

The primary ethical issue has been manipulation (Luthans and Kreitner, 1975). The argument is that behavior modification techniques put too much power in the hands of management, create debilitating dependencies on superiors, are essentially totalitarian rather than democratic in concept, and ignore the rights of the individual as well as the principle of individual consent. Behavior modification thus becomes a method of using others for one's own purposes at their expense. It is particularly unethical when techniques of punishment and avoidance learning are employed, because individual suffering is added to the manipulation.

The purpose here is not to debate these issues but to provide an awareness of reactions that may follow the introduction of an organizational behavior modification effort. Militant union officials, social activists, and dedicated liberals often have been at the forefront of the opposition. However, it is important to recognize that any valid theory of the kind discussed in this book could well elicit the same reactions. The reason that the other theories typically have not, and behavior modification has, is that the latter creates an explicit image of mindless obedience to the will of others, devoid of any voluntary component. The cognitive theories imply a greater degree of control over one's own behavior. In practice, however, when some people understand the theory fully and others are totally unaware of it, this difference may be misleading. Thus, as our knowledge of organizational behavior advances, the potential for misuse and manipulation for personal gain can become a basic social issue with regard to all theories.

A second matter of ethical relevance that probably is particularly germane to the behavioral approach, or at least to radical behaviorism of the Skinnerian type, is the implication that the individual is not responsible for his or her own behavior, that current behavior is entirely a consequence of the individual reinforcement history, and thus the person can do nothing about it (Mitchell, 1976). This denial of personal responsibility flies in the face of the assumptions underlying society's legal system, a free economic system, and practically every other aspect of our social fabric. If the basic theory is indeed correct on this matter, then a complete redesign of the social system is called for. Because of the implications of this denial of personal causation by the radical behaviorists, strong opposition to behavior modification programs on ethical grounds may be anticipated from certain quarters, including the very highest levels of management.

References

Adam, Everett E. Behavior Modification in Quality Control, *Academy of Management Journal*, Vol. 18 (1975), 662–679.

Aldis, Owen. Of Pigeons and Men, *Harvard Business Review*, Vol. 39, No. 4 (1961), 59–63.

Bandura, Albert. *Psychological Modeling, Conflicting Theories*. Chicago: Aldine-Atherton, 1971.

Berger, Chris J., Larry L. Cummings, and Herbert G. Heneman. Expectancy Theory and Operant Conditioning Predictions of Performance Under Variable Ratio and Continuous Schedules of Reinforcement, *Organizational Behavior and Human Performance*, Vol. 14 (1975), 227–243.

Blood, Milton R. Organizational Control of Performance Through Self Rewarding. In Bert King, Siegfried Streufert, and Fred E. Fiedler (eds.), *Managerial Control and Organizational Democracy*. New York: Wiley, 1978, pp. 93–103.

Feeney, Edward J. At Emery Air Freight: Positive Reinforcement Boosts Performance, *Organizational Dynamics*, Vol. 1, No. 3 (1973), 41–50.

Fry, Fred L. Operant Conditioning in Organizational Settings: Of Mice and Men? *Personnel*, Vol. 51, No. 4 (1974), 17–24.

Goldstein, Arnold P. and Melvin Sorcher. *Changing Supervisor Behavior*. New York: Pergamon, 1974.

Hamner, W. Clay. Reinforcement Theory and Contingency Management in Organizational Settings, In Henry L. Tosi and W. Clay Hamner (eds.), *Organizational Behavior and Management: A Contingency Approach*. Chicago: St. Clair, 1974, pp. 86–112.

Hamner, W. Clay. Worker Motivation Programs: The Importance of Climate, Structure, and Performance Consequences, In W. Clay Hamner and Frank L. Schmidt (eds.), *Contemporary Problems in Personnel*. Chicago: St. Clair, 1977, pp. 256–284.

Hamner, W. Clay and Ellen P. Hamner. Behavior Modification on the Bottom Line, *Organizational Dynamics*, Vol. 4, No. 4 (1976), 3–21.

Heiman, Gary W. A Note on Operant Conditioning Principles Extrapolated to the Theory of Management, *Organizational Behavior and Human Performance*, Vol. 13 (1975), 165–170.

Jablonsky, Stephen F. and David L. DeVries. Operant Conditioning Principles Extrapolated to the Theory of Management, *Organizational Behavior and Human Performance*, Vol. 7 (1972), 340–358.

Johnson, George A. The Relative Efficacy of Stimulus Versus Reinforcement Control for Obtaining Stable Performance Change, *Organizational Behavior and Human Performance*, Vol. 14 (1975), 321–341.

Kim, Jay S. and W. Clay Hamner. Effect of Performance Feedback and Goal Setting on Productivity and Satisfaction in an Organizational Setting, *Journal of Applied Psychology*, Vol. 61 (1976), 48–57.

Klein, Stuart M. Pay Factors as Predictors to Satisfaction: A Comparison of Reinforcement, Equity, and Expectancy, *Academy of Management Journal*, Vol. 16 (1973), 598–610.

Komaki, Judi, Willam M. Waddell, and M. George Pearce. The Applied Behavior Analysis Approach and Individual Employees: Improving Performance in Two Small Businesses, *Organizational Behavior and Human Performance*, Vol. 19 (1977), 337–352.

Korman, Abraham K., Jeffrey H. Greenhaus, and Irwin J. Badin. Personnel Attitudes and Motivation, *Annual Review of Psychology*, Vol. 28 (1977), 175–196.

Latham, Gary P. and Dennis L. Dossett. Designing Incentive Plans for Unionized Employees: A Comparison of Continuous and Variable Ratio Reinforcement Schedules, *Personnel Psychology*, Vol. 31 (1978), 47–61.

Locke, Edwin A. The Myths of Behavior Mod in Organizations, *Academy of Management Review*, Vol. 2 (1977), 543–553.

Luthans, Fred and Robert Kreitner. The Role of Punishment in Organizational Behavior Modification (O.B. Mod.), *Public Personnel Management*, Vol. 2, No. 3 (1973), 156–161.

Luthans, Fred and Robert Kreitner. *Organizational Behavior Modification*. Glenview, Ill.: Scott, Foresman, 1975.

Luthans, Fred and D. White. Behavior Modification: Application to Manpower Management, *Personnel Administration*, Vol. 34 (1971), July–August, 41–47.

Mawhinney, Thomas C. Operant Terms and Concepts in the Description of Individual Work Behavior: Some Problems of Interpretation, Application, and Evaluation, *Journal of Applied Psychology*, Vol. 60 (1975), 704–712.

Mitchell, Terence R. Cognitions and Skinner: Some Questions About Behavioral Determinism, *Organization and Administrative Sciences*, Vol. 6, No. 4 (1976), 63–72.

Moses, Joseph L. and Richard J. Ritchie. Supervisory Relationships Training: A Behavioral Evaluation of a Behavior Modeling Program, *Personnel Psychology*, Vol. 29 (1976), 337–343.

Nord, Walter R. Beyond the Teaching Machine: The Neglected Area of Operant Conditioning in the Theory and Practice of Management, *Organizational Behavior and Human Performance*, Vol. 4 (1969), 375–401.

Nord, Walter R. Improving Attendance Through Rewards, *Personnel Administration*, Vol. 33, No. 6 (1970), 37–41.

Otteman, Robert and Fred Luthans. An Experimental Analysis of the Effectiveness of an Organizational Behavior Modification Program in Industry, *Academy of Management Proceedings*, 1975, 140–142.

Pedalino, Ed and Victor U. Gamboa. Behavior Modification and Absenteeism: Intervention in One Industrial Setting, *Journal of Applied Psychology*, Vol. 59 (1974), 694–698.

Pritchard, Robert D., Dale W. Leonard, Clarence W. Von Bergen, and Raymond J. Kirk. The Effects of Varying Schedules of Reinforcement on Human Task Performance, *Organizational Behavior and Human Performance*, Vol. 16 (1976), 205–230.

Schneier, Craig E. Behavior Modification in Management: A Review and Critique, *Academy of Management Journal*, Vol. 17 (1974), 528–548.

Skinner, B. F. *Science and Human Behavior*. New York: Macmillan, 1953.

Skinner, B. F. *Beyond Freedom and Dignity*. New York: Knopf, 1971.

Skinner, B. F. *About Behaviorism*. New York: Knopf, 1974.

Skinner, B. F. The Steep and Thorny Way to a Science of Behavior, *American Psychologist*, Vol. 30 (1975), 42–49.

Skinner, B. F. and William F. Dowling. Conversation with B. F. Skinner, *Organizational Dynamics*, Vol. 1 (1973), Winter, 31–40.

Skinner, B. F. and Elizabeth Hall. Will Success Spoil B. F. Skinner? *Psychology Today*, Vol. 6, No. 6 (1972), 65–72, 130.

Sorcher, Melvin. A Behavior Modification Approach to Supervisory Training, *Professional Psychology*, Vol. 2 (1971), 401–402.

Stolz, Stephanie B., Louis A. Wienckowski, and Bertram S. Brown. Behavior Modification: A Perspective on Critical Issues, *American Psychologist*, Vol. 30 (1975), 1027–1048.

Weiss, Howard M. Subordinate Imitation of Supervisor Behavior: The Role of Modeling in Organizational Socialization, *Organizational Behavior and Human Performance*, Vol. 19 (1977), 89–105.

Wexley, Kenneth N. and Wayne F. Nemeroff. Effectiveness of Positive Reinforcement and Goal Setting as Methods of Management Development, *Journal of Applied Psychology*, Vol. 60 (1975), 446–450.

Whyte, William F. Skinnerian Theory in Organizations, *Psychology Today*, Vol. 6, No. 4 (1972), 67–68, 96–100.

Yukl, Gary A., Gary P. Latham, and Elliott D. Pursell. The Effectiveness of Performance Incentives under Continuous and Variable Ratio Schedules of Reinforcement, *Personnel Psychology*, Vol. 29 (1976), 221–231.

JOB CHARACTERISTICS THEORY OF WORK REDESIGN

9

In Chapter 4 the theory of job enrichment developed by Frederick Herzberg was considered, as was its relationship to motivation-hygiene theory. At that time it was noted that other theories of job enrichment and job redesign exist, and that orthodox job enrichment as advocated by Herzberg is not the only approach utilized in practice. The major *alternative* theoretical orientation emerged out of the collaboration of Edward Lawler and Richard Hackman, both at Yale University at the time (Hackman and Lawler, 1971). Lawler brought to this joint effort a strong predilection for, and research background with, expectancy theory, an orientation that he has continued to maintain (Lawler, 1969, 1973). Hackman, on the other hand, had done research and written on the ways in which different type of tasks and task characteristics influence behavioral outcomes (Hackman 1968, 1969a, 1969b). In his writing on job enrichment independent of Lawler, Hackman, although not rejecting expectancy theory formulations, has given them a less central role; it is Hackman who adopted the designation job characteristics theory to describe the formulations that are of major concern in this chapter.

Both sociotechnical systems theory and organization development theory (in certain of its variations) also deal with job enrichment; both make job enrichment an important aspect of their applications in practice. However, these theories are directly concerned with many factors other than the motivating effects of jobs on incumbents. In both practice and in the range of their primary variables they extend far beyond the immediate job or even the work group context in which the job is performed. For this reason they are better considered as theories of organizational process and structure rather than of organizational behavior.

DEVELOPMENT OF THE THEORY

Like many theories, job characteristics theory has undergone considerable expansion since its first statement, although actual revision has been minimal. In general this expansion has been devoted to achieving increased precision of predictions and to extending the boundaries within which the theory can operate.

The Original Hackman-Lawler Formulations

The basic theory rests on five propositions that are stated as follows:

1. To the extent that an individual believes that he can obtain an outcome he values by engaging in some particular behavior or class of behaviors, the likelihood that he will actually engage in that behavior is enhanced.

2. Outcomes are valued by individuals to the extent that they satisfy the physiological or psychological needs of the individual, or to the extent that they lead to other outcomes which satisfy such needs or are expected by the individual to do so.

3. Thus, to the extent conditions at work can be arranged so that employees can satisfy their own needs best by working effectively toward organizational goals, employees will in fact tend to work hard toward the achievement of these goals.

4. Most lower level needs (e.g., physical well-being, security) can be (and often are) reasonably well satisfied for individuals in contemporary society on a continuing basis and, therefore, will not serve as motivational incentives except under unusual circumstances. This is not the case, however, for certain higher order needs (e.g., needs for personal growth and development or feelings of worthwhile accomplishment).

5. Individuals who are capable of higher order need satisfaction will in fact experience such satisfaction when they learn that they have, as a result of their own efforts, accomplished something that they personally believe is worthwhile or meaningful. Specifically, individuals who desire higher order need satisfactions should be most likely to obtain them when they work effectively on meaningful jobs which provide feedback on the adequacy of their personal work activities (Hackman and Lawler, 1971, p. 262).

These general propositions draw upon both need hierarchy theory (Chapter 2) and expectancy theory (Chapter 6). They serve as a basis for the more specific hypotheses of the theory.

Characteristics of Motivating Jobs. In this early version of the theory four characteristics were proposed as essential to jobs constructed to engage higher order needs. Essentially what was hypothesized is that these four elements must be introduced into a job to enrich it and thus make it motivating for individuals with strong higher order needs. These four characteristics or task attributes are taken from earlier work by Turner and Lawrence (1965). The first is *autonomy*, defined as an indication of the degree to which individuals feel personally responsible for their work, and thus that they own their work outcomes. The authors consider autonomy as a necessary but not sufficient condition for experiencing personal responsibility for work or attributing performance to one's own efforts.

Second, there must be a high degree of *task identity*, defined as including a distinct sense of a beginning and an ending, as well as high visibility of the intervening transformation process itself, the manifestation of the transformation process in the final product, and a transformation process of considerable magnitude. As a subcomponent of this characteristic, the opportunity to use skills and abilities that are personally valued (and use them effectively) is noted.

In addition to task identity, another factor contributing to the meaningfulness of work is sufficient *variety*, the third task attribute specified by the theory. It is, however, only truly challenging variety that is included, variety that taps a number of different skills of importance to the worker.

Finally, the job must provide *feedback* on the level of accomplishment. Such feedback may be built into the task itself or it may stem from external sources (e.g., supervisors and coworkers). In any case it is the perception of feedback, just as it is the perception of autonomy, task identity, and variety, that makes the difference.

Task Characteristics and Outcomes. It is hypothesized that satisfaction, performance, and attendance should be higher when the four core characteristics are present in a job. The theory specifies that *all four* must be present for these consequences to accrue. Furthermore, these relationships are moderated by the level of higher order need strength in the individual. When higher order need strength is pronounced, the four core job dimensions should yield particularly high satisfaction, performance, and attendance levels. The implication is that many jobs in many organizations lack the core dimensions and that they should be redesigned (enriched) to provide them. Essentially this is the version of the theory to which Lawler has remained committed (Lawler, 1973).

The Hackman-Oldham Extensions

Job characteristics theory was explicated by Hackman and Oldham (1976). The number of core job characteristics was extended to five with the inclusion of *task significance* as a third contributor to the meaningfulness of work. Thus, the overall model is as follows:

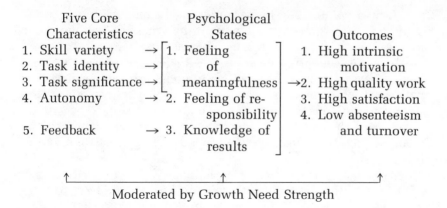

Five Core Characteristics	Psychological States	Outcomes
1. Skill variety →	1. Feeling of meaningfulness	1. High intrinsic motivation
2. Task identity →		→2. High quality work
3. Task significance →		3. High satisfaction
4. Autonomy →	2. Feeling of responsibility	4. Low absenteeism and turnover
5. Feedback →	3. Knowledge of results	

Moderated by Growth Need Strength

The new core characteristic, task significance, is defined as follows:

The degree to which the job has a substantial impact on the lives or work of other people, whether in the immediate organization or in the external environment (p. 257).

The psychological states are defined in the following terms:
1. Feeling of meaningfulness — the degree to which the individual experiences the job as one which is generally meaningful, valuable, and worthwhile.
2. Feeling of responsibility — the degree to which the individual feels personally accountable and responsible for the results of the work he or she does.
3. Knowledge of results — the degree to which the individual knows and understands, on a continuous basis, how effectively he or she is performing the job (pp. 256–257).

This model is explicitly employed to develop a formula to compute the motivating potential score (MPS) for a given job:

$$\text{MPS} = \frac{\text{Skill Variety} + \text{Task Identity} + \text{Task Signifcance}}{3} \times \text{Autonomy} \times \text{Feedback}$$

It should be noted that this formula departs slightly from the Hackman and Lawler (1971) view. There, all core characteristics had to be high; here, autonomy and feedback, as well as one or more of the three contributors to meaningfulness, must be high, but a zero on one of the latter three does not now have the potential for producing an overall zero MPS score.

A final point is that higher order need strength is now specifically defined as growth need strength in a manner that appears to follow Alderfer (1972), a colleague of Hackman's at Yale.

In a subsequent publication the moderating process was extended beyond growth need strength alone to include satisfaction with such job context factors as pay, job security, coworkers, and supervisors (Oldham, Hackman, and Pearce, 1976). The assumption here is that the broader work system must be healthy for the theory to operate effectively. The specific hypotheses are as follows:

1. When both work context satisfaction and growth need satisfaction are high, MPS-outcome relationships should be strong.
2. When both work context satisfaction and growth need satisfaction are low, MPS-outcome relationships should be near zero, or even negative.
3. When work context satisfaction is high, but growth need satisfaction is low (or the reverse), MPS-outcome relationships should be moderately weak.

The Moderating Effects of Organizational Climate

An additional moderating factor on performance outcomes that has been espoused by both Lawler (1973) and Hackman (1977) is the degree to which the organizational context of the job is of a mechanistic or organic type. This distinction follows that of Burns and Stalker (1961). *Mechanistic* systems are said to be consonant with the traditional concept of bureaucracy. The managerial hierarchy is tall, authority is centralized, and rules and procedures are well defined and consistently enforced. *Organic* systems, in contrast, are more flexible or variable, with operating approaches adapted to people and tasks. The managerial hierarchy is flat, and units are operated in whatever way serves overall organizational goals (Hackman, 1977).

Figure 9–1 sets forth hypothesized performance relationships when such organizational climate differences are taken into account. The figure has the added value of specifically indicating the expected consequences when low growth need employees are placed in enriched jobs. It does not, however, incorporate satisfaction with job context factors as a moderator variable; only the moderating effects of motivational patterns and organizational climates are considered. Thus, Figure 9–1 is not a full statement of the theory.

Existing Combination	Predicted Consequence
1. High growth need — enriched job — organic climate	Very high quality performance; high satisfaction; good attendance; low turnover.
2. High growth need — enriched job — mechanistic climate	Individual responds well to the job, but chafes at organizational overcontrol.
3. High growth need — routine job — organic climate	Individual will try to have the job changed; if unsuccessful, will resign.
4. High growth need — routine job — mechanistic climate	High frustration; low satisfaction; high turnover; high absenteeism.
5. Low growth need — enriched job — organic climate	Psychological withdrawal from the job; overt hostility; low job performance.
6. Low growth need — enriched job — mechanistic climate	Individual responds to the organizational cues and does not handle job effectively.
7. Low growth need — routine job — organic climate	Reasonably adequate performance; constant anxiety over perceived uncertainties.
8. Low growth need — routine job — mechanistic climate	Effective performance; adequate satisfaction; adequate attendance.

Figure 9-1. Predicted consequences of various combinations of individual need states, job scope, and organizational climate. (Adapted from Lyman W. Porter, Edward E. Lawler, and J. Richard Hackman. *Behavior in Organizations.* New York: McGraw-Hill, 1975, p. 309.)

Action Principles for Redesigning Jobs

A set of guidelines for enriching jobs, derived from the five core job characteristics of the theory, has been developed (Hackman, 1977; Hackham, Oldham, Janson, and Purdy, 1975). These so-called action principles represent specific hypotheses regarding how enriched jobs may be achieved. The five such principles noted below should be prefaced with the statement: If enriched jobs and increased motivating potential are to be achieved, then —

1. Natural work units should be formed, in order to increase *task identity* and *task significance*.
2. Tasks should be combined, in order to increase *skill variety* and *task identity*.
3. Client relationships with the ultimate user should be established, in order to increase *skill variety, autonomy,* and *feedback*.
4. The job should be vertically loaded with responsibilities and

controls formerly reserved for management, in order to increase *autonomy*.

5. Feedback channels should be opened, especially channels flowing directly from the job itself, in order to increase *feedback*.

These guidelines have much in common with those set forth for orthodox job enrichment, as discussed in Chapter 4. At the level of actual practice the two approaches have a good deal in common; at the level of theoretical origins they are considerably more diverse.

Designing Group Tasks

Recently extensions to job characteristics theory have focused on the design of group, as opposed to individual, tasks (Hackman, 1977, 1978; Hackman and Morris, 1975). The theorizing in this area is not as precise as that discussed to this point, but it does expand the boundaries of theoretical applications considerably.

Work group effectiveness is viewed as a consequence of the level of effort group members bring to the task, the amount of knowledge and skill relevant to task work the members have, and the appropriateness of the task performance strategies of the group. Thus group outcomes are considered to be a function of task factors. These so-called *interim criteria* are in turn hypothesized to result from group design factors such as the design of the group task, the composition of the group, and group norms about performance processes.

In essence what is proposed is that the five core characteristics be applied at the work group rather than the individual level. This means that there must be two additional job characteristics: (1) task-required interdependence, in that the task itself requires members to work together and rely on each other, and (2) opportunities for social interaction, in that members are in social proximity and conditions foster communication about the work. Group task performance, like individual task performance, assumes sufficient appropriate knowledge and skills to complete the task successfully.

The impacts of the group's effort, knowledge, and strategies are potentially constrained by the *technology*, a paced assembly line, for instance. They are also potentially constrained by imperfections in the *interpersonal processes* within the group, such as might be created by intense personal animosities, for instance. Thus, these two factors, technology and interpersonal processes, moderate the final impact of efforts, knowledge, and strategies emanating from the group on outcomes, including the overall quality of task performance.

Designing tasks on a group basis is recommended under the following conditions:

1. When the group can assume responsibility for a total product or service, but the nature of the work is such that individuals cannot. Thus, when the meaningful work potential of even the best possible individual job is low.
2. When the work is of such a nature that high interdependence among individual workers is essential.
3. When the workers involved have high social need strength, with the result that enrichment of individual jobs risks breaking up satisfying groups relationships.
4. When the motivating potential of the job would be expected to be much higher if arranged as a group task rather than as a set of individual tasks.

In contrast, individual (as opposed to group) task design is recommended:

1. When the individuals have high needs for personal growth but weak needs for social relationships at work.
2. When the prospect of dysfunctional conflict within a group is high.
3. When there is no inherent interdependence in the work of the individuals.
4. When the expertise needed to design group tasks, an inherently difficult process, is lacking.

In many cases technological or interpersonal factors will make group task design infeasible. In any event group task enrichment is a much more complex and less well understood process than individual job enrichment. Job characteristics theory has moved into this area recently, and it is far too soon to evaluate the theory adequately with respect to its formulations regarding group tasks; a sufficient amount of research has not been conducted. Thus, the discussion in the remainder of this chapter will focus on individual job enrichment and the applicable theoretical statements.

MEASUREMENT RESEARCH AND THE OPERATIONALIZATION OF THEORETICAL VARIABLES

One of the major strengths of job characteristics theory is that its variables are amenable to relatively easy operationalization. As a consequence the measurement problem was tackled at an early date and considerable progress was made. Among other considerations this has meant that direct tests of the theory could be carried out; also it has facilitated research directed at determining the conditions under which job enrichment efforts actually "take" and thus serve to expand job scope.

Early Developmental Research

The first major effort at measurement of job enrichment was conducted by Turner and Lawrence (1965). The indexes thus created had a considerable impact on the Hackman and Lawler (1971) measures that in turn formed the basis for the current Job Diagnostic Survey (Hackman and Oldham, 1975). Turner and Lawrence (1965) developed a number of scales to be used in rating jobs by those who had knowledge of them. Several of these scales were combined into a single overall measure called the Requisite Task Attribute Index. Included were items dealing with variety, autonomy, required interaction, optional interaction, knowledge and skill, and responsibility. An additional measure of task identity subsequently proved of considerable value, although it was not used in the composite index. All of these variables were intercorrelated at approximately the .50 level.

Hackman and Lawler (1971) drew items from the Turner and Lawrence measures to obtain their indexes of variety, autonomy, task identity, and feedback. They also developed measures of dealing with others (required interaction) and friendship opportunities (optional interaction) from the same source. The four job characteristics measures had reliabilities averaging .77, but the two social measures proved to be of unacceptable reliability. A measure of higher order need strength based on an employee rating of how much the individual would like to have an opportunity for growth, variety, a feeling of worthwhile accomplishment, and the like had a reliability of .89.

The Job Diagnostic Survey

The Job Diagnostic Survey (Hackman and Oldham, 1975) represents a considerable refinement of these preliminary measures. It contains measures of job dimensions (the five core characteristics, plus the dealing with others factor, and an index of feedback from external agents, not the job itself), critical psychological states (the three specified by the theory), affective reactions to the job (general satisfaction, internal work motivation, and specific satisfactions with regard to security, pay, coworkers, supervision, and growth opportunity), and growth need strength (both the index of what the individual would like from a job and a new one in which choices are made between alternative jobs). With the exception of the organizational climate moderators and certain variables introduced when the theory is extended to group tasks, the Job Diagnostic Survey provides a comprehensive coverage of both the primary and moderator variables of the theory. The reported reliabilities for individual scales range from .56 to .88 with a median of .72. There is good evidence that the instrument does discriminate among different jobs.

The feasibility of measuring the core job characteristic variables is further reinforced by the independent development of another instrument, also having its origins in the Hackman and Lawler (1971) measures (Sims, Szilagyi, and Keller, 1976). The scores derived from this second measure are quite comparable to those from the Job Diagnostic Survey but appear to be somewhat more reliable (Pierce and Dunham, 1978).

Some question has been raised as to the psychometric soundness of the Job Diagnostic Survey on the grounds that factor analytic studies yield varied dimensionality under different circumstances and that the factor structure emerging rarely matches the five core theoretical variables (Dunham, Aldag and Brief, 1977; Pierce and Dunham, 1976). In particular there is a question as to whether the measures of variety and autonomy really deal with separate constructs. Overall measures, such as the motivating potential score, can still be very useful in spite of these findings. Furthermore, if the differential validity of the various measures can be established, the lack of a consistently supportive factor structure is not necessarily indicative of defects in either the measures or the theory. In fact Turner and Lawrence (1965) argue for the value of their instruments on the grounds that they are highly intercorrelated, and thus presumably tap a general factor.

RESEARCH TESTS

Although direct tests of the hypotheses of job characteristics theory are not abundant, research has been conducted both by the originators of the theory at Yale and by others. In addition there is a second body of research that, although not conceptualized as a test of this particular theory, does bear on it. Some of these latter studies in fact pre-dated the formulation of the theory and exerted considerable influence on the form it has taken; in particular a full understanding of job characteristics theory requires knowledge of the research dealing with the moderating effects of the rural-urban variable on job enrichment outcomes.

The Rural-Urban Moderator

The initial formulations involving the rural-urban moderator were developed on an ad hoc basis to explain certain findings emerging from the Turner and Lawrence (1965) research. Since these findings were obtained only after an extensive search of the data, they may well have represented chance phenomena and thus must be considered hypotheses for further test.

In the primary analyses it was found that blue collar workers in more enriched jobs were generally absent less, but no clear relationships with job satisfaction were apparent. However, the secondary analyses revealed that the relationship with absenteeism characterized "town" workers only and that these same workers also exhibited the expected association between enriched jobs and satisfaction. For "city" workers of Catholic religion there was a negative relationship between enrichment and satisfaction.

Various possible explanations of these results are explored, although the Turner and Lawrence data do not permit reaching firm conclusions. Among the alternatives considered are the possibility that the town workers had stronger higher order needs in accord with need hierarchy theory, that they had strong achievment needs (and the city workers stronger affiliation motivation) in accord with achievement motivation theory, and that the city workers were characterized by anomie (or normlessness) while the town workers were not, in accord with various sociological conceptions.

The University of Illinois Research. A number of studies that bear on the rural-urban moderator hypothesis have emanated from the University of Illinois in the past ten years or so, as well as several analytic literature reviews (Hulin, 1971). Among the alternative Turner and Lawrence formulations regarding the moderator process, this research has come closest to emphasizing that of anomie. However, Hulin prefers to think in terms of alienation from middle class norms. Urban workers are said to be so alienated; rural workers are not, and in fact espouse these norms strongly. According to Hulin, the fact that writers and researchers in this area also come from middle class backgrounds accounts for the historical tendency to generalize that what is true of rural workers applies to all workers and thus to prescribe job enrichment as a panacea for everyone.

The early evidence amassed by Hulin (1971) bearing on the rural-urban, alienation hypothesis is generally favorable, as are the results of Hulin's own studies. However, there were, even in 1971, several conflicting findings. The data appear to support the idea of a moderator process, with job enrichment working for some people but not others. Hulin, like Turner and Lawrence before him, remains somewhat uncertain as to the exact nature of this process.

More Recent Findings.   As research has continued the idea that some type of value or norm differential moderates the job characteristics, outcome relationship has received increasing support. Thus, Robey (1974) found in a laboratory study that subjects with strong intrinsic work values were more satisfied and showed more performance improvement when working on an enriched task than those with strong extrinsic work values. Aldag and Brief (1975) found evidence for a similar kind of moderating effect among manufacturing employees using a measure of commitment to Protestant ethic values. In these studies and others, however, the relationships, although typically statistically significant, are not strong. One has the feeling that the moderators used are somehow hitting only the edges of the target and not the bull's eye.

Furthermore, as research continues, support for the type of gross rural-urban differential noted by Turner and Lawrence (1965) has become more and more tenuous. Aldag and Brief (1975) did not find their Protestant ethic value measure related to degree of urbanization. A recent review by Pierce and Dunham (1976) questions the value of the sociological explanations except as they served to point the way for more precise formulations such as those of job characteristics theory. A study by Castellano (1976) provides no support for the rural-urban moderator hypothesis when the size of the community in which the worker was raised is used to define the rural-urban variable. Given the trend of the findings and known changes in population characteristics, it seems likely that, although the rural-urban moderator concept may have possessed some validity at an earlier point in time, it no longer holds true. The increasing mobility of the population and changes in cultural values appear to have eliminated its explanatory power.

Research by the Authors of the Theory

The most extensive body of research on job characteristics theory has come from the authors of the theory. Of these, Hackman has been the most consistently involved. Lawler was a major contributor when he was with Hackman at Yale but not after he moved to the University of Michigan. Oldham has been a consistent contributor in recent years, beginning his work during his doctoral study at Yale and continuing it after joining the University of Illinois faculty.

The Original Hackman and Lawler Study. The first study, which pre-dated the full development of the Job Diagnostic Survey, was clearly an outgrowth of the earlier work involving rural-urban moderators (Hackman and Lawler, 1971). Data were obtained from individuals in telephone company plant and traffic units employed in thirteen different jobs. Data relevant to the theory are given in Table 9–1.

The findings for all subjects indicate a general tendency for the enrichment of jobs on various dimensions to be associated with favorable job outcomes; only in the case of quantity of work produced can this conclusion be questioned. It is interesting to note that quantity was accordingly dropped from subsequent statements of the theory (Hackman and Oldham, 1976). The findings also tend to support the use of higher order need strength as a moderator, although not consistently across dimensions. Variety and autonomy, which are highly intercorrelated, fare quite well with all moderator relationships in the predicted direction. However, task identity yields reversed relationships (except for job satisfaction), and many of the correlations are significant for the *low* higher order need strength employees. Furthermore the data for the feedback dimension yield far from consistent support for the theory. Unfortunately, the authors do not give the results of significance tests for the *differences* between high and low need strength correlations.

In spite of the uncertainties created by the data regarding the theoretical roles of certain job characteristics, it does appear that when the dimension scores are multiplied together to yield a score indicative of relatively high standing on all four, higher order need strength does tend to moderate the relation of this composite measure with the outcome variables; in all six instances the correlation differentials are in the predicted direction, although several of these differentials are rather small. The data do not permit tying these higher order need strength results back to rural-urban differences, however. Although there is a trend for employees from rural backgrounds to have elevated higher order need strength scores, this trend does not achieve accepted levels of statistical significance.

The Telephone Company Field Experiment. Lawler, Hackman, and Kaufman (1973) report a study in which the job of telephone company directory assistance operator was enriched. Before-after measures were taken using essentially the same instruments as in the previous research. The same operators also served as toll operators, and this aspect of their work was not enriched, thus providing a control condition.

Table 9-1.   CORRELATIONS BETWEEN JOB CHARACTERISTICS AND OUTCOME VARIABLES FOR ALL SUBJECTS AND WHEN MODERATED BY HIGHER ORDER NEED STRENGTH

Outcome Variable	Variety			Autonomy			Task Identity			Feedback		
	All Subjects	Need Strength High	Low	All Subjects	Need Strength High	Low	All Subjects	Need Strength High	Low	All Subjects	Need Strength High	Low
Level of intrinsic motivation	(.32)	(.56)	.15	(.30)	(.49)	.07	(.16)	.19	(.22)	(.18)	(.41)	(.25)
Rated performance												
quantity	−.03	−.02	−.24	(.13)	.09	−.09	.05	.01	.15	.00	.04	(.23)
quality	(.17)	.15	.05	(.16)	.17	−.05	.07	−.02	(.31)	.02	.12	.03
overall	(.20)	.09	.05	(.26)	.16	−.01	(.11)	.01	(.26)	−.03	−.04	.06
General job satisfaction	(.38)	(.41)	(.28)	(.39)	(.43)	(.29)	(.20)	(.27)	.18	(.28)	.17	(.33)
Absenteeism	.02	(−.29)	−.18	−.14	(−.24)	.01	(−.22)	.21	(−.26)	−.10	.04	.06

( ) Correlation statistically significant.

Adapted from J. Richard Hackman and Edward E. Lawler. Employee Reactions to Job Characteristics, *Journal of Applied Psychology*, Vol. 55 (1971), pp. 273, 279.

While no change was found for the control work as a toll operator, significant increases in variety and autonomy (but not task identity and feedback) did occur in the directory assistance work. However, these job characteristics changes were not coupled with improvements in job outcomes. Measures of work motivation, quality, and quantity revealed no before-after differences. Turnover and absenteeism did improve, but this appears to have been a function of economic conditions, not job enrichment. In most respects job satisfaction did not change, but those changes that did occur were in the direction of *less* satisfaction with interpersonal relationships at work. No direct test of the moderator hypothesis was carried out.

The Bank Stock Transfer Department Study. A second study involving the introduction of job enrichment in a work setting was conducted in the stock transfer department of a large bank (Frank and Hackman, 1975). The changes were introduced on a staggered basis, and some employees did not have their jobs enriched at all, so that it was possible to make experimental-control comparisons as well as before-after comparisons. The Job Diagnostic Survey was used for measurement purposes. The motivating potential score (MPS) was computed by the formula previously noted.

Within the stock transfer department as a whole MPS was related to a number of favorable job outcomes as the theory would predict. This was true for intrinsic work motivation, job satisfaction, and absenteeism. It was not true for work quality or any other measure of output. Thus, the introduction of job enrichment, which would be expected to raise MPS means, should have increased at least the first three types of outcome measures. The expected results did not occur, however; outcomes remained unchanged.

Comparisons of before-after and experimental-control measures of job characteristics indicated that if anything the supposedly enriched jobs were de-enriched, although the most common finding was that no real change had occurred at all. The authors present additional observational data to this same effect. Given the lack of change and the fact that moderator relationships were not considered, this study cannot be viewed as a true test of theory. Yet it does point up the fact that job enrichment must be made to "take" before it can affect outcomes and that getting it to take may not always be easy.

Tests of the Moderator Hypotheses. A comprehensive test of the theory was conducted by Hackman and Oldham (1976) with a large and diverse sample of employees in a wide range of jobs in seven organizations. Data were obtained using the Job Diagnostic Survey as well as absenteeism statistics and supervisory ratings of performance. The approach was entirely correlational as in the original study; no job enrichment intervention was involved.

In many respects the findings support the theory, as the data in Table 9–2 indicate. Yet as is evident from the blanks in that table, many relationships that bear on the theory's validity are not reported. Furthermore, although the version of the theory being tested emphasizes the quality of work outcome, the performance measure used is a composite of rated effort expenditure, quantity, and quality. Data to test the moderator hypothesis are reported for only one of the two growth need measures in the Job Diagnostic Survey. Within these limitations it appears that both the job characteristics and psychological states are related to the JDS measures of intrinsic motivation and satisfaction at a very respectable level. The absenteeism and performance correlations are much lower, and in a number of instances they are not statistically significant, even with the very large sample size. As the authors recognize, this pattern of results is of a kind that suggests that common method variance may well be contaminating the intrinsic motivation and job satisfaction relationships to some degree. The moderator findings also support the theory when they are restricted to analyses within the JDS, but to a much lesser degree when the independent outcome variables are used; with absenteeism there is no moderator effect at all.

It is important to note that negative correlations do not result for the low growth need strength employees — the interaction between enriched jobs and low need for growth does not have negative consequences. Data are also presented that generally support the mediating functions of the various psychological states as posited by the theory. The one exception is that experienced responsibility is affected by all of the five core dimensions, not just autonomy. Finally, the predictive power of the relatively complex MPS formula as specified by the theory is compared with that of other methods of combining the five job characteristic variables. The results appear to indicate that it does not matter a great deal what method is used; simply multiplying all five together yields the lowest correlations, but adding them is somewhat better than the theoretical formula.

Correlations between measured growth need strength and rural-urban status are .16 for rural place of work, .14 for rural current residence, and .02 for rural childhood residence. Although the first two values are statistically significant, they are not high.

Two other studies have considered not only growth need

Table 9-2. CORRELATIONS BETWEEN JOB CHARACTERISTICS AND PSYCHOLOGICAL STATE MEASURES AND OUTCOME VARIABLES FOR ALL SUBJECTS AND WHEN MODERATED BY GROWTH NEED STRENGTH

	Outcome Variables											
	Intrinsic Motivation			Job Satisfaction			Absenteeism			Composite Work Effectiveness		
	All Subjects	Need Strength		All Subjects	Need Strength		All Subjects	Need Strength		All Subjects	Need Strength	
		High	Low		High	Low		High	Low		High	Low
Job characteristics												
Skill variety	.34	—	—	.32	—	—	−.15	—	—	.07	—	—
Task identity	.25	—	—	.22	—	—	−.18	—	—	.15	—	—
Task significance	.31	—	—	.21	—	—	.16	—	—	.12	—	—
Autonomy	.31	—	—	.38	—	—	−.24	—	—	.19	—	—
Feedback	.35	—	—	.38	—	—	−.12	—	—	.21	—	—
MPS	.48	(.52	.27)	.43	.49	.32	−.25	−.25	−.23	.24	.44	.20
Psychological states												
Experienced meaningfulness	.64	—	—	.64	—	—	−.03	—	—	.13	—	—
Experienced responsibility	.65	—	—	.41	—	—	−.16	—	—	.16	—	—
Knowledge of results	.23	—	—	.33	—	—	−.11	—	—	.10	—	—
Product of all three	—	(.66	.48)	—	(.69	.36)	—	−.13	−.16	—	(.44	.12)

( ) Difference between correlations statistically significant.

Adapted from J. Richard Hackman and Greg R. Oldham. Motivation Through the Design of Work: Test of a Theory, *Organizational Behavior and Human Performance*, Vol. 16 (1976), pp. 263, 270.

strength but also various satisfaction indexes as moderators. The most comprehensive of these was conducted among various clerical employees of a large bank (Oldham, Hackman, and Pearce, 1976). Many of the measures were derived from the Job Diagnostic Survey. In addition, independent measures of rated overall performance effectiveness and salary per year of employment were obtained.

As indicated in Table 9–3, there was a general tendency for the more enriched jobs to be associated with more positive outcomes and for this assocation to be primarily characteristic of high growth need employees and those whose work was not disrupted by various sources of dissatisfaction. Although the moderator effects tend to be consistently in the hypothesized direction, only six of 21 are significant, and there are a number of instances in which there is clearly no moderator impact. Clearly something is moderating the effects of enriched jobs here, but the specific theoretical variables do not appear to be perfectly on target. In addition, it should be noted that the authors address themselves directly to the method variance issue noted previously. They present data indicating that when supervisors rather than incumbents independently evaluate the same jobs and create the MPS measures, the correlation with outcome variables for all subjects is at least as high as those reported in Table 9–3.

The second study is much less satisfactory in a number of respects, primarily because of the incompleteness of reporting

Table 9–3. CORRELATIONS BETWEEN MOTIVATING POTENTIAL SCORE AND OUTCOME VARIABLES FOR ALL SUBJECTS AND MODERATED BY GROWTH NEED STRENGTH AND VARIOUS SATISFACTION MEASURES

Outcome Variable	All Subjects	Growth Need Strength		Pay Satisfaction		Security Satisfaction	
		High	Low	High	Low	High	Low
Rated performance	.16	.25	.00	.21	.10	.25	.08
Salary	.22	(.44	.03)	.20	.24	.23	.20
Intrinsic motivation	.36	.36	.21	(.47	.25)	.32	.33

	Coworker Satisfaction		Supervisory Satisfaction		Combined Satisfaction		Growth Need Strength and Combined Satisfaction	
	High	Low	High	Low	High	Low	High	Low
Rated performance	(.33	.02)	.29	.08	.26	.13	(.32	−.19)
Salary	(.31	.05)	.29	.17	.30	.13	(.50	−.06)
Intrinsic motivation	.33	.26	.34	.26	.36	.25	.24	.15

( ) Difference between correlations statistically significant.

Adapted from Greg R. Oldham, J. Richard Hackman, and Jone L. Pearce. Conditions Under Which Employees Respond Positively to Enriched Work, *Journal of Applied Psychology*, Vol. 61 (1976), pp. 398–401.

Table 9–4. CORRELATIONS BETWEEN JOB CHARACTERISTICS AND INTRINSIC MOTIVATION MODERATED BY GROWTH NEED STRENGTH, COWORKER SATISFACTION AND SUPERVISORY SATISFACTION

Job Characteristics	Growth Need Strength		Coworker Satisfaction		Supervisory Satisfaction	
	High	Low	High	Low	High	Low
Skill variety	.53	.49	.51	.27	.42	.26
Task identity	.39	.14	.16	−.06	.19	.19
Task significance	.29	.11	.46	.06	(.57	−.17)
Autonomy	.58	.26	(.66	.17)	.48	.01
Feedback	.29	.34	.36	.20	.31	.22

( ) Difference between correlations statistically significant.

Adapted from Greg R. Oldham. Job Characteristics and Internal Motivation: The Moderating Effect of Interpersonal and Individual Variables, *Human Relations*, Vol. 29 (1976), p. 565.

(Oldham, 1976). The Job Diagnostic Survey plus additional outcome measures were obtained from a diverse array of manufacturing employees in one company. Only the moderator results noted in Table 9–4 are reported, although supervisory ratings of work quality, quantity, and effort, as well as absenteeism frequencies were also obtained. The data clearly indicate that the various indexes of job enrichment relate to intrinsic motivation, but one cannot help wondering how they relate to the other outcome measures, in which method variance is not an issue. Furthermore, only two of the 15 reported moderator effects are significant. With almost all of the correlation differentials in the hypothesized direction, it is apparent that the theory is not all wrong. Yet, given the unreported data and the problems of significance, questions must remain.

Independent Evaluations of the Theory

Research conducted by others having no inherent involvement in the development of job characteristics theory often has utilized components of the Job Diagnostic Survey but has drawn on other instruments as well. The most consistent focus of this research has been on the moderating hypotheses.

Tests of the Moderator Hypotheses. One of the most interesting studies was conducted to compare the relative effectiveness of three different moderators — rural-urban background as of the time of growing up, measured alienation from middle class norms, and higher order need strength (Wanous, 1974). The research was conducted with telephone operators, and the outcome variables were an independent measure of job satisfaction, absenteeism, and an overall rating index of job performance.

The moderator results involving the job satisfaction outcome are given in Table 9–5. The trend of the data is in the predicted direction for all three moderators, but significant differences between correlations are obtained only for higher order need strength. The other two outcome variables yielded nothing that would support one moderator hypothesis over the others; in fact in many cases there was little evidence of any relationship between job characteristics and outcome measures at all. In this study, as in several others previously noted, there was a minimal association between rural-urban status and higher order need strength. Overall the study supports the higher order need strength moderating hypothesis, when and if outcome relationships exist at all.

A second investigation conducted with state corrections department employees also utilized independent measures of job satisfaction variables, not the ones contained in the Job Diagnostic Survey; measures of absenteeism and performance were not obtained (Brief and Aldag, 1975). The all-subjects data produced consistently positive correlations for the various job characteristics. The median values were .25 for variety, .16 for task identity, .35 for autonomy, and .28 for feedback. However the effects of moderating by higher order need strength were not entirely as expected. For variety and task identity the trends were clearly in the predicted direction, and to a somewhat lesser extent this was true for autonomy, but there was no moderator effect in evidence for feedback. Statistically significant differences between correlations were few in number and when they did occur were often the reverse of what the theory predicts. There was no evidence of a dif-

Table 9–5. CORRELATIONS BETWEEN JOB CHARACTERISTICS AND JOB SATISFACTION MODERATED BY HIGHER ORDER NEED STRENGTH, ALIENATION FROM MIDDLE CLASS NORMS, AND RURAL-URBAN STATUS

Job Characteristics	Higher Order Need Strength		Alienated		Background	
	High	Low	No	Yes	Rural	Urban
Variety	(.50	.15)	.41	.10	.46	.45
Task identity	.30	−.07	.33	−.05	.34	.09
Autonomy	(.59	−.09)	.38	.21	.38	.02
Feedback	.41	.10	.24	.22	.34	.17

( ) Difference between correlations statistically significant.

Adapted from John P. Wanous. Individual Differences and Reactions to Job Characteristics, *Journal of Applied Psychology*, Vol. 59 (1974), p. 619.

ference in higher order need strength between workers of rural and urban backgrounds.

A third study is of primary interest because the measure of job characteristics used was developed separately from the Job Diagnostic Survey (Sims and Szilagyi, 1976). Independent measures of job satisfaction and performance were also employed. The subjects were support personnel in a large medical center.

The all-subjects correlations were consistently positive and in many cases significant. However, the median value for the satisfaction outcomes was .24 and for the performance outcomes only .15. In general the moderating effects for higher order need strength were as expected with the job characteristics of variety, autonomy, and feedback; no such effects were in evidence for task identity. An attempt to explore the potential of a measure of experienced internal versus external control as a moderator yielded no meaningful pattern of results, thus supporting the specific relevance of the growth need strength variable. Overall this study, conducted with measures of the theoretical variables that depart in a number of respects from those used in previous research, does yield support for the theory in many of its aspects, although the correlations tend to be rather low.

Evaluations of Nonmoderator Aspects.   Studies focusing on aspects of job characteristics theory other than the moderating effects of needs and satisfactions have produced mixed results. One such investigation provides data on unmoderated relationships between Job Diagnostic Survey job dimension measures and indexes of job satisfaction and involvement across a number of manufacturing jobs in 13 companies (Rousseau, 1977). The findings are important because, although significant relationships are consistently obtained, the correlations for the task identity variable are substantially below those for the other dimensions. Once again some doubt is raised about the theoretical importance of this factor.

In another instance comparisons were made among different groups of production employees in an electronics assembly plant who worked on a production line (Giles, 1977). One group volunteered to work on a proposed new production process designed to yield enriched jobs on all dimensions, another group volunteered to work on a newly established production line and thus to change to nonenriched jobs, and a third group did not wish to change at all. It was predicted that the enriched job group would be characterized by strong and at the same time unsatisfied higher order needs. This turned out to be the case. On the other hand, there was no evidence that the need satisfaction variable was related to the desire for job change, independent of enrichment. Thus the theoretical relevance of the motivational factor is established with a quite different research design from those used in previous studies.

Considerable evidence now has been developed that brings into question the superiority of both the straight multiplicative formula for combining job dimensions and the subsequent modification that treats skill variety, task identity, and task significance in an additive manner (Pierce and Dunham, 1976). The data clearly indicate that an entirely additive formula is at least as effective for purposes of predicting outcomes, and probably better.

Although little research has been conducted with reference to the organizational climate moderator, a study by Zierden (reported by Hackman, 1977) yields results that are at variance with the theory in a number of respects. The study utilized workers in two organizations and dealt only with the job satisfaction outcome. Data were obtained using the Job Diagnostic Survey and a measure of degree of participative management style as a surrogate for organizational climate. In general the data confirm expectations for the first four conditions shown in Figure 9–1, those involving high growth needs. In addition, the low growth need–routine job–mechanistic climate condition (number 8) produced results consistent with the theoretical expectations. But in the other three cells, in which the theory predicts negative outcomes, the satisfaction levels actually proved to be quite high in several instances and never below the moderate level. Overall, it appears that if climate factors are to be used effectively as moderators, revisions in the theory are necessary.

Related Research

There are a number of studies that, although not undertaken primarily as tests of job characteristics theory, bear in one way or another on its hypotheses. Thus, a study by Katz (1978) indicates that job longevity operates in a differential manner as a moderator of the various job characteristics' relationships with job satisfaction, and that this moderator effect occurs quite independently of that of higher order need strength.

Several recent investigations have utilized more specific needs as moderators rather than using global concepts such as higher order or growth needs. In particular this research has focused on the achievement motivation variable. One such study obtained a sizable moderator effect using an overall measure of performance as the outcome variable, as indicated in Table 9–6. The

Table 9–6. CORRELATIONS BETWEEN JOB CHARACTERISTICS AND RATED
OVERALL PERFORMANCE FOR ALL SUBJECTS AND
MODERATED BY ACHIEVEMENT MOTIVATION

Job Characteristics	All Subjects	Achievement Motivation	
		High	Low
Variety	−.07	(.20	−.33)
Task identity	.17	.28	.09
Autonomy	.11	(.34	−.08)
Feedback	.09	.22	−.02

( ) Difference between correlations statistically significant.

Adapted from Richard M. Steers and Daniel G. Spencer. The Role of Achievement Motivation in Job Design, *Journal of Applied Psychology*, Vol. 62 (1977), pp. 476–477.

subjects were managers from a single manufacturing firm. This achievement motivation measure does not meet the requirement that motivational variables be operationalized with projective instruments, as stressed in achievement motivation theory. However, other research supports the measure's usefulness in work settings (Steers and Spencer, 1977).

Other studies have dealt with the job satisfaction outcome rather than performance. In one case a clear moderating effect of achievement motivation was obtained; high need achievers were more satisfied in jobs permitting autonomy of action and more dissatisfied in highly structured positions (Stinson and Johnson, 1977). Yet there is some negative evidence as well (Stone, Mowday, and Porter, 1977). It is very difficult to compare these studies because of the different measures employed. Furthermore, none of the research has utilized a projective measure of the achievement motivation moderator. On balance, however, the data suggest a very fruitful area for future study.

A well-controlled simulation study noted previously, which dealt in large part with goal setting, also was concerned with the effects of job enrichment as evidenced by Job Diagnostic Survey scores (Umstot, Bell, and Mitchell, 1976). This is an experimental study that permits causal interpretations. The data indicate that enrichment does yield greater job satisfaction but that it has little impact on performance as measured in terms of the quantity of output. The research did consider the moderating effects of growth need strength as well, but no significant differences between correlations were obtained. Except for task identity, however, the overall trend of the data was generally in the hypothesized direction.

Research involving the introduction of job enrichment in ongoing work environments has produced a wide range of results. In a federal agency experimental and control group comparisons indicated that the job enrichment improved productivity, absenteeism, turnover, and grievance rates but had no impact at all on job satisfaction levels, which remained very low throughout the period of study (Locke, Sirota, and Wolfson, 1976). These findings are the reverse of those usually reported. In a sheltered workshop setting comparisons between job enrichment and mere job change without enrichment indicated little effect of enrichment per se; the changes could be accounted for in terms of the job alteration process alone (Bishop and Hill, 1971). If anything job enrichment produced poorer quality work among these handicapped workers.

There is other evidence that enriched jobs may well have negative consequences under certain circumstances. Sexton (1967) found that among assembly line workers in one plant job structure was positively correlated with a variety of types of need satisfaction and was unrelated to performance effectiveness. In this particular instance being in a more enriched job did not have any implications for performance levels, but it was associated with lower levels of need satisfaction.

Whether or not workers in general really want enriched jobs has been a matter of some controversy also. A study designed to look into this issue dealt with instances in two firms where workers voluntarily transferred to new positions (Simonds and Orife, 1975). The data indicate that the major characteristic of the new positions was a somewhat higher rate of pay. Since the more enriched jobs often paid better, they tended to be sought out. However, when pay was not a factor, neither enriched nor enlarged positions appeared to be especially attractive. The evidence clearly favors those who claim that most workers have no special preference for enriched jobs as such.

JOB ENRICHMENT IN PRACTICE

Most of the research investigations considered to this point have attempted to focus directly on the identification of motivational consequences likely to emanate from the change of *jobs* in a predetermined fashion. In contrast, many of the more widely publicized applications have involved numerous changes extending well beyond the individual job or even a group task (Walton, 1974). Under these circumstances it often is difficult to determine how important a role job enrichment per se may have played in the final outcome. Nevertheless, regardless of the scope of the change process, reports on specific applications have tended to be highly favorable (Davis and Cherns, 1975).

Applications at Bankers Trust Company

An application of job enrichment that appears to be relatively uncontaminated by other factors was carried out at Bankers Trust Company with various clerical operations involving the handling of deposits to customer checking accounts (Kraft and Williams, 1975). The description of changes in the regular and special accounts section provides a particularly good example of what is involved.

The job enrichment effort was undertaken because the section suffered from low productivity, high error rates, and considerable turnover, as well as a good deal of dissatisfaction over pay. The process began with a training program for supervisors during which a long list of possible job changes that might improve motivation was developed, and then pruned to a final set of practical plans. These plans called for the consolidation of three jobs concerned with comparing checks with signature cards, noticing dates and endorsements, and pulling mutilated checks. Thus, a previously divided natural unit of work was put back together.

In addition, all clerks were given greater responsibility for paying problem checks on their own initiative, including checks of considerable value. To do this it now proved practical to put the clerks in direct contact with branches and other inquiry sources, an activity previously handled by supervisors. A management–by–objectives type appraisal system was implemented to provide direct feedback to the clerks on their performance (in the process introducing goal setting as a confounding factor in interpreting the results of the program). These reported results were as follows:

1. Forgeries paid dropped 56 per cent.
2. Misfiled items decreased 19 per cent.
3. Complaints from branches declined approximately 25 per cent.
4. Staffing level was reduced 16 per cent for a somewhat increased volume of work.
5. A productivity level of 110 was attained in contrast to a 98 target figure.

Applications at Travelers Insurance Company

A second example is provided by a job enrichment program introduced into the keypunching operations at Travelers Insurance Company (Hackman et al., 1975). The objective was to enrich the keypunching job itself, again starting with a training program for supervisors out of which the basic plan emerged. At the time of initial implementation work output was deemed inadequate, the error rate excessive, and absenteeism too high. The keypunch job lacked skill variety, task identity, task significance, autonomy, or feedback as it was then designed. The changes introduced are described as follows:

1. *Natural units of work.* The random batch assignment of work was replaced by assigning to each operator continuing responsibility for certain accounts — either particular departments or particular recurring jobs.
2. *Task combination.* Some planning and control functions were combined with the central task of keypunching.
3. *Client relationships.* Each operator was given several channels of direct contact with clients. The operators, not their assignment clerks, now inspect their documents for correctness and legibility. When problems arise, the operator, not the supervisor, takes them up with the client.
4. *Feedback.* In addition to feedback from client contact . . . the computer department now returns incorrect cards to the operators who punched them, and the operators correct their own errors. . . . Each operator receives weekly a computer printout of her errors and productivity which is sent to her directly, rather than given to her by the supervisor.
5. *Vertical loading* . . . . Operators now have the authority to correct obvious coding errors on their own. Operators may set their own schedules and plan their daily work . . . Some competent operators have been given the option of not verifying their work (Hackman et al. 1975, pp. 68–69).

The reported results of implementing these action principles include a substantial reduction in the number of keypunch operators needed, increased quantity of output, reduced error rates, reduced absenteeism, improved job attitudes, and less need for controls. Actual first year savings totalled over 64 thousand dollars, with a potential annual saving of approximately 92 thousand dollars given expanded application.

Guidelines from Experience

In various places the authors of job characteristics theory have set forth a series of diagnostic steps to undertake and a list of guidelines for implementing job enrichment (Frank and Hackman, 1975; Hackman, 1975a, 1975b, 1977; Hackman et al., 1975). The diagnostic steps are predicated on the use of the Job Diagnostic Survey to gather information.

> *Step 1. Check scores in the areas of motivation and satisfaction to see if problems exist in these areas. If they do, and job outcomes are deficient, then job enrichment may well be called for.*

Step 2. Check the motivating potential scores of the jobs to see if they are low. If they are not, job enrichment is not likely to be the answer.

Step 3. Check scores for the five core dimensions to see what the basic strengths and weaknesses of the present job are. In this way it is possible to identify specific areas for change.

Step 4. Check to see what the growth need strength levels of job incumbents are. One can proceed with more confidence in enriching the jobs of high growth need employees since they are ready for the change.

Step 5. Check the scores for various aspects of job satisfaction and other information sources for roadblocks that might obstruct change or special opportunities that might facilitate it.

The prescriptive guidelines for implementation are as follows:

Guide 1. Diagnose the work system in terms of some theory of work redesign prior to introducing any change, to see what is possible and what kinds of changes are most likely to work.

Guide 2. Keep the focus of the change effort on the work itself, rather than other aspects of the work context, so that real job enrichment does occur.

Guide 3. Prepare in advance for any possible problems and side effects, especially among employees whose jobs are not directly affected by the change; develop appropriate contingency plans.

Guide 4. Evaluate the project on a continuing basis to see if anticipated changes actually are occurring, and using as many and as objective measures as possible.

Guide 5. Confront difficult problems as early in the project as possible.

Guide 6. Design change processes in such a way as to fit the objectives of the job enrichment. Thus if autonomy in work is to be an objective, autonomy should be respected in designing the new jobs in the first place; in other words be consistent with the theory guiding the change effort throughout.

The authors of the theory are well aware that many job enrichment efforts fail to achieve their objectives and that others die a natural death subsequent to the "pilot project" phase. A number of reasons for such failures are suggested. Adequate effort may not have been devoted to the initial diagnosis. There may be very little real change in the work itself. Unanticipated side effects in the surrounding work system may vitiate such initial changes as do occur. A lack of systematic evaluation may mean that little is learned from one project that could help in implementing the next more effectively. Insufficient knowledge of theory, strategy, and tactics of work design may undermine the effort. Traditional bureaucratic practices that are logically inconsistent with the objectives of job enrichment may creep into the process and dilute the effects. To the extent these factors pyramid, and they often do, a project is almost certain to fail. The authors are not entirely optimistic about the future of job enrichment as a result.

CONCLUSIONS

The discussion of job enrichment in connection with motivation-hygiene theory in Chapter 4 brought out the fact that even under the best of circumstances some employees do not respond to job enrichment. In blue collar jobs in particular the results often tend to be below expectations. Job characteristics theory represents an attempt to explain and predict these failures and successes. In this respect it contrasts sharply with motivation-hygiene theory and orthodox job enrichment. Potentially, at least, the job characteristics approach is the more powerful of the two theories, simply because it expands the boundaries of application to include failures as well as successes. It remains, however, to determine whether this potential has been realized.

Scientific Goals

The major strengths of job characteristics theory are its clear specification of what constitutes job enrichment and what does not and its introduction of the moderator concept. At a conceptual level the five core job dimensions appear to make considerable sense. The only real question involves whether job autonomy is an adequate way of representing the psychological state of experienced responsibility. Experienced responsibility requires that the job permit one to attribute successes and failures to one's own efforts; this would appear to be more than a matter of autonomy, and in fact the research data indicate that it is more. Autonomy is one of the best predictors of the outcome variables, but it is also closely related to skill variety and thus appears to account for relatively little criterion variance on its own. When multiple skills are invoked, close supervision of all aspects of the work becomes difficult, and thus a degree of autonomy is inevitable. It seems very likely that the introduction of a new dimension into the theory dealing directly with the opportunity to attribute results to one's own efforts would enhance the amount of outcome variance explained.

In general both autonomy and skill variety measures do appear to function in the manner the theory predicts with considerable consistency. Task significance has been studied much less extensively, but the results are typically positive. On the other hand, task identity has failed so often to relate to outcome measures (even moderating occasionally in a manner that is the reverse of that hypothesized) that its continued inclusion in the theory appears to be unwarranted. Feedback also has failed to yield expected results with some frequency but not often enough to place its theoretical status in serious question.

The original theory posited a multiplicative relation between job dimensions. This was later revised with the development of the MPS formula so that both multiplicative and additive relationships were invoked. Neither version has proved as effective as the simple addition of core dimensions scores. In this respect the theory clearly should be changed.

With regard to the moderator concept, there are a number of remaining uncertainties. The very profusion of moderators is a problem in itself. The theory specifies growth need strength, various types of job satisfaction, and organizational climate. In addition, the rural-urban factor and alienation from middle class norms, operating at a sociological rather than a psychological level, are conceptually congruent with the theory, and recent evidence suggests that job longevity and specific needs such as achievement motivation should be considered as well. All this leads to a very cumbersome prediction process, and one cannot help wishing for a more parsimonious formulation.

Both the organizational climate and longevity moderators have received very little empirical investigation, and thus judgment is premature. On balance the organizational climate extension of the theory as currently stated does not look promising. Of the various job satisfaction moderators proposed, satisfaction with coworkers and perhaps supervision appear to have the greatest support. The implication is that difficulties in dealing with people in the work environment can disrupt the job enrichment-outcome variable relationship, so that enrichment does not work as it should. If this is the case, direct measures of socially stimulated anger and anxiety should yield cleaner moderating effects than those obtained with the satisfaction measures.

The findings regarding the sociological moderators are muddied by a number of measurement problems. In different studies the definitions of rural and urban status have varied considerably. Turner and Lawrence (1965) defined their urban group not only in terms of city size but in terms of membership in the Catholic religion as well. Yet the latter aspect of their definition has received practically no attention in subsequent studies. Different investigations have varied the cutting point between rural and urban populations over a sizable range. Also there has been no consistency in handling suburban areas. Rural vs. urban childhood origins, current residence, and current employment location have all been used on occasion. The alienation variable lacks conceptual clarity and has been measured in various ways. It now seems apparent that rural-urban childhood background is not a moderator. The other proposed sociological moderators may yield mild differences in specific instances, but population changes appear to be obliterating their effects. Overall it would seem to be much more fruitful to concentrate on psychological moderators, as is done in job characteristics theory.

A recent review of the moderator literature takes an extremely critical position and concludes that the role of even psychological moderators has not been demonstrated (White 1978). The proclivity of the authors of job characteristics theory for partial reporting of their data does indeed raise questions. Again and again relationships, groups, and significance tests that the theory places in a position of salience are neglected in the published reports. Yet even with these shortcomings the data as a whole suggest that some kind of moderator effect of a motivational nature is present.

The difficulty is that higher order need strength, or growth need strength, yields a sizable number of moderator effects in the predicted direction, but few statistically significant differences between correlations; the moderator consistently falls short of full expectations. In part this may reflect the limitations of need hierarchy theory as discussed in Chapter 2. It may well be, however, that the problem resides in the specific designation of the moderator variable.

Turner and Lawrence (1965) suggested that their rural-urban moderator effects might be a consequence of anomie (alienation), higher order need strength, or achievement motivation. The first two have been studied in detail, with the results presented in this chapter; the third has only very recently begun to receive attention. Yet McClelland's description of the achievement situation as set forth in Chapter 3 closely parallels that for the job enrichment situation specified by job characteristics theory. Achievement situations primarily involve taking personal responsibility, intermediate risk, and feedback and secondarily involve novelty and planning. If such a situation is not enriched, it is hard to understand what is. Accordingly, it seems reasonable to anticipate that achievement motivation as measured by the Thematic Apperception Test should serve as an effective moderator of job characteristic-outcome relationships. One would anticipate that it would yield more precise differentiations than the more global higher order or growth need concepts.

The limited evidence does support this intuitive impression, especially in the area of job performance, where the current job characteristics theory has been least effective. Future research would benefit from the use of a projective measure of achievement motivation; in any event special attention should be given to the matter of construct validity. It may well be that some of the negative results reported are a consequence of a failure to truly measure the achievement motivation variable. Also there is a need to conduct studies in which enrichment is actively introduced in previously unenriched jobs to get at causal relationships. There are far too few such designs in the research bearing on job characteristics theory as a whole, and none in the research involving the need achievement moderator. The correlational studies across existing jobs are an important first step, but they do not tell us with certainty that job scope is the key factor — in any given instance pay differentials, job level, status considerations, or some other factor that co-varies with job scope may be the cause of the results. In addition, there may well be a difference between enriching jobs where no such expectation has existed previously and studying jobs widely known to have been enriched for years. At the very least the two should attract different kinds of people, in terms of achievement motivation levels, for instance.

There are also some problems with regard to the outcome variables specified by the theory. Quantity of output is not included, although the exclusion appears to be more on empirical grounds than on the basis of theoretical logic, and turnover is. Yet research tests, whether by the authors of the theory or others, have often incorporated quantity in the performance measure and neglected turnover entirely.

On the basis of the evidence it appears that job characteristics theory as currently stated relates to intrinsic motivation and job satisfaction quite well, absenteeism less well, and performance, including the quality factor, not very well at all. Apart from the method variance problem, which may have influenced at least some of the results, it does appear that the further one moves from the psychological states specified by the theory in the direction of actual job behavior, the less valid the theory becomes. This fact has led some to propose that the results obtained in research may be entirely explainable in terms of a kind of pretest sensitization in which employees about to undergo a job enrichment experience incorporate a mind-set that co-opts them into producing the expected results (Salancik and Pfeffer, 1978). The data to support or reject this hypothesis do not exist. It seems unlikely that the whole of job characteristics theory and its related research can be glossed over quite so lightly. Nevertheless, the relative failure of the theory in the job performance (behavior) area is a reality.

Managerial Goals

As a motivational technique, job enrichment has experienced a wave of popularity in recent years. It has been widely advocated not only as an application in its own right but also as a major component of organization development and various participative interventions, including those of a sociotechnical nature. A number of seemingly very practical arguments have been advanced in favor of the widespread application of the technique.

The Work in America Arguments.   In 1971 a special task force was convened by the Secretary of Health, Education, and Welfare to prepare a report on work in America (O'Toole et al., 1973). This report, which has received widespread circulation and discussion, advocated a number of changes in society's approach to work, including extensive redesign of jobs to make them more satisfying and challenging. The task force developed the thesis that changes in the values, desires, and capabilities of the work force have not been matched by an appropriate upgrading of jobs. As a result, large segments of society are disenchanted, dissatisfied, and alienated; they consider themselves to be engaged in "dull, repetitive, seemingly meaningless tasks, offering little challenge or autonomy." It takes little imagination to move from such a conception of the work force to the advocacy of job enrichment as it has been discussed in this chapter. Accordingly, the *Work in America* report has been cited widely in support of the use of the job enrichment approach.

Yet there are solid grounds for questioning the report's line of argument. Although there have been changes in attitudes, desires, and values in this country, there is little if any evidence that a sizable increase in real dissatisfaction and alienation has been the result. It appears that most people ultimately find a niche in the world of work that fits them quite well. Furthermore, there is no basis for concluding that a strong and frustrated desire for more challenging, meaningful, "humanized" work permeates the population. Most individuals, even in the younger age groups where changes have been greatest, appear to find jobs with a scope adequate to their desires. These conclusions are attested to by a sizable amount of data (Fein, 1975; Vogel, 1974; Wool, 1973). Job enrichment does often raise satisfaction levels, but there is also evidence that when dissatisfaction is really pervasive, enrichment does little to alleviate the situation (Locke, Sirota, and Wolfson, 1976). All in all, the *Work in America* arguments seem inadequate to justify a massive commitment to job enrichment by most companies.

The Basic Practicalities.   Rejecting the *Work in America* arguments for massive job enrichment does not mean that selective utilization under appropriate circumstances cannot prove to be a useful strategy. The authors of job characteristics theory have provided both measures and guidelines that can be effectively used in diagnosis and implementation. This is one of the major strengths of the theory and its application to practice.

It would appear that in many cases the desires of a company's work force for enriched work can be met simply through the traditional practices of upgrading and promotion, particularly if the company is growing and has a limited number of employees for whom enrichment is appropriate. However, there are many circumstances where work force composition and promotional opportunities make this an insufficient solution. At such times enrichment of existing jobs seems particularly appropriate.

There is a growing body of opinion to the effect that individuals at a particular time have what amounts to an optimal task scope that is ideal for their particular capabilities and personality makeup (Schwab and Cummings, 1976). In this view individual differences are pronounced and important. Jobs can be too enriched for a particular person, just as a person can be promoted "over his head" and fail because of an inability to cope emotionally or intellectually (Miner, 1975). Similarly, jobs can be insufficiently enriched, and it is in such cases that job characteristics theory or some modification of it becomes valuable as a guide.

It would appear likely that the kind of matching of people with job scopes recommended here will ultimately be built into regular personnel practice through job analysis, selection, and task assignment procedures. If so, the faddish aspect of many current job enrichment programs will disappear and the technique will become part of standard personnel practice as an ongoing activity. As the difficulties noted in the Scientific Goals section are resolved, it seems probable that job characteristics theory will make a useful contribution to this type of practice. The theory clearly moves in the right direction, but the exact form that it will finally take is not yet entirely visible.

References

Aldag, Ramon J. and Arthur P. Brief. Some Correlates of Work Values, *Journal of Applied Psychology,* Vol. 60 (1975), 757–760.

Alderfer, Clayton P. *Existence, Relatedness and Growth: Human Needs in Organizational Settings.* New York: Free Press, 1972.

Bishop, Ronald C. and James W. Hill. Effects of Job Enlargement and Job Change on Contiguous but Nonmanipulated Jobs as a Function of Workers' Status, *Journal of Applied Psychology,* Vol. 55 (1971), 175–181.

Brief, Arthur P. and Ramon J. Aldag. Employee Reactions to Job Characteristics: A Constructive Replication, *Journal of Applied Psychology,* Vol. 60 (1975), 182–186.

Burns, Tom and G. M. Stalker. *The Management of Innovation.* London: Tavistock, 1961.

Castellano, John J. Rural and Urban Differences: One More Time, *Academy of Management Journal.* Vol. 19 (1976), 495–502.

Davis, Louis E. and Albert B. Cherns. *The Quality of Working Life.* Volume Two: Cases and Commentary. New York: Free Press, 1975.

Dunham, Randall B., Ramon J. Aldag, and Arthur P. Brief. Dimensionality of Task Design as Measured by the Job Diagnostic Survey, *Academy of Management Journal,* Vol. 20 (1977), 209–223.

Fein, Mitchell. Job Enrichment Does Not Work, *Atlanta Economic Review,* Vol. 25, No. 6 (1975), 50–54.

Frank, Linda L. and J. Richard Hackman. A Failure of Job Enrichment: The Case of the Change That Wasn't, *Journal of Applied Behavioral Science,* Vol. 11 (1975), 413–436.

Giles, William F. Volunteering for Job Enrichment: Reaction to Job Characteristics or Change? *Journal of Vocational Behavior*, Vol. 11 (1977), 232–238.

Hackman, J. Richard. Effects of Task Characteristics on Group Products, *Journal of Experimental Social Psychology*, Vol. 4 (1968), 162–187.

Hackman, J. Richard. Toward Understanding the Role of Tasks in Behavioral Research, *Acta Psychologica*, Vol. 31 (1969a), 97–128.

Hackman, J. Richard. Nature of the Task as a Determiner of Job Behavior, *Personnel Psychology*, Vol. 22 (1969b), 435–444.

Hackman, J. Richard. Is Job Enrichment Just a Fad? *Harvard Business Review*, Vol. 53, No. 5 (1975a), 129–138.

Hackman, J. Richard. On the Coming Demise of Job Enrichment, In E. L. Cass and F. G. Zimmer (eds.), *Man and Work in Society*. New York: Van Nostrand Reinhold, 1975b, pp. 97–115.

Hackman, J. Richard. Work Design, In J. Richard Hackman and J. Lloyd Suttle (eds.), *Improving Life at Work: Behavioral Science Approaches to Organizational Change*. Santa Monica, Calif.: Goodyear, 1977, pp. 96–162.

Hackman, J. Richard. The Design of Self-Managing Work Groups, In Bert T. King, Siegfried S. Streufert, and Fred E. Fiedler (eds.), *Managerial Control and Organizational Democracy*. Washington, D. C.: Winston, 1978, pp. 61–91.

Hackman, J. Richard and Edward E. Lawler. Employee Reactions to Job Characteristics, *Journal of Applied Psychology*, Vol. 55 (1971), 259–286.

Hackman, J. Richard and Charles G. Morris. Group Tasks, Group Interaction Process, and Group Performance Effectiveness: A Review and Proposed Integration, In Leonard Berkowitz (ed.), *Advances in Experimental Social Psychology*, Vol. 8. New York: Academic Press, 1975.

Hackman, J. Richard and Greg R. Oldham. Development of the Job Diagnostic Survey, *Journal of Applied Psychology*, Vol. 60 (1975), 159–170.

Hackman, J. Richard and Greg R. Oldham. Motivation Through the Design of Work: Test of a Theory, *Organizational Behavior and Human Performance*, Vol. 16 (1976), 250–279.

Hackman, J. Richard, Greg Oldham, Robert Janson, and Kenneth Purdy. A New Strategy for Job Enrichment, *California Management Review*, Vol. 17, No. 4 (1975), 57–71.

Hulin, Charles L. Individual Differences and Job Enrichment — The Case Against General Treatments, In John R. Maher (ed.), *New Perspectives in Job Enrichment*. New York: Van Nostrand Reinhold, 1971, pp. 159–191.

Katz, Ralph. Job Longevity as a Situational Factor in Job Satisfaction, *Administrative Science Quarterly*, Vol. 23 (1978), 204–223.

Kraft, W. Philip and Kathleen L. Williams. Job Redesign Improves Productivity, *Personnel Journal*, Vol. 54 (1975), 393–397.

Lawler, Edward E. Job Design and Employee Motivation, *Personnel Psychology*, Vol. 22 (1969), 426–435.

Lawler, Edward E. *Motivation in Work Organizations*. Monterey, Calif.: Brooks/Cole, 1973.

Lawler, Edward E., J. Richard Hackman, and Stanley Kaufman. Effects of Job Redesign: A Field Experiment, *Journal of Applied Social Psychology*, Vol. 3 (1973), 49–62.

Locke, Edwin A., David Sirota, and Alan D. Wolfson. An Experimental Case Study of the Successes and Failures of Job Enrichment in a Government Agency, *Journal of Applied Psychology*, Vol. 61 (1976), 701–711.

Miner, John B. *The Challenge of Managing*. Philadelphia: W. B. Saunders, 1975.

Oldham, Greg R. Job Characteristics and Internal Motivation: The Moderating Effect of Interpersonal and Individual Variables, *Human Relations*, Vol. 29 (1976), 559–569.

Oldham, Greg R., J. Richard Hackman and Jone L. Pearce. Conditions Under Which Employees Respond Positively to Enriched Work, *Journal of Applied Psychology*, Vol. 61 (1976), 395–403.

O'Toole, James, et al. *Work in America: Report of a Special Task Force to the Secretary of Health, Education, and Welfare*. Cambridge, Mass.: MIT Press, 1973.

Pierce, Jon L. and Randall B. Dunham. Task Design: A Literature Review,

Academy of Management Review, Vol. 1, No. 4 (1976), 83–97.

Pierce, Jon L. and Randall B. Dunham. The Measurement of Perceived Job Characteristics: The Job Diagnostic Survey Versus the Job Characteristics Inventory, *Academy of Management Journal*, Vol. 21 (1978), 123–128.

Porter, Lyman W., Edward E. Lawler, and J. Richard Hackman. *Behavior in Organizations*. New York: McGraw-Hill, 1975.

Robey, Daniel. Task Design, Work Values, and Worker Response: An Experimental Test, *Organizational Behavior and Human Performance*, Vol. 12 (1974), 264–273.

Rousseau, Denis M. Technological Differences in Job Characteristics, Employee Satisfaction, and Motivation: A Synthesis of Job Design Research and Sociotechnical Systems Theory, *Organizational Behavior and Human Performance*, Vol. 19 (1977), 18–42.

Salancik, Gerald R. and Jeffrey Pfeffer. A Social Information Processing Approach to Job Attitudes and Task Design, *Administrative Science Quarterly*, Vol. 23 (1978), 224–253.

Schwab, Donald P. and Larry L. Cummings. A Theoretical Analysis of the Impact of Task Scope on Employee Performance, *Academy of Management Review*, Vol. 1 (1976), 23–35.

Sexton, William P. Organizational and Individual Needs: A Conflict? *Personnel Journal*, Vol. 46 (1967), 337–343.

Simonds, Rollin H. and John N. Orife. Worker Behavior Versus Enrichment Theory, *Administrative Science Quarterly*, Vol. 20 (1975), 606–612.

Sims, Henry P. and Andrew D. Szilagyi. Job Characteristic Relationships: Individual and Structural Moderators, *Organizational Behavior and Human Performance*, Vol. 17 (1976), 211–230.

Sims, Henry P., Andrew D. Szilagyi, and Robert T. Keller. The Measurement of Job Characteristics, *Academy of Management Journal*, Vol. 19 (1976), 195–212.

Steers, Richard M. and Daniel G. Spencer. The Role of Achievement Motivation in Job Design, *Journal of Applied Psychology*, Vol. 62 (1977), 472–479.

Stinson, John E. and Thomas W. Johnson. Tasks, Individual Differences and Job Satisfaction. *Industrial Relations*, Vol. 16 (1977), 315–322.

Stone, Eugene F., Richard T. Mowday, and Lyman W. Porter. Higher Order Need Strengths as Moderators of the Job Scope-Job Satisfaction Relationship, *Journal of Applied Psychology*, Vol. 62 (1977), 466–471.

Turner, Arthur N. and Paul R. Lawrence. *Industrial Jobs and the Worker: An Investigation of Response to Task Attributes.* Boston: Harvard Graduate School of Business Administration, 1965.

Umstot, Denis D., Cecil H. Bell, and Terence R. Mitchell. Effects of Job Enrichment and Task Goals on Satisfaction and Productivity: Implications for Job Design, *Journal of Applied Psychology*, Vol. 61 (1976), 379–394.

Vogel, Alfred. Challenging Work, *The Sampler*. No. 2 (1974), p. 3.

Walton, Richard E. Innovative Restructuring of Work, *In* Jerome M. Rosow (ed.), *The Worker and the Job: Coping with Change.* Englewood Cliffs, N. J.: Prentice-Hall, 1974, pp. 145–176.

Wanous, John P. Individual Differences and Reactions to Job Characteristics, *Journal of Applied Psychology*, Vol. 59 (1974), 616–622.

White, J. Kenneth. Individual Differences and the Job Quality-Worker Response Relationship: Review, Integration, and Comments, *Academy of Management Review*, Vol. 3 (1978), 267–280.

Wool, Harold. What's Wrong with Work in America? — A Review Essay, *Monthly Labor Review*, Vol. 96, No. 3 (1973), 38–44.

THEORY X AND THEORY Y

10

The theories of Douglas McGregor were first formally expounded in 1957. However, the values that underlie these theories, and many of the ideas as well, can be traced back in various articles and speeches to the early 1940s (McGregor, 1966). McGregor spent most of his professional career at Massachusetts Institute of Technology. He served there as executive director of the industrial relations section during the 1940s when his ideas were first developing and moved from that position to the presidency of Antioch College. After six years at Antioch he returned to MIT, where he remained until his death in 1964.

In order to understand McGregor's views it is important to put them in temporal perspective. McGregor was an advocate of humanism in the work place. He wrote at a time when ideas of this kind were beginning to achieve considerable popularity, and he shared with a

267

number of other theorists the task of promoting this popularity. Inevitably he was influenced by these people who shared his values and philosophical orientation — Maslow, Herzberg, Argyris, Likert, and others — and he drew heavily from them in his writings. This point is stressed by Bennis, a former student of McGregor's and for many years a colleague at MIT:

> He (McGregor) was a genius, not necessarily for the originality of his ideas, which were often "in the air" or developed by similarly creative spirits. He was a genius because he had clarity of mind, a rare empathy for the manager, and a flair for the right metaphor that established a new idea. . . . Theory X and Theory Y certainly existed before McGregor. But he named them, called them (Bennis, 1972, p. 148).

Management historians have noted applications of the kind McGregor advocated in the business world dating back to 1910 (Wrege and Lattanzio, 1977). McGregor, however, took what was "in the air" and gave it a continuing reality that it had not possessed previously.

McGREGOR'S STATEMENTS OF HIS THEORIES

There are three major statements dealing with theory X and theory Y — first a 1957 article, then a full scale book presentation in 1960, and finally some supplementary comments written in 1964 just before McGregor's death and published in a posthumous book (1967).

The Original Article

Theory X is set forth in a set of propositions and beliefs, hypothesized to be widely held in the ranks of management, that guide the formation of organization structures, policies, practices, and programs. It is thus a theory of the assumptions or working theories most managers use in carrying out their activities. The three propositions are:

1. Management is responsible for organizing the elements of productive enterprise — money, materials, equipment, people — in the interest of economic ends.
2. With respect to people, this is a process of directing their efforts, motivating them, controlling their actions, modifying their behavior to fit the needs of the organization.
3. Without this active intervention by management, people would be passive — even resistant — to organizational needs. They must therefore be persuaded, rewarded, punished, controlled — their activities must be directed. This is management's task (McGregor, 1957b, p. 23).

The five beliefs are:

4. The average man is by nature indolent — he works as little as possible.
5. He lacks ambition, dislikes responsibility, prefers to be led.
6. He is inherently self-centered, indifferent to organizational needs.
7. He is by nature resistant to change.
8. He is gullible, not very bright, the ready dupe of the charlatan and the demagogue (p. 23).

McGregor views this "conventional" managerial theory of the nature of man as incorrect in spite of its widespread acceptance. Instead, he proposes Maslow's need hierarchy theory (see Chapter 2) as a valid statement of man's motivational nature. Since lower level needs have been largely satisfied, higher needs are activated, but under theory X managerial assumptions, these higher needs remain deprived. Accordingly, people at work act with the indolence, passivity, resistance to change, lack of responsibility, willingness to follow the demagogue, and unreasonable demands for economic benefits that theory X leads one to expect. No amount of reward and punishment focused at the level of lower needs will change the situation, because these needs being satisfied are no longer operative.

What is required is a different set of managerial assumptions and practices attuned to the higher order needs of workers, the needs that have real behavior–producing potential at this point in time and which therefore reflect the nature of man as he currently is. The first proposition of this theory Y is the same as that of theory X; from that point on the two diverge sharply:

1. Management is responsible for organizing the elements of productive enterprise — money, materials, equipment, people — in the interest of economic ends.
2. People are not by nature passive or resistant to organizational needs. They have become so as a result of experience in organizations.
3. The motivation, the potential for development, the capacity for assuming responsibility, the readiness to direct behavior toward organizational goals are all present in people. Management does not put them there. It is a responsibility of management to make it possible for people to recognize and develop these human characteristics for themselves.
4. The essential task of management is to arrange organizational conditions and methods of operation so that people can achieve their own goals best by directing their own efforts toward organizational objectives (pp. 88–89).

Managing with a Y type working theory does not mean abdicating the managerial role or utilizing a laissez faire style. The shift from

X to Y involves substituting self-control and self-direction for external control and thus treating people as adults rather than children. Four different kinds of innovations in practice are discussed as consistent with theory Y — (1) decentralization and delegation, of the kind that might be expected when a flat organizational structure with wide spans of control is introduced; (2) job enlargement; (3) participation and consultative management, particularly as embodied in the Scanlon Plan (discussed later in this chapter); and (4) performance appraisal within a highly participative management–by–objectives framework, in which the individual sets his own objectives and evaluates himself.

The Expanded Version

In his subsequent book McGregor (1960) elaborates on many of the themes contained in his original article. Theory X is stated in somewhat more muted terms, but the assumptions of dislike of work, preference for direction, desire to avoid responsibility, limited ambition, and need for security above all remain, along with the belief that the managerial role is to coerce and control people to devote their efforts to organizational objectives. This theory is described as materially influencing managerial strategy in industry and as the basis for the principles of management derived from classical management theory; it is real, not a straw man. Workers who operate in a theory X context with their higher order needs deprived are being treated as children and exhibit symptoms of illness. In this discussion, as in certain other areas, McGregor draws heavily from the recently published theories of Argyris (1957). Only in dealing with professionals in the research and development context does McGregor believe there has been any significant movement away from theory X.

In general, McGregor rejects the human relations approach either as involving pseudo-participation and thus actually continuing to maintain a theory X orientation or as an abdication. However, he does elaborate more fully than previously on the assumptions inherent in theory Y:

1. The expenditure of physical and mental effort in work is as natural as play or rest.
2. External control and the threat of punishment are not the only means for bringing about effort toward organizational objectives. Man will exercise self-direction and self-control in the service of objectives to which he is committed.
3. Commitment to objectives is a function of the rewards associated with their achievement. The most significant of such rewards, e.g., the satisfaction of ego and self-actualization needs, can be

direct products of effort directed toward organizational objectives.

4. The average human being learns under proper conditions not only to accept but to seek responsibility.

5. The capacity to exercise a relatively high degree of imagination, ingenuity, and creativity in the solution of organizational problems is widely, not narrowly, distributed in the population.

6. Under the conditions of modern industrial life, the intellectual potentialities of the average human being are only partially utilized (McGregor, 1960, pp. 47–48).

The central principle of theory Y is one of integration whereby individuals "achieve their own goals best by directing their efforts toward the success of the enterprise"; this is in contrast to theory X, which operates according to the scalar principle of direction and control through the exercise of authority. McGregor's theory specifically states that operating on theory Y principles will create a more effective organization than operating on theory X principles, which by its very nature thwarts the satisfaction of operative needs. In this connection McGregor explicitly accepts not only need hierarchy theory but also motivation-hygiene theory as valid statements regarding human motivation.

Ultimately McGregor (1960, p. 103) came to associate theory Y directly with participative management — "The principle of integration requires active and responsible participation of the individual in decisions affecting his own career." Subsequently (p. 174) the role of the manager in this participative relationship is specified — "the most appropriate roles of the manager vis à vis his subordinates are those of teacher, professional helper, colleague, consultant. Only to a limited degree will he assume the role of authoritative boss. The line manager who seeks to operate within the context of Theory Y will establish relationships with his subordinates, his superiors, and his colleagues which are much like those of the professional vis à vis his clients."

In certain respects this view, although consistent with McGregor's overall values, appears to be at variance with his stated position at the time he left the presidency of Antioch College — "I believed, for example, that a leader could operate successfully as a kind of adviser to his organization. I thought I could avoid being a 'boss.' Unconsciously, I suspect, I hoped to duck the unpleasant necessity of making difficult decisions, of taking the responsibility for one course of action among many uncertain alternatives, of making mistakes and taking the consequences. I thought that maybe I could operate so that everyone would like me — that 'good human relations' would eliminate all discord and disagreement. I could not have been more wrong" (McGregor, 1954). By 1960 the impact of his prior experiences seems to have paled somewhat, and McGregor once again came to espouse an advisory, professional role for the manager rather than a hierarchic role. Yet there are hints of some uncertainties on this score throughout his writings.

The 1960 volume contains considerable elaboration on the author's views regarding management by objectives and on the Scanlon Plan as a method of participative management. In addition, McGregor endorsed various methods of improving managerial skills of social interaction, the kinds of skills a truly flexible, theory Y manager must possess. Psychotherapy is advocated with the recognition that at the present time it is not practical for most managers. Laboratory or T-group training thus becomes the method of choice for developing skills of social interaction.

Finally McGregor was realistic enough to recognize that there are subordinates who are incompetent, dishonest, and neurotically hostile, and there is such a thing as an incompatible relationship. "Under such conditions, it is nonsense to talk about creating positive expectations, mutual confidence, a healthy climate. The only real solution is to end the relationship, by transfer under some circumstances, or by termination of employment under others. If this is impossible, all that remains is to recognize that effective management in such a relationship is impossible, and to make the best of the situation" (McGregor, 1960, p. 142). Note that even in this situation a resort to approaches based on theory X assumptions is not advocated.

Supplementary Comments

The 1967 volume contains discussions of a variety of topics, many of them only tangentially related to theory X and theory Y. However, certain previous statements regarding those theories are re-emphasized and elaborated upon. In McGregor's view the best operating strategy out of a theory Y orientation is one that creates conditions whereby the subordinate can achieve his own goals, including self-actualization, most effectively by contributing to organizational goal achievement. This involves fostering integration, organizational commitment, and intrinsic motive satisfactions. It also means working to achieve conditions of mutual trust, support, and respect for the individual that will facilitate the emergence of self-actualizing behavior. McGregor clearly acknowledges that his espousal of this kind of managerial strategy is an outgrowth of his own strongly held values. These are said to be a belief in organized human effort, in the importance of meaningful work, in the undesirability of manipulation, and in the desirability of self-actualization.

McGregor (1967, p. 78) also returns to the case of the individual who does not respond to such a theory Y-based strategy. "It is to be anticipated that some percentage of any employee group (perhaps of the order of 10 per cent) will not respond at all or will take advantage of such a strategy. For such people the firm enforcement of limits, followed if necessary by dismissal, is the only feasible course. Otherwise there is danger that indulgence toward such individuals will affect the whole organization negatively." There is a definite ring of a more theory X-based approach in these statements than was evident in the 1960 discussion of the same topic.

The distinction between theories X and Y themselves, which are now referred to as cosmologies, and the various strategies that can grow out of them is clearly drawn. Theory X can yield a number of strategies including the hard approach of scientific management and the soft approach of human relations; so can theory Y. Theory X and theory Y are not poles of a continuum; they are qualitatively different, and other distinct managerial working theories are also possible. The view that the theory X cosmology is much more widespread in the ranks of management than theory Y is reiterated.

The discussion of applications in the 1967 book focuses on the team building approaches that now are widely utilized in organization development. In this connection McGregor draws heavily on his experiences as a consultant to Union Carbide Corporation and Bell Telephone Company of Pennsylvania.

EVIDENCE AND APPLICATIONS

There are very few direct tests of McGregor's formulations in the literature. In part this is a consequence of the philosophical, highly value-laden nature of many of his statements. Certainly this is a philosophy-theory in the sense considered in Chapter 1, and as such it becomes difficult if not impossible to test at some points; there are what appear to be occasional logical inconsistencies. Yet aspects of the theory certainly are testable. In all probability more has not been done because many researchers viewed McGregor's writings more as philosophical advocacy than as scientific theory. Furthermore, McGregor himself conducted no research related to his formulations; nor did he attempt to make his variables operational in any kind of measurement procedures. Under such conditions it is not uncommon for theories to fail to generate research.

There is, of course, considerable research evidence now bearing on the various theoretical positions that McGregor co-opted and also on the applications he espoused. Of this research the most relevant is that dealing with need hierarchy theory discussed in Chapter 2. McGregor made need hierarchy theory a central aspect of his own theoretical position, and the current lack of clear-cut support for Maslow's views is thus a damaging blow. The similar lack of support for motivation-hygiene theory (see Chapter 4) is not nearly as crucial, since McGregor merely added Herzberg's views to his own rather than incorporating them directly.

Among the large number of applications McGregor discussed and endorsed, only the highly participative, management–by–objectives approach to performance appraisal appears to be an outgrowth of the theory per se (McGregor, 1957a). The discussion in Chapter 7 of research on MBO and participative goal setting is relevant here; that research does not provide the universal evidence for the superiority of participative over assigned approaches that McGregor anticipated. Job enlargement is advocated, although with relatively little description of specific approaches, and thus the treatments of orthodox job enrichment in Chapter 4 and of job characteristics theory in Chapter 9 are both relevant. Research dealing with delegation and participative management is given specific attention in Chapter 13.

Confusions Over Tests of McGregor's Formulations

There is a great deal of uncertainty in the literature regarding what evidence can and cannot be used to support or oppose McGregor's views. Even when a study is explicitly stated to be a test of McGregor's hypotheses, there is often a question as to whether it really is. With regard to this confusion Edgar Schein, a colleague at MIT, says, "I believe that McGregor himself muddied the conceptual waters when he linked to his analysis of managerial cosmologies a value position that it was management's obligation to create opportunities for self-actualization" (Schein, 1975, p. 83). Without question McGregor did present his views in a manner that was both persuasively compelling and conceptually confusing. In reviewing the evidence bearing on the theory, therefore, every effort must be made to determine whether the data cited are germane to the theory.

Stogdill (1974) draws upon studies that show that on occasion greater job structure may be related to need satisfaction, that delegation is unrelated to either subordinate perception of supervisory consideration or job satisfaction, and that supervisor permissiveness does not relate consistently to either subordinate productivity or satisfaction, to argue against a "Theory Y type of leader behavior." On the latter point at least these conclusions may be questioned. On numerous occasions in his writings McGregor explicitly states that the strategies that emerge from theory Y assumptions, whatever else they may be, are not "soft," permissive, or laissez faire. Yet there are also many references to self-direction and self-control that imply a diminution of external forces of any kind; these may well have led Stogdill to interpret McGregor as he did.

Misconceptions regarding the exact type of leader behaviors that are manifestations of theory Y assumptions are so prevalent in the literature that it is almost impossible not to view a degree of theoretical imprecision as responsible. Thus, Morse and Lorsch (1970) take the theory to task because it does not allow for findings derived from contingency theory indicating that what is appropriate leader behavior in one context may not be in another. Schein (1975) points out, however, that one of the stated characteristics of a manager operating from theory Y assumptions is his greater flexibility in adapting to the needs of the situation, in contrast to the manager working from a theory X orientation, who is more rigid. Schein is correct in one sense — "The manager who finds the underlying assumptions of theory Y congenial will invent his own tactics provided he has a conception of the strategy involved. The manager whose underlying assumptions are those of Theory X cannot manage by integration and self-control no matter what techniques or forms are provided him" (McGregor, 1960, p. 75). Yet nowhere does McGregor clearly specify contingency variables and alternative behaviors. What should one do when? The theory leaves us hanging, and accordingly it is not surprising that others have put words in McGregor's pen.

Schein (1975) argues that theory X and theory Y, dealing as they do with managerial assumptions about the nature of man, have no necessary relationship to prescriptions that management should create conditions for higher order need satisfaction and self-actualization, should foster integration of personal and organizational goals, and should practice participative management. He points to his own findings in research with his students that indicates only a .60 correlation between theory Y assumptions and participative style as measured by self-report questionnaires. But the point is that McGregor, as part of his overall theory, did move beyond the more descriptive theory of X and Y to a normative theory of leadership behavior, however imprecisely stated, and he did link his normative formulations both to X and Y assumptions and to outcome variables such as organizational effectiveness and long-range profit. One can divorce theories X and Y from the rest of what McGregor said if one wishes, but then one has neither McGregor nor the reason for his sizable impact on management thought.

The Non-Linear Systems Experience

Starting in 1960 a small (225 employees) electronics firm in southern California called Non-Linear Systems began the introduction of procedures that were widely heralded as providing for a true test of the value of a theory Y-based approach. At the time these procedures were introduced, the company was eight years old and prospering. The president was the primary initiator of change.

Early Reactions.   McGregor apparently was fully familiar with the Non-Linear Systems changes and writes very approvingly of them; clearly he views them as consistent with theory Y. He notes that "productivity increased over two years by about 30 per cent. With respect to quality, customer complaints decreased by 7 per cent. As of today, there are virtually no quality defects" (McGregor, 1967, pp. 88–89). Furthermore, the company was able to weather a fairly severe market crisis in the fourth year of the experiment. Within this context the role of the supervisor is said to be that of "an expert source of help, a technical adviser, a teacher, a troubleshooter *by demand of the group*. He does not direct, control, or discipline in the conventional sense. He does not set standards of performance or exert pressure for improvement" (McGregor, 1967, p. 90).

Maslow spent a summer at Non-Linear Systems two years after the changes were first undertaken and wrote a book based on this experience (Maslow, 1965). He, too, endorses the procedures introduced there, at least under favorable economic conditions, and considers them to be consistent with his own and McGregor's views. Yet initially there is some feeling that McGregor may have gone too far — "a good deal of the evidence upon which he (McGregor) bases his conclusions comes from my researches and my papers on motivations, self-actualization, etc. But I of all people should know just how shaky this foundation is" (Maslow, 1965, p. 55). However, Maslow views the evidence for theory X as even less acceptable and, later in the book, clearly takes theory Y to be proven fact (p. 148).

Kuriloff (1963) served as vice-president for manager performance and development at Non-Linear Systems during the period of change. He, too, describes what was done as consistent with theory Y, noting the increases in mutual trust, the managerial emphasis on teaching and training rather than directing and controlling, and the shift to team production and decision-making. McGregor's reports of improved performance are generally endorsed, although the reduction in complaints from customers is stated to be 70 (not 7) per cent. Clearly the company has grown in number of employees and product lines. Yet there is no claim of increased profits, although they are anticipated. Furthermore, at the outset all employees were placed on salary, at a level well above that prevailing in the surrounding community, thus creating an apparent condition of overpay inequity (see Chapter 5).

Subsequent Interpretations. Five years into the change the company experienced severe financial difficulties and questioned most of the theory Y approaches. The president attributes many of the company's financial problems to these very approaches (Kay, 1973). Recently several postmortem analyses of theory Y at Non-Linear Systems have appeared in the literature that raise questions regarding what actually happened. These analyses have been hampered, however, by the fact that practically no written records were maintained during the period of the experiment, because such records might be used for purposes of external control on performance.

Malone (1975) concludes that in all probability no real increase in plant efficiency occurred at any point in the five years. He considers the reports of improved quality to be highly unreliable because of the lack of records. Job satisfaction appears to have increased for production workers but at the expense of those in management positions. Profits apparently declined over the five years, and bankruptcy was narrowly avoided at the time the company switched to a more traditional type of management. Overall, Malone concludes that the experiment simply did not work, and that similar results are to be expected whenever a firm is faced with highly competitive market conditions.

Another analysis, however, leads to a somewhat different conclusion. Gray (1978) notes that the lack of records and the failure to introduce changes in a sequential manner with adequate control conditions for comparison make it practically impossible to determine what caused what. He also believes that McGregor's views were in fact misapplied, especially as reflected in a lack of vertical participation and communication. Accordingly, he feels that one can conclude nothing from the Non-Linear Systems experience at all, at least insofar as McGregor's theories are concerned.

The Berkeley Studies

The largest body of research that does have implications for McGregor's theories has come from the University of California at Berkeley. In particular, this research has related to the distribution of theory X and theory Y assumptions in the managerial world.

International Research. Information was collected from some 3600 managers in 14 countries using a questionnaire that included items dealing with the degree to which people in general were believed to be capable of leadership and individual initiative, and with attitudes toward various managerial practices that might be

Table 10–1. ASSUMPTIONS REGARDING HUMAN NATURE AND ATTITUDES TOWARD RELATED ADMINISTRATIVE PRACTICES AMONG MANAGERS IN 14 COUNTRIES

Low scores reflect a theory X orientation and high scores a theory Y orientation (on a 1 to 5 scale).

Country	Assumptions Regarding Individual Leadership Capacity and Initiative	Attitudes Toward Administrative Practices		
		Sharing Information and Objectives	Subordinate Participation	Fostering Subordinate Self-control
United States	3.1	4.0	3.6	3.6
England	2.7	3.8	3.5	3.6
Germany	2.4	3.2	3.5	3.9
Denmark	2.5	3.1	3.7	3.9
Norway	2.5	4.0	3.5	3.9
Sweden	2.2	4.0	3.4	3.9
Belgium	2.3	3.7	3.9	3.7
France	2.4	4.0	3.8	3.8
Italy	2.4	3.6	3.2	3.7
Spain	2.5	3.6	3.7	3.8
Argentina	2.6	3.0	3.3	3.6
Chile	2.8	3.1	3.3	3.7
India	2.8	3.0	3.4	3.4
Japan	2.9	3.6	4.0	3.8
All countries	2.6	3.6	3.5	3.7

Adapted from Mason Haire, Edwin E. Ghiselli, and Lyman W. Porter. *Managerial Thinking: An International Study.* New York: Wiley, 1966, p. 22.

expected to indicate a theory Y orientation toward subordinates (Haire, Ghiselli, and Porter, 1966). The results given in Table 10–1 are noteworthy in a number of respects. There is a consistent pattern across all countries for the managers to hold assumptions about human nature that tend more toward theory X than do their prescriptions for managerial behavior. In essence they are saying, "We do not have much faith in people, but even so we favor sharing information, participation, and fostering internal control." Or, as the authors of the study expressed it (p. 24), the managers "want to build the techniques and practices of a Jeffersonian democracy on a basic belief in the divine right of kings."

What these findings appear to indicate is that most managers tend to hold theory X assumptions but have adopted human relations type strategies. Such a conclusion is not inconsistent with McGregor's views, especially those regarding the prevalence of theory X. On the other hand an average score of 2.6 on a scale with a midpoint of 3 is not exactly strong evidence. Additional possible sources of problems are the fact that McGregor considered theory X and theory Y as separate theories, not polar opposites, while the measuring instrument used violates this condition and the nature of the samples of managers. Most of the managers had been involved in management development programs in which they were taught human relations techniques. The effects of these factors on the results obtained are unknown.

Accounting Research.   A second study dealt with working theories held in the accounting field, especially with regard to cost control (Caplan, 1971). It should be noted in this connection that one of the first changes introduced at Non-Linear Systems was to abolish the accounting department as such in order to eliminate just this kind of external control. The data presented in Table 10–2 were derived from interviews with company accountants and accounting managers and other types of managers (primarily in production) in the same companies. The findings are based on relatively small samples, but as far as they go they support the hypothesis that theory X assumptions are quite widely held.

Research on Miles' Models of Managers' Theories.   Miles first became involved in research on managers' theories of management while at Stanford University (Yoder, Miles, McKibbin, Boynton, and England, 1963). However, it was after his move to Berkeley that he began to develop his own theories and to conduct research on them. The essence of his position is contained in Figure 10–1. His traditional model is largely synonymous with theory X and the human resources model with theory Y. The human relations model is in one

Table 10–2. RESPONSES OF COMPANY ACCOUNTANTS, ACCOUNTING MANAGERS, AND NON-ACCOUNTING MANAGERS TO QUESTIONS RELATING TO THEORY Y

	Per Cent Replying	
	Accounting Group	Non-Accounting Managers
Need to control costs?		
Yes—"because employees will either be deliberately wasteful or lazy, or will, at best, make no real effort to reduce costs on their own"	55	50
Yes—"because management might try to reduce cost on their own but would not have the necessary information to do so"	45	45
No—"because employees would do better without such control"	0	5
Company better off it it discontinued use of standard costing or variance analysis?		
Yes	0	10
No	100	90
Definition of management authority?		
Traditional definition—from above	80	65
Acceptance by others mentioned	20	15
Don't know	0	20

Adapted from Edwin H. Caplan. *Management Accounting and Behavioral Science.* Reading, Mass.: Addison-Wesley, 1971, pp. 73, 75, 78–79.

sense in between, but in all probability McGregor would consider it a particular manifestation of theory X involving pseudo-participation. In any event, it is clear that Miles' models draw heavily on McGregor, as Miles himself indicates, and that research on them relates back to theory X and theory Y (Miles, 1975).

The research data indicate that although most managers accept and endorse a participative strategy, they tend to doubt their subordinates' capacity for self-direction, self-control, and creative contribution. They rank their subordinates particularly low on responsibility, judgment, and initiative. This is the same pattern as found in the international research. In general, Miles interprets his findings as reflecting a predominant human relations orientation, and thus for all practical purposes they reflect theory X with a "soft" strategy. On the

Traditional model	Human relations model	Human resources model
Assumptions	*Assumptions*	*Assumptions*
1. Work is inherently distasteful to most people	1. People want to feel useful and important	1. Work is not inherently distasteful. People want to contribute to meaningful goals which they have helped establish
2. What workers do is less important than what they earn for doing it	2. People desire to belong and to be recognized as individuals	
3. Few want or can handle work which requires creativity, self-direction, or self-control	3. These needs are more important than money in motivating people to work	2. Most people can exercise far more creative, responsible self-direction and self-control than their present jobs demand
Policies	*Policies*	*Policies*
1. The manager's basic task is to closely supervise and control his subordinates	1. The manager's basic task is to make each worker feel useful and important	1. The manager's basic task is to make use of his "untapped" human resources
2. He must break tasks down into simple, repetitive, easily learned operations	2. He should keep his subordinates informed and listen to their objections to his plans	2. He must create an environment in which all members may contribute to the limits of their ability
3. He must establish detailed work routines and procedures and enforce these firmly but fairly	3. The manager should allow his subordinates to exercise some self-direction and self-control on routine matters	3. He must encourage full participation on important matters, continually broadening subordinate self-direction and control
Expectations	*Expectations*	*Expectations*
1. People can tolerate work if the pay is decent and the boss is fair	1. Sharing information with subordinates and involving them in routine decisions will satisfy their basic needs to belong and to feel important	1. Expanding subordinate influence, self-direction, and self-control will lead to direct improvements in operating efficiency
2. If tasks are simple enough and people are closely controlled, they will produce up to standard	2. Satisfying these needs will improve morale and reduce resistance to formal authority—subordinates will "willingly cooperate"	2. Work satisfaction may improve as a "by-product" of subordinates making full use of their resources

Figure 10–1. The three theories of management set forth by Miles. (Raymond E. Miles, *Theories of Management: Implications for Organizational Behavior and Development.* New York: McGraw-Hill, 1975, p. 35.)

other hand, the managers tended to espouse a human resources, theory Y model for their superiors in dealing with them and other managers at their level. This desire for theory Y treatment among managers is consistent with McGregor's hypotheses. However, it says nothing about how people at lower levels would respond.

Other findings indicate that the amount of confidence in subordinates (theory Y) is an important factor in the degree to which participative strategies yield satisfaction. Without such confidence participation is associated with somewhat lower levels of satisfaction than with it. In fact, "one can even imagine a theory Y or human resources manager actually consulting with his subordinates less often than some of his colleagues. Nevertheless, the nature and quality of participation employed by such a manager, when it occurs, would presumably be deeper and more meaningful, which would be reflected in high levels of subordinate satisfaction and — hopefully — performance" (Miles, 1975, p. 123). The use of the adverbs *presumably* and *hopefully* clearly reflects the lack of evidence on this score.

Other data confirm the relationship between a participative strategy and satisfaction, as well as performance, although to a somewhat lesser degree in the latter case. However, the relationships between holding theory Y assumptions and both satisfaction and performance are much less strong (Roberts, Miles, and Blankenship, 1968). The implication is that a resort to participation, even if not backed up by theory Y assumptions, may yield some positive consequences. In any event, the performance data raise consistent questions as to whether theory Y can be expected to yield the kinds of productivity and profit outcomes that McGregor said it would.

Other Relevant Research

Stogdill (1974) noted studies that indicate a considerable subordinate desire for structure from above, apparently in contradiction to McGregor's expectations. Subsequent research gives additional support to this conclusion (Kavanagh, 1975). There appear to be sizable individual differences in this regard. Some individuals prefer and prosper under a free climate in which superiors act as teachers and advisors when needed, in accordance with what McGregor recommended. Others want to know what they are expected to do, and they do best when such role prescriptions are provided. There are all shades of variation between the extremes. Such differences might be explained in terms of need hierarchy theory, with various individuals operating at different levels of the hierarchy. Given the lack of empirical support for that theory, however, it seems more appropriate to attribute the differences to long-standing personality predisposi-tions.

A study by Fiman (1973) is one of the few conducted specifically for the purpose of testing McGregor's propositions about managers' assumptions and thus theories X and Y per se. The research was carried out with clerical employees and office supervisors within a large retailing firm. Scales were developed directly from statements in McGregor's writings. Nevertheless, the theory X and theory Y measures turned out to be strongly negatively correlated. This is contrary to what one would expect from McGregor's discussions on this subject.

In general, the more theory X the supervisors were, the more they were perceived by their subordinates as providing more structure and being less considerate. The more theory Y a supervisor was, the less structuring her behavior and the greater the consideration exhibited. However, these assumption-behavior relationships hold only when the supervisor's theory as perceived by her subordinates is used. When the supervisors indicate their own working theories on the scales, no significant relationships are found. Furthermore, the self-reports by the supervisors of their theories were unrelated to either subordinate job satisfaction or subordinate performance measures. When the subordinates' reports of what they preceived their superi-or's position to be with regard to theory X and theory Y were used, a theory X orientation did go with lower levels of job satisfaction, but there were no associations with performance.

The findings consistently indicate a lack of relationship between the managers' theories, however measured, and subordinate perfor-mance. With regard to job satisfaction the results correspond to the theory when both the measures of theory X and theory Y orientation and the satisfaction measures come from the same people — the subordinates; otherwise there is no relationship. This one supportive finding could be a consequence of common method variance, in spite of the author's disclaimers on this score. In addition, the assumptions about human nature that a subordinate thinks his boss holds are not really what McGregor was talking about; he meant the real assump-tions that guide behavior. Overall, although Fiman interprets his results as supporting McGregor's views, it is apparent that they do so only in a very limited sense, if at all.

CONCLUSIONS

In drawing conclusions about McGregor's formulations it is important to recognize that among the various theories of managerial leadership this particular one is relatively dormant at the present time, at least in a scientific sense. It is not spawning much published research, and even references to McGregor's writings are not as prevalent as they were at an earlier time. The field appears, in fact, to have moved on to new concerns of the kind discussed in the remaining chapters of this book. Whether this situation is justified and appropriate in terms of the development of knowledge regarding organizational behavior is another matter, however. We need to look at this question both in terms of the advancement of scientific goals and in terms of guidelines for practice.

Scientific Goals

One line of argument against the validity of theory Y has been that such phenomena as militant unionism and employee restriction of output cannot be reconciled with a theory Y view of man. Schein (1975), on the other hand, contends that employee behavior of this kind does not represent evidence against the theory, on the grounds that the employees are "behaving consistently with theory Y. But the organization or group which has captured their involvement happens to be different from the employing organization" (p. 85). Whatever the merits of this type of argument in the first place, it would appear that Schein's interpretation is justified, although this may be so only because of the general looseness of McGregor's own theorizing.

In fact this looseness, the lack of conceptual clarity, the failure to state clear hypotheses in many areas, the "muddied conceptual waters," as Schein describes it, all represent major problems with the theory. It is very difficult to carry out an empirical test that everyone would agree is appropriate; there simply are too many escape valves left open. In part this is so because McGregor often says things slightly differently on different occasions; in part it is because he does not always distinguish between when he is expressing his value position and when he is presenting scientific theory; in part it is because, as Bennis (1972) notes, he treats the superior-subordinate relationship largely as if it existed in a void, leaving others free to extrapolate whatever environmental constraints, contingency statements, and the like they may wish. In reading McGregor one gets a strong impression of a very sensitive person with deeply held values who wants to be liked. These qualities may well not be as consonant with the construction of precise, logically consistent scientific theory as with the development of emotionally compelling social philosophy.

As a number of writers have pointed out, theories X and Y are in fact broad stereotypes. Managers may indeed think in such terms, but there is a real question as to whether they should. In this view both theories are wrong, simply because people come in all varieties of individual differences and thus *all* stereotypes are wrong. There is ample evidence of the great range of human variation on a host of dimensions (Miner, 1975). The effective manager will recognize these variations and deal with each individual in terms of the kind of person he or she really is rather than placing all (or most) together in a single category, no matter how that category is defined. To do otherwise is to perceive almost every subordinate incorrectly to some degree, and at least some by a very large degree indeed. It is interesting to note that none of the attempts to measure theory X and theory Y assumptions have pitted either of them against a "don't know" alternative that reads something like "it all depends on which subordinate, and what that individual is actually like." Had this been done the results might well have been different.

Some will argue that McGregor can handle individual differences through the medium of need hierarchy theory. Yet that theory can explain only motivational differences at best, utilizes broad social stereotypes, and probably for just this reason has failed in research confirmation to date. In any event, McGregor does not spell out in any detail how need hierarchy theory would relate to *individual* differences in the work place — such as the person who does not respond to a theory Y-based strategy, for instance.

The research evidence confirms that individual variation yields sufficiently wide fluctuations so that there are people who really want structure from above, authority relationships, hierarchic work contexts, and the like. Furthermore, there is no independent evidence that they are necessarily either emotionally ill or motivationally deprived. Clearly many people do want to work under theory Y managerial assumptions, but some want theory X also. Probably most individuals, given the choice, would prefer to work under assumptions (on the part of a superior) that are reasonably well meshed with the kind of people they actually are. That way unrealistic expectations would be avoided.

In the research, theory X has been pitted against theory Y with a negative correlation assumed, an assumption that now appears to be justified, and with the only possible alternative available being another stereotype, the human relations model, and that only in the Berkeley research. Overall, the human relations model, which we assume is a variant of theory X, emerges as the most frequently held under these circumstances. When only theory X and Y are available the data are conflicting — Caplan (1971) found a strong theory X emphasis and Fiman (1973) a theory Y predominance. Given the relatively small samples used in these studies it is probably best to base one's conclusions on the Haire, Ghiselli, and Porter (1966) international surveys. Their data suggest that McGregor was probably right in indicating a high incidence of theory X type thinking but that he may well have overestimated its prevalence. In this connection it is important to recognize that the 1957 and 1960 definitions of theory X are not the same. The more muted 1960 version would be expected to attract more adherents.

The research that has been conducted provides no real support for McGregor's hypothesis that a resort to theory Y will provide more favorable results at the level of outcome variables. Such positive findings as have been obtained involve job satisfaction, not performance or productivity. However, these findings suffer from the impossibility of unraveling the causal chain. It is just as likely that satisfied, happy employees cause theory Y managerial assumptions as the reverse. Certainly the Non-Linear Systems experience does nothing to generate confidence in the profit-making potential of theory Y. There are other similar efforts that have been undertaken in recent years, but these have arisen out of other theoretical orientations, such as socio-technical systems theory, and typically differ in a number of respects from what was done at Non-Linear Systems. It is not possible to establish relevance for McGregor's formulations. On balance it would appear that even a "pure case" theory X manager can be effective under certain circumstances and that the human relations approach may well be functional across a sizable band of situations.

A final point has been made by Bennis (1972). He feels that McGregor's ideal type theory Y manager is somehow not quite real or fully human. McGregor does not impute any motives or motive satisfactions to him, and thus it is not clear how a real human being would be able to function in accordance with the types of role prescriptions established. It is difficult to reconcile this model with what is known about managerial motivation from research on achievement motivation theory and managerial role-motivation theory (Miner, 1978). The importance of this problem is accentuated by one point on which observers of the Non-Linear Systems situation do agree. Middle and upper level management did not function well under the conditions of the experiment, and turnover at these levels was high. Many of these managers either did not assume the teacher-advisor role the theory prescribes or, even further removed from expectation, they did not do much of anything and became totally bored.

Managerial Goals

The basic question raised in the preceding section is whether a person really can be an effective theory Y manager within the context of a hierarchic organizational system. In a professional context or in

an entirely group-controlled system, this appears to present no problem, but within the hierarchy of an essentially bureaucratic organizational form, the evidence that a person can be at one and the same time
effective, theory Y, and a manager is far less convincing.

On Being an Effective Theory Y Manager. The problem here
goes back to an issue originally raised by Schein (1975). If a theory Y
manager means a person who operates (or uses a strategy to follow
McGregor's terminology) consistent with the professional model of
advisor, teacher, or consultant, then there is a basic conflict with the
managerial requirements of hierarchic systems, and it is hard to
conceive of such a person being considered effective. On the other
hand, if being a theory Y manager means having certain assumptions
about one's subordinates only, and it so happens that the particular
subordinates happen to match these assumptions reasonably well,
then it is indeed possible to be an *effective theory Y manager.*

Unfortunately, there will inevitably be many circumstances
under which subordinates will not even come close to matching
theory Y assumptions, with the result that managerial expectations
will be both quantitatively and qualitatively far removed from subordinate capabilities. As a result, it seems preferable to base one's
assumptions about subordinates on what one knows about them as
individuals and to develop strategies for dealing with them based on
this knowledge. True, it is impossible to have the knowledge of each
subordinate that a psychotherapist might have of each patient. But it
is possible to approximate such conditions to some degree, and any
such set of approximations will inevitably be superior to a single
gross categorization applied to all subordinates.

Based on the evidence it seems apparent that theory X and theory
Y have served their purpose in making managers aware of one set of
assumptions that can be important and that many managers may have
overlooked. But now it is time to move on, and accordingly, it
probably is best to leave theory X and theory Y in their current
dormant position.

The Scanlon Plan and Sensitivity Training. McGregor recommended a number of types of applications, and although most of these
were neither generated by his theories nor closely conceptually
linked to them, their effectiveness is relevant for managerial purposes. At various points in this book — before or after this chapter —
most of these applications are discussed in some detail. Two are
not — the Scanlon Plan and sensitivity or T-group training. Both
either originated at or received their major impetus from MIT at a time
when McGregor was a major force in that environment. It is important, therefore, to say something about these techniques before moving on to other more currently active theories of leadership.

The Scanlon Plan is described by McGregor (1960) as having two central features. The first is a kind of cost reduction sharing (built on top of the normal wage and salary structure) that yields a bonus and at the same time a considerable understanding of the economics of the firm. This mandatory feature is tied to a type of suggestion system that emphasizes creative (self-actualizing) contributions to the organization's goals (integration). Suggestions are considered and evaluated by committees (participation).

A recent review of the effectiveness of this approach, and it has been adopted by a number of companies, generally supports the technique; it surely can work, and sometimes dramatically (Geare, 1976). However, as so often happens, the Scanlon Plan typically involves introducing a number of changes at the same time. The best guess seems to be that the major contribution to organizational effectiveness derives from the performance-contingent compensation procedure rather than from participation, the fostering of self-actualization, or theory Y assumptions. Non-Linear Systems did not introduce either performance-contingent compensation or any other major aspect of the Scanlon Plan (Gray, 1978). On the evidence it is not clear why the Scanlon Plan works, and indeed sometimes it does not, but there is no clear evidence that the successes are a consequence of theory Y management.

Sensitivity, or T-group, or laboratory training underwent a period of considerable popularity in industry as a method of increasing social skills. However, this popularity has now tapered off sharply (Kearney and Martin, 1974). It has given way to the more pragmatic and organizationally pervasive organizational development approaches. McGregor's later concern with team building must be considered a major way station in the move from sensitivity training as a social skill-developing procedure to organizational development as a method of major organizational change or, as it is sometimes called, renewal.

Research on sensitivity training indicates that it is an effective management development device. It does change people, primarily in the humanistic direction that its techniques and advocates would lead one to expect. However, these changes appear to be antithetical to the needs of most modern corporations (Miner, 1974). The changes in motives, attitudes, and values produced do not appear to be consonant with the requirements of a hierarchic system. Thus, on the current evidence, one can assume only that sensitivity training tends to yield ineffective, theory Y *managers*, or at best individuals with strong conflicts in the corporate context. Probably this is the reason for the decline in popularity of the pure sensitivity training technique as a management development tool. This says nothing regarding the value of the approach for personal development, family therapy, community intergroup relations, and the like.

References

Argyris, Chris. *Personality and Organization.* New York: Harper, 1957.

Bennis, Warren G. Chairman Mac in Perspective, *Harvard Business Review,* Vol. 50 (1972), 140–149.

Caplan, Edwin H. *Management Accounting and Behavioral Science.* Reading, Mass.: Addison-Wesley, 1971.

Fiman, Byron G. An Investigation of the Relationships Among Supervisory Attitudes, Behaviors, and Outputs: An Examination of McGregor's Theory Y, *Personnel Psychology,* Vol. 26 (1973), 95–105.

Geare, A. J. Productivity from Scanlon-type Plans, *Academy of Management Review,* Vol. 1 (1976), 99–108.

Gray, Edmund R. The Non-Linear Systems Experience: A Requiem, *Business Horizons,* Vol. 21, No. 1 (1978), 31–36.

Haire, Mason, Edwin E. Ghiselli, and Lyman W. Porter. *Managerial Thinking: An International Study.* New York: Wiley, 1966.

Kavanagh, Michael J. Expected Supervisory Behavior, Interpersonal Trust and Environmental Preferences: Some Relationships Based on a Dyadic Model of Leadership, *Organizational Behavior and Human Performance,* Vol. 13 (1975), 17–30.

Kay, Andrew. Where Being Nice to Workers Didn't work, *Business Week,* January 20, 1973, 98–100.

Kearney, William J. and Desmond D. Martin. Sensitivity Training: An Established Management Development Tool? *Academy of Management Journal,* Vol. 17 (1974), 755–760.

Kuriloff, Arthur H. An Experiment in Management — Putting Theory Y to the Test, *Personnel,* Vol. 40, No. 6 (1963), 8–17.

Malone, Erwin L. The Non-Linear Systems Experiment in Participative Management, *Journal of Business,* Vol. 48 (1975), 52–64.

Maslow, Abraham H. *Eupsychian Management.* Homewood, Ill.: Irwin, 1965.

McGregor, Douglas. On Leadership, *Antioch Notes,* Vol. 31, No. 9 (1954).

McGregor, Douglas. An Uneasy Look at Performance Appraisal, *Harvard Business Review,* Vol. 35, No. 3 (1957a), 89–94.

McGregor, Douglas. The Human Side of Enterprise, *Management Review,* Vol. 46, No. 11 (1957b), 22–28, 88–92.

McGregor, Douglas. *the Human Side of Enterprise.* New York: McGraw-Hill, 1960.

McGregor, Douglas. *Leadership and Motivation: Essays of Douglas McGregor.* Cambridge, Mass.: MIT Press, 1966.

McGregor, Douglas. *The Professional Manager.* New York: McGraw-Hill, 1967.

Miles, Raymond E. *Theories of Management: Implications for Organizational Behavior and Development.* New York: McGraw-Hill, 1975.

Miner, John B. *The Human Constraint.* Washington, D.C.: Bureau of National Affairs, 1974.

Miner, John B. *The Challenge of Managing.* Philadelphia: W. B. Saunders, 1975.

Miner, John B. Twenty Years of Research on Role-Motivation Theory of Managerial Effectiveness, *Personnel Psychology,* Vol. 31 (1978), 739–760.

Morse, John J. and Jay W. Lorsch. Beyond Theory Y, *Harvard Business Review,* Vol. 48, No. 3 (1970), 61–68.

Roberts, Karlene, Raymond E. Miles, and L. Vaughn Blankenship. Organizational Leadership, Satisfaction and Productivity: A Comparative Analysis, *Academy of Management Journal,* Vol. 11 (1968), 401–414.

Schein, Edgar H. The Hawthorne Group Studies Revisited: A Defense of Theory Y, *In* E. Louis Cass and Frederick G. Zimmer (eds.), *Man and Work in Society.* New York: Van Nostrand Reinhold, 1975, pp. 78–94.

Stogdill, Ralph M. *Handbook of Leadership.* New York: Free Press, 1974.

Wrege, Charles D. and Bernice M. Lattanzio. The Human Side of Enterprise — Forty-five Years Before McGregor, the Work of Richard A. Feiss, Early Explorer in Human Relations, *Academy of Management Proceedings,* 1977, pp. 6–10.

Yoder, Dale, Raymond E. Miles, Lawrence McKibbin, Robert E. Boynton, and George W. England. Managers' Theories of Management, *Academy of Management Journal,* Vol. 6 (1963), 204–211.

11 CONTINGENCY THEORY OF LEADERSHIP

Contingency theory has been developed by Fred Fiedler, who was on the faculty at the University of Illinois for a number of years and now is at the University of Washington. The theory has had a long history, extending back to 1951, and has evolved slowly; it is still evolving. Fiedler has been extremely responsive to research results, both those generated by himself and those of others. As a consequence, it is very difficult to separate research and theory as we have done in discussing other theories; there is a constant interplay back and forth. The theory is almost entirely inductive in nature, and in fact some have questioned whether it should be labeled a theory at all (Ashour, 1973; Schriesheim and Kerr, 1977). In actuality, it is a set of continually changing empirical generalizations, although over the past 15 years the central body of propositions has maintained a certain common form.

Another distinguishing characteristic is that contingency theory has evolved around a measurement process. In fact, there was a measure before there was a theory. As a result, the usual procedures of theory construction have been reversed. Instead of proposing a set of theoretical constructs and then devising measures to match, Fiedler started with the measurement process and then sought to develop theoretical constructs to go with the measures and the research results obtained with them.

THE EVOLUTION OF CONTINGENCY THEORY

There have been two major stages in the development of contingency theory. The first, extending from the early 1950s to the early 1960s, was essentially exploratory. A sizable body of research data was collected, and various hypotheses were tried out in an attempt to explain the findings. During this period it is totally impossible to separate research from theory. The second stage began with the statement of contingency theory in a form much the same as that currently existing. This stage has continued to the present with the testing of these early propositions and of others that have emerged since.

The Exploratory Stage

Fiedler's original research interests involved the relationship between psychotherapist and patient, and the ways in which similarities and differences in ascribed self-concepts were related to effectiveness in such relationships (Fiedler, 1951). Self-concepts were measured originally using the Q-technique methodology, in which descriptive statements are sorted into categories in terms of the degree of approximation to perceived reality. This rather cumbersome approach was modified later as Fiedler's interests shifted to leader-member relationships in small task groups, but the concern with assumed similarities and differences among people remained.

The Assumed Similarity Between Opposites Measures. Through a gradual series of transformations the measurement process moved from the Q-technique to an approach of a semantic differential type (Fiedler, 1958). In this latter procedure the subject is asked to "think of the person with whom you can work best" and later to "think of the person with whom you can work least well." In both cases a description of that person then is obtained by having the subject place a mark on a six-point graphic scale between two polar adjectives such as careless-careful, gloomy-cheerful, efficient-inefficient, and the like. The differences between the numerical descriptions applied to the most and least preferred coworkers are then used to compute an Assumed Similarity Between Opposites Score (ASo) by summing over all the adjective pairs.

When the difference score is large it means that the least and most preferred coworkers are seen as quite disparate, and thus assumed similarity is minimal; when it is small the two are perceived as much the same. Essentially what is involved is that when ASo is low the person strongly rejects the least preferred coworker; job performance makes considerable difference in how people are judged.

The true meaning of the construct or constructs thus measured has presented difficulties from the beginning:

> One of the main problems in the research program has been in finding an adequate interpretation of Assumed Similarity scores, especially ASo. While we have no difficulty in designating the operations which define these scores, we have encountered considerable problems in attempting to anchor their meaning within a more general framework of psychological theory (Fiedler, 1958, p. 17).

The early resolution of this problem was as follows:

> The Assumed Similarity Between Opposites Score measures an attitude toward others which may best be described as emotional or psychological distance. A person with high ASo tends to be concerned about his interpersonal relations, and he feels the need for the approval and support of his associates. In contrast, the low ASo person is relatively independent of others, less concerned with their feelings, and willing to reject a person with whom he cannot accomplish an assigned task (Fiedler, 1958, p. 22).

Research Findings. The studies conducted during the 1950s utilized a variety of different approaches to the measurement of

ASo, and thus it cannot be assumed that the findings are entirely comparable. The measures were related to indexes of group effectiveness using basketball teams, surveying parties, bomber crews, tank crews, open hearth steel shops, farm supply cooperatives, and others (Fiedler, 1958; Godfrey, Fiedler, and Hall, 1959). The results indicated that ASo tends to relate to group performance only when moderated by some additional factor. These additional factors varied from study to study and were usually identified afterward. In some cases they were aspects of the task; in other cases they were aspects of the group's informal structure and sociometric choices or of the relationship between a leader and his key man.

Also, although generally the tendency was for the more psychologically distant, low ASo leader to be associated with success, there were occasions when this was reversed. Thus in the open hearth steel shops ASo was negatively correlated with effectiveness under certain task conditions (Cleven and Fiedler, 1956), and in the farm supply cooperatives the ASo of the general manager was negatively related to success under certain sociometric conditions (Godfrey, Fiedler, and Hall, 1959). However, in this latter study the ASo of the informal leader of the board of directors was positively related to organizational success, again when appropriate sociometric moderators operated.

After reading the reports of this early research one comes away with a feeling that there is something there, but no clear conception of what that "something" is. The lack of comparability across studies, the variations in moderators, many of them identified after an extensive empirical search of possible alternatives, and the uncertainty as to whether ASo might not be subject to considerable influence by environmental circumstances including management development, all contribute to a sense of uneasiness. There is a clear need for a theoretical structure to guide research, rather than continuing to permit the research to generate a procession of short-lived theories.

Formal Specification of Contingency Variables

In recognition of the need for a more stable theoretical structure, Fiedler articulated the major outlines of a contingency theory of leadership in the mid-1960s, drawing heavily on the research of the earlier, exploratory period. Fiedler's theory thus developed was first published in 1964, and its practical applications were elaborated in his 1965 work. The most comprehensive statement of this period appears in a subsequent book (Fiedler, 1967).

The Least Preferred Coworker Measure. One change that occurred at this point is that Fiedler dropped the use of ASo as a central theoretical variable and substituted one component of ASo, the least preferred coworker rating (LPC). Descriptions of the most preferred coworker were no longer employed. The semantic differential approach to measurement was utilized exclusively, but the actual adjective pairs incorporated tended to vary from study to study. The graphic scale was extended from six to eight points, and LPC was obtained by summing the values marked for each adjective pair in describing "the person with whom you can work least well." LPC and ASo are reported to correlate in the .80 to .90 range (Fiedler, 1967).

The struggle with the meaning of the central constructs appears not to have been affected by the shift from ASo to LPC.

> . . . it has been extremely difficult to develop an adequate and readily supportable interpretation of ASo and LPC scores. These scores do not measure attributes which correlate with the usual personality and ability tests or with attitude scales. Nor is there a one-to-one relationship between these scales and behaviors.

> . . . we visualize the high-LPC individual (who perceives his least-preferred coworker in a relatively favorable manner) as a person who derives his major satisfaction from successful interpersonal relationships, while the low-LPC person (who describes his LPC in very unfavorable terms) derives his major satisfaction from task performance (Fiedler, 1967, p. 45).

Classification of Interacting Task Groups. Fiedler's theory is initially presented as applying within the domain of groups that have a task to perform or a goal to achieve, and in which this task accomplishment requires interaction among members, not a series of entirely independent efforts. Within this domain groups may be classified with reference to three major factors — the leader's position power, the structure of the task, and the interpersonal relationship between leader and members.

Position power is a function of such considerations as legitimate authority and the degree to which positive and negative sanctions are available to the leader. It appears to assume the existence of an organization surrounding the group and a hierarchic means of conveying the power. The existence of position power makes the leader's job easier.

Task structure refers to the extent to which rules, regulations, job descriptions, policies — role prescriptions — are clearly and unambiguously specified. It is easier to lead in highly structured situations because structured tasks are enforceable. Task structure is presumed to exist when decisions are subject to clear-cut verifiability in terms of correctness, goals are clearly stated and understood, multiple paths to attaining the goals are not present, and only one correct answer or solution exists. Like position power, task structure is derived from the organization.

The relationship between the leader and group members is much more an internal matter. It is reflected in the degree to which the leader is accepted and members are loyal to him, and in the affective reactions of members to the leader. When leader-member relations are good, the leadership job is much easier. Good leader-member relations are reflected in a highly positive group atmosphere.

Using this set of classification factors, Fiedler developed a taxonomy for interacting task groups. The taxonomy does not deal with all possible alternatives. In keeping with the tendency to empirical generalization, it applies to groups of the kind that have been actually studied.

The results are as follows:

Group Category	Leader-Member Relations	Task Structure	Position Power
1	Good	High	Strong
2	Good	High	Weak
3	Good	Low	Strong
4	Good	Low	Weak
5	Moderately poor	High	Strong
6	Moderately poor	High	Weak
7	Moderately poor	Low	Strong
8	Moderately poor	Low	Weak
8–A	Very poor	High	Strong

The theoretical assumption is that these groups require different approaches to the leadership process to be effective. Subsequent analyses indicate that the degree of favorableness of the situation for the leader declines steadily from category 1 down. Actually, category 8–A was first labeled 5–A (Fiedler, 1964). However, it was later changed to 8–A to reflect its relative position on the favorableness scale (Fiedler, 1967).

Types of Groups, Leadership, and Effectiveness. Leader-member relations are the most important consideration in classifying groups, task structure is next, and position power least important. Empirically-based predictions regarding LPC-group effectiveness relationships are generated for each group using the degree of favorableness of the group situation for the leader as a moderator or contingency variable as follows:

Group Category	Relationship of LPC to Performance
1	Negative
2	Negative
3	Negative
4	Positive
5	Positive
6	Positive
7	Positive (but lower)
8	Negative
8–A	Negative

In presenting this contingency model Fiedler (1967) repeatedly refers to research data rather than to theoretical logic. Qualifications and uncertainties are numerous, again because findings from research raise questions regarding the influence of additional variables. There is no point at which Fiedler states exactly what his theory is, why it makes sense on logical grounds, and what its delimiting boundary statements are. In concluding his book he cites the need for:

1. A better method of measuring the favorableness of the leadership situation.
2. A method of weighting leader-member relations, task structure, and position power.
3. Knowledge of what really causes good or poor leader-member relations.
4. Information on the role of leader and member intelligence and ability.
5. Relating leader consideration, initiating structure, supportiveness, and so forth, to performance under varying degrees of situational favorableness.
6. Data on how task characteristics other than structure may operate.
7. Research on co-acting groups in which the members work independently.
8. Research on counteracting groups in which the members bargain with one another.
9. An understanding of individuals whose LPC scores fall in the middle range.
10. Specification of the influences of managers above the first level, line-staff status, and differing leadership styles among interacting managers.
11. Studies of the effects of training in diagnosing the favorableness of a leadership situation and in modifying it.

In none of these instances is a specific hypothesis stated, although hypotheses have been developed in some of the areas since. There is little attempt to posit a logically coherent theoretical system independent of the appeal to empirical data. The ambiguities surrounding the meaning of LPC make it almost impossible to do so.

Changes and Extensions

Since the early statements of the theory in the mid-1960s there have been a number of further developments, almost invariably as a result of subsequent research results. This continuing proliferation of both research findings and theoretical changes and extensions makes it difficult to determine which came first, and thus what is ad hoc theorizing and what is a test of theory. The following discussions will focus on what at one time or another have been statements of theory; in later discussions an effort will be made to identify true tests of these theoretical statements.

Changes in the Basic Model. In subsequent presentations of the model group, category 8–A has typically been eliminated, and leader-member relations in categories 5 through 8 often have been referred to as poor rather than as moderately poor (Mitchell, Biglan, Oncken, and Fiedler, 1970). However, there are subsequent statements that the situation can be even less favorable for the leader than octant 8 indicates. There is some ambiguity on this whole matter of extreme unfavorableness.

In addition, there is some inconsistency as to which octants are predicted and which are not. Negative LPC-performance relations are anticipated for octants 1, 2, and 8 and positive relationships for octants 4 and 5. The other octants are variously ignored or even specifically not predicted, or they are predicted. When predictions are made, octant 3 is expected to yield a negative correlation and octants 6 and 7 positive correlations (Fiedler, 1971; Fiedler and Chemers, 1974; Mitchell et al., 1970). The most recent statement of the theory appears to support the actual predictions noted (Fiedler, 1978b).

The original domain of the theory was that of interacting task groups. This subsequently has been extended to co-acting task groups but not to co-acting training groups that are said not to follow the contingency model (Fiedler, 1971; Fiedler and Chemers, 1974). The training groups referred to are those created to assist an individual to achieve his own goals, and in such groups a tentative suggestion is advanced that high LPC leaders consistently are more effective.

The situational favorableness dimension has been renamed *situation control and influence* in order to eliminate misunderstandings (Fiedler, 1978b). Also, a specific formula for weighting the three aspects of this dimension has been proposed. This formula calls for multiplying the leader-member relations score by four, the task structure score by two, and then adding these values to the position power score (Fiedler, 1978a; 1978b). Yet, it has been apparent for some time that situational control (or favorableness) is not simply a matter of the three basic factors:

> It must be pointed out, of course, that the three major sub-scales of leader-member relations, task structure, and position power by no means represent the only factors which determine the leader's situational control and influence. Other studies have pointed to situational stress as affecting the leader's control; cross cultural studies have shown that linguistic and cultural heterogeneity also play a major role in determining leader control. And leader experience and training also increase control. In unusual cases this formula may thus require appropriate modification, and specific rules governing these modifications still need to be developed (Fiedler, 1978b, p. 66).

Thus, in one study, the following hypothesis was tested:

> As environmental stress increases, the relationship-oriented leader will become relatively more effective in promoting member adjustment than task-oriented leaders. Hence, under conditions of high stress, high LPC leaders should have better adjusted groups than low LPC leaders, while under conditions of low stress, low LPC leaders should have better adjusted groups than high LPC leaders (Fiedler, O'Brien, and Ilgen, 1969).

As noted, the role of these additional factors is not stated specifically. Furthermore, there is ambiguity regarding the theoretical status of the middle LPC group, estimated to be some 15 to 20 per cent of the population. These individuals are considered to be different from either the high or low LPC groups and are labeled socioindependent without a clear picture of their actual characteristics (Fiedler, 1978b). As in other areas where the theory lacks clarity, the problem is that no inherent theoretical logic exists, and therefore hypotheses await empirical findings. Each step of theory development must depend upon the inductive theory-generating processes of dust-bowl empiricism, or it does not occur.

The Meaning of LPC. In the early writings LPC (or ASo, which is said to be essentially the same thing) was variously described as measuring psychological distance (Fiedler, 1958), controlling vs. permissive attitudes in the leadership role (Fiedler, 1964), and task vs. relationship orientations (Fiedler, 1967). More recently these categories have been described as oversimplifications, although not necessarily totally incorrect, and two additional construct definitions have been proposed.

Of these two Fiedler most consistently has supported what he calls the motivational hierarchy view (Fiedler, 1972a, 1973a,

1978b; Fiedler and Chemers, 1974). Essentially this view states that a leader will manifest his primary motives under conditions over which he has little control and influence, but that when control and influence are assured (favorableness is high), primary motives are easily satisfied and it is possible to move down the hierarchy and seek to satisfy motives of secondary importance. Thus, high LPC leaders will seek relatedness under unfavorable circumstances and seek to satisfy more task-related motives as conditions become more favorable. Low LPC leaders will manifest their primary task orientation in unfavorable situations but can be expected to shift to a more considerate, interpersonal relations-oriented pattern of behavior as their control and influence increase. In this view it is only under conditions of stress that the basic personality, or primary motive structure, reveals itself.

At present, however, Fiedler is somewhat hesitant about the motivation hierarchy view:

> These findings favor a motivational hierarchy interpretation, although other interpretations, consistent with these findings, are also tenable. Whatever the precise and final interpretation of the LPC score might turn out to be, there is very little question that it measures a personality attribute which has very important consequences for organizational behavior (Fiedler, 1978b, p. 103).

Consistent with this hesitancy is the fact that another formulation still remains viable and is in fact frequently mentioned in favorable terms by Fiedler. This second view is considered to be "quite compatible with the interpretation of LPC as an index of motivational hierarchy" (Fiedler and Chemers, 1974, p. 77). It is stated in the greatest detail in Foa, Mitchell, and Fiedler (1971).

This is a cognitive interpretation. The LPC scale contains a variety of adjective pairs. Some are task oriented, some are interpersonal in nature, and some are mixed, although the majority are interpersonal. The cognitively complex individual who differentiates among these types of adjectives is very likely to have a high LPC score because he describes his least preferred coworker positively on interpersonal adjectives and negatively on task adjectives. The low LPC, non-differentiating person will describe his least preferred coworker negatively not only with regard to task performance but in interpersonal terms as well — as inefficient, cold, rejecting, and the like. Thus, the degree of differentiation among types of adjective pairs is the key to interpreting LPC.

A moderately favorable leadership situation is characterized by considerable differentiation among the various aspects — some are positive and some negative insofar as leader control and influence are concerned. Thus, a high LPC leader who is cognitively complex would provide a good match and do well. Very favorable or very unfavorable situations are much less differentiated in terms of the three major classification variables, and the low cognitive complexity of the low LPC leader should be a positive value. In fact, greater differentiation might well introduce problems. The key to success is a matching of differentiation levels in the leader and in the task situation.

Extensions to Leadership Dynamics. The first extensions of contingency theory into the domain of leadership dynamics involved changes introduced by training and increasing experience. Fiedler (1972b) starts with the assumption that both leadership training and experience in the leadership role have not been shown to improve performance. He then uses an argument of the kind outlined in Figure 11–1 for training to show why this might be expected (Fiedler, Bons, and Hastings, 1975).

The primary consequence of the training is to increase leader influence and control through improved leader-member relations, task structuring, and position power. Such changes are equally likely to shift an individual into a good LPC-situation match or out of it, assuming that LPC itself is not changed. On the average, therefore, leadership performance will not be altered; an improvement in one person will be canceled out by the decreased effectiveness of another. In Figure 11–1 the extremely unfavorable situation beyond octant 8 is assumed to be rare but might occur with racially divided groups or when extreme stress is present; it

Before Training Perception of Situation	After Training Perception of Situation	Effective Performer	
		Before Training	*After Training*
1. Octant 4 ⟶ Octant 1 (Moderately favorable) (Very favorable)		High LPC	Low LPC
2. Octant 8 ⟶ Octant 4 (Unfavorable) (Moderately favorable)		Low LPC	High LPC
3. Beyond Octant 8 ⟶ Octant 8 (Extremely unfavorable) (Unfavorable)		High LPC (speculative)	Low LPC

Figure 11-1. Effects of leadership training on subsequent performance as moderated by situational favorableness — predicated on the hypothesis that training changes favorability as perceived by the leader to whatever next higher degree will reverse the leader effectiveness level. (Adapted from Fred E. Fiedler, P. M. Bons, and Limda L. Hastings. New Strategies for Leadership Utilization, In W. T. Singleton and P. Spurgeon (eds.), *Measurement of Human Resources.* New York: Halsted Press, 1975, p. 237.)

appears to have much in common with the original category 8–A, although the hypothesized LPC relationship to performance is reversed.

One approach suggested to achieve effective results from training is to teach managers how to modify the favorableness of a situation to match their LPC scores — how to engage in situational engineering. Another approach is to select for training only those individuals whose performance can be expected to improve because they will move into a good LPC-situation match, not out of it. Alternatively all might be trained, but the training must be selectively combined with job rotation so that some return to more challenging jobs, thus offsetting the increased favorableness induced by the training for these particular individuals. Rotation of some kind, including promotion, may be the only way of offsetting the automatic increases in situational favorableness that come with increased managerial experience.

What the dynamic theory posits is that as leader control and influence (favorability) increase, for whatever reason, the performance level of the *high* LPC leader will change as follows:

Octant	8	7	6	5	4	3	2	1
Performance	Low→	Low→	High	Medium→	High→	High→	Low→	Low→Low

For *low* LPC leader this pattern is reversed:

Octant	8	7	6	5	4	3	2	1
Performance	High→	High→	Low	Medium→	Low→	Low→	High→	High→High

It should be noted that these statements (Fiedler, 1978a, 1978b) are not consistent with other statements of the theory insofar as octant 7 is concerned. Also, octant 6 is labeled as unfavorable (low control), although from the theory one would expect it to be included in the moderate range (with octant 7). These inconsistencies appear in schematic representations of the theory and are not discussed in the texts; thus the reasons for them are unclear.

The dynamic theory indicates that in selecting individuals for leadership positions a decision should be made as to whether high initial performance is needed, or whether it is desirable to wait and permit training and experience to shift favorableness and performance levels. Also, as experience in a given job accumulates there comes a point at which rotation into a new, less familiar position is advisable. The theory is not specific in any general sense as to exactly how much experience is required before these hypothesized performance changes can be anticipated, although the degree of structure and complexity of the work and the intelligence of the leader are viewed as relevant (Fiedler, 1978a).

There is also some ambiguity regarding the effects of different kinds of training programs. Fiedler (1972b) describes human relations training as improving the leader-member relations factor and thus increasing favorableness, yet later (Fiedler, 1978b) he notes that training in participative management (which human relations training certainly is) reduces position power and accordingly decreases favorableness.

The theory also deals with changes in the degree of turbulence and instability in the organizational environment. With greater turbulence there is greater uncertainty and thus less leader control and influence. Personnel shakeups, reorganizations, new product lines, and the like introduce turbulence. Under continuing turbulent conditions the downward shift in favorableness can be expected ultimately to bring about a situation in which low LPC leaders are needed.

RESEARCH RELATED TO MEASUREMENT

Contingency theory is intermeshed closely with measurement. There can be no question that the continuing concern with developing measures of the theory's key variables has provided a major impetus to research. It is important, however, to evaluate the measures used in terms of the usual criteria of psychometric soundness.

Reliability and Stability of LPC

Contingency theory anticipates not only a reliable measure of LPC but a stable one — thus whatever the nature of the construct underlying the LPC measure, it is expected to be of an enduring quality. Furthermore, although the particular adjective pairs used to measure LPC have varied in both number and nature, this fact is considered to be irrelevant to the results obtained.

On the latter point there now appears to be little question — one LPC instrument is not necessarily the same as another and the results of studies over the years may well have been influenced by these differences (Fox, 1976). In particular, the scales have been found to contain both task competence and interpersonal items in varying degrees, although the latter tend to predominate. The two types of items are independent of each other and relate to external factors in different ways (Rice, 1978).

Probably the best measures of LPC reliability are provided by internal consistency indexes (such as those yielded by the odd-even approach) and short-term test-retest correlations. In both cases the data indicate good reliability for the LPC measures (Rice, 1978).

On the other hand, the stability of the instrument over longer time intervals has been severely questioned (Fox, 1976; Stinson and Tracy, 1974). There appears to be a drop in retest correlations over time. However, many of the lowest correlations were obtained across significant educational, training, or management development experiences (Rice, 1978). There is ample evidence from research in other areas that such experiences can reduce test-retest correlations significantly (Miner, 1965). Although studies extending beyond six months are rare, it does appear that under normal circumstances stability coefficients in the low .70s can be anticipated; much lower values can be expected if training intervenes.

The Measurement of Leader-Member Relations

The primary contingency variable of leader-member relations has been measured in different ways under different circumstances. On occasion, the responses of subordinates have been utilized, but more frequently the leader has provided the information. In recent years a semantic differential scale, not unlike that used to measure LPC, has been introduced to measure group atmosphere, although this has now been replaced with a questionnaire index (Fiedler, 1978b).

There have been problems associated with the similarity of LPC and group atmosphere measures and with the fact that in many studies, especially those of a laboratory nature, leader-member relations must be assessed after task completion under conditions in which group performance may influence the responses. Furthermore, there is a problem because different cut-off points have been used to establish good, moderately poor, or poor leader-member relations in different studies. In many instances these specifications have not been made before the fact but rather with full knowledge of score distributions, thus permitting capitalization on chance to enter into the calculations.

These and other considerations raise serious questions regarding the comparability of results obtained from different studies. Sometimes these problems are known to influence the results, sometimes not; more often we do not know. What is clear is that the findings from different studies cannot be assumed to be fully cumulative (McMahon, 1972).

The Measurement of Task Structure

Task structure also has been measured in different ways and with variable cut-off points. The typical procedure is to have various dimensions of the work that are related to structuring rated by judges. Although there are some difficult theoretical questions as to why certain aspects of structure are incorporated in the measures used while others are not, the task structure measurement process has been relatively free of criticism.

The Measurement of Position Power

Often it is argued that the position power factor can be judged merely from knowledge of position titles. Managers, foremen, supervisors, and superintendents in the business world have high position power, while committee chairmen and leaders of collegial groups do not (Fiedler and Chemers, 1974). Thus, in a number of studies no formal measure is obtained at all. However, various rating scales also have been used. In certain cases these scales have incorporated measures of a variety of bases of power inherent in the individual, not just in the position (McMahon, 1972). The result is considerable construct confusion. Recent measures appear to be more directly focused on the appropriate theoretical construct but have not been widely used (Fiedler, 1978b).

Combining the Contingency Variables

Recently Fiedler has proposed a formula for combining the three contingency variables to obtain an overall index of situational favorableness or leader control and influence. Research conducted by Nebeker (1975) tends to support the weightings Fiedler suggests, in that a multiple regression analysis and the Fiedler procedure yielded practically identical results. However, as Schriesheim and Kerr (1977) note, the fact that in this research position power had no variance (it was assumed to be constant) and task structure was measured by amount of training or experience raises a question as to the generality of this finding. Other data also support the significance of the role played by leader-member relations, while placing the relative status of task structure and position power in considerable doubt.

When the three moderator variables are combined into a single index of situational favorableness, or, as Fiedler now prefers to call it, control and influence, it appears that the most appropriate designation is in terms of experienced environmental certainty (Nebeker, 1975). When the situation is favorable for leadership, leaders perceive various aspects of the world around them as certain, and thus decision-making as relatively easy; under conditions of unfavorability, uncertainty is at a high level.

Construct Validity and Meaning of LPC

Given that LPC can serve as a predictor of group performance under certain circumstances, this provides only a partial approximation to the goals of science. Ideally it is possible to understand and explain phenomena as well as predict them, and this is when the LPC measure and its related theory experience difficulty. Various construct explanations have been offered, and at least two are currently viable. Evaluating these explanations is a matter for research investigation.

The Motivational Hierarchy Interpretation. Fiedler (1972a) reviews a considerable body of research that raises serious doubts regarding the earlier view that low LPC leaders are characterized by a task orientation and high LPC leaders by a relationship orientation. It turns out that a number of studies have produced results just the reverse of this expectation. These conflicting results are explained in terms of the motivational hierarchy concept whereby actual leadership behavior is posited to be a consequence of the individual's primary and secondary motive systems in interaction with the degree of threat, stress, or unfavorableness inherent in the situation.

Although Fiedler (1972a, p. 406) appears to feel confident of this new formulation and in fact says, "it appears that we may have begun at long last to unravel the enigma of the Least Preferred Coworker score," certain cautions are in order. One cannot use the findings from which the theory was developed at one and the same time to validate that theory. Thus, it is necessary to turn to the post-1972 literature to evaluate the motivational hierarchy interpretation.

When this is done, one finds a number of studies that for various reasons prove to be inadequate in design, measurement, executions, and the like and that therefore say relatively little one way or the other. However, several studies, most of them conducted recently, do constitute adequate evaluations. The data of Table 11–1 derive from one such investigation. In this instance simulations were used to establish favorable and unfavorable situations,

Table 11-1.   PROPORTION OF BEHAVIORS OF AN INTERPERSONAL
AND TASK NATURE FOR LOW AND HIGH LPC
LEADERS UNDER VARYING CONDITIONS OF
SITUATIONAL FAVORABLENESS

	Highly Favorable Situation	Highly Unfavorable Situation
Low LPC Leaders		
Proportion of behaviors that are interpersonal	41	41
Proportion of behaviors that are task oriented	59	59
High LPC Leaders		
Proportion of behaviors that are interpersonal	37	43
Proportion of behaviors that are task oriented	63	57

Adapted from Stephen G. Green and Delbert M. Nebeker. The Effects of Situational Factors and Leadership Style on Leader Behavior, *Organizational Behavior and Human Performance*, Vol. 19 (1977), p. 373.

and the verbal responses of preselected low and high LPC subjects were scored for interpersonal and task orientations (Green and Nebeker, 1977). The data both support and refute the motivational hierarchy view.

The high LPC individuals do exhibit more interpersonal behavior under unfavorable circumstances and exhibit less under favorable conditions — as the theory predicts. But the low LPC leaders do not change, and thus their behavior fails to confirm expectations. This tendency to vary behavior in accordance with the situation among high LPC leaders, while low LPC leaders remain essentially the same, has been noted in other research as well (Rice and Chemers, 1975). In a study by Larson and Rowland (1973) the low LPC individuals appeared to shift in the predicted directions but not nearly to the same extent as the high LPCs.

A study by Schneier (1978) tends to confirm the findings given in Table 11–1 for low LPC leaders. In this instance the leaders were predominantly low LPC, and the analysis was restricted to octant 2, a favorable leadership situation. The theory predicts a predominance of relationship behavior, but, as in the Green and Nebeker (1977) study, the reverse proved to be the case. Overall, it is clear that the motivational hierarchy view receives much greater support among high LPC individuals than among low.

The Cognitive Complexity Interpretation. Early research prior to the formal theoretical formulation tended to favor the cognitive complexity interpretation (Foa, Mitchell, and Fiedler, 1971), but the problem of ad hoc theory validation is just as acute here as in the case of the motivational hierarchy interpretation. Subsequent findings have been rather mixed.

Several of the studies discussed in the preceding section do tend to support the cognitive complexity view in one way or another (Green and Nebeker, 1977; Rice and Chemers, 1975; Schneier, 1978), although more frequently with regard to low LPC leaders than high. The latter of these investigations yielded a correlation of .49 between LPC and a measure of cognitive complexity.

There also is evidence that low LPC people are often responding to an imaginary stereotype of their least preferred coworker rather than to a specific individual (Shiflett, 1974). Such stereotyping might be expected of cognitively more simple individuals, and these findings therefore reinforce the cognitive complexity view, at least for low LPC individuals. Other research indicates that cognitive simplicity is related to low LPC scores, although the relationship breaks down at higher LPC levels (Evans and Dermer, 1974).

There are results of a less convincing nature, but the overall pattern of findings suggests that the cognitive complexity formulation does have some validity, most frequently with regard to low LPC leaders, in contrast to the motivational hierarchy view, which applies primarily to high LPC leaders. Further support for differentiation by LPC level is found in Fiedler's discussion of the intermediate group:

> There is some evidence of a middle LPC group which differs in behavior and attitudes from both high and low LPC persons. These individuals, who comprise about 7 to 10 per cent above and below the population mean of 60, either have a "mixed" motivation pattern or else a distinctly different leadership approach. They seem less concerned about the opinions and attitudes of others and less dependent on superiors' and subordinates' evaluations as well as less desirous of accepting a leadership position. Further research is needed to describe this group in a more adequate manner (Fiedler, 1978b, p. 91).

It appears not at all unlikely on the evidence that the LPC measure taps different constructs at different levels and that it is for this reason that it has proved so resistant to interpretation. In all likelihood it should be broken down into two, or perhaps three, separate measures.

RESEARCH TESTING THE THEORY

At various points in time Fiedler has provided reviews of the research literature related to contingency theory and has stated his

Table 11–2. MEDIAN VALIDITY COEFFICIENTS IN STUDIES
REVIEWED BY FIEDLER, CLASSIFIED BY OCTANT
WHERE POSSIBLE AND OTHERWISE BY GENERAL
SITUATIONAL FAVORABLENESS

Octant	Median Correlation
1	−.59
2	.04
3	−.23
4	.37
5	.19
6	.13
7	.17
8	−.35
Favorableness	
High	−.37
Intermediate	.20
Low	−.30

Adapted from Fred E. Fiedler. The Contingency Model and the Dynamics of the
Leadership Process, In Leonard Berkowitz (ed.), *Advances in Experimental Social
Psychology*. Vol. 11. New York: Academic Press, 1978, pp. 68–70.

conclusions as to the validity of the theory (Fiedler, 1967; Fiedler,
1971; Fiedler, 1978b; Fiedler and Chemers, 1974; Mitchell et al.,
1970). The results of the most recent efforts to summarize LPC-
group performance relationships are given in Table 11–2 using
median correlation values. Where possible the findings have been
assigned to a specific octant of the model; otherwise they have
been classified more broadly into favorable (octants 1–3), intermediate (octants 4–7), and unfavorable (octant 8) situational categories. These are all evidential studies conducted since the formal
statement of the theory, and the most recent of them was published in 1973. Certain research that Fiedler believes is not adequate to provide a legitimate test of the theory has been excluded.

In general, the data of Table 11–2 support the theory, and this
fact is attested to by the finding that overall binomial tests of such
distributions have consistently proved to be statistically significant. However, very few of the constituent correlations obtained in
individual studies have achieved significance. This disparity is explained in part at least by the fact that testing contingency theory
requires group rather than individual performance data with the
result that Ns are often small in individual studies, and thus statistical significance is difficult to attain.

It should be noted that the values indicated in Table 11–2 are
generally closer to .00 than were those of the exploratory research
from which the theory was developed. The only exceptions (and

these are not large) are in octants 1 and 7. The data for octant 2 are inconsistent with the theory; all other correlations are in the predicted direction. Fiedler's own most recent conclusion is that "on the whole there is now little question about the basic validity of the Contingency Model. The evidence is very clear. . . . These findings are quite strong for octants 1, 4, 5, and 8, in which correlations account for substantial portions of the variance, that is, about 36 per cent, 16 per cent, 15 per cent, and 12 per cent respectively. Octant 3 appears to account for about 8 per cent of the variance, while the variance accounted for by octants 2, 6, and 7 is negligible" (Fiedler, 1978b, pp. 72–73). An independent reviewer, considering much the same literature, concludes that "only for octants I and IV of the eight octants proposed by the model were the composite correlations of all studies significant" (Ashour, 1973, p. 371). Clearly, it is important to look deeper into the research.

Comprehensive Tests

Ideally, research studies would be conducted that bridge all octants of the theory. The advantage of this approach is that comparability of measurement can be maintained, and thus the relative effectiveness of predictions from the theory in various octants can be determined within a common set of conditions. Group performance, leader-member relations, task structure, position power, even LPC have been measured in many different ways in different studies; the comprehensive studies tend to hold these measurement processes constant across octants to provide more comparable data.

Fiedler's Belgian Navy Study. The Belgian Navy research (Fiedler, 1966) was carried out in a period contiguous with the formulation of the basic model, and there is some possibility that preliminary results may have influenced some statements of that model, especially the book presentation (Fiedler, 1967). The study utilized laboratory tasks but manipulated position power through the use of real officers in the Belgian navy. It also varied group homogeneity and heterogeneity by utilizing leaders speaking the same or different languages from other group members.

Fiedler analyzed the data of the study in various ways, some of which were not consonant with previous statements of the theory. In particular, the homogeneity-heterogeneity factor was introduced into the calculation of the situational favorableness dimension even though it had not been previously specified (Graen,

Table 11–3.   CORRELATIONS BETWEEN LPC AND GROUP
PERFORMANCE IN VARIOUS OCTANTS OF THE
CONTINGENCY THEORY USING TWO
STRUCTURED TASKS AND DIFFERENT TASK
ORDERS

| | | Correlations | | | | |
| | | Homogeneous Groups | | Heterogeneous Groups | | |
Octant	Predicted Relationship	Unstructured Task First	Structured Task First	Unstructured Task First	Structured Task First	Median Correlation
1	Negative Task 1	−.20	.59	−.49	−.09	−.15
	Task 2	−.77	−.72	.03	.77	
2	Negative Task 1	.67	−.43	−.49	−.25	.06
	Task 2	.37	.50	.77	−.53	
3	Negative	−.16	−.54	.20	−.26	−.21
4	Positive	.08	.13	−.89	.70	.11
5	Positive Task 1	.36	−.03	.54	.09	.09
	Task 2	.16	.03	.08	−.19	
6	Positive Task 1	.10	−.72	−.13	.30	.09
	Task 2	.07	.14	.53	−.90	
7	Positive	.26	−.27	−.37	.08	−.10
8	Negative	−.37	.60	−.36	−.60	−.37
Number of correlations in predicted direction		10	6	6	9	

Adapted from Fred E. Fiedler. The Effect of Leadership and Cultural Heterogeneity on Group Performance: A Test of the Contingency Model, *Journal of Experimental Social Psychology*, Vol. 2 (1966), p. 255.

Alvares, Orris, and Martella, 1970). The result was to produce cells of the nature of octant 8–A and beyond. However, as Table 11–3 indicates, there is no empirical basis in the study for this procedure; the number of correlations having the same directionality as the theory in the heterogeneous language groups is essentially the same as in the homogeneous groups. Given the fact that the theory itself does not consider language heterogeneity as a contingency variable, it seems most appropriate to consider homogeneity and heterogeneity of groups, as well as task sequencing, as providing independent validation data for the same basic model.

When this is done, as Table 11–3 indicates, 31 of the 48 correlations are in the predicted direction, although only two are statistically significant; 24 of 48 would be expected by chance. The median values are in the reverse direction from those predicted for octants 2 and 7, and with the exception of octant 8 they are minimal in size. Furthermore, the range of correlations within octants is very large in a number of cases — in octant 1 from −.77 to +.77; in octant 2 from −.49 to +.67; in octant 3 from −.54 to

+.20; and so on. Overall, one must challenge Fiedler's (1966, p. 262) conclusion that "the data clearly support the major hypothesis of the Contingency Model." As others have noted also (Graen et al., 1970), the data of this study, when related directly to prior theoretical formulations, yield only very weak support at best.

The Graen, Orris, and Alvares Laboratory Studies. A second set of investigations, again utilizing laboratory tasks but with undergraduate students, provides even less support (Graen, Orris, and Alvares, 1971). None of the correlations, as presented in Table 11–4, are statistically significant; somewhat less than half are in the predicted direction. This research suffers from the possibility that the task structure and position power manipulations may not have been strong enough to produce the expected results. However, the leader-member relations differentiation is not in question, and this is the most important contingency variable of the theory. Certainly there is nothing in these two studies that would support the contingency theory and much that would refute it; at best the research is mute on the theory's validity.

The Chemers and Skrzypek Research with West Point Cadets. The strongest support for the theory from a comprehensive study derives from a laboratory experiment conducted with cadets at the U. S. Military Academy at West Point (Chemers and Skrzypek, 1972). In this instance special care was taken to introduce

Table 11–4. CORRELATIONS BETWEEN LPC AND GROUP PERFORMANCE IN VARIOUS OCTANTS OF THE CONTINGENCY THEORY

		Correlations	
Octant	Predicted Relationship	First Study	Second Study
1	Negative	.47	−.13
2	Negative	−.41	.18
3	Negative	.46	.02
4	Positive	.33	−.08
5	Positive	.25	−.52
6	Positive	−.39	−.43
7	Positive	.43	.45
8	Negative	−.33	.44

Adapted from George Graen, James B. Orris, and Kenneth M. Alvares. Contingency Model of Leadership Effectiveness: Some Experimental Results, *Journal of Applied Psychology*, Vol. 55 (1971), p. 198.

strong manipulations of the theoretical variables. The resulting LPC-group performance correlations for the octants were:

1.	−.43	5.	.28
2.	−.32	6.	.13
3.	.10	7.	.08
4.	.35	8.	−.33

These data yield directional support for the theory in all cells except octant 3. Although the correlations consistently fall short of statistical significance when considered individually, a subsequent application of analysis of variance to the total data set does yield significance (Shiflett, 1973). This analysis also indicates that leader-member relations and task structure are sufficient to account for the results and that position power could be eliminated from consideration with no diminution in predictive power.

The Utecht and Heier Study of Successful Military Leaders. A considerably different approach to the theoretical question is taken in a study by Utecht and Heier (1976) of officers in the various branches of the armed forces who had been selected to attend the senior service colleges such as the War Colleges and the Industrial College of the Armed Forces. By definition these are highly successful leaders. One would anticipate, therefore, that they would have held positions prior to selection that were appropriate to their LPC scores.

LPC scores were obtained as well as information that permitted the classification of the last six positions held prior to selection for a service college into the appropriate octant. Using the time served in each position it was then possible to determine whether the officers had spent the majority of their time in positions appropriate to their LPC scores. On an overall basis the data do not support this hypothesis; the contingency theory predictions do not exceed chance levels of accuracy. However, this overall finding reflects two competing trends. The results for low LPC officers do tend to follow theoretical expectations; they did serve predominantly in positions expected to be appropriate for success — octants 1, 2, 3, and 8. The reverse was true for high LPC officers, however. In particular, the data for octants 5 and 7 were contrary to theoretical expectations.

Although the results of this study can be generalized only to similar settings in which position power is usually high and task structure strong, the overall lack of theoretical support, and in particular the marked departures from theory in octants 5 and 7, should be a source of concern. On the other hand, it could be argued that the results do not bear directly on the theory because group performance was not the dependent variable, and less successful officers were not included.

Vecchio's Research with Air Force Personnel. A recent laboratory study utilizing a number of different tasks with Air Force enlisted personnel has been reported by Vecchio (1977). An analysis in terms of rank order correlations between LPC and group task performance, the approach preferred by Fiedler, yields no support for the theory at all. In fact, there is some tendency for the correlations to move in a direction opposite to that predicted by the theory rather than being consistent with it.

When analysis of variance procedures is applied there is some marginal support for the theory on certain low structure tasks (when a very stringent leader-member relations differentiation is applied). These findings are so few in number relative to the number of relationships studied and so specific to particular types of tasks that they cannot be interpreted as supporting contingency theory as a general theory of leadership.

Fiedler (1978b) has dismissed the results of this study on the grounds that the leader-member relations manipulation was inappropriately carried out. However, independent checks on group atmosphere levels, as well as separate analyses utilizing extreme groups on the group atmosphere index of leader-member relations (discussed in the Vecchio article) clearly appear to refute Fiedler's contentions. In all, the research would seem to have been well designed and conducted.

Tests in Specific Octants

Research yielding results only in specific octants of the theory is much more numerous than the comprehensive types of tests discussed in the previous section. At least in recent years, it would appear likely that such partial tests are most likely to be accepted for publication if they yield significant results; accordingly, the published findings for specific octants may not be truly representative. In any event, a number of significant relationships have been reported.

Hovey (1974) conducted studies in octants 4 and 8 using student subjects who worked on a group project. Measures of both group effort and the quality of the group product were correlated with LPC scores. In octant 4 all five effort correlations were positive as predicted, but the three quality correlations were negative; some of the eight values achieved significance. In octant 8, however, seven of the eight correlations were in the anticipated negative direction, and two of these were significant. A very similar study by Schneier (1978) that was restricted to octant 2 produced strong support for the theory with a validity coefficient of $-.55$, significant at the .01 level.

Csoka (1975) utilized Army mess hall stewards and correlated their LPC scores with ratings of their performance in octants 1, 3, 5, and 8. The resulting correlations were $-.66$, $-.69$, .80, and $-.80$, all significant in the predicted direction. In addition, he was able to show that the organizational climate was mechanistic in octants 1, 3, and 8, and organic in octant 5. Low LPC scores were associated with success in the mechanistic contexts and high LPC scores with success in the organic situation.

The Hovey (1974), Schneier (1978), and Csoka (1975) studies, taken together, offer solid support for the theory in octants 1, 2, 3, 5, and 8, and some partial support in octant 4. They do not consider octants 6 or 7. The picture thus created is much more favorable to the theory than that obtained from the comprehensive research.

Research Bearing on the Leadership Dynamics Formulations

Research relating to the dynamic effects of training, experience, organizational turbulence, and the like is not nearly as voluminous as research on the basic model. A number of studies that preceded the formal specification of the dynamic hypotheses have been quoted in support of them (Fiedler, 1972b; Fiedler, Bons, and Hastings, 1975). However, this seems hardly justified, and the amount of truly relevant research is reduced substantially.

Fiedler (1972b) starts with the assumption that research generally has failed to find support for the position that leadership training and development increase performance levels. This contention seems to be based on a very limited view of the research literature. A comprehensive consideration of this research extending back over a considerable time period indicates that management training and development can indeed have a sizable impact on a large number of participants (Miner, 1965). This, however, does not invalidate the contingency model's dynamic hypotheses regarding the effects of training and certainly has no bearing on formulations in the areas of experience, turbulence, and the like. More direct tests are needed to gain insight into these views.

A series of studies of military leaders (artillery sergeants, petty officers, company commanders) by Csoka and Fiedler (1972) indicates some support for the training hypotheses. The subjects had received varying amounts of training, primarily of the knowledge and

Table 11–5.   RELATIONSHIPS BETWEEN LPC AND PERFORMANCE
RATINGS FOR LEADERS IN VARIOUS OCTANTS AND
WITH LOW OR HIGH TRAINING

	Octant 1 High Training	Octant 3 Low Training	Octant 5 High Training	Octant 8 Low Training
Artillery sergeants	−.47	−.78	.75	−.66
Navy petty officers	−.50	−.57	.67	−.75
Company commanders	−.71	−.66	.22	−.47

Adapted from Louis S. Csoka and Fred E. Fiedler. The Effect of Military Leadership Training: A Test of the Contingency Model, *Organizational Behavior and Human Performance*, Vol. 8 (1972), p. 404.

skill type, although the company commanders had had some supervisory training. Degree of training was treated as an analogue for task structure in the basic model.

Because training was not varied systematically and movement across octants observed, this research more closely approximates a test of the basic than of the dynamic theory. Nevertheless, the results, as noted in Table 11–5, are those the theory would predict. On the other hand, the placement of the poor leader-member relations and low training leaders in octant 8 appears highly questionable. All the other military leaders were assumed to have had high position power. If poor leader-member relations and low task structure automatically mean low position power, then octant 7 does not exist, and prior research results should be reviewed with this consideration in mind. On the evidence, it would appear that octant 7, not 8, was tested, and if so these results are opposite to what the theory would predict. Also, the contingency effects as reflected in the positive correlations of octant 5 are minimal for the company commanders. This is important because this is the only group that participated in anything approximating the typical management development experience.

A subsequent study provided for a greater degree of control of the training variable in that leaders who received and did not receive special knowledge training related to the laboratory tasks used were compared (Chemers, Rice, Sundstrom, and Butler, 1975). The data indicate that low LPC leaders perform better when untrained (in octant 8) and more poorly when trained (in octant 6); the reverse is true of high LPC leaders. Unfortunately, this study did not compare performance levels on the same group before and after training, and accordingly a full test of the dynamic theory, as opposed to the basic model, was not possible.

A study of infantry squad leaders dealt with the effects of organizational change as reflected in either reassignment of the leader or reassignment of the superior (Bons and Fiedler, 1976). The data indicate that organizational turbulence of the kind introduced by such reassignments does reduce situational favorability but only for inexperienced leaders. However, this study did not utilize actual measures of performance at either the group or the leader level. Consequently no direct test of the dynamic theory as a whole was possible.

Overall, the research findings are consistent with the dynamic theory more often than not, but comprehensive longitudinal tests of a kind that would extend beyond the basic model are not yet available. The research in this area, in contrast to that on the basic model, has been conducted almost entirely by individuals closely associated with the development of the theory itself.

THE LEADER MATCH APPLICATION

For some time contingency theorists have advocated a process of situational engineering whereby an individual leader is placed in a situation appropriate to his or her LPC score (Fiedler, 1965). For this approach to work for a given organization, LPC would have to be stable over time, and performance levels would have to be essentially the same across octants. In other words, with LPC appropriate to the situation, it should not matter whether octant 1, or 5, or 8, or whatever, was used. Furthermore, this approach assumes that it is easier to change aspects of the situation, either by re-engineering the job itself or by transfer to a different position, than it is to change the person, and in particular those aspects of the person that LPC measures. All of these assumptions and expectations are built into the Leader Match procedure whereby individuals learn to modify their leadership situations so as to provide a degree of situational favorableness or control appropriate to their LPC.

The Nature of Leader Match

Leader Match training utilizes a programmed learning test (Fiedler, Chemers, and Mahar, 1976). The process starts with a self-measurement of LPC and then with measures of the various aspects of the leadership situation — leader-member relations, task structure, and position power — to obtain an index of situational favorableness. Next, the individual learns how to match leadership style (LPC level) with the situation and subsequently to influence or self-engineer it to his or her personality. This may be done through the use of a variety of techniques, from influencing one's superior to actually moving to a new position. There is also a section on how to engineer the leadership situations of subordinate managers for those at the second level of supervision and above.

The training is self-paced with appropriate measurement instruments incorporated in the text. It adheres closely to the theory and utilizes theoretical discussions, problems, questions, and feedback statements. As a programmed learning text, it appears to be conceptually adequate. However, the real test is in the research.

Research Evidence

There are two kinds of research evidence to be considered. The first bears on the basic validity of the situational engineering concept itself. Do the assumptions involved hold up? Second, what is the evidence as to the effectiveness of Leader Match as a training device? Does it yield more effective leadership performance?

Evidence Related to Situational Engineering. We have already discussed the stability of LPC. Under normal, unchanging circumstances it too remains stable. But there clearly are conditions under which considerable variation can be expected (Bons and Fiedler, 1976; Rice, 1978). This suggests the possibility that concerted efforts to change LPC in a consistent manner might prove successful. The lack of reports of results from such efforts in the literature does not demonstrate that situational engineering is more easily accomplished. The problem is that as long as the true nature of LPC remains an enigma, it is hard to develop training programs to change it.

With regard to the stability of mean performance levels across octants, the following quote from a review of relevant research provides a good picture of the situation:

> . . . data reported by Fiedler (1967, p. 259) show a steady decline in performance from favorable to unfavorable situations for an unstructured task and rather erratic variations for two structured tasks. Yet Fiedler (1965) has suggested situational engineering as an alternative to leadership training. In other words change the situation — shift a group up or down on the favorableness dimension — to fit the leadership style. But if mean productivity is not constant across situations, one might find that a leader who has the wrong leadership style in one situation may become even less effective when his group is changed to a second situation where, according to the model, his leadership style is right (Shiflett, 1973, pp. 435–436).

The problem noted in the quote is illustrated in some detail using data from the Chemers and Skrzypek (1972) research.

A direct test of the situational engineering hypothesis was carried out by Shiflett and Nealey (1972) using octants 3 and 4 and manipulating leader position power, which is the factor differentiating these octants. In this instance, the same leaders were moved from one octant to the other and comparisons made. The study failed to yield significant results and did not support hypotheses derived from contingency theory. Not only was there a lack of support for situational engineering but the octant 3 LPC-performance correlation of .16 was opposite in direction to that predicted by the basic model, and the octant 4 correlation of .05 was too low to be meaningful.

Studies of Leader Match Itself.   A certain amount of research has been conducted that focuses directly on the performance effects of Leader Match training. In one instance comparisons were made between groups of naval officers who did and did not receive the training (Leister, Borden, and Fiedler, 1977). The trained officers studied the programmed text (Fiedler, Chemers, and Mahar, 1976) and also viewed a related film and participated in a short discussion. Performance ratings by superiors on both experimental and control subjects were obtained prior to the time of training and again six months later. The changes noted are summarized in Table 11–6. Overall, the data appear to be consistent with the expectation that the Leader Match approach does improve performance levels.

A second series of studies was conducted with West Point cadets assigned as platoon leaders (Csoka and Bons, 1978). The designs were similar to that of the preceding research except that training was restricted to self-instruction with the text. In two separate studies evidence was obtained indicating improved performance among the trained, as opposed to control, subjects. However, in one of these studies evidence was obtained indicating that a sizable majority of the trained individuals really did not understand the material and thus were in no position to manipulate situational variables in the prescribed manner. Furthermore, certain subjects tended to reject LPC scores inconsistent with their self-concepts and even, on occasion, to alter their scores; those in the middle range on LPC typically did not know what to do to increase their situational favorableness. The

Table 11–6.   MEAN CHANGE IN PERFORMANCE RATINGS FOR SUBJECTS PARTICIPATING IN LEADER MATCH TRAINING AND CONTROLS

	Experimental Group (Received Training)	Control Group (No Training)
Naval air station officers	(+.53	−.59)
Destroyer officers	+.92	−.18
Combined means	(+.57	−.46)

( ) Difference statistically significant.

Adapted from Albert Leister, Donald Borden, and Fred E. Fiedler. Validation of Contingency Model Leadership Training: Leader Match, *Academy of Management Journal*, Vol. 20 (1977), p. 468.

authors of the study indicate considerable doubt that situational engineering was in fact responsible for the results. They suggest that the training may well have increased confidence or merely sensitized the subjects to significant aspects of the leadership situation, thus improving performance. In any event, the data raise questions as to exactly how Leader Match training works and whether other approaches, completely divorced from the contingency model, might not yield the same results.

CONCLUSIONS

Contingency theory of leadership has been the subject of a considerable amount of criticism. Because the theory is essentially a set of empirical generalizations the research that has generated it, changed it, and tested it also has become involved in this critical process. As has been noted several times, the theory and the results of research are intertwined so closely that it is often difficult if not impossible to separate one from the other. Theory of this kind tends to change frequently, being highly responsive to the research evidence, and in fact contingency theory also has been criticized on this score. Fiedler's response to this point is characteristic:

> A number of the Contingency Model's critics have charged that ". . . the theory keeps changing to fit the data" and that it is becoming increasingly complex. Both of these observations are accurate. . . . The theory will, of course, continue to change as new data become available. . . . We simply have to live with the fact that any attempt to predict pretzel-shaped relationships will require the development of pretzel-shaped hypotheses (Fiedler, 1973b, p. 113).

As in the above instance, Fiedler has consistently and staunchly defended his approach, theory, research, and interpretations of the research evidence. There are numerous rejoinders and counter-rejoinders in the literature. It remains, therefore, to attempt to sift through the controversy and see where contingency theory has gotten us.

Scientific Goals

There clearly are problems inherent in contingency theory and its related research that justify matching Fiedler's own optimism with an equivalent amount of skepticism. For one thing, the various measures of theoretical constructs used in the research have varied considerably from study to study, with the result that treating these research results as in some way additive or cumulative is highly questionable.

The primary theoretical variable is LPC, or in an earlier period,

ASo. Both of these measures have been used in a variety of forms in different studies. At the present writing Fiedler (1978b) has proposed a purified LPC measure that eliminates task-related adjective pairs and stresses those of an interpersonal nature, which have always predominated. It remains to be seen whether this revision will yield new and different results.

The moderator variables also have changed from one investigation to another. Although the theory has continued to emphasize leader-member relations, task structure, and position power, a variety of indexes of these variables have been employed and many other factors have been substituted in specific studies. The problem of substitute or additional moderators has been noted by Fiedler himself:

> No procedure has been specified to date as to how these measures should be combined with the usual factors in the favorability dimension. Moreover, the adequacy of these measures as measures of situation favorability typically was not established. This leaves the possibility open of generating supporting results for the Contingency Model by choosing from among the many measures, which are purported to be of situation favorability, those which produce the curvilinear relationship between LPC and performance. This is obviously not tenable from a methodological point of view (Mitchell et al., 1970, p. 265).

In other words, there is a possibility of capitalization on chance in the selection of moderators, just as there has been in the development of other aspects of the theory and in the formulation of research hypotheses.

A similar problem arises in the selection of the high, low, weak, strong, good, poor, and moderately poor designations to indicate cutting points on the moderator variables. To the extent this is done on an ad hoc basis after the data are available for inspection, there is a prospect of capitalization on chance. In various studies these cutting points have been established using median splits, normative distributions, and the like. Comparability clearly is not present, and the wide variation in cutting points used suggests that capitalization on chance may have occurred in some instances.

Given these divergences between studies, the practice of combining correlations that are in themselves not significant into a single distribution to calculate an overall significance level from multiple studies is questionable; the studies are not that similar. Furthermore, we do not know that the published studies are representative. Many studies are not accepted for publication, and this tends to be particularly true of those that do not yield significant results. On the other hand, there are significant findings in most, if not all, octants of the theory. The point is that these significant results are few in number relative to the published nonsignificant results, and there may be many other even less impressive findings that have not found their way into print. Furthermore, calculating binomials from studies (most of which cross several octants) is not justified because of the lack of independence of the correlations taken from the same study. Even the use of median correlation values for octants can be called into question when the medians summarize data with as wide variations as the contingency theory research has produced. Overall, we simply do not know whether contingency theory has been validated or not, although there is reason to believe that the probability of validity varies from octant to octant.

The construct validity of LPC also represents a major problem. Over the years a variety of definitions have been proposed, but Fiedler (1978b) remains uncertain even today, and with good empirical reasons. The most likely interpretation at present is that LPC taps different constructs in the low, middle, and high ranges, and that clarification awaits the establishment of multiple measures as a substitute for the single LPC dimension. What this would do to the theory as a whole remains an open question; certainly it would make it much more complex. In any event the fact that LPC continues to be a measure in search of a meaning is one of the most theoretically confusing phenomena in the whole leadership field.

There can be no question that contingency theory suffers from inconsistencies of presentation. Diagrams, numerical calculations, and verbal statements often are at variance with one another, although some of these inconsistencies may represent shifts in conceptual position in response to new empirical data that are not clearly stated for what they are. Yet compared to the problems in defining LPC, these theoretical contradictions, or seeming contradictions, are of relatively minor importance.

A final problem relates to causality. There are sufficient studies in which LPC has been administered prior to other measures to establish that LPC can be a causal factor. However, it may not be a determinant in this sense very often, and the results reported from various studies may be influenced in only very small measure by the cause-effect relationship from LPC to performance. Thus the variance accounted for by LPC may be quite small, so small that contingency theory would become rather trivial as an explanation of the leadership process.

A series of studies reported by Mitchell, Larson, and Green (1977) indicates that the experience of success can have a strong influence on overall situational favorability measures. Success leads to higher favorability scores and failure to lower. Group atmosphere is particularly likely to be viewed favorably when the group experiences success. The authors do not contend that their findings can account for all of the contingency theory results, but they do note:

> These results suggest that leadership theorists who use such situational percep-
> tions as moderator variables must be extremely cautious in the process of

classification, and the inferences drawn from correlational analyses. Perception of performance may be confounding both these classifications and the resulting interpretations (Mitchell, Larson, and Green, 1977, p. 265).

Given all of these problems, it is still possible to ask whether contingency theory has any validity at all, and if so in which of its aspects. Ashour (1973) indicates that it may well have some validity in octants 1 and 4. The comprehensive studies across all octants taken as a whole are not very supportive except for the Chemers and Skrzypek (1972) investigation, and it, too, yields the largest correlations in octants 1 and 4. If one considers the literature since 1973 (as well as before), there is reason to believe that if contingency theory has any validity at all it exists in octants 1 and 4, and also in octants 5 and 8. In this interpretation the present analysis is in complete agreement with Fiedler (1978b). The theory simply appears to be irrelevant to octants 2, 3, 6, and 7, if one looks at the research in a comprehensive manner.

These conclusions give rise to some interesting speculations. Octants 1 and 8 yield negative LPC-performance correlations, yet they differ on all three contingency variables. Octants 4 and 5 yield positive LPC-performance correlations, yet they too differ on all three contingency variables. The uniformities are that negative LPC-performance relationships occur when the contingency variables are all in the same direction, and positive relationships occur when they are not, and either leader-member relations alone are high or the other two (lesser) variables together are high. In this connection it should be remembered that leader-member relations scores are typically multiplied by 4, and task structure and position power by 2 and 1 respectively. Thus, the sum of the weights is much the same if one considers leader-member relations as one moderator and the conceptually similar task structure and position power taken together as the other.

It would be desirable to go beyond this and posit a new or alternative contingency theory. However, without a fuller understanding of the meaning of LPC this is impossible. All that can be said is that low LPC appears to relate to high performance under consistent environmental conditions — perhaps mechanistic climates, to utilize the Csoka (1975) interpretations. High LPC, on the other hand, relates to high performance under inconsistent or conflicting environmental conditions — in what would appear to be more organic climates.

Managerial Goals

For managerial purposes contingency theory sets forth guidelines for such personnel actions as transfer, rotation, selection, training, job modification, and the like. These are embodied in the recommendations related to situational engineering and Leader Match training.

It is not now possible to endorse Fiedler's recommendations in these areas. Although the LPC measure does appear to be reliable, it is not sufficiently stable over long time periods to justify the situational engineering approach; in particular its stability appears to be jeopardized by interventions such as those introduced by management development programs. Furthermore, the idea of a change in situational favorableness with experience, with a consequent need for rotation, transfer, or some other change has not been substantiated, and in any event the theory is not at all clear as to how and when to carry out such changes. Given the problems regarding scientific goals, this type of application should be held in abeyance pending clarification of the scientific issues. The problems involved in carrying out the engineering approach are well stated in the following excerpt:

> Make no mistake about what Fiedler and his associates are suggesting here. Despite the ever-present possibility of leader change through illness or transfer, they are seriously recommending that in some circumstances good leader-member relations should intentionally be harmed, or goal clarity impaired, or other elements of situational favorableness altered so as to establish congruence with a leader's LPC score, even though the chance of a substantial shift in LPC by even the same leader, after only a few weeks time, is quite likely (Schriesheim and Kerr, 1977, p. 54).

There is indeed some support for the dynamic theory with regard to knowledge and skill training, although further studies that move individuals across cells (1 ↔ ↗ 4, 5 ↔ ↗ 8) are needed. But there is no basis for concluding anything about management development efforts, especially those that deal with motives, attitudes, values, and the like. In these areas Fiedler's equating of training with experience seems hardly justified, and other evidence discussed previously in this volume with regard to the effects of training and development efforts raises considerable doubt about contingency theory formulations.

The studies of Leader Match do indicate that a change occurs because of the training, but the content of that training appears irrelevant. Perhaps the change that occurs in the training setting is that people come to think more about the leadership process, a change that is less likely to occur in control subjects. This could explain the changes produced by a wide range of management development programs. Accordingly, Leader Match would be no different from any other such approach. If this is true, then the Leader Match training findings have no specific implications for the validity of the contingency theory formulations.

There is also the possibility that LPC can be altered rather easily through training, and thus that LPC change rather than situational engineering is the appropriate procedure within the confines of the theory. No doubt Fiedler's statements regarding the unmodifiability of LPC and the uncertainty surrounding its meaning have combined to thwart efforts to modify LPC in a consistent manner. Yet training of this kind does appear possible; if it were successful, sizable insights into the LPC construct itself might also result.

On the evidence, the only application of contingency theory results that appears to have a sufficient degree of support to warrant its use at the present time would be the utilization of LPC as a selection instrument when the leadership situation in which the person is to function can clearly be specified as meeting the requirements of octants 1, 4, 5, or 8. Such prediction without true understanding is not an ideal practice, but it can be justified on the grounds that some probability of successful placement is preferable to a strictly trial and error process.

References

Ashour, Ahmed Sakr. The Contingency Model of Leadership Effectiveness: An Evaluation, *Organizational Behavior and Human Performance*, Vol. 9 (1973), 339–355, 369–376.

Bons, Paul M. and Fred E. Fiedler, Changes in Organizational Leadership and the Behavior of Relationship and Task-Motivated Leaders, *Administrative Science Quarterly*, Vol. 21 (1976), 453–473.

Chemers, Martin M., Robert W. Rice, Eric Sundstrom, and William M. Butler. Leader Esteem for the Least Preferred Coworker Score, Training, and Effectiveness: An Experimental Examination, *Journal of Personality and Social Psychology*, Vol. 31 (1975), 401–409.

Chemers, Martin, M. and George J. Skrzypek. Experimental Test of the Contingency Model of Leadership Effectiveness, *Journal of Personality and Social Psychology*, Vol. 24 (1972), 172–177.

Cleven, Walter A. and Fred E. Fiedler. Interpersonal Perceptions of Open-Hearth Foremen and Steel Production, *Journal of Applied Psychology*, Vol. 40 (1956), 312–314.

Csoka, Louis S. Relationship Between Organizational Climate and the Situational Favorableness Dimension of Fiedler's Contingency Model, *Journal of Applied Psychology*, Vol. 60 (1975), 273–277.

Csoka, Louis S. and Paul M. Bons. Manipulating the Situation To Fit the Leader's Style: Two Validation Studies of Leader Match, *Journal of Applied Psychology*, Vol. 63 (1978), 295–300.

Csoka, Louis S. and Fred E. Fiedler. The Effect of Military Leadership Training: A Test of the Contingency Model, *Organizational Behavior and Human Performance*, Vol. 8 (1972), 395–407.

Evans, Martin G. and Jerry Dermer. What Does the Least Preferred Coworker Scale Really Measure?: A Cognitive Interpretation, *Journal of Applied Psychology*, Vol. 59 (1974), 202–206.

Fiedler, Fred E. A Method of Objective Quantification of Certain Countertransference Attitudes, *Journal of Clinical Psychology*, Vol. 7 (1951), 101–107.

Fiedler, Fred E. *Leader Attitudes and Group Effectiveness.* Urbana, Ill.: University of Illinois Press, 1958.

Fiedler, Fred E. A Contingency Model of Leadership Effectiveness, *In* Leonard Berkowitz (ed.), *Advances in Experimental Social Psychology.* Vol. I.

New York: Academic Press, 1964, pp. 149–190.

Fiedler, Fred E. Engineer the Job To Fit the Manager, *Harvard Business Review*, Vol. 43, No. 5 (1965), 115–122.

Fiedler, Fred E. The Effect of Leadership and Cultural Heterogeneity on Group Performance: A Test of the Contingency Model, *Journal of Experimental Social Psychology*, Vol. 2 (1966), 237–264.

Fiedler, Fred E. *A Theory of Leadership Effectiveness*. New York: McGraw-Hill, 1967.

Fiedler, Fred E. Validation and Extension of the Contingency Model of Leadership Effectiveness: A Review of Empirical Findings, *Psychological Bulletin*, Vol. 76 (1971), 128–148.

Fiedler, Fred E. Personality, Motivational Systems, and Behavior of High and Low LPC Persons, *Human Relations*, Vol. 25 (1972a), 391–412.

Fiedler, Fred E. The Effects of Leadership Training and Experience: A Contingency Model Interpretation, *Administrative Science Quarterly*, Vol. 17 (1972b), 453–470.

Fiedler, Fred E. Personality and Situational Determinants of Leader Behavior, *In* Edwin A. Fleishman and James G. Hunt (eds.), *Current Developments in the Study of Leadership*. Carbondale, Ill.: Southern Illinois Press, 1973a, pp. 41–61.

Fiedler, Fred E. Predicting the Effects of Leadership Training and Experience from the Contingency Model: A Clarification, *Journal of Applied Psychology*, Vol. 57 (1973b), 110–113.

Fiedler, Fred E. Situational Control and a Dynamic Theory of Leadership, *In* Bert King, Siegfried Streufert, and Fred E. Fiedler (eds.), *Managerial Control and Organizational Democracy*. New York: Wiley, 1978a, pp. 107–131.

Fiedler, Fred E. The Contingency Model and the Dynamics of the Leadership Process, *In* Leonard Berkowitz (ed.), *Advances in Experimental Social Psychology*. Vol. 11. New York: Academic Press, 1978b, pp. 59–112.

Fiedler, Fred E., P. M. Bons, and Limda L. Hastings. New Strategies for Leadership Utilization, *In* W. T. Singleton and P. Spurgeon (eds.), *Measurement of Human Resources*. New York: Halsted Press, 1975, pp. 233–244.

Fiedler, Fred E. and Martin M. Chemers. *Leadership and Effective Management*. Glenview, Ill.: Scott, Foresman, 1974.

Fiedler, Fred E., Martin M. Chemers, and Linda Mahar. *Improving Leadership Effectiveness: The Leader Match Concept*. New York: Wiley, 1976.

Fiedler, Fred E., Gordon E. O'Brien, and Daniel R. Ilgen. The Effect of Leadership Style Upon the Performance and Adjustment of Volunteer Teams Operating in a Stressful Foreign Environment, *Human Relations*, Vol. 22 (1969), 503–514.

Foa, Uriel G., Terence R. Mitchell, and Fred E. Fiedler. Differentiation Matching, *Behavioral Science*, Vol. 16 (1971), 130–142.

Fox, William M. Reliabilities, Means, and Standard Deviations for LPC Scales: Instrument Refinement, *Academy of Management Journal*, Vol. 19 (1976), 450–461.

Godfrey, Eleanor P., Fred E. Fiedler, and D. M. Hall. *Boards, Management, and Company Success*. Danville, Ill.: Interstate Printers and Publishers, 1959.

Graen, George, Kenneth Alvares, James B. Orris, and Joseph A. Martella. Contingency Model of Leadership Effectiveness: Antecedent and Evidential Results, *Psychological Bulletin*, Vol. 74 (1970), 285–296.

Graen, George, James B. Orris, and Kenneth M. Alvares. Contingency Model of Leadership Effectiveness: Some Experimental Results; Some Methodological Issues, *Journal of Applied Psychology*, Vol. 55 (1971), 196–201, 205–210.

Green, Stephen G. and Delbert M. Nebeker. The Effects of Situational Factors and Leadership Style on Leader Behavior, *Organizational Behavior and Human Performance*, Vol. 19 (1977), 368–377.

Hovey, Donald E. The Low-Powered Leader Confronts a Messy Problem: A Test of Fiedler's Theory, *Academy of Management Journal*, Vol. 17 (1974), 358–362.

Larson, Lars L. and Kendrith M. Rowland. Leadership Style, Stress, and Behavior in Task Performance, *Organizational Behavior and Human Performance*, Vol. 9 (1973), 407–420.

Leister, Albert, Donald Borden, and Fred E. Fiedler. Validation of Contingency

Model Leadership Training: Leader Match, *Academy of Management Journal*, Vol. 20 (1977), 464–470.

McMahon, J. Timothy. The Contingency Theory: Logic and Method Revisited, *Personnel Psychology*, Vol. 25 (1972), 697–710.

Miner, John B. *Studies in Management Education*. Atlanta, Ga.: Organizational Measurement Systems Press, 1965.

Mitchell, Terence R., Anthony Biglan, Gerald R. Oncken, and Fred E. Fiedler, The Contingency Model: Criticism and Suggestions, *Academy of Management Journal*, Vol. 13 (1970), 253–267.

Mitchell, Terence R., James R. Larson, and Stephen G. Green. Leader Behavior, Situational Moderators, and Group Performance: An Attributional Analysis, *Organizational Behavior and Human Performance*, Vol. 18 (1977), 254–268.

Nebeker, Delbert M. Situational Favorability and Perceived Environmental Uncertainty: An Integrative Approach, *Administrative Science Quarterly*, Vol. 20 (1975), 281–294.

Rice, Robert W. Psychometric Properties of the Esteem for Least Preferred Coworker (LPC) Scale, *Academy of Management Review*, Vol. 3 (1978), 106–117.

Rice, Robert W. and Martin M. Chemers. Personality and Situational Determinants of Leader Behavior, *Journal of Applied Psychology*, Vol. 60 (1975), 20–27.

Schneier, Craig E. The Contingency Model of Leadership: An Extension to Emergent Leadership and Leader's Sex, *Organizational Behavior and Human Performance*, Vol. 21 (1978), 220–239.

Schriesheim, Chester A. and Steven Kerr. Theories and Measures of Leadership: A Critical Appraisal of Current and Future Directions, In James G. Hunt and Lars L. Larson (eds.), *Leadership: The Cutting Edge*. Carbondale, Ill.: Southern Illinois University Press, 1977, pp. 9–45, 51–56.

Shiflett, Samuel C. The Contingency Model of Leadership Effectiveness: Some Implications of Its Statistical and Methodological Properties, *Behavioral Science*, Vol. 18 (1973), 429–440.

Shiflett, Samuel C. Stereotyping and Esteem for One's Least Preferred Coworker, *Journal of Social Psychology*, Vol. 93 (1974), 55–65.

Shiflett, Samuel C. and Stanley M. Nealey. The Effects of Changing Leader Power: A Test of Situational Engineering, *Organizational Behavior and Human Performance*, Vol. 7 (1972), 371–382.

Stinson, John E. and Lane Tracy. Some Disturbing Characteristics of the LPC Score, *Personnel Psychology*, Vol. 27 (1974), 477–485.

Utecht, R. E. and W. D. Heier. The Contingency Model and Successful Military Leadership, *Academy of Management Journal*, Vol. 19 (1976), 606–618.

Vecchio, Robert P. An Empirical Examination of the Validity of Fiedler's Model of Leadership Effectiveness, *Organizational Behavior and Human Performance*, Vol. 19 (1977), 180–206.

PATH-GOAL THEORY OF LEADERSHIP

12

Path-goal theory has its origins in expectancy theory; in fact, it is in large part an expansion of expectancy theory concepts into the leadership domain. Thus the discussion in Chapter 6 provides a backdrop for what is said here.

Two individuals have been the major contributors, both of them now located at the University of Toronto. Martin G. Evans first developed his ideas in the area as a doctoral student at Yale and incorporated them in his dissertation, which was completed

327

in 1968. Robert J. House presented his views first while a faculty member at Baruch College of the City University of New York in the early 1970s. Both the Evans and House versions have gone through several stages. Because of the strong roots in expectancy theory all versions are more similar than they are different. Yet, it is meaningful to differentiate the contributions of the two major proponents of path-goal theory.

STATEMENTS OF PATH-GOAL HYPOTHESES

The Evans Formulations

The basic model as originally set forth by Evans (1970a, 1970b) contained five steps. These are elaborated in Figure 12–1. The process starts with the supervisor or leader behaving in certain ways. Two kinds of behavior are stressed, drawing upon the conceptual scheme originally developed at and long associated

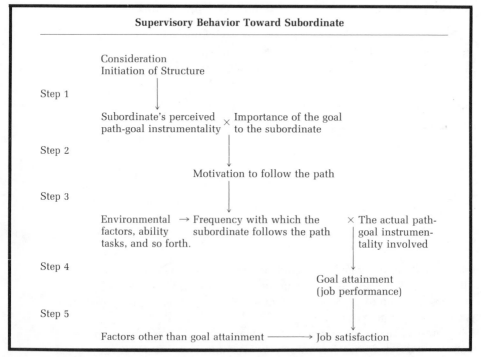

Figure 12–1. Steps in the Evans path-goal model. (Adapted from Martin G. Evans. The Effects of Supervisory Behavior on the Path Goal Relationship, *Organizational Behavior and Human Performance*, Vol. 5 (1970), pp. 279–282.)

with Ohio State University (Fleishman, Harris, and Burtt, 1955; Stogdill and Coons, 1957). The first type of behavior involves indications of trust, respect, warmth, concern for personal needs, and the like in dealing with subordinates and is reflected in considerable two-way communication and subordinate participation in decision-making; it is labeled *consideration*. The second type of behavior, called *initiation of structure*, is focused more directly on organizational goals, and includes organizing and defining work, establishing role prescriptions for subordinates, assigning tasks, planning work, and pushing for desired performances.

The behaviors affect the subordinate by influencing perceptions of path-goal instrumentalities — the extent to which following a certain path (behaving in a certain way) is seen as likely to lead to goal attainment or to hinder the achievement of goals. These perceived path-goal instrumentalities in turn are multiplied with the importance of the goals involved to the subordinate (their valence) to yield the level of motivation to follow a path or engage in a specific behavior.

However, motivation is only one contributor to actual job behavior; environmental factors, including the nature of the task (as well as particular individual abilities), also exert an influence. The resulting frequency with which the subordinate does follow the path and exhibit a particular kind of behavior, when multiplied with the actual path-goal instrumentality (the extent to which that behavior really does contribute to attaining the goal and is not merely perceived as doing so), produces the level of goal attainment. Goal attainment in turn is viewed as a partial measure of job satisfaction.

Leadership Hypotheses. The focus of the theory is at the level of supervisory behavior. How can a supervisor influence path-goal instrumentalities? For one thing, the subordinate must perceive the superior as being in a position to influence rewards and punishments. Given this, a considerate supervisor would be seen as an abundant source of rewards and a source that fits the rewards given to the desires of the individual. An inconsiderate supervisor would differentiate less in terms of individual needs or goals.

Also, the subordinate must see these rewards as linked to, or contingent upon, specific behaviors. Initiation of structure is the process by which rewards are tied to specific behavior paths. A supervisor who does not structure this way fails to indicate what paths should be utilized and distributes rewards without reference to the path followed.

In order to influence performance a supervisor must make judgments as to which are high performance paths and which are low. Although usually these judgments are easily made, there are instances in which only the highly considerate supervisor can make them. In particular, the considerate supervisor will perceive: (1) being given suggestions by subordinates, and (2) helping fellow workers as high performance paths; less considerate supervisors will not. Accordingly, these two so-called *variable* paths can be expected to be perceived as having higher path-goal instrumentalities when the supervisor is high in consideration.

The resulting hypotheses regarding the effects of different supervisory behaviors on perceived path-goal instrumentalities are as follows:

For *high* performance paths —

1. High consideration and high structure→highly positive instrumentalities (following the high performance path will help goal attainment).
2. High consideration and low structure→low positive or even neutral instrumentalities.
3. Low consideration regardless of structure→neutral instrumentalities for the high performance paths.

For *low* performance paths —

1. High consideration and high structure→highly negative instrumentalities (following the low performance path will hinder goal attainment).
2. High consideration and low structure→somewhat negative or neutral instrumentalities.
3. Low consideration regardless of structure→neutral instrumentality for the low performance paths.

For the two *variable* paths —

1. High consideration and high structure→highly positive instrumentalities.
2. High consideration and low structure→low positive instrumentalities.
3. Low consideration regardless of structure→neutral instrumentality for the variable paths.

The remaining hypotheses extend the theory to other aspects of the model set forth in Figure 12–1:

1. The higher the sum of the products of path-goal instrumentality and goal importance, the higher the path frequency (steps 2 and 3).
2. The higher the sum of the products of path frequency and path-goal instrumentality, the higher the goal attainment (step 4).
3. When supervisory behavior is related to path-goal instrumentality (step 1) and when the product of path-goal instrumentality and path frequency is related to goal attainment (step 4),

then supervisory behavior will be related to goal attainment — and to job satisfaction (the total model) (Evans, 1970b, p. 285).

Subsequent Extensions. Based upon the results of research carried out to test the initial leadership hypotheses, Evans (1974) developed several extensions to his theory. These involve the introduction of three types of moderators into the relationships hypothesized at steps 1 and 2 of the model. The moderator variables are the degree of upward hierarchic influence with his superiors that the supervisor has in the organization, the amount of role conflict the subordinate is experiencing, and the extent to which the subordinate is predominantly internal or external in locus of control — i.e., views himself as master of his own destiny or largely at the mercy of influence processes controlled outside the self.

These variables are incorporated in the theory as it relates to the prediction of motivation to follow a particular type of path through the following hypotheses:

1. The more considerate the supervisor, the higher the motivation is for high performance paths.
   a. The greater the upward influence of the supervisor, the more likely that he could offer and deliver many rewards (consideration) to the employees, thus influencing their expectancies and increasing their motivation.
2. The greater the initiation of structure, the higher the motivation is for high performance paths.
   a. The higher the role conflict experienced by the subordinates (in that different role senders had clearly different expectancies of how the individual should behave), the less effect the supervisor has on making the distribution of the rewards contingent on performance (initiating structure).
   b. The more internally controlled the subordinate, the stronger the relationship (Evans, 1974, p. 173).

House's Path-Goal Theory

As originally presented, House's path-goal theory was said to differ from that of Evans "in that its (Evans') predictions are not contingent on situational variables, and it is not an attempt to account for the conflicting findings" (House, 1971, p. 322). The two approaches moved closer together when Evans added his subsequent extensions, since both then utilized moderator variables.

In his first statement House (1971) presented a view of motivation as a combination of intrinsic and extrinsic valences and path instrumentalities of various kinds and then showed how these factors might be influenced by leader behaviors. A set of general propositions was then advanced followed by certain illustrative hypotheses intended to show how the propositions might be made operational. These hypotheses dealt with leader consideration, initiating structure, closeness of supervision, hierarchical influence, and authoritarianism, as well as a number of other variables. As a theoretical statement this first effort is complex and at times difficult to follow; it is not at all clear why certain variables are introduced and their role in the theory is often unclear.

Subsequent statements (House and Dessler, 1974; House and Mitchell, 1974) have attempted to rectify these problems and do indeed present a much cleaner theoretical framework. It seems appropriate, therefore, to start our discussion with this revised version.

General Propositions. The general propositions of the theory have been stated as follows:

1. ... leader behavior is acceptable and satisfying to subordinates to the extent that the subordinates see such behavior as either an immediate source of satisfaction or as instrumental to future satisfaction.
2. ... the leader's behavior will be motivational, i.e., increase effort, to the extent that (1) such behavior makes satisfaction of subordinate's needs contingent on effective performance, and (2) such behavior complements the environment of subordinates by providing the coaching, guidance, support and rewards necessary for effective performance (House and Mitchell, 1974, p. 84).

Thus, the inputs of the theory are various types of leader behaviors, and the outputs are the leader acceptance, job satisfaction, and motivation to performance of subordinates. Within this framework the role of the leader becomes one of recognizing and arousing subordinate desires for outcomes or goals that the leader can influence, increasing the personal payoffs to the subordinate for attainment of work goals, utilizing coaching and direction to make the paths to these personal payoffs easier to travel, helping subordinates to clarify expectancies, reducing frustrating barriers, and increasing opportunities for personal satisfaction contingent on effective performance.

Stated less formally, the motivational functions of the leader consist of increasing the number and kinds of personal payoffs to subordinates for work-goal attainment and making paths to these payoffs easier to travel by clarifying the paths, reducing road blocks and pitfalls, and increasing the opportunities for personal satisfaction en route (House and Mitchell, 1974, p. 85).

This quote appears in almost identical form in other statements of the theory (House, 1971; House and Dessler, 1974) and represents the essence of the theoretical view. The types of leader behaviors through which these functions are performed are directive (initiating structure), supportive (consideration), achievement-oriented, and participative.

Contingency Factors.   These leader behaviors influence subordinate outputs in different ways depending upon the manner in which certain contingency variables moderate the relationships. One set of contingency variables involves characteristics of subordinates. Typical hypotheses of this kind are:

> Subordinates with a high need for affiliation see high leader consideration as a source of satisfaction.
> Subordinates with a high need for achievement view leader behavior that clarifies path-goal relationships and provides feedback (achievement oriented behavior) as more satisfying.
> Subordinates with a high need for extrinsic rewards (pay, for instance) perceive leader directiveness or coaching as more satisfying.
> Subordinates who perceive a strong internal locus of control experience a participative leadership style as more satisfying.
> Subordinates who are highly authoritarian are more receptive to directive leader behavior.
> Subordinates who consider their ability relative to task demands to be high will find leader directiveness and coaching (initiating structure) less acceptable.

Although schematic statements of the theory note only subordinate authoritarianism, locus of control, and ability as personal moderators, it is clear from the above statements that the actual list is considerably longer.

A second set of contingency variables derives from pressures and demands in the work environment. Thus:

> When the task is routine, clear group norms exist, and objective controls derive from the formal authority system, directive (structuring) leader behavior will be considered redundant and as representing excessively close supervision with resulting lowered subordinate satisfaction and leader acceptance.

Theoretical statements tend to be consistent in emphasizing the task, the formal authority system, and the primary work group as environmental moderators.

In a more recent publication, certain contingency hypotheses have been stated using the four types of leader behavior specified in the theory as a starting point (Filley, House, and Kerr, 1976). The first of these behaviors, supportive leadership, is defined as "behavior that includes giving consideration to the needs of subordinates, displaying concern for their well-being, status, and comfort, and creating a friendly and pleasant climate." This type of leadership is hypothesized to yield its most positive effects on satisfaction when the work is stressful, frustrating, or dissatisfying.

Participative leadership involves the "sharing of information, power, and influence between supervisors and subordinates," thus treating subordinates largely as equals and allowing them to influence supervisory actions and decisions. It is hypothesized that when the task is clear and the subordinates are not ego-involved in the work, participative leadership will contribute to satisfaction and performance only for highly independent, nonauthoritarian subordinates. On ambiguous, ego-involving tasks, participative leadership will have positive effects regardless of subordinate personality.

Instrumental leadership "features the planning, organizing, controlling, and coordinating of subordinate activities by leaders." Such directiveness is expected to yield positive results when the task is ambiguous and when organizational procedures and policies are unclear or conflicting; with greater clarity and certainty it will be a hindrance.

Achievement-oriented leadership "is characterized by leaders who set challenging goals, expect subordinates to perform at their highest level, continuously seek improvement in performance, and show a high degree of confidence that the subordinates will assume responsibility, put forth effort, and accomplish challenging goals." Leadership of this kind is expected to induce striving for high standards and confidence in meeting challenging goals, especially among individuals working on ambiguous, nonrepetitive tasks.

These more recent hypotheses are often intertwined with research, and in several cases are stated on an ad hoc basis. Thus, some of the difficulties considered in the previous chapter in discussing Fiedler's contingency theory of leadership re-emerge here. House is well aware of the problems associated with introducing contingency variables when needed rather than on *a priori* theoretical grounds. Accordingly, he views his approach as more of a useful theoretical framework than a fully developed, internally consistent theory.

RESEARCH ON CONSIDERATION AND INITIATING STRUCTURE

Both versions of path-goal theory have been tied closely to the Ohio State University research on leader behavior from their origins and remain so in their current forms. House now has adopted a somewhat different terminology, using words such as supportive and instrumental (directive) rather than consideration and initiating structure, but both his descriptions of his variables and the operationalizations applied in much of his research indicate comparable constructs. Accordingly, it becomes important to determine how solid an underpinning the Ohio State conceptualizations provide for path-goal theory.

In their original form these conceptualizations were relatively simple and straightforward (Fleishman, 1973). Consideration and initiating structure were viewed as two independent dimensions rather than as opposite ends of a single continuum; thus, they were assumed to be uncorrelated with each other, either positively or negatively. Each was important to leadership success, so that being above average on both consideration and structure was particularly likely to bring about effective behavior in leadership situations. Furthermore, the appropriate method of measuring the key variables was assumed to be reports by qualified observers, primarily subordinates. It is in this basic form that the approach has been popularized under the title of the *managerial grid* (Blake and Mouton, 1964), using a 9-point scale for each construct. More recent theoretical extensions have introduced a long list of moderators into the relationships between leadership behaviors and performance/satisfaction. Path-goal theory incorporates a number of these moderator variables, but others have been utilized as well.

Evidence of Validity

Although the preferred method of obtaining evidence bearing on the consideration and initiating structure constructs has been some type of behavior description questionnaire, a leadership opinion questionnaire also has been used that elicits attitude data on how the leader believes he should behave in his role. This latter measure has yielded few significant relationships with either performance or satisfaction measures over the years and is also somewhat peripheral in its relationship to the theory (Kerr and Schriesheim, 1974; Korman, 1966). Accordingly, it will be given little attention here.

Leader Behavior Descriptions. The early studies utilizing descriptions by subordinates provided very mixed results (Korman, 1966). There were sufficient instances of nonsignificant findings or even relationships in a direction opposite to what the theory would predict so that considerable skepticism seemed warranted.

More recent research has provided a much more positive picture in that significant correlations have been obtained with some consistency (Kerr and Schriesheim, 1974). This appears to have occurred, however, as a result of the introduction of moderator variables into the research designs. In particular the use of situational pressure, task-related satisfaction, subordinate need for information, job level, subordinate expectations, congruence of leadership styles in the hierarchy, subordinate's organizational independence, and leader upward influence have served to enhance correlations between the leader behavior measures and outcome variables (Kerr, Schriesheim, Murphy, and Stogdill, 1974). Thus, the basic theory itself remains highly questionable, although there clearly are instances when it works.

An interesting example of such a positive outcome involves relating consideration and initiating structure scores obtained from university students in describing their instructors to the students' ratings of teaching effectiveness (Lahat-Mandelbaum and Kipnis, 1973). The results are given in Table 12–1. Clearly, considerate behavior earns a professor high ratings, and, at least among lower division students, initiating structure earns low ratings. In general, these instructor behaviors make less difference to graduate students than to undergraduates.

The Hi-Hi Hypothesis.   The idea that leaders who are high on both consideration and initiating structure will be the most effective has been the subject of a sizable body of research (Larson, Hunt, and Osborn, 1976; Nystrom, 1978). In a wide range of organizations the hypothesis has failed to achieve support. In all but a very few cases when leader behaviors did relate to criteria, either consideration alone or structure alone predicted as well as the

Table 12–1.   RELATIONSHIPS BETWEEN INSTRUCTOR BEHAVIOR DESCRIPTIONS OBTAINED FROM UNIVERSITY STUDENTS AND TEACHER EVALUATIONS

	Student Groups		
	Lower Division (Freshman-Sophomore)	Upper Division (Junior-Senior)	Graduate
Consideration	.79*	.79*	.49*
Initiating structure	−.34*	−.05	.15

*Statistically significant.
Adapted from Bat-sheva Lahat-Mandelbaum and David Kipnis. Leader Behavior Dimensions Related to Students' Evaluation of Teaching Effectiveness, *Journal of Applied Psychology*, Vol. 58 (1973), p. 251.

combination posited by the theory. Since path-goal theory tends to emphasize moderated relationships, and the hi-hi hypothesis is stated without reference to additional variables, this finding is of only tangential interest for present purposes. However, it does question the view that a really effective leader must be adept at dealing with *both* socio-emotional and productivity aspects.

The Problem of Causality

In the early period it was generally assumed that when a correlation between leader behavior and subordinate performance levels was obtained, it reflected a causal flow from the leader to the subordinates. Over a time this assumption was questioned. There is now a sizable body of research indicating that the performance levels of subordinates can act on the leader and serve to bring about different kinds of behaviors toward the subordinates (Miner, 1978). This has been demonstrated for a wide range of leader behaviors including consideration and initiating structure. However, just as these leader behaviors sometimes do and sometimes do not correlate with group performance indexes, so also different performance levels may or may not produce changes in consideration and structuring.

The data of Table 12–2 are reasonably typical of those obtained in other studies. In all three experiments comparisons were

Table 12–2. MEAN CONSIDERATION AND INITIATING STRUCTURE SCORES ASCRIBED TO LEADERS OF HIGH AND LOW PERFORMING GROUPS

	High Performing Group	Low Performing Group
Study 1		
Consideration	33.4	29.3
Initiating structure	(25.6	20.8)
Study 2		
Consideration	(35.9	29.6)
Initiating structure	(31.2	26.1)
Study 3		
Consideration	42.2	40.0
Initiating structure	31.6	30.2

( ) Difference statistically significant.
Adapted from Terence R. Mitchell, James R. Larson, and Stephen G. Green. Leader Behavior, Situational Moderators, and Group Performance: An Attributional Analysis, *Organizational Behavior and Human Performance*, Vol. 18 (1977), pp. 260, 262, 264.

made among behavior descriptions of leaders when the group performance was presented as either high or low to those providing the descriptions, and all other factors were held constant (Mitchell, Larson, and Green, 1977). Thus only the differences in performance levels could account for the changed descriptions. Although in this instance performance level was manipulated by leading the subjects to believe that a group performed either well or poorly, similar results have been obtained when actual group behavior was observed (Barrow, 1976).

These findings do not permit one to conclude that leader behavior does not influence subordinate performance at all. The amount of co-variation typically accounted for by the effects of performance on leader behavior descriptions is less than the total variation, and there is independent evidence that the causal flow occurs in both directions (Herold, 1977). Nevertheless, one can assume that when significant correlations between consideration (or initiating structure) and performance are obtained, a sizable component of the relationship can be attributed to the effects of subordinate performance on leader behavior, not the reverse. Thus, the basic theory turns out to be much less powerful than the mere correlational data would suggest.

Measurement Considerations

The dimensions of consideration and initiating structure arose out of studies in which large numbers of items were subjected to factor analysis to determine what kinds of groupings emerged. Thus, the constructs of the theory are intimately related to the measurement procedures used. Accordingly, it is not suprising that a full evaluation of the Ohio State concepts requires an exploration of measurement factors.

Independence of Dimensions. The original view that consideration and structure represent two independent dimensions has come into increasing question. Whether the theory is supported in this regard appears to depend on what measures are used. As noted previously, both leader opinion and behavior description questionnaires have been developed. However, there are at least three different versions of the behavior description questionnaire that have been used extensively in research.

These versions had been assumed to measure the same constructs. Recent evidence indicates that although this is true for consideration, it is not true for initiating structure (Schriesheim, House, and Kerr, 1976). The latter measures differ considerably in the extent to which they include items of a punitive, autocratic, or production oriented nature. When these items are extensively included, consideration and structure typically do not emerge as significantly correlated; when they are included only minimally, a positive correlation on the order of .50 can be anticipated. These differences cannot be attributed to variations in the reliabilities of the measures, since there appear to be only minimal differences in this regard, and all measures yield quite satisfactory values (Schriesheim and Kerr, 1977). On balance, the evidence indicates that whether the dimensional independence hypothesis is supported depends on how the initiating structure construct is defined and made operational. In any event, certain problems of construct validity exist.

Different Measures, Different Validities.   The construct validity problems manifest themselves not only in correlations between measures but also in correlations between these measures and outcome criteria. Although the various consideration scales tend to yield essentially the same validities, this is not true of initiating structure. Contradictory results can be obtained when different measures are used; thus, at least part of the variation in validity results from one study to another may be attributed to measurement differences. A version that does not contain many autocratic, punitive, or production oriented items consistently has been found to correlate positively with job satisfaction, while a version with more of these items yields negative correlations (Schriesheim, House, and Kerr, 1976; Szilagyi and Keller, 1976).

Bias Associated with Subordinate Descriptions.   The preferred method of measuring leader behavior in the Ohio State research was through the use of descriptions provided by subordinates, either individually or as a group. These tend to be summary statements based on what the subordinates remember and what they have perceived. Both memory and perception can be in error, and thus a potential source of bias exists.

A study dealing with this issue was conducted comparing subordinate descriptions subsequent to a laboratory experience with ongoing recordings of leader behavior during the laboratory by trained observers (Ilgen and Fujii, 1976). The findings suggest some serious problems as indicated in the following statements (pp. 648–649):

> ...behavior ratings from subordinate group members created two problems. First, they were unable to detect relationships between leader behaviors and member performance. In general, lower performing members received more initiation-of-structure behavior from their leaders than did higher-performing members. A reliance upon only member ratings would

not have detected this relationship. A second and more serious problem is that of overinterpretation of the satisfaction data. With independent observers, it would have been concluded . . . that the behavior of the leader strongly influenced the extrinsic and general satisfactions of group members. Observer ratings did not support this conclusion. Overinterpretation is most likely to occur when leader behaviors obtained from group members' descriptions are related to other responses from the same group members such as their satisfaction. . . . This response-response mode allows response styles as well as general perceptual biases to inflate any correlations with leader behavior descriptions obtained from the same individuals.

This same study identifies another problem with special implications for research on path-goal theory. When leader descriptions obtained from subordinates were considered separately for each subordinate, agreement with the observer descriptions was minimal, but when the data for the various subordinates of the same leader were combined to yield a composite index, correlations with the observers rose dramatically; presumably the composites neutralized the effects of individual biases. Yet path-goal theory assumes an individual level of analysis because individual differences are part of the theory; moderator variables by their very nature tend to foster the use of the individual as the unit of study rather than the work group.

The indications that subordinate descriptions may be severely biased emanating from the Ilgen and Fujii (1976) research receive support from other sources as well (Lord, Binning, Rush, and Thomas, 1978; Rush, Thomas, and Lord, 1977). The demands on subordinate memory required by the Ohio State measures appear excessive, and as a result it seems likely that stereotypes and implicit theories are often substituted for fact, thus reducing information processing requirements. Forgotten details are filled in from assumptions about how a good supervisor ought to act. Presumably, this type of bias would be minimized if the subordinates made separate ratings over short time intervals at the point at which behaviors actually occurred, thus reducing memory requirements. The Ohio State measures, however, rely heavily on summary statements. To that extent the resulting scores appear to have only a very limited relationship to actual leader behavior.

TESTS OF THE COMPREHENSIVE THEORY

It is apparent that reliance on the consideration and initiating structure constructs does not always serve path-goal theory well. The research clearly indicates that these constructs are more likely to relate to outcome criteria significantly when moderators are introduced, and current versions of path-goal theory do specify moderated relationships. Thus, the real test is provided by research focused directly on the hypotheses of the theory rather than on the original Ohio State concepts.

Research Conducted by the Theorists

Both Evans and House utilize post hoc interpretations of prior studies as a basis for developing their own formulations. Although this approach has the advantage of placing the resulting theories at the forefront of knowledge, the studies thus used cannot be considered as providing evidence in support of hypotheses that were in fact derived from them. The present discussion will accordingly concern itself with *a priori* tests only.

Evans' Research. Evans (1970b) reports two studies, one conducted with blue collar workers in a public utility and one with nurses in a general hospital. In both cases a questionnaire was used to collect data relevant to certain goals such as respect from one's supervisor, skill development, doing a good job, and pay. *Path-goal instrumentality* was measured by questions regarding the utility of such behaviors as performing well, giving suggestions to the boss, and doing low quality work for goal attainment. *Path frequency* was indicated with reference to each of these paths, and estimates of *goal attainment* (How much is there now?) and *goal importance* (How important is it to you?) also were obtained. Indexes of *job satisfaction* and supervisory *consideration* and *initiating structure* were included in the questionnaire.

The theory generally predicted path-goal instrumentalities in the utility but failed to do so in the hospital. Predictions of path frequency from path-goal instrumentality (see Figure 12–1) were highly successful in the utility but less so in the hospital, although in neither case did goal importance make the expected contribution. Goal attainment was predicted from the combination of path-goal instrumentality and path frequency reasonably well in both organizations. The comprehensive hypothesis extending from supervisory behavior through to goal attainment and job satisfaction was supported strongly in the utility but rarely in the hospital.

The subsequent extension of the theory through the addition of moderator relationships represented in large part an attempt to handle the disparate results obtained in the utility and the hospital (Evans, 1974). To test these relationships Evans carried out a study using employed MBA students, again utilizing questionnaire measures obtained from his subjects for all of the variables.

The overall results do not provide strong support for the extended theory. The self-rating of performance was not predicted differentially at different levels of any of the moderator variables. There was some evidence that internal-external orientation moderated the relationship between consideration and job motivation in the expected manner. However, the hypothesis as stated deals with initiating structure, not consideration, while only consideration data are presented. It is not possible, even in this one instance, to determine whether the theory is confirmed.

House's Research. House (1971) conducted three studies to test hypotheses derived from his initial formulation of path-goal theory. In the first study he was able to demonstrate that role ambiguity did moderate the relationship between supervisor initiating structure and subordinate satisfaction among individuals performing quasi-professional or administrative work. However, the tendency for structuring to relate to greater satisfaction in ambiguous situations was far from strong.

The second study used task autonomy and job scope as moderators and tested the following hypotheses:
1. Initiating structure→high satisfaction (where autonomy is high)
2. Initiating structure→high performance (where autonomy is low)
3. Consideration→high satisfaction (where autonomy is low)
4. Consideration→high performance (where autonomy is low)
5. Consideration→high satisfaction (where job scope is low)
6. Consideration→high performance (where job scope is low)

The results obtained are summarized in Table 12–3. Tests of significant differences between correlations indicate clear support for hypotheses 4 and 6, and some directional support for hypotheses 1, 2, and 3. Only hypothesis 5 involving job scope is clearly not supported. The results involving performance are particularly encouraging since the performance ratings were made independently.

A third study attempted to replicate the second with regard to hypotheses 3, 4, 5, and 6, all involving the consideration variable, using a different sample (see Table 12–3). None of the correlation differences is significant, although hypothesis 6 and now also hypothesis 5 receive directional support, as does hypothesis 3 to a mixed degree. Hypothesis 4, which was strongly supported in the previous study, no longer is supported.

As a whole this early research appears to provide some support for the path-goal theory, while suggesting that additional

Table 12–3.   CORRELATIONS BETWEEN LEADER BEHAVIORS AND
SATISFACTION AND PERFORMANCE AS MODERATED
BY TASK AUTONOMY AND JOB SCOPE
(House's Studies 2 and 3)

	Low Group		Medium Group		High Group	
	Study 2	Study 3	Study 2	Study 3	Study 2	Study 3
	Task Autonomy					
Initiating Structure vs.						
Satisfaction (hypothesis 1)	.19	–	.21	–	.33	–
Performance (hypothesis 2)	.47	–	.18	–	.18	–
Consideration vs.						
Satisfaction (hypothesis 3)	.37	.45	.30	.28	.23	.36
Performance (hypothesis 4)	.42	−.15	.11	−.06	.08	−.06
	Job Scope					
Satisfaction (hypothesis 5)	.36	.38	.30	.24	.30	.19
Performance (hypothesis 6)	.52	.33	.02	.18	.09	.04

Adapted from Robert J. House. A Path-Goal Theory of Leader Effectiveness, *Administrative Science Quarterly*, Vol. 16 (1971), pp. 331, 334, 336.

moderator variables may need to be considered. A second series of studies leads to much the same conclusion (House and Dessler, 1974).

In this latter research the moderating effects of task structure were investigated for instrumental (similar to initiating structure), supportive (similar to consideration), and participative leadership behavior. In general, instrumental leadership was related to positive outcomes as hypothesized when there was little structure in the task, and supportive leadership was related similarly when there was considerable structure. As in the prior research, however, results did not always replicate from one sample to another and significant differences between high and low task structure condition correlations occurred for only nine of 22 comparisons.

Participative leadership was studied using certain items from the Ohio State measure of consideration plus additional, comparable items. The expectation was that participative leadership might operate as a means of clarifying role expectations and thus would be most effective under conditions of low task structure. The data did not support this conclusion, and there was no real evidence that task structure moderated relationships between participative leadership and outcomes.

Studies of the Moderating Effects of Task Factors

Although path-goal theory proposes a wide range of moderators, House's concentration on task factors, and in particular task structure, appears to have exerted a strong influence on other researchers. Tests of the theory have been predominantly in this area and have focused on considerate or supportive, and directive or structuring leader behaviors much more than those of a participative or achievement-oriented type.

The Pennsylvania State University Research.   As in other studies the Pennsylvania State University research dealt with the positive relationship between initiating structure and outcomes on unstructured tasks, and the tendency for consideration to moderate in the reverse direction. The subjects were managers and machine operators in a steel company, and the initial analyses were of a concurrent nature (Downey, Sheridan, and Slocum, 1975).

The results obtained for initiating structure provided no support for the theory. Performance and motivational variables were essentially unmoderated by task structure, as inferred from the manager-operator position distinction. Various job satisfaction indexes were moderated in one direction as often as in another. The results for consideration were somewhat more consistent with the theory, especially when performance motivation and satisfaction with supervision were used as dependent variables. However, there were a number of other dependent variables that did not yield findings in support of theoretical predictions.

A subsequent extension of this study involved the collection of longitudinal data at a one-year interval (Downey, Sheridan, and Slocum, 1976). Although some results were consistent with theoretical predictions, there were at least as many instances of reversed findings. Task structure did not operate consistently as a moderator in the manner the theory posits. Furthermore, attempts to establish causal paths from leader behavior to job performance, motivation, and satisfaction were not successful. The longitudinal analyses indicated a pattern of predominantly interactive relationships with leader behavior operating as a result as much as a cause.

Studies of this kind have been criticized to the extent that they confound participative with supportive items in the consideration measure, and punitive or autocratic items with role clarification items in the initiating structure measure (Schriesheim and Von Glinow, 1977). Although several of the earlier studies often cited in support of the theory also involve confounding on one or both of these bases, it is still possible that the generally negative results of the Pennsylvania

State research might be reversed with more differentiated leader behavior measures.

Accordingly, Sheridan, Downey, and Slocum (1975) carried out separate analyses in which items from the Ohio State measures were grouped into role clarification, supportive, participative, and autocratic categories. The results, however, continued to provide little support for path-goal theory. None of the four kinds of leader behaviors measured showed consistent relationships of the kind the theory predicts. Task structure did not moderate as anticipated, and leader behavior relationships to dependent variables were reciprocal rather than causal. This research must be considered as nonsupportive for path-goal theory. It is particularly important because it considers the causal hypotheses emanating from the theory — a matter of special concern given the previously noted problems with regard to the direction and nature of causality operating generally in studies of consideration and initiating structure.

Other Studies of Task Moderators. Several additional studies have failed to identify task structure moderator effects in various contexts, including a hospital (Sheridan and Vredenburgh, 1978) and a manufacturing firm (Dessler and Valenzi, 1977). However, there are findings of a more positive nature. The typical result tends to be some partial support for the theory.

Thus, Stinson and Johnson (1975) conducted a study in which task structure, task repetitiveness, and task autonomy were measured separately as moderators, and the leader behavior dimensions were established on a purified basis by purging punitive and participative items from the Ohio State measures. As noted in Table 12–4, the data for initiating structure do not support the theory with regard to the task autonomy moderator and are antithetical to it for the other two task moderators. Yet, the results for consideration consistently support the theory across all moderators. The authors suggest that the contradictory findings for initiating structure may be a function of the sample used — administrative and technical personnel with a relatively high level of education.

This view that job level actually operates as an additional moderator receives support from another study conducted with operative level employees in a paper plant in rural Quebec (Johns, 1978). In this case initiating structure relationships were moderated in the predicted manner by task variables for both job satisfaction and turnover intentions, although not for absenteeism. The consideration findings were less strong, although they were clearly as predicted for the turnover intention outcome.

Table 12–4. CORRELATIONS BETWEEN LEADER BEHAVIORS AND VARIOUS SATISFACTION INDEXES UNDER DIFFERENT TASK CONDITIONS

	Task Structure		Task Repetitiveness		Task Autonomy	
	Low	High	Low	High	High	Low
Initiating structure vs.						
Intrinsic job satisfaction	(−.25	.22)	.22	.18	.17	−.01
Satisfaction with supervision	−.11	−.01	(−.28	.20)	−.06	−.04
Job satisfaction generally	.18	.33	−.08	.28	.22	.16
Consideration vs.						
Intrinsic job satisfaction	(.15	.58)	.24	.49	.52	.56
Satisfaction with supervision	(.68	.87)	(.72	.88)	(.72	.90)
Job satisfaction generally	(−.25	.55)	.43	.43	.40	.61

( ) Difference statistically significant.
Adapted from John E. Stinson and Thomas W. Johnson. The Path-Goal Theory of Leadership: A Partial Test and Suggested Refinement, *Academy of Management Journal*, Vol. 18 (1975), pp. 248–249.

Subordinate Authoritarianism as a Moderator

Most of the research on subordinate authoritarianism as a moderator variable has involved the hypothesis that participative leadership will contribute to satisfaction among nonauthoritarian individuals only on repetitive tasks. On nonrepetitive tasks of a kind more likely to arouse intrinsic motivation, participative behavior on the part of the leader will be satisfying regardless of the degree of authoritarianism of the subordinate (Filley, House, and Kerr, 1976). Schuler (1976) tested this formulation using a diversified sample of individuals from a large manufacturing firm, and it was supported.

In other research aimed at investigating relationships among subordinate authoritarianism, task type, and leader behavior, the focus was on the effects of differences in consideration and initiating structure (Weed, Mitchell, and Moffitt, 1976). The research was conducted in a laboratory setting and leader behaviors were actually manipulated to permit causal statements. Only on difficult tasks of an ambiguous nature did leader behavior interact with subordinate personality to determine performance outcome. Predominantly structuring behavior produced better performance on such tasks from authoritarian subordinates, while predominantly considerate behavior yielded the best results with nonauthoritarian subjects. These results provide qualified support both for the effects of leader behavior on performance and for the role of subordinate authoritarianism as a moderator. However, it is important to note that these moderator effects occurred with only one of the four types of tasks studied and then only for task performance, not satisfaction.

Results with Nontask Moderators

Research related to the hypotheses of path-goal theory that do not involve task factors as moderators has been very slow in developing. The most frequently studied such moderator has been role clarity-ambiguity, and even this factor might well be interpreted as primarily of a task nature.

A study by Szilagyi and Sims (1974) found that initiating structure was related to high satisfaction when little role clarity existed. Furthermore, this same structuring behavior was related to low performance levels when role clarity was pronounced, a result that also has been reported by Schriesheim and Murphy (1976). However, these kinds of findings that are consistent with theoretical expectations do not occur in all groups studied. It is not entirely clear when the hypothesized relationships will appear and when they will not, although there is some basis for concluding that they are more likely at higher occupational levels.

Path-goal theory also utilizes job stress as a moderator, although this factor has often been made operational in terms of task characteristics. Some research has been conducted, however, using on-the-job anxiety as a stress index (Schriesheim and Murphy, 1976). Contrary to theoretical expectations, consideration was more negatively related to satisfaction (and performance) when anxiety levels were high. Under such stressful anxiety-provoking circumstances, initiating structure is more likely to produce positive results.

O'Reilly and Roberts (1978) have conducted an investigation that bears upon several of the earliest formulations by Evans and House. When upward influence is used as a moderator there is evidence that work satisfaction is highest when consideration is high and the supervisor has considerable influence. However, consideration is positively related to satisfaction even for low influence supervisors, and no such effects are reported for performance. Thus, Evans' hypothesis is partially supported.

When subordinate mobility aspirations are introduced as a moderator, there is a facilitation of the initiating structure-outcome relationship. "These results are consistent with some of the findings from path-goal leadership studies indicating that high initiating structure has a positive impact when it acts to clarify the path to desired outcomes, and a negative effect when it does not contribute to subordinate accomplishment of desired goals" (O'Reilly and Roberts,

348 PATH-GOAL THEORY OF LEADERSHIP

1978, pp. 100–101). The findings with regard to both the upward influence of the supervisor and the upward mobility aspirations of the subordinate are of rather small magnitude, however, and thus probably of limited practical significance.

CONCLUSIONS

Managerial Goals

An early statement by Evans (1970a) offered some promise that path-goal theory might make important contributions to managerial practice. However, the current state of affairs is best epitomized in the following statement:

> We are optimistic about the future outlook of leadership research. With the guidance of path-goal theorizing, future research is expected to unravel many confusing puzzles about the reasons for and effects of leader behavior that have, heretofore, not been solved. However, we add a word of caution: the theory, and the research on it, are relatively new to the literature of organizational behavior. Consequently, path-goal theory is offered more as a tool for directing research and stimulating insight than as a proven guide for managerial action (House and Mitchell, 1974, p. 94).

Applications have not been developed and guidelines for managerial action have not been specifically spelled out. Given this situation, it appears premature to draw inferences about the use of the theory in management practice.

Scientific Goals

There is no question that the purported research tests of path-goal theory provide equivocal results. A more basic question is whether the theory has really been tested at all. Almost without exception these tests have drawn in one way or another on the Ohio State scales. Yet these scales have been shown not to provide comparable measures of what might appear to be the same constructs (Schriesheim and Von Glinow, 1977). Untangling the confounding thus created appears to be an almost impossible process. Results previously reported to be supportive of the theory may not be if one uses a later operationalization of the variable, and so on. It is easy to accept positive results as positive, and negative as negative, regardless of the measure used, but when the measures are clearly not the same, the possibility of capitalization on chance through selection of measures is a real danger.

Furthermore, it now appears quite possible that leader behavior descriptions of the type the Ohio State measures provide may identify implicit theories and existing biases more often than true behaviors. Accordingly, there is a real prospect that studies using measures of this kind have not tapped the actual leader behaviors specified by the theory.

An additional problem arises because the theory is considerably more comprehensive than the research on it. The outcomes specified are job satisfaction, acceptance of leader, and motivational behavior.

Although the latter construct has been assumed to include only motivational components by some (Schriesheim and Kerr, 1977), it certainly has been tested primarily at the level of actual performance, and there appears to be sufficient theoretical support to justify this approach. Acceptance of the leader as an outcome has not been studied at all. Among the various leader behaviors, published research on achievement-oriented behaviors is for all practical purposes nonexistent; and research on participative behavior is much less than might be desired. Among the various environmental moderators noted, those of a task nature have been studied extensively, but such factors as existing authority systems and work group norms have received practically no attention. At the individual subordinate level, authoritarianism has received the most attention; other factors, especially those of an ability and motivational nature, have gone almost unrecognized.

Given this uncertainty regarding the nature and scope of the research, it is still possible to ask where the current research leads. Certainly there are sufficient findings that appear to support the theory, especially for task moderators, to rule out a purely chance explanation. However, the frequent negative findings have typically elicited a resort to additional moderators as explanations, and thus ad hoc extensions to the theory. Thus, job level differences have been added in order to explain contradictory findings with regard to task structure. Job level also has been used to explain similar disparities when role clarity is a moderator, but in this instance the relationships are completely reversed, even though task structure and role clarity would appear to be closely related concepts.

The use of such ad hoc moderators on a case by case basis seems likely to fail on logical grounds alone, while making the theory so complex that it violates all meaningful concepts of parsimony. An alternative approach might be to attempt to define primary moderators (and perhaps leader behaviors also) in somewhat different terms — terms that might more precisely match the realities of the organizational world and also avoid the problems inherent in the Ohio State constructs and measures.

An example of such an approach would be the schema (Miner, 1975) wherein various types of control (or inducement) systems are posited as moderator variables. These inducement sources include hierarchic sanctions, professional norms, task pushes and pulls, and group pressures. Leader behavior that reflected a willingness and ability to resort to initiating structure and even autocracy (if required) would be expected to yield maximum results in hierarchic systems. On the other hand, professional systems would be expected to produce their best outcomes when there is a managerial style that emphasizes the use of expert power, expertise, and professional accomplishment. Task-based systems such as those inherent in the entrepreneurial role are entirely intrinsic in the pure case, and thus outcomes are maximized when there is no external leadership at all. Finally, consideration produces its best results under group systems; in such instances a strong measure of employee-centered behavior is essential for leader survival and the effective operation of the system. There are other approaches of this type including views emphasizing substitutes for leadership (Kerr and Jermier, 1978, Schriesheim and Kerr, 1977). The major point is that path-goal theory might achieve greater precision with somewhat different moderators and leader behavior variables (Miner and Dachler, 1973). In fact, there are serious questions as to whether expectancy theory and the Ohio State leadership dimensions are theoretically compatible, deriving as they do from such different origins.

The close tie that path-goal theory posits between leadership and subordinate motivation has a compelling logic to it that other theories have not achieved. One cannot help concluding that in this respect path-goal theory is on the right track, and it is probably for this reason that a number of significant findings have been obtained. However, the origins of path-goal theory in expectancy theory would appear to indicate that the limitations of the motivational theory should hold for the leadership theory as well. As indicated in Chapter 6, expectancy theory (whatever its pretensions) is bounded within a rather limited domain; it applies to the world of hedonistic, maximizing decisions and is concerned with a rational, conscious model of human behavior. So too is path-goal theory, and it is probably for just this reason that it so frequently strikes out. A number of the research studies appear to have extended beyond the presumed boundaries of the theory, and if this is so, it is not surprising that they have failed to yield supportive results. One of the difficulties with path-goal theory is that its boundary conditions have not been clearly specified.

A recent article has proposed that the hypotheses and data of path-goal theory may be explained and subsumed under behavior modification and operant learning interpretations (Mawhinney and Ford, 1977). The logic is compelling, but a question remains whether one should do this. The answer, as noted in Chapter 8, appears to lie in the relative power of the underlying theoretical stances. As indicated there:

> . . . when one looks at the limited amount of comparative research available, the data do tend to favor expectancy and goal setting formulations over those of behavior modification. Thus, on the evidence, there is good reason to question whether behavior modification *theory* makes a useful independent contribution at the present time.

Extrapolating from expectancy theory to path-goal theory, a presumably entirely appropriate procedure, one must end by favoring the cognitive formulations on the evidence. This is not to say that predictions from behavior modification theory are wrong, merely that they do not achieve the same level of explanatory impact as is obtained from the combined power of expectancy and path-goal formulations.

A final point relates to the current activities of the major originators of path-goal formulations in the leadership area. Evans has contributed little to the development of the theory in recent years. House remains a strong advocate and is continuing to conduct related research. He also has proposed a theory of charismatic leadership that utilizes the path-goal framework to only a limited degree, and that deals with a somewhat different set of phenomena (House, 1977). Perhaps the goal of extending expectancy theory into the leadership domain has been achieved, and future contributions will derive primarily from the broader expectancy framework. Should this be the case, path-goal theory will still have made a contribution in melding leadership and motivation constructs and in pointing up the guiding, coaching role of leadership as it relates to motivation.

References

Barrow, Jeffrey C. Worker Performance and Task Complexity as Causal Determinants of Leader Behavior Style and Flexibility, *Journal of Applied Psychology*, Vol. 61 (1976), 433–440.

Blake, Robert R. and Jane S. Mouton. *The Managerial Grid*. Houston, Texas: Gulf, 1964.

Dessler, Gary and Enzo R. Valenzi. Initiation of Structure and Subordinate Satisfaction: A Path Analysis Test of Path-Goal Theory, *Academy of Management Journal*, Vol. 20 (1977), 251–259.

Downey, H. Kirk, John E. Sheridan, and John W. Slocum. Analysis of Relationships Among Leader Behavior, Subordinate Job Performance and Satisfaction: A Path-Goal Approach, *Academy of Management Journal*, Vol. 18 (1975), 253–262.

Downey, H. Kirk, John E. Sheridan, and John W. Slocum. The Path-Goal Theory of Leadership: A Longitudinal Analysis, *Organizational Behavior and Human Performance*, Vol. 16 (1976), 156–176.

Evans, Martin G. Leadership and Motivation: A Core Concept, *Academy of Management Journal*, Vol. 13 (1970a), 91–102.

Evans, Martin G. The Effects of Supervisory Behavior on the Path-Goal Relationship, *Organizational Behavior and Human Performance*, Vol. 5 (1970b), 277–298.

Evans, Martin G. Extensions of a Path-Goal Theory of Motivation, *Journal of Applied Psychology*, Vol. 59 (1974), 172–178.

Filley, Alan C., Robert J. House, and Steven Kerr. *Managerial Process and Organizational Behavior*. Glenview, Ill.: Scott, Foresman, 1976.

Fleishman, Edwin A. Twenty Years of

Consideration and Structure, In Edwin A. Fleishman and James G. Hunt (eds.), Current Developments in the Study of Leadership. Carbondale, Ill.: Southern Illinois University Press, 1973, pp. 1–37.

Fleishman, Edwin A., Edwin F. Harris, and Harold E. Burtt. Leadership and Supervision in Industry. Columbus, Ohio: Bureau of Educational Research, Ohio State University, 1955.

Herold, David M. Two-Way Influence Processes in Leader-Follower Dyads, Academy of Management Journal, Vol. 20 (1977), 224–237.

House, Robert J. A Path-Goal Theory of Leader Effectiveness, Administrative Science Quarterly, Vol. 16 (1971), 321–338.

House, Robert J. A 1976 Theory of Charismatic Leadership, In James G. Hunt and Lars L. Larson (eds.), Leadership: The Cutting Edge. Carbondale, Ill.: Southern Illinois University Press, 1977, pp. 189–207.

House, Robert J. and Gary Dessler. The Path-Goal Theory of Leadership: Some Post Hoc and A Priori Tests, In James G. Hunt and Lars L. Larson (eds.), Contingency Approaches to Leadership. Carbondale, Ill.: Southern Illinois University Press, 1974, pp. 29–55.

House, Robert J. and Terence R. Mitchell. Path-Goal Theory of Leadership, Journal of Contemporary Business, Vol. 3, No. 4 (1974), 81–97.

Ilgen, Daniel R. and Donald S. Fujii. An Investigation of the Validity of Leader Behavior Descriptions Obtained from Subordinates, Journal of Applied Psychology, Vol. 61 (1976), 642–651.

Johns, Gary. Task Moderators of the Relationship Between Leadership Style and Subordinate Responses, Academy of Management Journal, Vol. 21 (1978), 319–325.

Kerr, Steven and John M. Jermier. Substitutes for Leadership: Their Meaning and Measurement, Organizational Behavior and Human Performance, Vol. 22 (1978), 375–403.

Kerr, Steven and Chester Schriesheim. Consideration, Initiating Structure, and Organizational Criteria — An Update of Korman's 1966 Review, Personnel Psychology, Vol. 27 (1974), 555–568.

Kerr, Steven, Chester A. Schriesheim, Charles J. Murphy, and Ralph M. Stogdill. Toward a Contingency Theory of Leadership Based upon the Consideration and Initiating Structure Literature, Organizational Behavior and Human Performance, Vol. 12 (1974), 62–82.

Korman, Abraham K. Consideration, Initiating Structure and Organizational Criteria — A Review, Personnel Psychology, Vol. 19 (1966), 349–361.

Lahat-Mandelbaum, Bat-sheva and David Kipnis. Leader Behavior Dimensions Related to Students' Evaluation of Teaching Effectiveness, Journal of Applied Psychology, Vol. 58 (1973), 250–253.

Larson, Lars L., James G. Hunt, and Richard N. Osborn. The Great Hi-Hi Leader Behavior Myth: A Lesson from Occam's Razor, Academy of Management Journal, Vol. 19 (1976), 628–641.

Lord, Robert G., John F. Binning, Michael C. Rush, and Jay C. Thomas. The Effect of Performance Cues and Leader Behavior on Questionnaire Ratings of Leadership Behavior, Organizational Behavior and Human Performance, Vol. 21 (1978), 27–39.

Mawhinney, Thomas C. and Jeffrey D. Ford. The Path-Goal Theory of Leadership Effectiveness: An Operant Interpretation, Academy of Management Review, Vol. 2 (1977), 398–411.

Miner, John B. The Uncertain Future of the Leadership Concept: An Overview, In James G. Hunt and Lars L. Larson (eds.), Leadership Frontiers. Kent, Ohio: Kent State University Press, 1975, pp. 197–208.

Miner, John B. The Management Process: Theory, Research, and Practice. New York: Macmillan, 1978.

Miner, John B. and H. Peter Dachler. Personnel Attitudes and Motivation, Annual Review of Psychology, Vol. 24 (1973), 379–402.

Mitchell, Terence R., James R. Larson, and Stephen G. Green. Leader Behavior, Situational Moderators, and Group Performance: An Attributional Analysis, Organizational Behavior and Human Performance, Vol 18 (1977), 254–268.

Nystrom, Paul C. Managers and the Hi-Hi Leader Myth, Academy of Management Journal, Vol. 21 (1978), 325–331.

O'Reilly, Charles A. and Karlene H. Roberts. Supervisor Influence and Subordinate Mobility Aspirations as Moderators of Consideration and Initiating Structure, *Journal of Applied Psychology*, Vol. 63 (1978), 96–102.

Rush, Michael C., Jay C. Thomas, and Robert G. Lord. Implicit Leadership Theory: A Potential Threat to the Internal Validity of Leader Behavior Questionnaires, *Organizational Behavior and Human Performance*, Vol. 20 (1977), 93–110.

Schriesheim, Chester A., Robert J. House, and Steven Kerr. Leader Initiating Structure: A Reconciliation of Discrepant Research Results and Some Empirical Tests, *Organizational Behavior and Human Performance*, Vol. 15 (1976), 297–321.

Schriesheim, Chester A. and Steven Kerr. Theories and Measures of Leadership: A Critical Appraisal of Current and Future Directions, *In* James G. Hunt and Lars L. Larson (eds.), *Leadership: The Cutting Edge*. Carbondale, Ill.: Southern Illinois University Press, 1977, pp. 9–45.

Schriesheim, Chester A. and Charles J. Murphy. Relationships Between Leader Behavior and Subordinate Satisfaction and Performance: A Test of Some Situational Moderators, *Journal of Applied Psychology*, Vol. 61 (1976), 634–641.

Schriesheim, Chester and Mary Ann Von Glinow. The Path-Goal Theory of Leadership: A Theoretical and Empirical Analysis, *Academy of Management Journal*, Vol. 20 (1977), 398–405.

Schuler, Randall S. Participation with Supervisor and Subordinate Authoritarianism: A Path-Goal Theory Reconciliation, *Administrative Science Quarterly*, Vol. 21 (1976), 320–325.

Sheridan, John E., H. Kirk Downey, and John W. Slocum. Testing Causal Relationships of House's Path-Goal Theory of Leadership Effectiveness, *In* James G. Hunt and Lars L. Larson (eds.), *Leadership Frontiers*. Kent, Ohio: Kent State University Press, 1975, pp. 61–80.

Sheridan, John E. and Donald J. Vredenburgh. Usefulness of Leadership Behavior and Social Power Variables in Predicting Job Tension, Performance, and Turnover of Nursing Employees, *Journal of Applied Psychology*, Vol. 63 (1978), 89–95.

Stinson, John E. and Thomas W. Johnson. The Path-Goal Theory of Leadership: A Partial Test and Suggested Refinement, *Academy of Management Journal*, Vol. 18 (1975), 242–252.

Stogdill, Ralph M. and Alvin E. Coons. *Leader Behavior: Its Description and Measurement*. Columbus, Ohio: Bureau of Business Research, Ohio State University, 1957.

Szilagyi, Andrew D. and Robert T. Keller. A Comparative Investigation of the Supervisory Behavior Description Questionnaire (SBDQ) and the Revised Leader Behavior Description Questionnaire (LBDQ-Form XII), *Academy of Management Journal*, Vol. 19 (1976), 642–649.

Szilagyi, Andrew D. and Henry P. Sims. An Exploration of the Path-Goal Theory of Leadership in a Health Care Environment, *Academy of Management Journal*, Vol. 17 (1974), 622–634.

Weed, Stan E., Terence R. Mitchell, and Weldon Moffitt. Leadership Style, Subordinate Personality, and Task Type as Predictors of Performance and Satisfaction with Supervision, *Journal of Applied Psychology*, Vol. 61 (1976), 58–66.

13 DECISION TREE AND RELATED TYPES OF LEADERSHIP THEORIES

What has now come to be called the decision tree approach in leadership theory dates back to an article published by Tannenbaum and Schmidt in 1958. The article treats how managers select or decide upon the behaviors they will use in different situations and with different subordinates. It also focuses on the degree to which these behaviors are boss-centered or subordinate-centered, i.e., participative. These same concerns, the choice of leader behaviors and the degree of participativeness, also have characterized the theories that have followed.

The most comprehensive of these theories has been proposed by Victor Vroom and various colleagues. The original work was done while Vroom was on the faculty at Carnegie-Mellon University (Vroom and Yetton, 1973); it has been expanded upon following Vroom's move to Yale. Over much the same time period, starting in the late 1960s, two other theoretical frameworks have emerged with quite similar orientations. The first is Frank Heller's work, which began at the University of California at Berkeley and has continued at the Tavistock Institute in Great Britain (Heller, 1971). The second is the vertical-dyad linkage model proposed by George Graen and various colleagues. This latter approach developed out of the author's original work in expectancy theory at the University of Illinois (Graen, 1969) and has continued at the University of Cincinnati.

VROOM'S THEORY OF PARTICIPATIVE LEADERSHIP

As with his concern with motivation and expectancy theory (see Chapter 6), Vroom's interest in leadership, and particularly participative leadership, extends back to the period of his doctoral study at the University of Michigan (1960). During this early period, and subsequently in his formulation of a decision tree theory of leadership, Vroom was influenced strongly by the thinking of Norman Maier. This influence is manifest in the distinction between sharing decisions with individual subordinates and with the subordinate group as a whole, for instance, and in the differentiation between decision quality and decision acceptance (Maier, 1970). Yet Maier's formulations do not meld into a formal, cohesive theory of leadership of the kind Vroom and his coworkers have achieved.

Tannenbaum and Schmidt – "How To Choose a Leadership Pattern"

Vroom and Yetton (1973, p. 18) comment as follows on the Tannenbaum and Schmidt article:

The most comprehensive treatment of situational factors as determinants of the effectiveness and efficiency of participation in decision-making is found in the work of Tannenbaum and Schmidt (1958). They discuss a large number of variables, including attitudes of the manager, his subordinates, and the situation, which ought to enter into the manager's decision about the degree to which he should share his power with his subordinates. But they stop at this inventory of variables and do not show how these might be combined and translated into different forms of action.

Since the Vroom and Yetton theory and the extensions that have followed build upon these views and do attempt to combine the variables and translate them into action, it is instructive to begin with the Tannenbaum and Schmidt formulations. In essence, these formulations deal with a range of leadership behaviors that a manager may draw upon:

1. The manager makes and announces the decision.

2. The manager sells his decision to subordinates.

3. The manager presents ideas and invites questions.

4. The manager presents a tentative decision subject to change.

5. The manager presents a problem, invites suggestions, and then decides.

6. The manager defines the limits of a decision the group makes.

7. The manager permits his subordinates to function within the same limits imposed on him.

Boss-centered leadership

Subordinate-centered leadership

The particular type of leadership behavior that a manager chooses to employ in a given situation depends on a variety of factors in the manager, the subordinates, and the situation itself:

Manager factors
  The manager's value system, including the value placed on decision sharing
  The manager's confidence and trust in subordinates
  The manager's basic inclination toward directive or team leadership
  The manager's security in the face of the uncertainty produced by delegation
Subordinate factors
  The level of independence needs among subordinates
  The readiness to assume responsibility of subordinates

The degree of tolerance for ambiguity possessed by subordinates

The extent to which subordinates are interested in the problem and believe it to be important

The understanding subordinates have of organizational goals and their identification with them

The knowledge and experience subordinates bring to the problem

The extent to which subordinates expect to share in decision making

Situation factors

The type of organization including, in particular, its values vis à vis participation, and the size and geographical dispersion of units

The effectiveness of the work group as a smoothly functioning team

The nature of the problem relative to the capabilities of the manager and the group

The degree to which time pressure exists, thus limiting subordinate involvement

The successful manager is defined as one who accurately and flexibly adjusts his behavior to these various situational constraints on the choice of a leadership pattern.

The Group Decision Sharing Theory

The Vroom theory differentiates between instances when, if decision sharing occurs, it will be with two or more subordinates and thus of a group nature, and cases when only a single subordinate would be involved (Vroom and Yetton, 1973). Under the group condition, the following leader behaviors are specified:

The manager solves the problem or makes the decision himself, using information available at the time (A1)

The manager obtains the necessary information from subordinates, then decides the solution to the problem himself (A2)

The manager shares the problem with relevant subordinates individually, getting their ideas and suggestions without bringing them together as a group, and then makes the decision himself (Cl)

The manager shares the problem with subordinates as a group, obtaining their collective ideas and suggestions, and then makes the decision himself (C2)

The manager shares the problem with subordinates as a

group, serves in a role much like that of a chairman in attempting to reach a consensus on a solution, and is willing to accept any solution that has the support of the group (G2)

Decision Rules.   A number of decision rules have been developed to guide the use of these leadership behaviors. The first three rules are intended to protect the quality of decisions and the last four their acceptance.

The information rule: If the quality of the decision is important, and if the leader does not possess enough information or expertise to solve the problem by himself, A1 behavior is eliminated.

The goal congruence (or trust) rule: If the quality of the decision is important and if the subordinates do not share the organizational goals to be obtained in solving the problem (cannot be trusted to base their efforts to solve the problem on organizational goals), G2 behavior is eliminated.

The unstructured problem rule: When the quality of the decision is important, the leader lacks the necessary information or expertise, and the problem is unstructured, A1, A2, and C1 behaviors are eliminated.

The acceptance rule: If acceptance of the decision by subordinates is critical to effective implementation, and if it is not certain that an autocratic decision made by the leader would receive acceptance, A1 and A2 behaviors are eliminated.

The conflict rule: If acceptance of the decision is critical, an autocratic decision is not certain to be accepted, and subordinates are likely to be in conflict or disagreement, A1, A2 and C1 behaviors are eliminated.

The fairness rule: If the quality of decision is unimportant and if acceptance is critical and not certain to result from an autocratic decision, A1, A2, C1, and C2 behaviors are eliminated.

The acceptance priority rule: If acceptance is critical, not assured by an autocratic decision, and if subordinates can be trusted, A1, A2, C1, and C2 behaviors are eliminated.

These decision rules incorporate certain of the factors noted by Tannenbaum and Schmidt, although by no means all of them; included are the importance of decision quality, the manager's level of information, the extent to which the problem is structured, the criticalness of subordinate acceptance, the probability of subordinate acceptance of an autocratic decision, the degree to which subordinates are motivated to attain organizational goals, and the amount of subordinate conflict.

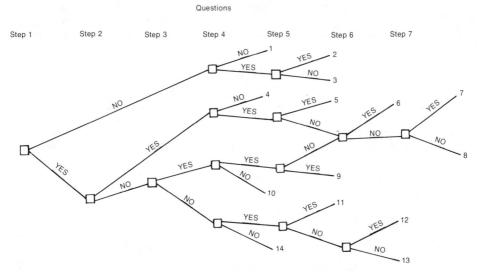

Figure 13–1. Decision tree for arriving at feasible sets of leader behaviors for different group problem types. (Adapted from Victor H. Vroom and Philip W. Yetton. *Leadership and Decision-making.* Pittsburgh: University of Pittsburgh Press, 1973, p. 188.)

Decision Trees. When the decision rules are applied, they yield a feasible set of acceptable behaviors for different types of problems. To arrive at the feasible set for a given type of problem, one answers a series of questions either yes or no. The process involved can be depicted as a decision tree. Several variants of this tree for the group situation may be found in the literature (Vroom, 1973, 1974, 1975, 1976a; Vroom and Yetton, 1973). The version given in Figure 13–1 is somewhat easier to follow than some of the others. It yields 14 problem types and requires that answers be provided for seven questions:

Step 1: Is there a quality requirement such that one solution is likely to be more rational than another?
Step 2: Do I have sufficient information to make a high quality decision?
Step 3: Is the problem structured?
Step 4: Is acceptance of decision by subordinates critical to effective implementation?
Step 5: If I were to make the decision by myself, is it reasonably certain that it would be accepted by my subordinates?
Step 6: Do subordinates share the organizational goals to be attained in solving the problem?
Step 7: Is conflict among subordinates likely in preferred solutions?

Table 13–1. FEASIBLE SETS OF LEADER BEHAVIORS FOR EACH OF 14 PROBLEM TYPES

	Total Feasible Set				
	Behavior Calculated to Minimize Man Hours Spent	*Behaviors Providing for Increasing Amounts of Team Development* $\longrightarrow$			
Problem Type					
1	A1	A2	C1	C2	G2
2	A1	A2	C1	C2	G2
3	G2				
4	A1	A2	C1	C2	G2*
5	A1	A2	C1	C2	G2*
6	G2				
7	C2				
8	C1	C2			
9	A2	C1	C2	G2*	
10	A2	C1	C2	G2*	
11	C2	G2*			
12	G2				
13	C2				
14	C2	G2*			

*Within the feasible set only when the answer to the step 6 question is Yes.

Adapted from Victor H. Vroom and Philip W. Yetton. *Leadership and Decision-making.* Pittsburgh: University of Pittsburgh Press, 1973, p. 37.

The feasible sets of behaviors remaining after the decision rules are applied are noted in Table 13–1 for each of the problem types, indicated by the numbers to the right of Figure 13–1. The behaviors specified in the second column of Table 13–1 are those that should be used to minimize the number of man hours devoted to the problem. As one moves to the right across the third column, time minimization is increasingly traded off against subordinate team development.

The Individual Decision-Sharing Theory

Like the group theory, the theory for dealing with individual subordinates specifies what kinds of manager behaviors are feasible in different problem situations; it, too, states what a manager should and should not do in a normative sense but specifically when the problem would affect only one subordinate.

The A1, A2, and C1 behaviors considered in the group theory are equally applicable to the individual situation. However, C2 and G2 are no longer appropriate, and two new behaviors become possible (Vroom and Jago, 1974; Vroom and Yetton, 1973):

The manager shares the problem with the subordinate, and together they analyze it and arrive at a mutually agreeable solution (G1).

The manager delegates the problem to the subordinate, providing him with relevant information but giving him responsibility for solving the problem (D1).

Decision Rules. With the change in relevant behaviors, certain changes in decision rules also become necessary. The goal congruence rule now serves to eliminate D1 and G1 behaviors. The unstructured problem rule eliminates A1 and A2 behaviors. The conflict rule is no longer relevant. A new rule, the subordinate information rule, indicates that if the quality of the decision is important and the subordinate lacks the information to solve the problem, D1 behavior is eliminated.

Decision Trees. The individual situation has not been depicted in a separate decision tree. However, various combined group and individual versions are available. Figure 13–2 presents a decision tree of this kind. In this instance step 7 is not relevant for individual problems, since it relates to conflict among subordinates and only one subordinate exists for the individual case. A new question is added at the end:

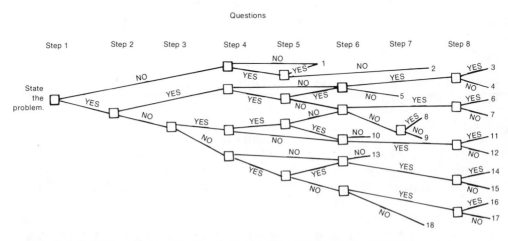

Figure 13-2. Decision tree for arriving at feasible sets of leader behaviors for different group and individual problem types. (Adapted from Victor H. Vroom and Philip W. Yetton. *Leadership and Decision-making.* Pittsburgh: University of Pittsburgh Press, 1973, p. 194.)

Step 8: Do subordinates have sufficient information to make a high quality decision?

The feasible sets for the 18 problem types noted in Figure 13–2 for individual problems only are:

1. A1 D1 A2 C1 G1
2. D1 G1
3. A1 D1 A2 C1 G1
4. A1 A2 C1 G1
5. A1 A2 C1
6. D1 G1
7. G1
8. C1
9. C1
10. A2 C1
11. D1 A2 C1 G1
12. A2 C1 G1
13. C1
14. D1 C1 G1
15. C1 G1
16. D1 G1
17. G1
18. C1

In the above listing the minimum man-hour solution is given first and the most participative behavior is given last. Although Figure 13–2 may be used with group problems, it is more cumbersome than Figure 13–1 for that purpose.

RESEARCH TESTS AND APPLICATIONS OF THE VROOM DECISION TREES

By far the largest amount of research on the decision tree formulations has been conducted by Vroom himself and those who have been associated closely with him in the development of the theory. Furthermore, the research has been primarily of a descriptive nature comparing what the models say managers should do with what they actually do. This represents a weak type of test for a normative theory. The real need is to determine whether managers do better when they follow the theory, and in this area the research evidence is limited.

Descriptive Research by the Theory's Authors

Much of the research conducted by Vroom and his colleagues has utilized managers participating in management development programs (Vroom and Yetton, 1973). These managers typically report how they would deal with a particular problem or how they have dealt with it in the past. The data are thus of a self-report nature; how a manager actually behaves in different problem situations is not known with certainty.

Recalled Problems. In one variant of the research procedure the managers were asked to select a problem from their experience that affected at least two subordinates. Data were then obtained about which of the leader behaviors specified by the theory was utilized and about the various aspects of the problem situation that go into the decision tree. The results from a comprehensive study of all theoretical variables and from an earlier, less complete, study conducted as the theory was being developed are given in Table 13–2.

The findings provide rather strong support for the view that the perceived locus of information is related to the degree of participation in the decision; to a lesser degree, decision-sharing appears to be a function of the extent to which subordinates can be trusted. The other findings tend to be equivocal except for some

Table 13–2. CORRELATIONS BETWEEN VARIOUS ASPECTS OF THE PROBLEM SITUATION AND PARTICIPATIVENESS OF THE LEADER BEHAVIOR REPORTED

	Level of Participation	
Aspects of the Problem Situation	Comprehensive Study	Partial Study
Importance of a quality decision	(.12)	−.02
Amount of leader information	(−.36)	(−.34)
Amount of subordinate information	(.43)	not measured
Degree to which the problem is structured	(−.15)	not measured
Importance of subordinate acceptance	(.24)	.02
Probability of an autocratic decision being accepted	(−.23)	not measured
Extent to which subordinates can be trusted to accept organizational goals	(.21)	(.18)
Amount of subordinate conflict	.08	−.01

(　) Statistically significant.

Adapted from Victor H. Vroom and Philip W. Yetton. *Leadership and Decision-making.* Pittsburgh: University of Pittsburgh Press. 1973, pp. 81–82.

evidence indicating that when it appears probable that an autocratic decision will be accepted, participation is less likely. Subordinate conflict does not appear to be a relevant consideration.

Standardized Problems. A second research procedure utilized a set of standardized problem situations, and the managers were asked to place themselves in these situations. The various aspects of problem situations considered by the theory and built into the decision trees were incorporated deliberately in the problems, and the managers indicated for each problem which of the leader behaviors they would choose.

One important finding was that differences in the nature of the problem situations accounted for nearly three times as much variation in responses as differences between individuals. There was a tendency for managers to choose a more or less participative style with some consistency, but the tendency to vary one's style depending on the situation was much more pronounced. In all probability this situational effect was inflated in the research over what would be found in any one actual managerial situation, because the case problems covered an atypically large range of situations. Nevertheless, the theoretical expectation that situational factors do matter is supported.

The research using standardized problems also indicates that the various situational attributes of the theory are related to level of participation in the expected manner across eight different managerial samples. Among the variables of the theory, only the quality requirement fails to yield a significant relationship sufficiently often to bring the theoretical hypothesis into question. These latter results are in general agreement with more recent data that were obtained using a somewhat improved set of standardized problems as a measure (Jago, 1978). In this recent study the quality requirement also failed to show the predicted relationship on occasion, as did subordinate conflict.

Comparisons with Normative Expectations. It is possible to make direct comparisons between what managers indicate as their behavior and what the theory calls for, using both the recalled and standardized data. When this is done the managers portray themselves as somewhat more participative and less variable in their behavior than the theory would prescribe. As indicated in Table 13–3, there is a strong tendency to avoid A1 behavior when it would be theoretically appropriate, and to a somewhat lesser extent G2 behavior; C1 behavior is clearly overstressed and so also is C2. In these comparisons the most time-conserving behavior alternative is taken as the ideal.

Table 13–3. COMPARISONS: THEORETICALLY PRESCRIBED AND PERSONALLY DESCRIBED BEHAVIORS

	Managerial Behavior				
	A1	A2	C1	C2	G2
Recalled Problems					
Theoretical expectation	27%	10%	5%	19%	39%
Behavior described	11%	9%	22%	30%	28%
Difference	−16%	− 1%	+17%	+11%	−11%
Standardized Problems					
Theoretical expectation	40%	14%	3%	23%	20%
Behavior described	25%	15%	19%	26%	15%
Difference	−15%	+ 1%	+16%	+ 3%	− 5%

Adapted from Victor H. Vroom and Philip W. Yetton. *Leadership and Decision-making.* Pittsburgh: University of Pittsburgh Press, 1973, pp. 139–140.

When the single most theoretically appropriate behavior is used in the comparison, agreement occurs in something over a third of the cases; when the whole feasible set is used, this proportion is doubled. Violation of the various decision rules is much more likely to occur with regard to acceptance than quality. The fairness rule, the acceptance priority rule, and the conflict rule are often violated; the goal congruence rule and the information rule practically never are. Thus, it appears managers are much more likely to risk implementation of a decision by subordinates than the basic quality of the decision itself.

Studies Extending to Individual Decision Sharing. While the early studies dealt with group situations only (Vroom and Yetton, 1973), more recent investigations have utilized standardized problems of both a group and an individual nature (Vroom and Jago, 1974). The results from these latter studies indicate that the individual situation elicits less participative behavior than the group. Once again situational differences were found to account for about three times as much variation on group problems as individual differences, but on individual problems this ratio jumped to 5 to 1, indicating a much greater situational impact.

In general, the findings with regard to the effects of the various problem aspects are consistent with the theory for both group and individual problems. There are, however, certain departures from theoretical expectations in the case of the importance of a quality decision on individual problems (a low quality requirement yields *more* participation) and subordinate conflict on group problems (more conflict yields *more* participation).

Agreement with the feasible set occurred 68 per cent of the time on group problems, thus replicating prior findings. It rose to 83 per cent for individual problems, wherein decision rule violation occurs predominantly with regard to the acceptance priority rule; it is quite rare for the rules designed to protect decision quality. On group problems the fairness and acceptance priority rules are again frequently violated, and the leader information rule is not. The most pronounced finding, however, is the much greater agreement with the theoretical model obtained with the individual problems.

Superior and Subordinate Perceptions. A possible problem with the methodology used in the descriptive research is that the reports of managers as to what they would do in the case situations might have little relationship to what they actually do in such situations. To investigate this hypothesis, responses to the cases were obtained from a group of managers and also from their subordinates (Jago and Vroom, 1975).

When the subordinates were asked to indicate how their superiors would respond in each situation, substantial agreement was found among subordinates of the same superior. However, the expected agreement between subordinates and superiors was not obtained. Further analysis suggested that several sources of bias existed in the subordinate descriptions, in particular a tendency to attribute behaviors to the superior that the subordinates also attributed to themselves. There was consistent underestimation of the variability of superior behavior and overestimation of the degree of autocratic behavior on the part of superiors, in comparison with the superior's own self descriptions. A similar "autocratic shift" also has been noted by Vroom and Yetton (1973) and by Jago and Vroom (1977). On the evidence this shift appears to be a function of perceptual error rather than behavioral fact.

The results of this study indicate that obtaining attributed descriptions of superiors from subordinates is a highly questionable method of determining the validity of the standardized case procedure. It may be that the problem is inherent in the use of situations not typically observed as such by the superiors or the subordinates. This line of research has neither proved nor disproved the value of the methodology used in the descriptive studies. Standardized observation of ongoing manager behavior appears to be needed. A study of this kind has been conducted but not yet published. It is described in a preliminary report as "producing favorable but nonetheless modest results" (Jago, 1978, p. 386).

Normative Tests by the Authors

The real need in validating decision tree theory is not for descriptive findings, although these can prove useful in an inferential sense, but for normative findings that tie the theoretical variables to indexes of managerial success and failure. A preliminary effort of this kind is reported by Vroom and Yetton (1973, p. 183) In this instance managers were asked to describe a situation using the recalled problems design and then to rate both the quality and the acceptance of the decision. The expectation was that decisions outside the feasible set for the problem would be rated less effective.

The results indicated a tendency for decisions within feasible sets to be viewed as more effective. However, their superiority over decisions outside the feasible set was minimal and not statistically significant. A problem in interpreting these data is that the number of decision rule violations was minimal, and the rated effectiveness level was consistently high. Thus, there was sufficient restriction of range on the criteria to make the lack of significant findings difficult to interpret. The study does not yield clear evidence one way or another. Subsequent research has attempted to overcome these difficulties (Vroom, 1976b; Vroom and Jago, 1978).

Although essentially the same procedure was used subsequently, the managers were asked to provide two stories, one successful and one unsuccessful, in order to extend the range of criterion variance. The results of this investigation, shown in Tables 13–4 and 13–5, give much greater support to the theory. This sup-

Table 13–4.   RATED EFFECTIVENESS OF DECISIONS WITHIN AND OUTSIDE THE FEASIBLE SET FOR EACH TYPE OF MANAGERIAL BEHAVIOR

		Decision Effectiveness*					
		Overall		*Quality*		*Acceptance*	
Managerial Behavior	*Type*	*Within Set*	*Outside Set*	*Within Set*	*Outside Set*	*Within Set*	*Outside Set*
Autocratic	A1	5.1	2.2	4.9	3.3	4.8	2.1
↑	A2	6.4	3.4	5.6	3.6	5.9	2.6
	C1	4.6	3.9	4.3	4.7	5.2	3.8
↓	C2	5.4	5.0	5.4	5.5	5.4	5.5
Participative	G2	5.2	2.6	5.0	2.6	5.8	4.8

*Rated on a scale from 1 (low) to 7 (high).

Adapted from Victor H. Vroom and Arthur G. Jago. On the Validity of the Vroom-Yetton Model, *Journal of Applied Psychology*, Vol. 63, (1978), p. 157.

Table 13–5. RATED OVERALL DECISION EFFECTIVENESS ON PROBLEMS INVOLVING VIOLATION AND NONVIOLATION OF DECISION RULES

Decision Rule Involved	Overall Decision Effectiveness*	
	Rule Not Violated	Rule Violated
Quality rules		
1. Leader information	(4.7	1.9)
2. Goal congruence	3.9	2.6
3. Unstructured problem	(5.2	3.2)
Acceptance rules		
4. Acceptance	(4.8	2.4)
5. Conflict	4.5	2.0
6. Fairness	(5.0	2.6)
7. Acceptance priority	(5.6	3.8)

*Rated on a scale from 1 (low) to 7 (high).
( ) Difference statistically significant.
Adapted from Victor H. Vroom and Arthur G. Jago. On the Validity of the Vroom-Yetton Model, *Journal of Applied Psychology*, Vol. 63 (1973), p. 159.

port is stronger for rated decision acceptance than for decision quality, however, and tends to be concentrated in the A and G behavior types at the extremes of the participative continuum rather than in the C behaviors (see Table 13–4). Furthermore, the analysis by type of decision rule in Table 13–5 fails to provide clear evidence substantiating the goal congruence and conflict rules.

In spite of these variations in the extent of support for the theory, the overall result is distinctly encouraging. On the other hand, the research design used leaves much to be desired. As the authors themselves recognize, there are sources of potential error and confounding in the approach employed, and additional, more sophisticated investigations are needed:

> Because the measurement of all variables is based on self-reports provided by the same subjects, there exists the possibility that reported correlations among variables could in part reflect such correlated errors. . . . Those who conduct future research to assess the validity of the Vroom-Yetton model would do well to obtain independent estimates of the decision process used, problem characteristics, and decision outcomes. If managerial perceptions are to be used, it would be highly desirable to conduct a longitudinal study in which perceptions are measured prior to the resolution of the problem and before information concerning decision effectiveness is available (Vroom and Jago, 1978, pp. 160–161).

Independent Evaluations of the Theory

Decision tree theory is relatively new, at least in a form that permits ready testing, and accordingly it has spawned little research to date beyond what the authors themselves have done. The research conducted by Frank Heller (to be discussed later in this chapter) does bear on the theory, but it was not designed as a specific test of it.

There is considerable research (much of it antedating the actual formulation of the theory) that supports the importance of the specific factors built into the theory for decision-making and leader behavior. Thus, for example, the significance of subordinate information has been demonstrated by Ashour and England (1972), and of trust and goal congruence by Rosen and Jerdee (1977). However, integrated, comprehensive tests are practically nonexistent. One exception to this conclusion is a study by Hill and Schmitt (1977) that utilized a somewhat abbreviated decision tree in a descriptive investigation of group decision-sharing. The findings generally are consistent with those previously reported from descriptive research and add further evidence of construct validity in that a rather different and much simpler measurement procedure was substituted for the standardized problems used by Vroom.

Applications and Their Value

There are two related types of applications of the Vroom version of decision tree theory that have received attention in the literature. One is merely the use of the theory to guide managerial decisions in the hope of improving both their quality and acceptance. The second involves training in the use of the theory.

Using the Theory To Make Decisions. The essential argument for applying the theory in actual managerial decision-making is that in doing so a manager will achieve more effective decisions and thus better leadership. With regard to this point the authors conclude their major normative study with the following statement:

> Using the data collected in this investigation, we can estimate that agreement with the model in all cases would have increased the number of successful decisions form 52 per cent to 68 per cent in our sample and increased the overall effectiveness of decisions from 4.45 to 5.19 (on a 7-point scale). The latter effect is due more to the usefulness of the model in enhancing decision acceptance (where the expected increase would be from 4.62 to 5.41) as opposed to decision quality (from 4.56 to 4.97). It is of course difficult to translate these estimates into economic terms. . . . Although the use of the model is no guarantee of an effective decision and evidence obtained has already suggested avenues for its improvement, its use even in the present form can be expected to reduce many of the errors to be found in current managerial practice (Vroom and Jago, 1978, p. 162).

To use the theory a manager would answer the questions at steps 1 through 7 of Figure 13–1 or steps 1 through 8 of Figure 13–2 in a yes or no manner with reference to a particular problem facing him. The selection of the particular decision tree to use would depend on whether a single subordinate or more than one was affected. Ultimately, this process yields a single problem type number. Using this number, a feasible set of decisions for the particular problem can be identified; these are the decisions that do not violate one or more decision rules. If minimizing the man hours spent on the problem (and thus the time to decision implementation) is important, one selects the first alternative in the feasible set. To the extent participation is desired and time constraints are less important, one moves to the right in the feasible set.

To facilitate carrying out this process a "black box" has been constructed with switches that may be set in either yes or no positions to describe the problem. The manager than depresses a button that illuminates lights to indicate the appropriate feasible set. The light for the least man hours alternative is the brightest, and brightness declines as one moves to the right in the feasible set (Vroom, 1973).

Leadership Training. A training program to introduce understanding and changes in a manager's leadership behavior has been developed and reported upon in various publications (Vroom, 1973, 1974, 1975, 1976b; Vroom and Yetton, 1973). To date no formal evaluation research to determine the effects of this training has been reported, although Vroom (1976b) does indicate that research of this type is in process. However, the approach used is sufficiently novel to warrant discussion.

Although the procedures used have varied somewhat over time, the Vroom and Yetton (1973) description provides an example of how the training is conducted. It starts with a general familiarization with the basic components of the theory and practice in using this information to describe oneself and others. Films are used in this phase. The participants then describe their own leadership behavior using one or another set of standardized cases. Next comes a certain amount of practice in simulated contexts in the use of different leadership behaviors, particularly G2, which is likely to be unfamiliar. Standard human-relations exercises are used to demonstrate the effects of participation on decision quality and acceptance. The normative model is then presented (including decision trees and feasible sets) and practice in using it is provided through application to another set of standardized cases.

Probably the key aspect of the training is the feedback of information on each manager's leadership style via computer print-out, utilizing data from responses to the standardized cases. A manual is provided to help in interpreting these data. The computer feedback provides answers to the following questions:

1. How autocratic or participative am I in my dealings with subordinates in comparison with other participants in the program?
2. What decision processes do I use more or less frequently than the average?
3. How close does my behavior come to that of the model? How frequently does my behavior agree with the feasible set? What evidence is there that my leadership style reflects the pressure of time as opposed to a concern with the development of my subordinates? How do I compare in these respects with other participants in the class?
4. What rules do I violate most frequently and least frequently? How does this compare with other participants? On what cases did I violate these rules? Does my leadership style reflect more concern with getting decisions that are high in quality or with getting decisions that are accepted?
5. What circumstances cause me to behave in an autocratic fashion; what circumstances cause me to behave participatively? In what respects is the way in which I attempt to vary my behavior with the demands of the situation similar to that of the model? (Vroom, 1973, pp. 79–80).

The results from the printout typically result in considerable soul searching and reanalysis of the cases. Small group discussions often are used to facilitate this process. Presumably this is the point at which change occurs, if it does occur, since the manager is inevitably under some pressure to shift his behavior toward that of others and toward the normative model.

HELLER'S THEORY AND RESEARCH DEALING WITH THE INFLUENCE-POWER CONTINUUM

A parallel development to the Vroom decision tree approach has been Heller's work on decision-sharing, primarily at top managerial levels. Although Heller's theoretical statements lack the precision achieved by Vroom, they have been adequate to guide an extensive program of research. The Heller theory utilizes a decision-sharing continuum very similar to Vroom's, but the contingency variables are only partially overlapping. Furthermore, the theory is primarily, although not entirely, descriptive rather than normative.

Theoretical Statements

To some extent the Heller theory has been evolutionary, like so many other theories in the field of organizational behavior, changing to adapt to new research findings. The first preliminary statements in Heller and Yukl (1969) were followed by a major exposition (Heller, 1971) and then certain subsequent revisions and extensions (Heller, 1973; 1976).

The Influence-Power Continuum. Originally Heller set forth a continuum with five different decision-making styles extending from very high influence and power in the superior to a similar situation for subordinates:

The manager makes the decision without discussion or explanation.

The manager makes the decision but subsequently explains it.

The manager makes the decision but only after consultation with one or more subordinates.

The manager makes the decision jointly with subordinates, usually honoring a majority view.

The manager delegates the decision, so that it is actually made at the subordinate level.

Subsequently, following up on an idea originally considered only in passing in a footnote (Heller and Yukl, 1969), the last, delegation style was subdivided into short-term delegation, in which a review of the decision occurs rather quickly, and long-term delegation, in which review and evaluation occur much later and intervention is rare (Heller, 1976). Unlike Vroom, Heller does not specifically differentiate group and individual decision-sharing.

Specific Hypotheses. A number of hypotheses are proposed to describe perceptions between superior and subordinate, and how various factors influence the choice of a decision-making style (Heller, 1971):

1. Both superior and subordinate will believe more skills are necessary in their own jobs.
2. When superior and subordinate both estimate the time subordinates would need to acquire the skills and qualities necessary to perform the superior's job, the superior's estimates will be the larger.
3. Subordinates see themselves as having more influence and power in relation to the superior's decision than the superiors do.
4. Superiors who perceive large differences in skills or skill re-

quirements between themselves and subordinates will use more centralized, less participative decision procedures than in the absence of such a skill gap.

5. A large span of control for the superior will be associated with time-saving decision styles at the extremes of the continuum, either highly centralized or decentralized.
6. Superiors whose jobs have a small degree of freedom will use a more centralized decision-making style.
7. Superiors in the line function of management, having a smaller degree of freedom than those in staff, will utilize more centralized decision-making.
8. The locus to which a decision applies (immediate subordinates, all those at any lower level, the subordinates of subordinates) will influence the superior's decision style (direction is not specified).
9. When decisions are more important to the business as a whole and to the superior than the subordinate, more centralized procedures will be used; when they are more important to a subordinate, power-sharing will be greater.
10. The greater the experience (age, tenure in position, tenure with the company) of the superior, the more centralized his decision behavior.
11. The greater the experience of the subordinate, the more the superior will utilize power-sharing styles.
12. Belief in participatory practices on the part of the superior will be associated with power-sharing.

The concern with the moderating effects of such factors as skill level, experience, and importance of the decision to the business results in some similarities between the Heller and Vroom theories. However, there are major differences as well, and the Heller hypotheses are not stated in normative form.

Expanded Contingency Specification. In more recent publications Heller (1973, 1976) has extended the list of contingency variables to cover a wide range of factors, many of them far removed from the immediate job situation. Thus, there are not only the various characteristics of the manager (experience, skill), situational variables close to the decision maker (job function, who the decision effects), and micro-structural variables (span of control, department size) but also macro-structural variables such as organization size and workflow technology, and ecological variables such as environmental turbulence and level of economic development. The specific factors listed vary somewhat from one publication to another, and directional hypotheses are not stated consistently. Macro-structural and, in particular, ecological variables rarely are measured in actual research; the theory must be considered very loose in its expanded version.

This interpretation holds equally for the stated linkage between contingency variables and normative outcomes. Other things being equal, the power-sharing methods are to be preferred because they harness more of the existing reservoir of skills in the organization, thus increasing motivation, satisfaction, and performance effectiveness. "Other things being equal" refers to the operation of the contingency variables. However, the specific manner in which these variables should moderate power-sharing to produce desired outcomes is not indicated. Thus, the normative theory is incomplete.

Research Evidence

Heller's research has utilized a variety of questionnaire measures that are administered to a dyad consisting of a senior manager and a single immediate subordinate, usually the most senior subordinate. The questionnaires measure various theoretical variables and, in particular, the overall tendency to utilize power-sharing along the influence-power continuum. Typically, the questionnaires are administered in a small group setting and the results fed back to the managers for discussion and interpretation.

The United States Study. The most comprehensive analysis of U.S. data utilized 130 managerial dyads from 15 companies located in California, the superiors being vice-presidents or major division heads (Heller, 1971). The findings consistently support the first three hypotheses of the theory relating to perceptual differences within the dyad. Contingent effects on decision-making of skill differences and span of control in line with hypotheses 4 and 5 also were obtained, and there was some support for hypothesis 6 in that general managers and personnel managers used the greatest amount of power-sharing, while production and finance managers used the least. Hypothesis 7 relating to line-staff differences was not confirmed. Decisions involving the subordinate's subordinates were more likely to be shared than those affecting the subordinate only, consistent with hypothesis 8. The predicted relationships involving the importance of decisions to the business and to the subordinate (hypothesis 9) were demonstrated. With regard to the role of experience the data are mixed; the role of superior experience is not confirmed, but the age of subordinates does operate in the expected manner. Hypothesis 12 involving a belief in participatory practices achieves little support.

The data indicate considerable variation in the degree of power-sharing for the same manager depending on the various contingent circumstances. The major stated reason for such sharing is to improve decision quality.

International Research. In recent years the research program has been extended to a number of other countries including Great Britain, the Netherlands, Germany, France, Sweden, Israel, and Spain (Heller, 1976; Heller and Wilpert, 1979). In the process measures of new variables, especially contingency variables, have been added. Thus, this research provides certain tests of the original theory while dealing with components of the expanded theory not considered in the U.S. research. Unfortunately, only partial reports have been published to date. The international research utilized well over 1000 managers from more than 100 companies.

The published findings provide further support for hypothesis 2 (that there are perceptual differences in the estimated time to learn the superior's job), hypothesis 3 (that subordinates perceive more power and influence in relation to superior's decisions), hypothesis 4 (that more centralized decision making goes with large perceived skill and skill-requirement differences), and hypothesis 8 (that the locus to which a decision applies makes a difference). In addition, the new hypotheses (that when skills and educational levels are high, decisions tend to be decentralized, and that when environmental turbulence and complexity are high, decentralization also occurs) receive support. The effects for education are quite strong; those for turbulence are much less so.

Finally, comparisons across nations indicate that differences are present. Managers from Great Britain, Germany, and Israel appear to utilize more centralized approaches, while managers from Sweden and France are more participative. When the United States data are added in, the U.S. managers appear to be in the more centralized category.

Conflicts Between Heller and Vroom. The Heller and Vroom researches both provide strong support for the view that participation is not a stable leadership style that characterizes certain managers but rather that it is a variable behavior that managers may or may not use depending on the situation. There are many other similarities between the two sets of results. However, there appears to be a discrepancy in that the Vroom data suggest that subordinates perceive their superiors as more autocratic, while the Heller findings consistently indicate a more participative perception.

Initially, these differences were attributed to measurement differentials — Vroom used group problems and Heller individual, for instance — and there were differences in the specificity of the questions as well. More recently, Vroom has interpreted these measurement differentials in a somewhat different manner and has come to accept a view much closer to that of Heller:

> ... it seems more likely that use of participative methods does increase with level and that this occurs both as a result of beliefs concerning the utility and appropriateness of participative practices, which are more characteristic of higher level managers, and differences in the nature of decisions to be made as one ascends the organizational hierarchy.
> ... A member may feel powerless when confronted with decisions that affect him but in which he did not actively participate. He may equate this feeling of powerlessness with the use of autocratic decision methods even if the actual process was highly participative but involving only levels above his own (Jago and Vroom, 1977, pp. 141–142).

In any event, the convergent nature of many of the findings from the two approaches provides strong evidence in support of both, at least at the descriptive level.

GRAEN'S VERTICAL DYAD LINKAGE MODEL

The formulations put forth by George Graen and his colleagues might appear at first exposure to differ rather sharply from those we have been considering. However, they have in common the fact that they, too, deal with differences in the way a manager behaves toward different subordinates and with the degree of participativeness characterizing this behavior. In large part Graen's ideas represent a reaction against the tendency to consider leader behaviors as averages that apply to all subordinates (or all subordinate perceptions), as was done in the early Ohio State University research on consideration and initiating structure (see Chapter 12). In developing his own alternative views, Graen appears to have been influenced by the ideas of Katz and Kahn (1966) regarding the processes of role taking in organizations and by Jacobs' (1971) conceptions of the various kinds of exchange occurring in the leadership context.

Theoretical Statements

Graen's concept of the vertical dyad refers to the relationship between a supervisor and an individual subordinate. There are as many such dyads in a work group as there are immediate subordinates to the unit's manager. For theoretical purposes two types of dyadic relationships are important. These are variously referred to as relationships with informal assistants and ordinary members (Graen, 1976), leadership and supervisory relationships (Dansereau, Graen, and Haga, 1975), in-group and out-group relationships (Graen and

Cashman, 1975), or high- and low-quality relationships (Graen and Schiemann, 1978).

The Role of Dyadic Relationships. The essential concept is that when the relationship between manager and subordinate is of the informal assistant, leadership, in-group, high-quality type, very different kinds of outcomes in terms of job performance ratings, job satisfaction (including turnover), and experienced job problems are to be anticipated. Specifically, under these circumstances performance ratings will be higher, subordinate satisfaction greater (and turnover lower), and problems with supervision fewer.

The process involved has been summarized as follows:

> ... the inputs to team development are the characteristics of each member and those of their leader. These characteristics are harnassed to outputs, such as member performance, satisfaction, and job problems, through their interactions with leader-member exchanges. Based on the compatibility of some combination of member's characteristics and some combination of leader's characteristics, a leader initiates either an in-group or an out-group exchange with his member early in the life of the dyadic relationship (Graen and Cashman, 1975, pp. 154–155).

The major early indicator of what type of relationship will subsequently emerge is the degree to which negotiating latitude is extended by the manager. When the manager is relatively open in extending individualized assistance to work through job problems, an in-group relationship is likely. Such relationships:

> ... involve interlocking different task behaviors and forming different working relationships than do out-group exchanges. Specifically, in-group exchanges will involve first, the interlocking of more responsible tasks accepted by members and higher levels of assistance provided by leaders; and second, working relationships will be characterized by greater support, sensitivity, and trust than occurs in outgroup exchanges. Furthermore, the mechanism of this interlocking of member and leader behaviors probably is reciprocal reinforcement ... once these structures emerge, they demonstrate high stability over time. Thus, until the nature of the linkage becomes altered, both member and leader behavior can be both understood and predicted over time (Graen and Cashman, 1975, p. 155).

When an in-group relationship develops, leadership occurs in that behaviors depend upon the interpersonal exchange, not formal authority. The leader gives resources at his command and the member gives expanded effort and time. The leader loses control and becomes more dependent on the outcomes of negotiations with the member, while the member risks receiving less than equitable rewards and the unilateral institution of supervision. In contrast, under an out-group relationship supervision does exist, and the employment contract with its implicit acceptance of legitimate authority in exchange for pay and benefits governs.

The in-group relationship exhibits many of the characteristics of participative decision-making and of job enrichment as well:

> The superior for his part can offer the outcomes of job latitude, influence in decision making, open and honest communications, support of the member's actions, and confidence in and consideration for the member, among others. The member can reciprocate with greater than required expenditures of time and energy, the assumption of greater responsibility, and commitment to the success of the entire unit or organization, among others (Dansereau, Graen, and Haga, 1975).

Extensions to the Model.   Recently the basic dyadic model has been extended one level upward to include the manager's superior as well as his subordinate (Cashman, Dansereau, Grean, and Haga, 1976). The hypothesis is that the nature of this manager-superior relationship (in-group or out-group) will affect the extent to which the manager can bring resources to the manager-subordinate relationship and thus exert an indirect effect on subordinate outputs such as satisfaction, job problems, termination, and the like.

A second extension relates to the matter of agreement between the manager and the dyadic subordinate (Graen and Schiemann, 1978). Two hypotheses are stated:

> If a leader and a member have a high-quality dyadic relationship, the leader should be more aware of the problems confronting the member on the job. Hence, their perceptions should be more alike regarding the severity of job problems than those of a leader and a member in a low-quality relationship.

> Another important set of variables . . . includes sensitivity of the leader to the member's job and attention, information, and support given the member by the leader . . . if the quality of the interdependencies is high, leader and member should agree more accurately about these variables than those locked into lower quality relationships (Graen and Schiemann, 1978, pp. 206–207).

Research Evidence

Initial research by Graen and his coworkers utilized the leader behavior description measures of consideration and initiating structure but employed an individual subordinate level of analysis rather than average data for each work group as in the original Ohio State studies. The nature of the analytical approach used in this research was highly consistent with the vertical dyad linkage model. However, the studies were not carried out as tests of that particular set of theoretical hypotheses; rather they test certain hypotheses related to the relative predictive power of expectancy and equity theories (Dansereau, Cashman, and Graen, 1973), to the validity of the man-in-the-middle interpretation of managerial role stress (Graen, Dansereau, and Minami, 1972b), and to the nature of performance feedback (Graen, Dansereau, and Minami, 1972a; Graen, Dansereau, Minami, and Cashman, 1973). These studies are important, nevertheless, because they represent the empirical base from which vertical dyad linkage theory subsequently developed.

Indirect Criteria of Dyadic Relationships. The next set of studies moved closer to providing specific tests of theoretical formulations without actually achieving this goal. In these cases actual measures of the quality of the dyadic relationships were not obtained, but other indexes that yielded results consistent with theoretical expectations were used to differentiate the groups studied.

Thus, in one case newly hired clerical employees at a university were differentiated into those who separated relatively quickly and those who did not. Analysis of data obtained over a period of 16 weeks indicated that there was greater role conflict and ambiguity in relationships with superiors among those who subsequently left employment (Johnson and Graen, 1973). The design of this study does not permit direct extrapolation to vertical dyad linkage hypotheses, but the relationships are consistent with them.

The same is true of another analysis of additional data obtained from the same subjects (Graen, Orris, and Johnson, 1973). In this instance the group was differentiated not by job tenure but in terms of the extent to which the individual viewed the job as career relevant. Those who did not consider the job to be career relevant tended to have more turnover, but they also evidenced less communication with superiors, including less participation in decisions, as well as other responses consistent with an out-group status.

In another case, a group of university housing and food service managers was split in terms of their degree of professionalism and studied over a nine-month period subsequent to an extensive reorganization (Haga, Graen, and Dansereau, 1974). The findings are consistent with an interpretation that describes the professionals as possessing in-group status. In particular, they appear to be engaged in a sizable amount of role-making or role-altering behavior that is entirely consistent with theoretical expectations under conditions of negotiated roles.

Direct Tests of the Theory. A subsequent analysis of data obtained from this same group of university managers is more directly supportive of the theory (Dansereau, Graen, and Haga, 1975). In this case, a measure of negotiating latitude perceived by the dyadic subordinate early in the relationship was used as a basis for differentiation. This early index of negotiating latitude proved to be a good predictor of in-group and out-group status throughout the nine months of the study. In-group members received more supervisory attention and greater support, experienced fewer job problems, perceived their superior as more responsive to their needs and as communicating with them more, were evaluated as behaving in a manner closer to superior expectations, indicated more job satisfaction, and were less likely to separate. This pattern of results is quite congruent with the theory.

A replication study with a new sample that extended the measures to include communication frequency, bases of influence, and dyadic loyalty provides further support (Graen and Cashman, 1975). Clearly the in-group members were more involved in all aspects of their work and expended greater time and effort; they influenced decisions more and were in a better position to do so. Outcomes such as rated performance, job satisfaction, and job problems were all more positive for in-group members, and as expected, dyadic loyalty and trust were greater in these exchanges.

Table 13–6 presents the data for the use of various bases of influence or power. Referent and expert power characterize the in-group exchanges, consistent with their more participative, negotiated nature. There is also some basis for concluding that coercive or legitimate (bureaucratic) influence characterizes the out-group exchanges; which of the two is characteristic appears to depend on who is doing the perceiving. In any event, these findings are consistent with the hypothesized leadership-supervision distinction.

A study by Graen and Ginsburgh (1977) partially replicates the earlier study involving the career relevance of the job (Graen, Orris, and Johnson, 1973) and extends it by investigating the quality of the dyadic relationship, in this instance as perceived by the superior, not the subordinate, as in previous studies. Although university clerical employees also were used in this study, they were not new employees. The sample is essentially the same as that used in the Graen and Cashman (1975) research.

Table 13–6. REPORTED BASES OF INFLUENCE (POWER) IN IN-GROUP AND OUT-GROUP EXCHANGES

	Superior Report		Subordinate Report	
Bases of Influence	In-Group	Out-Group	In-Group	Out-Group
Referent	(3.4	2.7)	(3.8	2.0)
Expert	(3.8	3.1)	(4.0	2.8)
Reward	3.0	3.1	3.2	2.5
Coercive	2.4	2.7	(1.7	2.7)
Legitimate	(3.5	4.0)	4.1	4.2

( ) Difference statistically significant.

Adapted from George Graen and James F. Cashman. A Role-Making Model of Leadership in Formal Organizations: A Developmental Approach, In James G. Hunt and Lars L. Larson (eds.), *Leadership Frontiers*. Kent, Ohio: Kent State University Press, 1975, p. 161.

The findings indicate that in-group subordinates were given greater amounts of sensitivity and self-determination by their superiors. They also were rated as better performers. However, the anticipated job satisfaction differences did not emerge, even though turnover was greater among out-group subordinates. Taken as a whole, the data show that the quality of the dyadic relationship is associated with work outcomes but that the career relatedness of the work accounts for additional variance.

Research on the Extended Model. A reanalysis of the original data derived from university housing and food managers (Dansereau, Graen, and Haga, 1975) extends those findings to the level of the superior's superior (Cashman et al., 1976). The data do provide some support for the view that whether a superior has an in- or out-group relationship with the person above him affects the outcomes from his dyadic relationships with subordinates. In particular, when the upward exchange is of an out-group nature, subordinates tend to perceive job problems, especially problems in bringing about change. They are also less satisfied with their rewards and the technical competence of their superior. Although the findings with regard to the impacts of higher level relationships are less pervasive than those for the immediate dyad, significant results do occur. This study did not yield the expected results for the turnover outcome, however.

A later study, also conducted within the administrative components of a university, yields similar support for the impact of the quality of the upper level dyadic relationship at lower levels (Graen, Cashman, Ginsburg, and Schiemann, 1977). However, the specific types of job problems and other factors affected are frequently quite different. These differences in results in the two settings are attributed to variations in the organizational contexts of the studies — in flux in the first instance and stable in the second.

An investigation carried out to determine whether greater perceptual agreement within the dyad was to be anticipated as a function of the quality of the relationship provides generally supportive results (Graen and Schiemann, 1978). In this case quality was measured at the subordinate level with a measure of known good reliability. Again the samples were obtained within the administrative contexts of universities and overlapped prior studies. The findings indicate that perceptual agreements are consistently less pronounced when out-group dyads are involved.

Overall, the research conducted has been quite consistent with predictions from the vertical dyad linkage model. However, once again research by individuals not associated with the development of the theory appears to be nonexistent. It would be desirable to have more research and a more diverse array of studies. The Graen research has tended to draw on a very small number of subject pools to test a much larger number of hypotheses, and it has relied heavily on university-based samples. There is therefore a need for more evidence on which to base generalization of the findings.

CONCLUSIONS

The theories and research considered in this chapter provide further support for a contingency approach to leadership, although not necessarily the same contingency approaches as were considered in previous chapters. Even within the context of participative vs. nonparticipative behaviors, which is the essential domain of these three theories, there is far from total agreement on what constitute the key contingency factors.

The difficulty with the lack of agreement generated by these contingency theories is that since they are new, research evidence to accept or dispute their contentions is minimal. Almost all the research has been conducted by the authors of the theories themselves, and even that has been so delimited in terms of method and samples as to make generalization difficult. Thus, we are left at present with some promising approaches that lack sufficient empirical substantiation.

Scientific Goals

The most advanced of the theories both in conceptual sophistication and in the amount of research conducted is the Vroom decision tree theory. The logical consistency of the theory and the precision of its statements are persuasive. Yet, in line with the inherent conservatism of scientific judgment, a decision to withhold full endorsement seems appropriate.

The most obvious problem with the research conducted on the theory is that it consistently has used perceptual, self-report data with little attempt to relate these data to independent, outside criteria (Hoffman, 1974). Even the normative research fails to utilize success criteria free from influence by the subjects. Thus, the findings may be a consequence of logic-tight processes within the managers themselves, perhaps strongly influenced by the management development experience rather than a reflection of real-world relationships. That the theory's authors are well aware of this problem does not make it go away. In the one instance when external factors were considered, and the managers' perceptions compared with those of subordinates, evidence of construct validity was not obtained. One cannot help wondering whether a study in which managers' agreement with the feasible set scores were correlated with independent measures of their on-the-job effectiveness would yield more favorable results.

A second type of problem underlying this research is considered in the following:

> ... there is a serious question as to whether the method of measurement employed in many of these studies may not overestimate the degree to which decisions are in fact shared. Basically, the research related to behavioral decision theory utilizes the perceptions of those involved. Yet it is clear from the research of Mulder (1971), and Mulder and Wilke (1970), that senior managers may attempt to share decisions without actually being able to do so because their expert power in fact determines the decision at the outset. Thus, both senior manager and subordinate may *perceive* decision sharing where indeed the decision has already been foreordained by the perceived expertise of the superior (Miner, 1975, p. 199).

This participative shift may well be accentuated by the fact that managers feel they should be more participative than they are (Jago and Vroom, 1975). The operation of processes of this kind could well account for the reported finding that the use of the model in decision-making appears to enhance decision acceptance much more than decision quality (Vroom and Jago, 1978). Subordinates respond to the attempt at participation even though in reality they have little impact on what is done.

If one nevertheless assumes some validity for the measures used, then there is support, at the descriptive level at least, for a number of the contingency variables of the decision tree theory. Only the requirements for a high quality decision and subordinate conflict fail to operate in the expected manner sufficiently often to question their contributions. Additional evidence for the roles played by leader and subordinate information and the extent to which subordinates can be trusted to support organizational goals comes from the research conducted by Heller. The Graen findings appear to fit best with the idea that trust and loyalty (and thus goal commitment) moderate leadership relationships, although there is probably more to the in-group and out-group concepts than that. The three theories, and their related research, do appear to reinforce each other to some extent in telling us something about when participation will occur. They are much less helpful in telling us when it should occur.

Of the three theories, that proposed by Heller comes closest to achieving the breadth originally envisioned by Tannenbaum and Schmidt. Yet in achieving this breadth the latest versions of that theory have become so loose and imprecise that conducting appropriate research tests is difficult, if not impossible. In addition, several of the macro variables recently introduced present severe measurement problems, and effective operationalization remains to be achieved.

The research on vertical dyad linkage theory has been questioned on much the same grounds as that on decision tree theory because of a heavy reliance on self-report, perceptual data (Cummings, 1975). To some degree this criticism is warranted. However, the perceptions of both members of a dyad are typically obtained, and convergence is reported in a number of instances. The outcome variables considered — perceived (or superior *rated*) performance, perceived problems, perceived satisfaction — are clearly not measured independently of other theoretical variables. However, turnover is not only an independent factor but also a behavioral one. Unfortunately, tests of the theory have not always included the turnover variable, and when they have the results have not always been confirming. The fact that the theory is mute regarding relationships to actual performance does serve to reduce its value.

A major limitation of the research on vertical dyad theory is that the studies bearing directly on its hypotheses all have been conducted in a university setting. The possibility that negotiated relationships may occur more frequently and play a more important role in such a setting has not been ruled out and in fact seems highly likely. Thus, generalization to business organizations is not warranted at the present time.

An additional difficulty relates to the fact that the theory indicates a range of outcome variables, and in a number of studies more than one index of each dependent variable has been utilized. This provides a very large target to shoot at, and although the various studies have invariably hit the target somewhere, they have not hit it consistently in the same places. This would appear to indicate that the incorporation of additional contingency variables (beyond the quality of the dyadic relationship) in the theory should increase the predictive accuracy. It might thus be possible to specify in advance where in the broad target of outcome measures a bullet from the theoretical gun might land.

On balance, it would appear that these theories are moving toward an effective contingency mapping of the participative leadership domain. We lack the data at present, however, to say whether any of them has done the job either accurately or completely. The old saw "more research is needed" is perhaps more applicable to these theories than to any others in this book.

Managerial Goals

Even given the fact that managers must act and scientists should wait, the problems of research support elaborated in the previous section should give a manager pause. Of the three theories only

Vroom's has been actively advanced as providing solutions to present practical problems. Graen, for instance, says the following:

> Should this model of leadership prove under further testing to provide valid descriptions of leadership processes, it may have implications for training leaders and members in team building skills. . . . the outcomes of team building may be enhanced by coaching both parties to the leader-member exchange both before and during the process. In addition it may have implications for normative models of operating. For example the decision-making model of Vroom and Yetton (1973) may need to be modified to include consideration of team structure. It may change the prescriptive decision of whether or not to let a member who holds needed information participate in a decision (Graen and Cashman, 1975, p. 163).

In contrast to this tentative note, decision tree theorists have advocated the use of their normative model and their management development program and have actively promoted application through a consulting firm. Yet evidence of the actual practical value of theory is tangential at best and nonexistent for the management development program. If the latter does subsequently prove to improve performance, the possibility that it may do so primarily by sensitizing a manager to the leader role appears high. Accordingly, comparisons with other management development approaches in a tandem type of research design should be carried out before concluding that decision tree theory is the source of the training power.

The Vroom theory has been criticized on the grounds that it stops at the level of the decision and does not proceed to skill development and application (Hoffman, 1974). Accordingly, a manager might learn how to make the right decision regarding his leadership behavior without being able to execute that decision effectively, whether the intended behavior was autocratic or participative. Certainly this is an important problem in application, although not an insurmountable one, as Maier (1970) has shown. Skill training, in both autocratic and participative modes, should be introduced along with any cognitive training.

A more difficult problem relates to whether under the stress of day-to-day activities managers actually can carry out the highly rational, conscious processes the theory requires. Doing so with hypothetical cases, stripped of personal emotional impact in an educational context far removed from the job is one thing; doing it in reality is another. This is why validation of the theory against solid criteria of managerial effectiveness is so urgently needed.

There is much in the three theories considered in this chapter that a manager may wish to extract and use as part of his or her own personal working theory of leadership behavior. The quality of a dyadic relationship, or perceived skill differences, or the importance of decision acceptance may be well worth considering in deciding what to do in a particular situation with a particular subordinate. However, none of the theories in toto appears to warrant widespread

acceptance and application yet. Our mapping of the participative
leadership domain continues, but decision tree and related theories
have not completed the task for us, or if they have we are not yet well
enough informed to know it. In all probability future theory will draw
on all three of these formulations and perhaps from the much earlier
Tannenbaum and Schmidt (1958) concepts as well. The problem is to
achieve parsimony in terms of the number of contingency variables
and to achieve simplicity of application while retaining strong predictive power.

References

Ashour, Ahmed S. and George England. Subordinate's Assigned Level of Discretion as a Function of Leader's Personality and Situational Variables, *Journal of Applied Psychology*, Vol. 56 (1972), 120–123.

Cashman, James, Fred Dansereau, George Graen, and William J. Haga. Organizational Understructure and Leadership: A Longitudinal Investigation of the Managerial Role-Making Process, *Organizational Behavior and Human Performance*, Vol. 15 (1976), 278–296.

Cummings, Larry L. Assessing the Graen/Cashman Model and Comparing It with Other Approaches, In James G. Hunt and Lars L. Larson (eds.), *Leadership Frontiers*. Kent, Ohio: Kent State University Press, 1975, pp. 181–185.

Dansereau, Fred, James Cashman, and George Graen. Instrumentality Theory and Equity Theory as Complementary Approaches in Predicting the Relationship of Leadership and Turnover Among Managers, *Organizational Behavior and Human Performance*, Vol. 10 (1973), 184–200.

Dansereau, Fred, George Graen, and William J. Haga. A Vertical Dyad Linkage Approach to Leadership within Formal Organizations: A Longitudinal Investigation of the Role Making Process, *Organizational Behavior and Human Performance*, Vol. 13 (1975), 46–78.

Graen, George. Instrumentality Theory of Work Motivation: Some Experimental Results and Suggested Modifications, *Journal of Applied Psychology Monographs*, Vol. 53, No. 2 (1969).

Graen, George. Role-Making Processes Within Complex Organizations, In Marvin D. Dunnette (ed.), *Handbook of Industrial and Organizational Psychology*. Chicago: Rand, McNally, 1976, pp. 1201–1245.

Graen, George and James F. Cashman. A Role-Making Model of Leadership in Formal Organizations: A Developmental Approach. In James G. Hunt and Lars L. Larson (eds.), *Leadership Frontiers*. Kent, Ohio: Kent State University Press, 1975, pp. 143–165.

Graen, George, James F. Cashman, Steven Ginsburg, and William Schiemann. Effects of Linking-Pin Quality on the Quality of Working Life of Lower Participants, *Administrative Science Quarterly*, Vol. 22 (1977), 491–504.

Graen, George, Fred Dansereau, and Takao Minami. Dysfunctional Leadership Styles, *Organizational Behavior and Human Performance*, Vol. 7 (1972a), 216–236.

Graen, George, Fred Dansereau, and Takao Minami. An Empirical Test of the Man-in-the-Middle Hypothesis among Executives in a Hierarchical Organization Employing a Unit-Set Analysis, *Organizational Behavior and Human Performance*, Vol. 8 (1972b), 262–285.

Graen, George, Fred Dansereau, Takao Minami, and James Cashman. Leadership Behaviors as Cues to Performance Evaluation, *Academy of Management Journal*, Vol. 16 (1973), 611–623.

Graen, George, and Steven Ginsburgh. Job Resignation as a Function of Role Orientation and Leader Acceptance: A Longitudinal Investigation of Organizational Assimilation, *Organizational Behavior and Human Performance*, Vol. 19 (1977), 1–17.

Graen, George, J. Burdeane Orris, and Thomas W. Johnson. Role Assimilation Processes in a Complex Organization, *Journal of Vocational Behavior*, Vol. 3 (1973), 395–420.

Graen, George and William Schiemann. Leader-Member Agreement: A Vertical Dyad Linkage Approach, *Journal of Applied Psychology*, Vol. 63 (1978), 206–212.

Haga, William J., George Graen, and Fred Dansereau. Professionalism and Role Making in a Service Organization: A Longitudinal Investigation, *American Sociological Review*, Vol. 39 (1974), 122–133.

Heller, Frank A. *Managerial Decisionmaking: A Study of Leadership Styles and Power-sharing among Senior Managers*. London: Tavistock, 1971.

Heller, Frank A. Leadership, Decision Making, and Contingency Theory, *Industrial Relations*, Vol. 12 (1973), 183–199.

Heller, Frank A. Decision Processes: An Analysis of Power-Sharing at Senior Organizational Levels, In Robert Dubin (ed.), *Handbook of Work, Organization, and Society*. Chicago: Rand, McNally, 1976, pp. 687–745.

Heller, Frank A. and Bernhard Wilpert. Managerial Decision Making: An International Comparison, 1979.

Heller, Frank A. and Gary Yukl. Participation, Managerial Decision-Making and Situational Variables, *Organizational Behavior and Human Performance*, Vol. 4 (1969), 227–241.

Hill, Thomas E. and Neal Schmitt. Individual Differences in Leadership Decision Making, *Organizational Behavior and Human Performance*, Vol. 19 (1977), 353–367.

Hoffman, L. Richard. Review of Leadership and Decision Making, *Journal of Business*, Vol. 47 (1974), 593–598.

Jacobs, T. O. *Leadership and Exchange in Formal Organizations*. Alexandria, Va.: Human Resources Research Organization, 1971.

Jago, Arthur G. A Test of Spuriousness in Descriptive Models of Participative Leader Behavior, *Journal of Applied Psychology*, Vol. 63 (1978), 383–387.

Jago, Arthur G. and Victor H. Vroom. Perceptions of Leadership Style: Superior and Subordinate Descriptions of Decision-Making Behavior, In James G. Hunt and Lars L. Larson (eds.), *Leadership Frontiers*. Kent, Ohio: Kent State University Press, 1975, pp. 103–139.

Jago, Arthur G. and Victor H. Vroom. Hierarchical Level and Leadership Style, *Organizational Behavior and Human Performance*, Vol. 18 (1977). 131–145.

Johnson, Thomas W. and George Graen. Organizational Assimilation and Role Rejection, *Organizational Behavior and Human Performance*, Vol. 10 (1973), 72–87.

Katz, Daniel N. and Robert L. Kahn. *The Social Psychology of Organizations*. New York: Wiley, 1966.

Maier, Norman R. F. *Problem Solving and Creativity: In Individuals and Groups*. Belmont, Calif.: Brooks/Cole, 1970.

Miner, John B. The Uncertain Future of the Leadership Concept: An Overview, In James G. Hunt and Lars L. Larson (eds.), *Leadership Frontiers*. Kent, Ohio: Kent State University Press, 1975, pp. 197–208.

Mulder, Mauk. Power Equalization through Participation, *Administrative Science Quarterly*, Vol. 16 (1971), 31–38.

Mulder, Mauk and Hans Wilke. Participation and Power Equalization, *Organizational Behavior and Human Performance*, Vol. 5 (1970), 430–438.

Rosen, Benson, and Thomas H. Jerdee. Influence of Subordinate Characteristics on Trust and Use of Participative Decision Strategies in a Management Simulation, *Journal of Applied Psychology*, Vol. 62 (1977), 628–631.

Tannenbaum, Robert, and Warren H. Schmidt. How to Choose a Leadership Pattern, *Harvard Business Review*, Vol. 36, No. 2 (1958), 95–101.

Vroom, Victor H. *Some Personality Determinants of the Effects of Participation*. Englewood Cliffs, N.J.: Prentice-Hall, 1960.

Vroom, Victor H. A New Look at Managerial Decision Making, *Organizational Dynamics*, Vol. 1 (1973), 66–80.

Vroom, Victor H. Decision Making and the Leadership Process, *Journal of Contemporary Business*, Vol. 3 (1974), 47–64.

Vroom, Victor H. Leadership Revisited, *In* Eugene L. Cass and Frederick G. Zimmer (eds.), *Man and Work in Society.* New York: Van Nostrand, 1975, pp. 220–234.

Vroom, Victor H. Leadership, *In* Marvin D. Dunnette (ed.), *Handbook of Industrial and Organizational Psychology.* Chicago: Rand, McNally, 1976a, pp. 1527–1551.

Vroom, Victor H. Can Leaders Learn to Lead? *Organizational Dynamics,* Vol. 4, No. 3 (1976b), 17–28.

Vroom, Victor H. and Arthur G. Jago. Decision Making as a Social Process: Normative and Descriptive Models of Leader Behavior, *Decision Sciences,* Vol. 5 (1974), 743–769.

Vroom, Victor H. and Arthur G. Jago. On the Validity of the Vroom-Yetton Model, *Journal of Applied Psychology,* Vol. 63 (1978), 151–162.

Vroom, Victor H. and Philip W. Yetton. *Leadership and Decision-making.* Pittsburgh: University of Pittsburgh Press, 1973.

CONTRIBUTIONS OF THEORY IN ORGANIZATIONAL BEHAVIOR

14

In the preceding chapters a variety of theories of organizational behavior have been considered one at a time, and each has been evaluated against existing criteria of theoretical soundness, research support, and practical utility. One may also ask what contributions these theories and their related research have made to understanding, prediction, and managing in various areas. Where have these theories contributed the most to our knowledge of or-

389

ganizations and the ability to influence the course they take? Which theories have produced the greatest yields in the various areas? These questions imply a comparative or relative type of approach that focuses on particular topic areas and then attempts to determine what each theory has to offer in that area.

One immediate question involves the extent to which the theories have provided a comprehensive mapping of the organizational behavior field. What domains have been studied well, inadequately, or not at all? Also, what constructs have been developed and clearly identified so that they can be used in thinking about and communicating about organizations? Are adequate measures of these constructs available for use in research and for analyzing organizations and learning about the people who work in them?

A major concern of the theories considered has been the prediction of performance. Who, under what circumstances, with what kind of leadership will do well and who poorly? Who will be reasonably satisfied and who will be dissatisfied, with all that this means for cooperative working relationships, continued job tenure, and the like? Who would profit most from preparing for and entering one type of job in a particular organizational context, and who would profit from a completely different kind of work? What supplies of talent are available in society to provide for various types of organizational needs? How can people be trained and developed or influenced in other ways to help them contribute more to organizational effectiveness; and, accordingly, how may talent shortages be overcome?

MAPPING DOMAINS

In establishing domains for the various theories, the boundary statements set forth by the theorists, are, of course, of primary significance. However, such statements do not exist for all theories, and in other instances the terrain covered does not turn out to be identical with that anticipated. Thus the research evidence, the areas in which the theory works and those in which it does not, must also be considered in reaching conclusions about domains.

The Grander Theories

Several of the theories considered have been proposed as extending across the whole field of organizational behavior and even beyond it — in fact, some are completely lacking in delimiting boundary statements of any kind. The theories of this grander type are need hierarchy, motivation-hygiene, expectancy, behavior modification, and (to a somewhat lesser degree) theory X and theory Y.

In general, it would appear that our capacity to formulate broad theories of this kind that will actually work across such a wide spectrum is not great. Within the limitations of the measures and research designs used, need hierarchy theory has characteristically failed of consistent support in any domain studied. Theory X and theory Y, which incorporate the need hierarchy formulations and focus them more specifically on hierarchic organizations, have suffered a similar lack of research confirmation. Motivation-hygiene theory has fared better at the hands of research only when the incident method is used. This might suggest that the theory applies to a somewhat narrower domain than the author envisioned. However, to use a measurement-defined domain is theoretically meaningless. The theory seems to gain what apparent support it does for reasons other than the stated motivation-hygiene formulations.

The idea of a theory applying to a smaller domain than anticipated does have some validity in the case of expectancy theory. For expectancy theory to work, contingencies must be established in a concrete manner between effective job performance and attaining favorable outcomes. It is a theory for situations involving conscious, highly rational, maximizing, hedonistic decision-making. This suggests that it is a theory for certain kinds of people who think this way, much more than for others. From an organizational standpoint the domain is one in which people are rewarded in relation to performance levels, merit increases are based on performance, recognition is given for good work, and people with ability are seen as having a promising future. Although hierarchic structures with legitimized authority would seem to provide an ideal arena for the theory to operate in, this is not a necessary condition.

Behavior modification and operant learning appear to overlap the theoretical space covered by expectancy theory, perhaps expanded by goal-setting theory, to such an extent that they cannot meaningfully be said to possess a theoretical domain of their own. Given the empirical and conceptual limitations of the behavior modification formulations, they must be considered to perform less effectively within this conjoint domain; and it is apparent that the domain, like that of expectancy theory, is much smaller than at first thought.

Theories of More Limited Domain

The remaining theories opt for relatively smaller components of the theoretical landscape, but while attempting less they generally achieve more. Typically, these theories fill a limited domain defined or definable either in terms of one or more basic motives residing in the individual or in terms of some area or aspect of work such as a set of task characteristics, or both.

Achievement motivation theory deals with three kinds of motives — achievement, power, and affiliation — although only the former two receive major attention. Achievement motivation is linked to entrepreneurial effort and performance at both the organizational and societal levels. Power motivation is linked to hierarchic management. Job characteristics theory also operates in a domain defined by motives (higher order needs) and tasks (degree of job enrichment). It may prove ultimately to be a special case within achievement motivation theory in which higher order needs are defined more specifically as achievement striving, and job enrichment is defined as entrepreneurial.

In spite of efforts to incorporate them within expectancy theory, equity and goal setting theories both appear now to cover domains definable primarily in terms of types of motives — the needs for equity and competitive striving. In both instances boundary statements related to work areas or tasks are lacking, and research has not as yet charted the true limits of application. The origin of both theories in laboratory studies provides another parallel. It is possible that these two theories may be much more closely allied than at first appeared evident.

The various leadership theories considered all introduce a set of contingency variables that operate as boundary statements. In most cases they deal with leader behaviors rather than leader motives, and it is not entirely clear what kind of transformation might be used to convert the behavioral statements to a motivational calculus. LPC, however, is not a behavioral variable, although the uncertainty surrounding it makes a clear domain definition impossible. The theories of Vroom, Heller, and Graen all deal somewhat narrowly with degrees of participative or closely related behavior; they could be fitted into the broader framework of path-goal theory, but how they relate to the contingency theory of leadership remains unknown because of the lack of knowledge regarding LPC. The concern with conscious, rational decision-making also gives path-goal and decision tree theories considerable commonality.

These leadership theories deal with a wide range of contingency variables. Unfortunately, each theory tends to develop or utilize its own measures of these variables. For this reason, as well as a lack of comparative research, a parsimonious telescoping has not occurred. It seems likely that such telescoping will become possible, as for instance with the various statements related to task structure. Also, there is a high probability that many of the contingency variables will prove extraneous for most purposes. The early statements of Tannenbaum and Schmidt and the more recent ones by House and Heller resemble taxonomies of possible contingency variables more than they resemble theoretical statements.

The Unmapped Landscape

The tendency for motivational theories to utilize motivational variables and leadership theories to focus on behavior has created an artificial barrier between the two, to the detriment of both. It would be highly desirable to fill in the blanks so that each theory is stated at both the motivational and the behavioral levels. In this way overlapping domains could be recognized more clearly, and limited domain theories could be combined more easily to move back toward the arenas of the grand theories. What are the motives behind consideration behavior and the behaviors associated with power motivation in a leadership context? What behaviors and motives relate to LPC? Even when hypotheses of this type have been developed, they have tended either to prove relatively unfruitful or to have spawned insufficient research.

Also, there has been a much greater emphasis on charting the domain of conscious, rational decision-making than on unconscious, nonrational (at least from the organizational viewpoint) processes. Presumably, this is because problems of measurement appeared easier to surmount in the rational domain. Some theories deal only with conscious processes, some with conscious and unconscious, but none primarily emphasizes the unconscious as does psychoanalytic theory in the field of psychopathology. Among the major theories in the organizational behavior field, this is a clear gap that needs filling.

Finally, the limited domain theories tend to apply either explicitly or implicitly to contexts in which legitimate, hierarchic authority operates in some form (or should operate). Equity theory, for instance, assumes a source creating (primarily pay) inequities, and contingency theory of leadership introduces position power, presumably derived from hierarchic status. Yet, there are other ways of organizing human work, notably the professional and group-centered approaches. Our theories at the micro level, dealing strictly with organizational behavior in such terms as motivation and leadership, have largely ignored these domains. Extensions beyond the hierarchic form have occurred only with entrepreneurship. There is a large, uncharted area remaining for the theorist.

ESTABLISHING CONSTRUCTS

It has not proved easy to develop constructs of known, satisfactory validity in the field of organizational behavior. Problems have often arisen because of imprecise and inadequate definitions of constructs. There have been numerous instances in which constructs have not operated in the anticipated manner when inserted into research. Although problems of measurement and construct validity are often so closely intertwined that they cannot be separated, there is still sufficient independent evidence that all of the theories suffer somewhat from problems of construct definition.

The Theories with More Valid Constructs

Although some questions exist regarding the achievement motivation theory constructs (based on the lack of correlation between TAT and other measures), there is good reason to believe that the non-TAT measures may fail to tap the constructs set forth in the theory. However, research does not support the hypothesized roles of either independence training for male children, or Protestantism in the development of achievement motivation — thus introducing a need for modifications in the construct. Other constructs of the theory receive considerable support, especially the specification of the factors inherent in a situation that arouses achievement motivation. Research on the various types and stages of power motivation has not yet progressed to where the exact nature of these variables can be specified. There is better evidence as to the fear of failure–achievement motivation differentiation.

Goal setting theory predicts that the performance effects of knowledge of results, time limits, and monetary incentives can be accounted for in terms of implicit goal setting; such predictions to related phenomena give considerable meaning to the goal setting construct. Overall, the research results tend to support the idea that goal setting often is implicit in these phenomena. Although goal setting does not account for all of the variance, the fact that these extrapolations work at all injects considerable confidence in the underlying validity and power of the goal setting construct.

Of the leadership theories, the decision tree approach of

Vroom and the vertical dyad linkage model of Graen appear to have faced the fewest difficulties in defining constructs, although both have been criticized in this respect. The Vroom problems appear to be more in measurement than in construct specification per se. Graen has not been entirely consistent in operationalizing the in-group and out-group constructs (using superior and subordinate perceptions interchangeably), but overall the research relationships do tend to support the validity of his theoretical constructs.

Theories with Construct Validity Problems

The remaining theories have all suffered at one time or another from serious construct validity problems, although in many instances these theories have generated constructs that have proved to be very useful in thinking about and studying organizations. The problems that path-goal theory has experienced may be more historical than current. The construct confusion surrounding the consideration and initiating structure variables clearly hampered the early development and application of theory. More recently, House has approached these problems by differentiating supportive, participative, instrumental, and achievement-oriented leader behaviors. This appears to be a definite theoretical advance. However, research evidence establishing construct validities with full confidence is not yet available.

Job characteristics theory also appears to be in the process of redefining constructs to achieve greater precision and validity, although it has not yet advanced as far as path-goal theory. The growth need moderator does not operate to produce clear predictions. However, the characteristics of enriched jobs and of the achievement situation are so similar that one would expect that the use of a component of the global growth need variable, achievement motivation, might produce more substantial differentiations. The data that are available tend to support this conclusion, suggesting that growth need strength works largely because it incorporates the achievement construct.

Of the job satisfaction moderators, satisfaction with coworkers and with supervision appear to receive the greatest support, apparently because they relate to the disruption of the enrichment-outcome relationship. If so, direct measures of socially stimulated anger and anxiety should yield cleaner moderating effects and a more precise construct definition.

Finally, there is a serious question whether autonomy is an adequate representation of the psychological state of experienced responsibility and whether it differs from skill variety. The existence of skill variety almost guarantees autonomy from supervision, and thus the two constructs may not be meaningfully separable. Experienced responsibility would thus be better represented by a dimension concerned with the opportunity to attribute results to one's own efforts.

Equity theory also suffers from a need to redefine constructs, but progress here has been minimal. It seems increasingly apparent that the central construct of the theory should be equity motivation or perhaps two constructs involving guilt or shame reduction and anger or hatred reduction. This would tend to make it a content theory rather than the process theory it usually has been called.

There has been considerable controversy about the experimental results being a consequence of inequity or insecurity, and studies by Adams and others have adduced evidence on this. It now appears that inequity alone can produce the hypothesized results, although insecurity may well have been an added factor in the early studies.

Some attention has been given to individual differences in responsiveness to inequitable circumstances, primarily pay inequity. Those who are strongly responsive to inequity stimuli turn out not to be risk takers and gamblers but may be high on achievement motivation. The need exists for greater knowledge of such people, and thus of the construct. Furthermore, the theory lacks precision regarding what factors operate as inputs or as outputs under what circumstances and how different individuals reduce inequity in a given instance. Without direct measures of equity-related variables, the central constructs of the theory tend to remain cloudy.

Similar construct validity problems plague expectancy theory. Different measures of what is supposed to be the same construct often do not correlate well. The problem may derive in part from the multiple versions of the theory, but also it is due to a general tendency toward loose formulations that permit bending the theory to handle unexpected results. There is a need for more precise theoretical definitions of constructs, especially that of expectancy.

Within need hierarchy theory, the self-actualization construct is often described by Maslow in philosophical, even mystical, terms. This makes it very difficult to determine the real nature of this variable. There is reason to believe that many of the measures developed have not coincided with what Maslow meant. Also, Maslow's own efforts at measurement in this area were singularly unsuccessful, in part at least because there are some logical inconsistencies among his own statements regarding it. One of the key variables of the theory thus remains very uncertain in meaning even now. However, other motivational variables specified have proved to be very useful in conceptualizing human motivation in organizational contexts.

Need hierarchy theory's problems with the self-actualization construct also plague theory X and theory Y. However, the conceptual confusion is extended in this instance because value and scientific constructs are mixed, and construct definitions are not stated consistently. Much the same situation exists in motivation-hygiene theory. The use of the self-actualization concept and the tendency to describe aspects of the theory in somewhat vague philosophical, often biblical terms cloud the meanings of constructs. In addition, there is some equivocation on the true position of pay in the theory. However, the major problems of a construct validity nature in motivation-hygiene theory relate to the fact that the incident method and other approaches do not yield the same results. As a result, one must question whether the motivators and hygienes operate as specified by the theory.

The long history of construct validity problems surrounding LPC need not be repeated. We still have a measure without a clear conceptual base, although recent evidence that multiple constructs are confounded in the measure opens up new theoretical ground. Also, the situational favorableness dimension suffers from the confusion over what occurs beyond octant 8, what contingency variables should be incorporated beyond the basic three, and what the true meanings of the three are — whether position power includes personal power, for instance. Being as close to empirical generalization as it is, contingency theory of leadership often predicts without generating understanding. As a result, problems of construct validity are paramount.

Finally, behavior modification theory faces a problem unique to its approach to theory construction; it might be called a problem of nonconstruct validity. According to radical behaviorism, there are no internal constructs. Yet, one can ask whether this black box approach is not a misinterpretation of the facts, whether the nonconstructs are not really constructs. In a number of respects the research results from behavior modification do parallel those from intentional goal setting very closely — in particular the decrease in performance effects over time and the negative effects on performance in interacting jobs. Furthermore, a number of the reported performance effects from behavior modification programs occur in a considerably shorter time span than that required for operant learning. Expectancy theory or goal setting theory can explain these rapid changes; behavior modification theory cannot.

When dealing with complex organizational contexts, behavior modification theorists (even some who profess a radical Skinnerian orientation) often do invoke internal constructs. This occurs particularly with modeling or imitation and self-control. Such constructs are introduced to deal with the fact that full reinforcement histories are, in a practical sense, impossible to obtain for mature working adults. Yet, some alternative method of representing these forces is required. It appears that the nonconstructs of the radical theory are frequently constructs after all, and that in this highly unusual sense construct validity (or nonconstruct validity) is not obtained.

Changing Constructs

Clearly, we do have some solid constructs on which to build in the field of organizational behavior — a variety of content motives, goal setting, participative behaviors, and in-group and out-group relationships, to name a few. However, there is a pronounced tendency for theoretical constructs to evolve, differentiate, or change in some manner as a theory is exposed to research. This tendency is particularly pronounced when the theory's original constructs were derived from some other source, perhaps a pre-existing theory or a previously developed measure. Examples are the ultimate differentiation of higher order need strength in job characteristics theory to focus on achievement motivation and House's alterations in the original Ohio State formulations regarding leader behaviors.

These and other examples suggest that theorists in the field may be relying too heavily on historically important constructs (and measures) that have in fact outlived their usefulness. When one is engaged in the difficult mental processes of theory formulation it is easy to fill in the blanks with constructs from another theory or with constructs for which measures already exist. Yet later on these constructs may need to be drastically revised to handle the research results and new measures created. This argues for the precise defining of *new* constructs at the outset, even though this may force a long and laborious process of measure development before research to test the theory can be conducted.

CREATING MEASURES

The field of organizational behavior has been relatively successful in evolving measures of its constructs, given the fact that it has had such a short history.

Availability and Appropriateness of Measures

Most theorists of recent origin have generated measures of key constructs rather quickly. This was not true of certain older theories such as need hierarchy and theory X and theory Y; the resulting stifling of research or, at best, delay in its conduct was clearly unfortunate, in that uncritical acceptance, which subsequently proved to be unwarranted, occurred.

A much greater problem currently is the tendency for measures not to operationalize fully an underlying construct or, for important constructs of the theory, to remain unmeasured in spite of the availability of measures for other constructs. The matter of incomplete (or perhaps somewhat off center) operationalization has been a major problem in leadership theory. It turns out that existing consideration and initiating structure measures did not measure exactly the leader behavior variables of path-goal theory; self-reports to standardized stimuli are not the same as the actual behaviors of managers in the work place specified by decision tree theory; and the measures that finally developed related to theories X and Y do not permit other alternatives (including nonstereotyping responses), even though McGregor said such alternatives exist.

In the motivational area there has been a tendency to utilize self-report measures operating entirely at the conscious level, even though the constructs of the theory include unconscious components. This has been a particular problem with need hierarchy theory, and it appears to explain why projective and self-report measures of achievement motivation theory variables have not correlated well; the projective measures appear to be most appropriate to the theory.

For behavior modification theory the basic measurement need is to obtain precise behavioral measures of the central performance variables during a baseline period and under conditions of contingent reinforcement. This is much easier for manual work than for professional and managerial positions, and primarily for that reason applications and research have tended to focus on lower level positions. In any application of the theory there is always a risk that ease of measurement rather than centrality of the variable will determine what performance factor is reinforced; as a result, little if any job-related change may occur. Thus, here too, measurements can well be off-center in terms of theoretical specifications.

Such off-center measurement of the dependent variable is particularly characteristic when the measures are all taken at the same time from the same person under self-report conditions, thus permitting response bias to enter. Of the various measures, the critical incident method used in testing motivation-hygiene theory and the standardized problem approach used with decision tree theory seem most susceptible to this source of error.

The problem of insufficient operationalization of theoretical constructs appears to be most pronounced when the theory has been tested primarily in the laboratory setting. Thus, job characteristics theory with a complex array of constructs has still produced a corresponding set of measures. Equity theory, on the other hand, has not generated the measures of inequity tension, prevailing strength of equity motivation, inequity thresholds, and inequity tolerances that are needed to move the theory forward at the present time. Similarly, goal setting theory lacks indexes of theoretical constructs such as values and emotional reactions. Accordingly, research related to these aspects of the theory is practically nonexistent.

Yet, the failure to measure all theoretical variables is not restricted to theories tested mostly in the laboratory. Need hierarchy theory, for instance, has never produced any direct measures of cognitive and aesthetic needs. And Heller's recent expanded list of contingency variables influencing the use of participation contains a number of unmeasured constructs.

Reliability

The theories have been surprisingly diverse in the extent to which reliable operationalizations of variables have been developed. Job characteristics theory measures, the critical incident approach to measuring motivation-hygiene variables, and the indexes of vertical dyad linkage constructs provide examples of good reliability; so, too, does LPC, once certain problems of stability over time are eliminated.

The TAT measures used with achievement motivation theory, however, have not exhibited good test reliability, in spite of very satisfactory scorer reliabilities, suggesting that more items are needed. Expectancy theory variables, too, often have been measured unreliably, even though it is now clear that good reliabilities can be obtained with adequate attention to this factor. Variations in reliabilities of measures used within a single study present a special problem in that the relative contributions of the different theoretical variables cannot be determined. In general, problems of unreliability appear to be closely related to the use of excessively short measures or to ambiguity in the definition of the underlying construct.

Changing Measures and the Cumulative Nature of Research

A final problem relates to the use of the different measures of the same construct in studies that differ on a number of other parameters. The use of different measures in this manner when other factors remain the same, thus approximating a replication, can contribute valuable information regarding construct validity. But when a number of factors vary, including the measures, it is impossible to account for variations in results. Thus, the cumulative nature of the research becomes questionable; to have additive research data, one must hold the measurement process constant.

This consideration has been noted in questioning the combining of nonsignificant results from a variety of sources to evaluate the contingency theory of leadership. The measures of contingency theory variables keep changing to a point where older findings simply cannot be added to the newer ones without better evidence of the comparability of measures than currently exists. Path-goal theory, also, suffers from this phenomenon in its research, as does expectancy theory. In contrast, much of the laboratory research on equity theory and goal setting has systematically varied measures while holding other design factors constant for the specific purpose of establishing the validity and generality of constructs.

Certainly a comparison of the knowledge generated by theories that have utilized the same measures across many studies, or measures of known high comparability, with that generated by theories with varying measures argues strongly for the former approach. Measures should be established, studied, and perfected before moving on to substantive research. To continually tinker with measures that were used originally before they were ready to become operational seriously undermines the value of research programs. There is ample evidence in this book to substantiate this fact.

PREDICTING PERFORMANCE

From a pragmatic viewpoint, the most important requirement of a theory is to predict performance in one of its aspects. Although several of the theories considered do not explicitly state performance prediction as a goal, all have been tested against this criterion merely because of its significance.

Instances When Performance Has Not Been Predicted

Very little has been done to test need hierarchy theory's predictions regarding performance. One would anticipate that the particular needs that are independently established as providing the predominant motivational force for an individual at one time would be most closely associated with performance, and that higher order needs would generally be better predictors than lower ones. The sparse evidence available in this area tends to be nonsupportive, but it is insufficient.

One tangential approach to the problem is through the research on theory X and theory Y. The performance-related research in this instance also is limited, but what has been done supports neither the superiority of the theory Y concept of leadership nor the need hierarchy formulations.

Another tangential approach is through the research on job characteristics theory, since higher order need strengths are used as a moderator in that theory. However, predictions from job characteristics theory to job performance have been relatively ineffective. Quantity of output is actually not incorporated in the theory, although it has been included in actual tests. It makes little difference; the performance results are not impressive. If one moves back a level to intrinsic motivation (force), the findings are much more encouraging, although in some cases they may be enhanced by a bias produced by common method variance. There is little reason to believe that need hierarchy theory or theories that incorporate it, either in part or as a whole, have much value in predicting performance per se.

This same conclusion extends to motivation-hygiene theory. Studies of performance relationships have all included a potential for response bias; independent measures of performance have not been employed. Furthermore, even these relationships are better explained in terms of direct satisfaction-dissatisfaction associations rather than through the motivator and hygiene constructs. Studies of job enrichment interventions are often invoked in favor of the performance-relatedness of the theory, but it is not at all clear how job enrichment ties back to the theory and in any event it has nothing to do with the hygiene aspects. It is apparent that the theory has not demonstrated a capacity to predict performance.

The other major theoretical framework that has not demonstrated a capacity to predict performance is the decision tree approach to leadership. Here, however, the lack of relevant research is so great that no real conclusions can be drawn. Decision tree theory itself has not been tested using independent performance measures, and the Heller theory has not been related to performance in any form. Vertical dyad linkage theory has demonstrated some predictive power in relation to supervisor rated performance, but the theory itself predicts bias in these ratings, and independent measurement of true performance has not been attempted.

Effective Predictors and Delimiting Conditions

The remaining theories have proved successful in predicting performance although, typically, not under all circumstances. In general, one cannot help feeling more confident of the predictive power of the motivational theories than of those in the realm of leadership.

Achievement motivation theory has proved quite effective in guiding research on the relationship between achievement motivation and entrepreneurship, entrepreneurial success, and societal economic development. Consistent evidence of positive relationships with organizational and societal performance criteria has been developed. The record with regard to the hypothesized role of socialized power motivation in business management performance is less strong, in part because the theoretical differentiation between personalized and socialized power is of recent origin, and sufficient research has not yet evolved. The theory overall has not yielded good predictions for females, but this can be explained because these predictions have been attempted outside the domain.

The evidence that both overreward and underreward inequity can have the hypothesized effects on the quality and quantity of performance is convincing. There is a question as to how long these effects typically last before being corrected by cognitive manipulations, but the data indicate that they can last at least a week. In all probability, under appropriate circumstances, they can last much longer. There certainly are studies that have failed to obtain the hypothesized performance effects, but inadequacies of conceptualization and design are sufficiently apparent in these instances to explain the results. On balance, the theory does seem to predict performance, at least over short periods of time.

Goal setting theory predicts performance levels relatively well but not for everyone and not under all circumstances. Generally, goal specificity, goal difficulty, and participation in goal setting are related positively to performance but not for all persons. Apparently, Locke obtained consistently positive results in his studies largely because he used college students as subjects and because the assigned goal approach he used works best with such a group.

There is also evidence that positive performance effects are contingent on independent (rather than on interacting tasks) in which coordination of effort is not required. Individual goal setting in a top management team can create problems. Also, the motivating effects of difficult goals have a distinct tendency to dissipate over time, and specific efforts are required to reactivate them.

A large number of investigations have attempted to predict performance criteria from expectancy theory variables. The early research produced support for the theory but not very strong support. More recently, with certain improvements in design and measurement, much more impressive results have been obtained. These improvements include using short lists of outcomes generated individually by subjects, analyses of the data within subject rather than between subjects, and conducting research that falls squarely within the domain of the theory using consistently reliable measures.

There is ample evidence that contingent reinforcement as utilized in behavior modification influences performance. However, such findings are equally derivable from expectancy theory. Where the two theories depart, with expectancy theory emphasizing continuous reinforcement and behavior modification theory variable reinforcement, and especially variable ratio reinforcement, the data support the expectancy theory formulations. In the organizational context, continuous reinforcement is much more powerful than behavior modification theory presumes.

In general, behavior modification techniques appear to work best in improving performance in highly controllable contexts and with variables of an independent and separate nature such as absenteeism. In more complex situations involving quantity-quality interactions and interdependent tasks, they work less well. Efforts to use them in quality control have not been successful. There is also evidence from a number of broad scale applications in organizations that performance effects tend to peak and then taper off over a time.

The problem with the leadership theories is that they seem to work at some times but not at others. Contingency theory of leadership yields causal predictions to performance only in octants 1, 4, 5 and 8, and even in these cases the evidence is mixed. Similarly, path-goal theory yields very unstable results. In fact, the Evans version must be considered not well supported at all in the performance area. The House version has yielded predictions of performance only with regard to supportive and instrumental leadership, and even then the causal impact of leader behavior may not be large.

Overall, we can be confident that certain motivational theories—achievement motivation, equity, goal setting, and expectancy, in particular — can prove useful in predicting performance, and that performance can be predicted also from leadership theories, although we are less certain as to when and how. It is equally evident that these predictions are severely restricted by the domain of the theory and apply to certain individuals under certain circumstances. There is no such thing as a general theory of performance at present, and there is little reason to believe one will emerge in the near future.

PREDICTING WORK SATISFACTION

A number of the theories are not concerned with satisfaction or related outcomes, and the research has been so guided by the theoretical hypotheses that practically no predictions of satisfaction have been attempted from the theories. The epitome of this situation is provided by behavior modification theory, which does not view internal, mental states such as satisfaction as appropriate for scientific study at all. It is not surprising, given this theoretical orientation at least on the part of the radical behaviorists, that behavior modification theory has not been used to predict work satisfaction.

A similar tendency to neglect work satisfaction characterizes several of the leadership theories, particularly contingency theory and decision tree theory, including the work of Heller. It would be useful to determine whether these theories predict work satisfaction, but their general thrust tends to preclude such research.

Successful Prediction

The lack of concern with satisfaction also characterizes achievement motivation theory, and the accumulated research reflects this emphasis. However, there are some data indicating that satisfaction measures may be predicted from the variables of the theory. For instance, the limited confirmatory research in the area of power motivation has dealt primarily with measures related to work satisfaction.

In the leadership area and in motivation theory, predictions of satisfaction, when made, have tended to be better than predictions of performance. Often this has been attributed to common method bias rather than to true differences in the two outcomes. It is evident, for instance, that motivational effort or force tends to be better predicted than performance, and that effort or force measures also may be characterized by greater response bias of this kind. However, satisfaction is better predicted than turnover and absenteeism, both of which are independent behavioral concomitants of dissatisfaction at work. Thus, the pattern of results may be more a matter of the theoretical distance between independent and dependent variables than of measurement-based biases. This conclusion is reinforced by the findings from studies in which opportunities for response bias seem to have been effectively eliminated.

In the leadership arena satisfaction does appear to have been predicted with at least some consistency, when the theory anticipates it. This is particularly true of path-goal theory and of vertical dyad linkage theory, although there are more problems in predicting turnover. Theory X and theory Y also show some relationship to satisfaction variables, although the direction of the causal arrow is not clear.

The best predictions of satisfaction have come from expectancy and equity theories. The research on expectancy theory has tended to emphasize performance factors more than work satisfaction, but when satisfaction has been studied it often has been effectively predicted. Overreward inequity has been shown to produce dissatisfaction as a continuing state. The same is true of underreward inequity; in addition, underreward has contributed to a propensity to separate from the organization, to actual separation (in subsequent studies), and also to increased absenteeism. There are even instances when inequities have resulted in refusal to participate in laboratory studies and severely disruptive behavior within the context of such studies. The data give strong support to equity theory in the area of work satisfaction.

Less Certain Results

In contrast with performance, need hierarchy theory has spawned a sizable amount of research dealing with satisfaction variables. The results of this research are quite mixed, but the tendency in many studies to utilize measures of higher order needs that are not yet engaged or activated for the subjects raises questions regarding the theoretical relevance of a number of the investigations. More appropriately designed longitudinal studies focusing directly on the prepotency of need categories in the hierarchy consistently have failed to support the theory. In general, it would appear that need satisfaction can be an important contributor to satisfaction at work but not necessarily in accordance with Maslow's hierarchic processes.

Given these results from tests of the Maslow hypotheses, one might anticipate somewhat better support for job characteristics theory in the area of satisfaction. Indeed, predictions of satisfaction measures have been much more successful than those for performance, and although common method variance is on occasion a problem, there are a number of instances when it is not. Satisfaction-related variables such as actual absenteeism statistics are predicted less well. Turnover, which is included in the basic statement of job characteristics theory, has hardly been studied at all. It appears that when dissatisfaction is really pervasive, not even job enrichment can alleviate it. The hypothesized organizational climate moderator (organic-mechanistic) has been studied only in relation to satisfaction and has not produced results matching the theory.

In many respects motivation-hygiene theory also appears much stronger as a predictor of satisfactions. The results obtained using the incident technique often support the theory. However, opportunity for growth, which should be a self-actualizing motivator, is a source of dissatisfaction just as often. Pay, interpersonal relations, status, and security are not just sources of dissatisfaction — they are just as frequently contributors to satisfaction. In certain groups some of them may well be predominantly so. Achievement and the work itself are found repeatedly to be sources of dissatisfaction as well as satisfaction. Furthermore, there is considerable reason to believe that even the confirmatory results are method bound. Defensiveness clearly contributes to the tendency to attribute dissatisfaction to hygiene factors. Given the findings, it is not possible to conclude that the two-factor concept provides a valid formulation even of the work attitude relationships that are generally considered the central focus of the theory.

As opposed to the preceding theories characterized as producing uncertain results, goal setting theory suffers primarily from a lack of research rather than from any disconfirming evidence. Although the theory is explicit in its statements that dissatisfaction is a consequence of discrepancies between performance and either goals or values, relatively little reserach has been done on these hypotheses. What exists has been done by Locke and is confirmatory, but there is a need for more investigation, especially since the research has consisted entirely of laboratory studies.

Given the fact that consistent relationships between satisfaction and performance variables are not found in the literature, the tendency for certain theories, such as expectancy and equity, to predict both is not entirely expected. It would appear from the evidence that we need not develop separate theories for each type of outcome variable; a single theory can handle both. Therefore, it seems entirely possible that certain of the theories developed to focus on a particular outcome, most typically performance, may in fact be capable of predicting both types of outcomes. It would be valuable to extend the research in this regard.

GUIDING VOCATIONAL CHOICE

The theories considered in this book have been devoted much more to the processes of operating organizations than to guiding individual actions. This is to be expected, given the level of aggregation at which organization study operates. As a result, concern with individual vocational or organizational choice has not been extensive; there are many other theories that focus on this matter exclusively and that do not fall within the purview of organizational behavior. Nevertheless, some of the theories discussed do speak directly to the matter of vocational choice.

Theories Bearing on Vocational Choice

Perhaps the best example of a theory dealing directly with vocational choice is expectancy theory. Vroom's original formulation contained explicit propositions dealing with vocational choice, performance, and satisfaction. The research on vocational choice has not only been sizable in volume but has also yielded predictions more consistently and generally at a higher level than those for either performance or satisfaction. Often nonexpectancy theory variables such as peer and family pressures have been added into the predictor sets in these studies with quite favorable results. This very fact, however, appears to underline the limited scope of expectancy theory itself.

Achievement motivation theory also has been a major source of research. The primary data involve relating achievement motivation scores to occupational choices, such as the choice of an entrepreneurial role. There also is evidence that high achievement motivation people make quite realistic occupational decisions, whereas high fear of failure individuals do not; the latter carry their avoidant tendencies into the choice process itself and do not obtain needed information. There is other evidence that children from entrepreneurial families tend to develop high achievement motivation that then conditions their own occupational decisions. Considerable research has been done in the vocational area related to the theory, generally supporting it.

Studies explicitly designed to investigate the implications of need hierarchy theory for vocational choice are lacking, in spite of the fact that the theory has been used as a factor in the classification of occupations. On the other hand, the theory has generated a considerable amount of research which, although often not providing a true test of theoretical hypotheses, does indicate how the variables relate to such factors as managerial level, line-staff status, company size, and the like. This research can prove useful entirely independent of the theory.

Job characteristics theory also has generated some research on vocational choice, although less than might be anticipated. There is evidence that those with high, unsatisfied growth needs prefer enriched jobs rather than job change. The theory appears to offer considerable potential for studying vocational choice, particularly if it proves feasible to integrate it more fully with achievement motivation theory. However, this potential remains relatively unexploited at present.

Theories Not Concerned with Choice

The remaining theories are not directly concerned with guiding vocational choice and have not typically spawned research in this area, although some would appear to offer potential.

The two theories furthest removed from this question appear to be behavior modification and motivation-hygiene. For the former the term "choice" is antithetical, since it implies internal mental processes. Motivation-hygiene theory lacks the concern with individual differences essential to research on vocational choice.

The leadership theories also have been mute on this matter, despite the need to attract and select individuals who will lead well. This is one of the major problems facing industrial psychology and personnel management. There is the implication in Fiedler's writings related to situational engineering that LPC scores might be used to help individuals find their appropriate leadership situations. This prospect faces a number of difficulties related to the stability of LPC, uncertainties regarding the middle range of LPC scores, and the like. Nevertheless, more reseach in this area does seem warranted.

More fruitful, perhaps, would be studies relating equity and goal setting theories to vocational choice. Equity motivation might well emerge as a major factor in job and career choice — the choice of a legal career, for instance, or union steward, or labor arbitrator. Unfortunately, neither the theory nor the research has been extended in this direction. Similarly, goal setting theory has not concerned itself with vocational choice to date, although it might well make a contribution to predicting the occupational level a person would strive for and achieve. There is a potential here, also, that has not been realized.

The theories of organizational behavior consistently utilize variables that have implications for vocational and organizational choice. Yet, only a few of the theories have been extended to deal with this question. When such an extension is made, as with expectancy theory and achievement motivation theory, the results tend to be both useful and supportive of the theoretical statements. On the evidence, it would appear that the matter of vocational choice is one to which the field of organizational behavior could fruitfully devote much more theoretical and research attention than it has in the past.

IDENTIFYING TALENT SUPPLIES

What information have the various theories generated regarding the availability of different types of talent in the population? This question is not far removed from the matter of guiding vocational choice, and it is therefore not surprising that the theories that have made contributions in one of these areas tend to contribute in the other.

One of the major approaches used in research on achievement motivation theory is to plot measures of motivation against economic indexes for countries and cultures. This has been done for the United States, and the curves are remarkably congruent. Achievement motivation rose steadily from 1800 to 1890, peaked, and has continued to decline. There is, however, some reason to believe that in the present world of large multinational firms a decline in achievement motivation may not necessarily bring economic downfall as it has in the past if the motives required to manage the corporations, such as socialized power needs, remain in good supply. Although data on socialized power motivation per se are lacking, there is considerable evidence that managerial motivation in many of its aspects is on the decline. Thus, overall, the findings indicate shortages of talent defined in motivational terms.

Data related to expectancy theory yield a similar conclusion. The implication of the theory is that given a suitably rationalized, reward contingent organization, one would want to employ people as high on the various expectancy theory measures as possible. Although knowledge of such individuals is far from complete, it is apparent that they tend to be internals who view events in their lives as subject to their own control. Direct data on talent supplies for the expectancy constructs are lacking, but there is evidence that external thinking, not internal, is widely prevalent in the younger generation. Thus, as with achievement motivation, expectancy motivation (effort) appears to be in relatively short supply at present.

It is clear that Maslow considered self-actualization to be a variable that society needs badly, and one that is in very short supply. Ultimately, he decided that operating out of self-actualization motivation for any meaningful period is practically impossible for young people and is very rare below the age of 50. One of the difficulties with the various measuring instruments developed is that they consistently yield a much greater incidence of self-actualization than either Maslow's own research or his theory would anticipate. At this point, therefore, the talent supply question cannot be considered to be adequately answered directly from need hierarchy theory.

However, evidence related to theory X and theory Y indicates that theory X assumptions are widely held, much more so than theory Y. This is at least theoretically consistent with the view that a talent shortage exists insofar as managers are concerned and appears to support Maslow regarding the dearth of self-actualization motivation. Furthermore, there is no basis for concluding that a strong desire for more meaningful, challenging, enriched work of the kind envisaged by need hierarchy and job characteristics theories permeates the population. Most individuals, even in the younger age groups, appear to find jobs with a scope at least equal to their needs. There is no reason to believe that a large reservoir of talent for enriched jobs exists in the population at this time; quite the contrary. Assuming that expanding technology will generate more demanding work, it again appears likely that talent shortages can be anticipated.

The remaining theories have not addressed the talent supply issue at all, although some of them appear to have this potential. Thus, among the leadership theories, contingency theory would require information regarding how frequently each octant actually occurs in the world of work. These data could then be compared with the results of surveys of LPC levels in the population to determine whether high or low LPC might be needed.

Goal setting theory indicates a need for evidence of the proportion of the population likely to accept hard goals and the proportion actually responsive to goal setting. For equity theory the question of talent supplies will remain unanswered until adequate measures of equity-related constructs are developed. How many people are highly responsive to overreward inequity, for instance? Until we can answer such questions it will not be possible to say how significant the theory really is.

Talent for behavior modification theory is a product of genetic and environmental histories. In order to truly measure talent, one would have to obtain a complete picture not only of a person's history of reinforcement but also of his genetic background. As might be anticipated the impracticalities of doing this have stifled research on talent supplies. This situation is unlikely to change. Similarly, for motivation-hygiene theory the position has been that most people will respond to motivation and hygienes in accord with the basic theory, and that if they do not they are often mentally ill. However, data bearing on the actual frequency of this kind of mental illness in the population have not been developed in a systematic manner and probably will not be, given the current state of research on the theory.

Although the theories consistently have not produced information with regard to talent supplies, a number have, and it is apparent that we know a great deal more about such matters because of the theories. The overall picture is compellingly consistent—major shortages of motivational and leadership talent are in evidence, and without some change in this situation, sizable difficulties in organizational functioning appear inevitable.

TRAINING, DEVELOPING, AND INFLUENCING PEOPLE

A major method of dealing with the shortages identified through research related to the talent supply question is to introduce change efforts that will alter motivational and cognitive patterns to erase the shortages. The question then becomes — to what extent have the theories actually generated training, development, or influence approaches that can accomplish this type of objective?

Management Development

A number of the theories have either produced their own management development programs or become closely allied with particular kinds of programs that were already in existence. Not surprisingly, such a pattern is especially characteristic in the case of the leadership theories. Thus theory X and theory Y have become tied closely to sensitivity training, in that this training appears to teach theory Y values and inculcate theory Y assumptions. The training has brought about changes in people, although not necessarily of a kind that will improve performance in hierarchic organizations. Efforts to design sensitivity training to develop higher order needs have been undertaken, but their effectiveness remains undetermined. At the present time, broad organization development programs extending beyond management development and beyond the scope of this book appear to be more characteristic of attempts to introduce theory Y assumptions than sensitivity training.

Contingency theory of leadership is the source of leader match training that has as its goal teaching managers to manipulate their environments to make them match their LPC. Although research appearing to support this approach has been conducted, it is likely that the effects are a result of sensitization to the leadership role more than of the learning of the constructs of the theory. No programs intended to change LPC itself have been developed.

The other management development approach stemming from a theory of leadership is the decision tree training devised by Vroom to shift managers toward the normative model. In this case evaluation research is entirely lacking. However, the complexity of the learning required suggests that if changes occur they may well parallel those obtained from the leader match procedure. Sensitization to the managerial role may be the major contribution.

Achievement motivation theory deals at some length with the processes of motive development and how management development programs may be used for this purpose. Achievement motivation training clearly does accomplish its goals and does foster entrepreneurial activity. This has been demonstrated with regard to black capitalism in the United States, economic growth in the developing countries, and motivational development among disadvantaged school children. Power motivation training also gives some evidence of promise, especially as regards shifting from personalized to socialized manifestations, although the evidence is insufficient in this area. It is clear from all of this research that an explicit effort to change motives is necessary if results are to be obtained; mere exposure to organizational climates of various kinds is not sufficient.

Since behavior modification theory is, strictly speaking, a theory of learning processes and not motivation, we are dealing entirely with effects of external influences. This is particularly evident in the case of shaping and modeling techniques and in the whole process of applied learning as a management development procedure. These approaches, when utilized with managers to teach them to manipulate contingencies of reinforcement for their subordinates, do appear promising. Positive results relating to both subordinate absenteeism and supervisory behavior are reported. It is also evident that teaching managers to utilize behavior modification techniques is not easy. A major component of this teaching is the use of behavior modeling through role playing. However, evidence from achievement motivation and managerial role motivation training indicates that mental modeling can be at least as effective, and perhaps because it is less threatening, even more effective. It seems likely, therefore, that other techniques could be used to the same ends if the theory has incorporated the necessary internal constructs.

There is a frequent suggestion from research dealing with theoretically based management development programs that when changes occur they are occasioned not so much by the interjection of specific theoretical constructs into the training as by a role sensitization process. The training gets the participants actively involved in thinking about and evaluating a role (such as manager or entrepreneur) that they are expected to perform or anticipate performing. As a result, they explore new sources of satisfaction and behaviors and subsequently change in certain ways predictable from the specific role requirements, not necessarily from the particular theory. This explanation clearly lacks empirical confirmation, but it does serve to reconcile the findings from studies that seem to show that a wide range of management development approaches can yield comparable change effects.

Job Enrichment and Goal Setting

A second grouping of change procedures, in addition to management development, includes various types of job enrichment, goal setting, and management by objectives. Two theories are closely allied with job enrichment programs — motivation-hygiene and job characteristics. In the case of the former, there is some evidence that orthodox job enrichment can yield positive outcomes, particularly in areas related to work satisfaction. However, its relationship to motivation-hygiene theory is tangential at best. It involves motivators only, not hygienes, and among the latter the so-called generators — the work itself, responsibility, opportunity for growth, and advancement. Achievement and recognition, which (based on the research evidence) one would expect to see emphasized, are downplayed. Even in the best of circumstances, 10 to 15 per cent of the participants do not respond to job enrichment and in some contexts, particularly those of a blue collar nature, the results are frequently nil. The theory provides no basis for predicting these failures and pays little attention to individual differences in any form.

In-contrast, job characteristics theory makes specific predictions as to when job enrichment as an external influence will actually affect motivation. It clearly says that many job enrichment programs may not "take." The theory is very specific as to how jobs should be redesigned to achieve motivational effects. The findings suggest that one does best to be very selective in applying the technique, picking people and situations with considerable care based on findings from some instrument such as the Job Diagnostic Survey. Within these constraints, however, job enrichment can influence motivation.

Much the same conclusion holds for goal setting and management by objectives. Again, the research evidence is far from universally favorable. Difficulties appear to arise because of the interactive nature of much managerial work, the tendency for the motivating effects of difficult goals to dissipate over time, and the failure of certain individuals to be responsive to goal setting. The evidence suggests that isolated goal setting in the dyadic superior-subordinate relationship can be much more effective than a comprehensive management by objectives program that shortly loses its legitimacy. In this context, whether goals should be assigned or influenced strongly by the subordinate appears to depend on the subordinate, the nature of the relationship, and the question at issue. Decision tree theory might prove useful in reaching conclusions in this regard.

Direct Influence Guided by Theory

The theories also have produced a number of procedures for exerting direct influence on people, although the extent to which these have been subjected to appropriate research tests varies considerably. Need hierarchy, expectancy, and equity theories all contain implications for changing motivation and behavior, but none of these has been adequately tested in an ongoing organizational setting.

Need hierarchy theory predicts that the needs operating to affect a person's behavior can be influenced by systematically varying the levels and types of need satisfaction provided. With the exception of research related to theory X and theory Y, there is only limited evidence of this kind that can be explicitly tied to need hierarchy theory. The research that can be so traced is either not sufficiently well controlled to reach conclusions or yields negative results. The research on prepotency is sufficiently discouraging to make the conduct of programs of this kind a rather poor bet at best.

In contrast, both expectancy and equity theories generate approaches that would appear to have considerable potential. The ideal way to activate the processes of expectancy theory is through the design of a highly rationalized, reward-contingent organization with rewards tailored to individual wants, sizable opportunities for both extrinsic and intrinsic rewards available to good performers, and considerable opportunity to see that performance really matters. Cafeteria compensation systems and the elimination of pay secrecy are consistent with these objectives. Unfortunately, we know little about what effects a comprehensive influence system of this kind would have; the needed field research has not been done. Deci's theory and research suggest that the consequences would be disastrous, because intrinsic motivation would be undermined. However, given that high levels of intrinsic motivation tend to be impervious to extrinsic effects and that the phenomena described by Deci do not appear to operate when there is an implicit inducement-contributions norm, as there is in the employment context, the relevance of this theory can be questioned.

Although the laboratory studies have typically manipulated pay inequity externally, there is no research in which this has been done systematically in an organizational setting, and certainly no instance in which effects on equity motivation have been determined. There is a need for this kind of research. Can equity motivation be stimulated or aroused in ongoing organizations? Can it be increased or diminished? The answers to these questions do not exist. However, the prospects that applications of this kind might yield important consequences for an organization seem good.

Another approach to influencing behavior, specifically that of leaders, is situational engineering within the context of contingency theory. This procedure assumes a stable LPC over a long period and an increase in situational favorableness with experience, neither of which can be relied upon with certainty. Given this situation and the existing research evidence, the situational engineering approach must be considered more experimental than operational at present.

Actually, the only one of the direct influence procedures considered in this section that has the needed amount of research support is behavior modification. However, this procedure requires a large element of environmental control for adequate utilization. The nonorganizational applications have been with children, often school children, hospitalized mental patients, prisoners, and (originally) animals. Organizational application has involved either lower level jobs or the highly controlled context of a formal management development program. Although the domain of the theory may extend to relatively noncontrollable situations, it cannot actually be applied there. Nevertheless, no matter what theoretical base one uses to derive them, the techniques of behavior modification can produce major changes under the right circumstances.

The evidence indicates that the theories have produced the most advanced procedures for application in the areas of management development, job enrichment, and objective setting. With the exception of behavior modification techniques, many of the other theoretical applications to influencing people at work remain just that — theoretical. Yet there is a great deal of promise for future breakthroughs. Without question theories of organizational behavior will continue to provide a major source of innovation in operating organizations. Given the trends now clearly in evidence, there is every reason to believe they will become *the* source of such innovations.

CONCLUSIONS

The various theories of organizational behavior have generated a considerable body of knowledge. As a result, our understanding, capacity to predict and ability to manage the future have been expanded in a variety of ways. This is what theories are supposed to do, and if one takes the total body of knowledge in the field of organizational behavior as a base, there is little question that theories and theory-generated research have contributed the great majority of that knowledge. Yet at the same time, certain of the theories, particularly some of the grander ones, have not proved very helpful. Some have even had negative consequences in that they have taken us up blind alleys, thus wasting research efforts and introducing unjustified applications.

An ideal outcome for a book such as this would be that the theories considered could be ranked on certain dimensions, so that it would be possible to make a choice of which ones to follow. However, the very fact that the theories are spread over such a wide range of domains makes this approach meaningless. It may well be appropriate to follow a not very good theory that deals with a unique domain simply because there is nothing better available, while rejecting a very good theory in a more cluttered domain because there is something better already there.

Clearly, there is a need to tie the various theories, with their differing levels of effectiveness and their different domains, together in some manner to yield the kind of "big picture" that general managers, corporate strategists, and even broadly concerned scientists desire. At the present stage in the development of the science, this is not possible. There is a clear need for research at the boundaries of theories and of their domains, and for more comparative analyses in which one theory is pitted against another to see which will do best in handling a particular problem. Some such research has been conducted; we need much more.

Finally, it is important to emphasize that our discussion of theories in organizational behavior has been limited primarily to theories operating at the individual and work group levels. We have not been concerned with inter-group organizational matters, except in the most cursory manner, nor have we extended our purview beyond the organization into its environment. Yet, the theories of organizational process and structure are also of major significance in organizational study. The need to integrate them with the organizational behavior theories is just as great as the need to find common ground within the theories of organizational behavior. To stop with the field of organizational behavior is to know only half of what the functioning of organizations is all about.

NAME INDEX

Page numbers followed by (t) indicate tables. Page numbers in italics indicate illustrations.

SUBJECT INDEX

Page numbers followed by (t) indicate tables. Page numbers in italics indicate illustrations.